ELSE WHERE

Neil Macdonald

NEWSAGENT

NEWSAGENT

Newspapers

Newspapers

Sold

Here

BATSFORD

Elsewhere

Contents

COVER
Curtis McCann, Meanwhile 2, 1991, by James Hudson
PREVIOUS PAGE
Car park ejection, 1991, by James Hudson
FROM LEFT TO RIGHT
[1] Broadmarsh, Nottingham, by Sean Keef
[2] Chris Roderick, Edinburgh, by Andy Horsley
[3] Dan Cates, Buckingham Palace fountain, by Wig Worland
[4] Mark Brewster and Kevin Parrott, Broadgate, by Wig Worland

Elsewhere

Introduction

This book exists now because it didn't already. The story of the people who progressed UK – and therefore global – skateboarding during the era when everything was happening for the first time, street skating was taking over, and suddenly skateboarding wasn't so much about observing the American superstars as it was about what you could do with the kerb outside your house and some 'borrowed' ply – or a big yellow gas pipe – has never been properly told.

The generation that started at the end of the 1980s, and whose focus was almost entirely street skating – and not travelling to a ramp, getting padded up and waiting in line until it was your turn – changed the direction of not only skateboarding but culture itself, globally.

The things that happened by chance, the relationships that were formed, the experiments that worked, the inspiration and ideas in UK skateboarding during this time have truly gone on to change the world.

1987 to 2002 is the pivotal era for modern skateboarding, from the beginning of the street skating revolution to the thoroughly overground mainstream monetisation of it brought on by corporate sponsors, mainstream coverage and 'extreme' festivals. The race to jump down the biggest sets of stairs took over from stylishness. Post-millennium cultural malaise set in and for the first time, youth cultures began referring to their own history in order to progress, and like never before, everything came to exist simultaneously.

Skateboarding in the UK progressed in a different direction to what we were seeing in the US magazines and videos. It adapted to the climate and terrain, and the scarcity of dry days and smooth ground led to a different style of skateboarding altogether, one which came with its own fashion more suited to cold, dark days and nights.

Even within the UK regional differences were clear. In the North, with its Victorian brick warehouses abandoned following Thatcher's sweeping closures of industry, there was suddenly free – or cheap – space to build indoor ramps, and the yuppie-fication of London opening up more available street skating opportunities, especially at the weekend when huge swathes of the city were devoid of human life.

During this era of unprecedented progression in skateboarding, art and culture, there are so many stories beyond what was reported in the magazines or recorded on video, and it turns out that when you start asking questions, a lot of people have got a lot to say.

Telling the story as completely as possible came about through hundreds of hours of interviews with the skateboarders, company owners, photographers, shop owners, videographers and artists over five years, and the openness and honesty with which people spoke – often about subjects that had never been discussed before – says so much about how much what went on during this era meant, and how much it shaped people. So many of the people in this book have moved on to do incredible things in skateboarding, fashion, art, music and culture, and I think this drive comes from living through a period where you could try things, you could make things up and see what happened.

Neil Macdonald

Elsewhere

Foreword

Right place, right time?

1987 to 2002 was the pivotal era in the skateboard world.

We went from the do-it-yourself culture of the mid- to late 1980s – still skating our delaminated decks for months – to the banality of the X-Games, via the most stylish and arguably the most significant development in what was and is possible to do with, on or near, a skateboard.

In the mid- to late 1980s I was finishing secondary school, having learned more from the magazines I collected in my lunch break than from the lessons themselves. Because of the images in those magazines, I knew I wanted to be a photographer, but I didn't know that would take more than learning how to use a camera.

A lucky connection to Mon Barbour and his 'backyard' ramp in rural Oxfordshire via an Archigram-designed play centre in Milton Keynes ultimately connected me to the most important people in the skateboard industry at the time. I don't need to mention names. You know who you are. At the same time I was also lucky enough to be learning the technicalities of photography through a Thatcher-era government training scheme. The irony is not lost on me.

Though the main innovation in the skateboarding world had previously always seemed to come from the epicentre of the industry in California, by the early '90s some ideas seemed to be flowing the other way. The skateboarding youth of the UK, who had brought themselves up on the big US company video parts, released on VHS, had taken the videos for literal reality and believed all the tricks were landed every time rather than through hours of footage collection. It created some skateboarders who were more consistent than their American counterparts at the time.

In the early 1990s I had the opportunity to travel to California to work at the very centre of the industry at the time. It didn't last; I wanted to get back to the characters and the scenes in the UK. That is what actually meant something to me. The weather in the UK also suited the idea I wanted to pursue in photography. Not for no reason is Hollywood located in LA. The light is strong and clear over there, whereas I wanted to set up a studio in the street and decide where the light would come from myself.

It was absolutely the right thing for me to come back to the UK and carry on the good work started by Tim Leighton-Boyce [TLB] and the crew that did *RAD* magazine. We tried to build on that, first with *System* magazine and then *Sidewalk Surfer* – an odd name for a UK-based magazine, I always thought.

We thought we knew what we were doing, but many of the early issues of *Sidewalk* are unreadable now and unfortunately can't be deleted like a MySpace page. Things got better as we brought more people in to help us, and the people and the scene shaped the project over time.

Just as we thought we knew everyone, along came another set of skateboarders we'd never heard of before. I remember being as excited by seeing the Ipswich scene video, *Tough Guys*, in 1995 as when we first visited the city. Probably not more than a week later we had another brilliant scene to report on. Meeting the people along the way was always the best thing.

The early years at the print magazine, where we could travel anywhere and do whatever we wanted, were the creative days of our lives. Looking back, I'd probably have spent more time photographing the people and not so much the tricks. But film was finite and the magazines wanted bright colourful images of skateboard stunts to make the publication jump off the shelf at the newsagents.

By the early 2000s we'd all perhaps begun to lose our heads. I started to carry around a full Hasselblad kit, including a Polaroid instant film back to check exposure before loading the real film for the real moves. All of this, along with the weight, the lights and the other paraphernalia I'd decided was necessary at the time, was to make every picture 'special'. This level of production made the skateboarding superstars feel important, but looking back, it really altered the feeling of the average session. But as the gaps started to open up, the handrails got longer, and the whole scene was being fuelled by seemingly bottomless energy drinks. It seemed like the right thing to do.

All of the editorial staff of *Sidewalk* had tried to keep the worst excesses of the late 1990s skateboard boom away from the pages of the magazine. We'd done our best to keep the magazine true to its UK roots. We invited American pros to the UK, some of whom racked up huge expenses for the UK distributor, rather than taking the easy route of using pictures, sometimes offered for free, from the USA.

But we couldn't hold back the tide. The commodification of skateboarding that had begun in 1995 with the advent of the X-Games had taken a wider grip. Perhaps machismo was the dominant force? We'd ended up taking the money from the soft drink companies and in the process perhaps subverted our own values?

By the early to mid-2000s I sensed something was off and pulled back, and I had essentially stopped shooting skateboarding by 2005. I couldn't put my finger on it at the time but, looking back, everything had changed and I didn't like what I could see.

I'm not sure any of us have any idea of the significance of the times we live through. Whether now or then. But those last few years before the internet really took hold of our lives do now seem very significant. Maybe we can't see the importance of something clearly until we're miles or years away from it.

Wig Worland

9

Elsewhere

1987

David Morpeth, Walker Wheels, by Dave Duff

One of the biggest wake-up calls was in '87, when us older generation used to meet each other at Southbank at one o'clock in the afternoon. This American skate magazine called me up and said they wanted to do some stuff with me at Southbank, and they asked me to be there for nine o'clock in the morning. I arrived at ten o'clock, thinking it was going to be dead, but there must have been 200 skaters there.

I'm looking round and thinking that six months ago there was 15 people there, and now there's a couple of hundred at ten o'clock in the morning. I was just watching them pushing around, rolling in and rolling out, trying ollies and falling and trying again. Not even carving and working the banks, it was all basics. It was all new to them. No lines or nothing like that. That's the first wake-up call I got of, 'This is it, it's started'. If that was going on at ten o'clock in the morning there, what else is going on around the country?

Then that was it, it completely went out of control. A whole new generation arrived overnight. You thought, 'Wow, how did we get here?'
SHANE O'BRIEN

1991

Tim Leighton-Boyce (TLB)

Because of my connection with Alpine Sports and *Alpine Action*, and getting into BMX, I had been dealing with *BMX Action Bike*. We were running adverts – because it was the only place that we could – for our BMX stuff. We kept wanting to do skateboard ads, but they were still very much, 'No, this is BMX, and skateboarding went out with the dinosaurs'. They were part of that world. Nevertheless, I was someone who was into photography and wanting to do photographs, so I ended up gradually getting sucked into that world and moving closer and closer and I started to photograph BMX races for them. I started to do more and more stuff like that, and generally being part of the group of people around the organisation.

I introduced them to Dobie Campbell, and he started taking photographs too, and the other thing that Dobie did was set up a dark room in the toilets at that building, so he started printing for them. So there was both me and Dobie floating around within this world in which everybody knew we were totally into skating and wanted skating in the magazine and hated when they made rude comments about skating.

Gradually, the people running *BMX Action Bike* became aware that we were on to something, that it was legit and there was an interest, so they started putting a bit of skate stuff in, which me and Dobie were very happy to provide. At that point nobody had any idea that skateboarding would ever come back, so it was our dream to try to get some coverage for skateboarding, and if it's going to be in a BMX magazine, so be it. I look back on this period and we were so snotty and up our own arses with skateboarding. Getting skating back was the dream.

Nick Philip was this brilliant young designer figure running this brand called Anarchic Adjustment who had gravitated into the circle of the magazine through his advertising for Anarchic Adjustment, and had already been providing huge amounts of editorial steer. It was decided that Nick could do the design and paste up, and they gave him an office – they had a floor in a grotty old building in Tooley Street – so Nick sat in there and drew, and started being the designer. More and more it was me producing the content, Nick doing the design, and that being sold to these other people as a package. Then it got to the point of them saying that it still doesn't make sense, and to just have Nick and I do the whole thing.

So the Croftward Publishing people said they'd go for that, 'Tim and Nick will do it'. They had a mate around the corner from their offices, who was this designer and paste-up studio bloke called Graeme Baldock, and Graeme could rent them a desk space in his studio, so we moved our computer there and we produced it from there.

The other thing that was going on, was that the writing was on the wall that it needed to become much more of a skating mag than anything else, and they totally knew that that was what I wanted to do and that that was part of it. We agreed from the get-go that it was going to morph into *Read and Destroy*.

We were going to do that across three issues, but the key issue here is that the distribution deal with Comag was for a BMX magazine called *BMX Action Bike*. If we'd gone to Comag and said we were changing the name, they'd have said, 'Wait a minute, that's a different magazine, and by the way, now that we're looking at sales figures, *BMX Action Bike* is going down, so let's start over'. So we had to tell them that it was still *BMX Action Bike* but we were rebranding it a bit. And gradually it became *Read and Destroy*. The 'Read and Destroy' text disappeared because the distributors didn't like that; it sounded a bit nasty to them, so it became *RAD*.

Nick was so integral to that magazine, and people tend to think of it as something I did – I was certainly the leading figure and I was old enough that I was trusted to do it – but he shaped that thing. It wasn't just the design, and everybody talks about Nick's design because that was such a strong, stand-out feature, but the whole content and attitude of it was hugely, hugely influenced by him. →

RAD Magazine

[1–9]   Selection of *RAD* magazine covers, 1987

Elsewhere

BMX *Action Bike* — March 1987 No 50 85p

GO FOR IT!

SKATING
STEVE DOUGLAS EXCLUSIVE

FREESTYLE
CARDIFF, BRIGHTON & THE BANKS WITH NO NAME

BMX *Action Bike* — April 1987 N°51 85p

Full on aggro

WIN! 3 RAD SCOOTS UP FOR GRABS!

SKATING: Wind & Surf Show

OUT THERE: Birmingham & Milton Keynes

More Colour Skating and More Colour Freestyle than Any Other UK Mag

BMX? *Action-Bike* — May 1987 N° 52 85p

R.A.D — READ AND DESTROY

FREESTYLE OUT
Bristol
Goff Shreds Kidlington

SCOOTERS!

SKATING Webster Shreds Warrington

ANTI-AUTHENTIC ISSUE

BMX *Action-Bike* — JUNE 1987 85p No 53

READ AND DESTROY

R.A.D

EXCLUSIVE LANCE MOUNTAIN

THREE RAD NEW RAMPS!

BMX *Action-Bike* — JULY 1987 85p Issue 54

READ AND DESTROY

R.A.D

AMERICANS IN EUROPE
CABALLERO GONZALES STAAB

R.A.D GOES RACING
NBMX Crewe National

WIN GNARLY NINJA SCOOTECH RAW R.A.D SHIRTS RACING PAGER BOARDS ROLLERSKATES

SAVE £2 Money off voucher inside

Wheel Aggro

READ AND DESTROY — AUGUST 1987 85p Issue 55

BMX *Action-Bike*

SICK! GONZ'S 8 FOOT OLLIE

UNRULY! WOKING INDIAN AIR

HARD! GILLINGHAM SKATEPARK ACTION

PLUS:
+ Racing from Farnham
+ Street from Sheffield and Bristol
+ Words from Kevin Staab
+ Skating for Cash at Banbury

READ AND DESTROY — SEPTEMBER 1987 85p ISSUE No. 56

BMX *Action-Bike*

GON in The UK

PULL-OUT POSTER INSIDE!

SPEED! SKATING AT 50 PLUS

HOFFMAN DESTROYS THE MOST INTENSE BMX ACTION YE

BUILD A FLY-OFF RAMP FULL PLANS INSIDE

WIN! Skateboards Surfwear Snowboard Video Frisbees Hacky Sacks

R.A.D STICKER

FREE 30 Skate, Surf, BMX Computer Game

R.A.D — OCTOBER 1987 85p ISSUE No. 57

BMX *Action-Bike*

The Only Magazine for SKATEBOARDS FREESTYLE & STREET ACTION!

SKATEPARK SCOOP Southsea's New Ramp

SKATE IN A PUB! STRANGE but TRUE

FREESTYLE AND BANKS Tricks you can Do

CONTORTION! Bikers Tweak the Rules

FLAT Hot New Tricks

FREE FREE FREE FREE FREE FREE

R.A.D — CHRISTMAS 87 85p ISSUE No. 58

BMX *Action-Bike*

NUMBER ONE FOR SKATEBOARDS FREESTYLE & STREET ACTION!

LUCIAN HENDRICKSE SKATING'S MR BAD SPEAKS OUT

EXCLUSIVE! WORLDS HOTTEST RAMP CABALLERO and HOSOI at RAGING WATERS

HOLESHOT PREVIEW AMERICAN SKATERS AND FREESTYLERS COMING HERE!

WIN! NEW PACER SCOOTERS

RAGING BMX AIR Canning Contorts

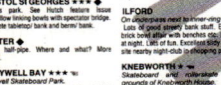

Nick Philip

My friend at school and I wanted to do something, so we were going to import and sell Vans, because at that point you could order customised Vans, so you could have 'I'd rather be surfing' or whatever around the edge. So we did that, got some really amazing shoes back, and we sold them to all our mates, and they were the best Vans in London because no one else was going to the trouble of getting custom Vans. Every pair was different and there were some bangers and there were some clunkers, but nonetheless they sold.

I thought I'd keep doing it, and so a friend said I'd need to come up with a name, and I came up with 'Anarchic Adjustment' because at that point I was studying Politics, Modern History and Sociology, and the first day I walked into my Politics class, my teacher said, 'I think it's ethically correct of me to tell you what my political views are before I teach you A-level politics – I'm an Anarchist'. My Sociology teacher was a Marxist Feminist, and my History teacher was a kind of a Centralist. So I was thinking about those kind of things in my head when I started this project.

It's surprising that it was actually as successful as it was considering how bloody difficult it is to pronounce, but what makes it interesting is that it's a sort of contradiction. The common misconception of what anarchy is, is that it's chaos and punk and all that, and to adjust is to put something into order, so that's why I came up with that name. It's not saying there should be complete anarchy, no, but we should always want to change things in a way in which we're trying to go against the dominant hierarchy. That's not just a political thing, that's the dominant hierarchies of what people accept in all aspects of culture. That seeming contradiction is what made it interesting, I think.

A friend had said that I should make t-shirts with Anarchic Adjustment on them because it was a cool name, so I made a t-shirt and I went to *Action Bike* to put an advert in the magazine. I really didn't know what I was doing with graphic design, and I have no formal art training at all. My mother was an art teacher so in a sense I got my own private art history lesson all my life, which I'm very grateful for, but in terms of paste-up – which is what it was then because it was before desktop publishing – I didn't know what I was doing.

So I go down to *Action Bike* and say that I want to put an advert in the magazine for t-shirts I'm making, and I ask them how I do that. They were like, 'Well, you better go and try and figure that out, mate'. So I went, very briefly, to a night school class and I learned how to do paste-up.

I came back to *Action Bike* with an advert ready for Anarchic, and I gave it to them, and I remember Boycey – Tim Leighton-Boyce – later said to me that they were impressed with how quickly I'd learned to do it or whatever, so I had an ad in the mag.

Richard Grant was the editor at the time, and they were selling *Action Bike* to a different publisher. BMX had peaked, so they wanted to sell the property quick, and I think that pretty much all the staff were out of there, they were going to move on to other things. So it was basically just Boycey.

I think – and this is me speculating – that what happened was they were thinking, 'Fuck, we can't sell it with just Boycey, we need someone that we can say is the Art Director as well', and I think they looked at my stuff and thought, 'Well, this kid's maybe going to do some stuff and he'll probably work for cheap because he's only 17', and so they asked if I wanted to do it and I said yes. Then the transition from *Action Bike* to *RAD* happened.

The cover of April 1987[2] was a bit of a thing. I made that cover by hand, and I got griptape and stuck it all together, and I gave that physical collage – with actual skateboard griptape on it – to this guy Bob that used to do all the separations and the scans for the magazine. He had a very expensive drum scanner that would scan the slides at the high resolution that was required for the printing, and it has to be calibrated, they have to get all the dust out of it, and it's an expensive, delicate piece of hardware. I presented him with this piece of artwork that could easily damage and fuck up their really expensive machine, and he was cool. He let us do it.

May 1987[3] with the distorted *RAD* logo was something that Dave Currie started. I had a lot of respect for him, and I thought he was a really cool guy. He had already been working on that cover, and what he'd done helped to be the basis of the *RAD* logo.

I took some bits and redid it, but he was the inspiration for what ended up being the *RAD* logo. Today it still looks really fresh, because every other logo is some minimal, flat, clean bollocks, which is great but this really did get across what we were trying to do.

I was in the right place at the right time. I walked in there when that transition was going on, and I was a young kid. I made a lot of mistakes, I did a lot of shit like where I'm reversing green type out of yellow on red backgrounds, I mean this was pre-desktop publishing so you spec'ed colours manually: 20% cyan, 50% black, all that, but basically you didn't know what it looked like until it came back, and I'm a kid who's used to making zines and then I've got the opportunity to basically make a zine, but make it colour. There were a lot of mess ups because I had a little bit of training but I learnt the rest on the job and thankfully there wasn't horrible corporate wankers looking over our shoulder saying no.

Steve Douglas

I had five days to get that interview[13] together and it's totally unreadable. It's yellow print on a red background and you can't read a fucking word of it. It's bittersweet that I got on the cover, and the disappointment was always going to be that I got my interview but you couldn't read it.

Go For It was the name of my magazine,[15] which obviously I got from the Stiff Little Fingers album *Go For It*, and one of my Schmitt graphics is a take-off of that album. My go-to is always 'Go for it'. Someone says they want to start a company? I'm just like, 'Man, you've just got to go for it'.

Mike John

Tim was the facilitator and he was great at bringing people in and letting you do your own thing. He was providing the canvas for us.

When it switched to a skate magazine, more of the skate photographers got involved. I knew Paul Sunman and Dobie from Southbank – we were all Southbankers – so the three of us were taking photos, but Tim was doing the majority himself. He was very pragmatic and I think the reason he did that was to save money. What you'd notice in *RAD* was how many photos didn't have a photo credit, and if there was no photo credit that meant Tim took it and he was so modest that he didn't want to put his name on it. He'd take all these great photos and not even put his name on them. When we took them he made sure we got a photo credit and he made sure we got paid the proper rates. He's absolutely brilliant, Tim. Without him nothing would have happened.

Dobie Campbell

Tim was the older dude, and he was kind of the leader. He was always asking us what we thought of things, and he was always really open to us pitching ideas to him.

Mike Manzoori

Pretty much as soon as travel cards [14] were available, we went everywhere. From looking at *RAD* mags, at the page in the back where you could see where things were,[12] it was on. ●

CLOCKWISE FROM TOP LEFT
[10] *RAD*, October, designed by Nick Philip, photo by TLB
[11] *RAD*, September, photo by TLB
[12] *RAD*, Where? Guide, December
[13] *RAD*, Steve Douglas interview, designed by Nick Philip
[14] £2 Capitalcard travel card
[15] *Go For It!* zine, 1985

    1987

Nick Philip

At first I was screening the t-shirts myself, at my parents' house, and that ended up just being too much work and too messy. I got some trouble from my dad because I would wash the screens out in our bath, and he didn't like that. Screenprinting is dirty work – ink gets everywhere, you have to clean the screens, you have to burn screens, all that, so I did some at my house until I found a vendor that could do some more numbers for me. I would paste up the artwork in kind of the same way as I would for the magazine, and then I would give it to the vendor and they would have a stat camera, and they would shoot that to make the film, and then the film would burn the screens.

My friend did the logo, [2] and there was one logo that had the 'A' that was not as legible, and I made stickers of it that we used to put up on the ramps and all that business, and everyone was all, 'Oh yeah, Narchic Adjustment, that's cool!', and I was like, 'Oh shit, you're not getting it', so I sort of art directed my friend – his name's Alistair MacKenzie – and explained that it needed to look more like an 'A' because no one was getting it. It was all hand drawn with a rOtring pen.

I was living in Muswell Hill, and one morning, all around Muswell Hill Broadway, were the outlines of people. As I understand it, it was an agitprop protest by CND, representing that if a nuclear bomb dropped you would just be vaporised, and these figures all around Muswell Hill were meant to be a visual representation of a vaporised body. So I just put an Anarchic sweatshirt on there because it looks like he's dancing.[2] I was sort of taking the piss a little bit, and I'm sure there were some people at CND that maybe saw that and thought it was a travesty, but I was only 16 or something. Tim took that photo,[1] and that's me. I used to do that hand signal, and then all these kids in Japan started doing it too.

Wig Worland

Nick Philip put an Anarchic Adjustment ad in *RAD*[2] that included his address. Me and two of my mates turned up at it, and it was his house. We turned up at this address in Muswell Hill on a Saturday morning thinking it was a shop and it was his house. He was like, 'Err, OK? Come in.' He had one frame and two pairs of really expensive handlebars or whatever, but he gave us some stickers. He was a bit confused but I think he realised what he'd done and he can't put his parents' address in the mag because people will turn up. ●

LEFT TO RIGHT
[1] Anarchic t-shirt print, Nick Philip, by Tim Leighton-Boyce
[2] Anarchic logos and ads
[3] Variflex XP ad
[4] Variflex XPS ad
[5] Variflex dealer list

Variflex

Chris Allen

In 1987 we distributed Variflex, cheap Variflex completes that I would consider in today's sense as being toys, but we also did the better ones as well, things that they called the 'Variflex XP Series',[3] and the 'Variflex XPS Series advert',[4] which were pro models of skateboarders who were not considered good enough to be on a US branded company and have a pro deck. The boards were Canadian maple, and they had a 66mm wheel on them that was better than the other completes, so they were like premium completes, and they had a retail price of about £100.

Variflex had boards that retailed from £20 up to £100, so different categories of them sold to different shops. We sold the cheaper ones to people like Toys 'R' Us because that was when Toys 'R' Us first came to the UK, and we sold the ones that retailed between £20 and £60 through sports shops, generally, and then the better ones, and things like Powell and Santa Cruz and those sorts of things, we sold to specialist independent bike shops.

Curtis McCann

My first memory of really wanting to skate was when I saw a Variflex skateboard in a DC comic... when I saw how wide skateboards had become I decided right away I wanted one.

Soon I started travelling regularly to a model shop in Croydon just to look at skateboards and watch skate videos like the first 'Bones Brigade' videos... soon after, I found Mud Machine and started buying a skateboard in instalments. I remember before my mum was able to pay off the £70 I would go into the shop regularly just to look at it... when it was paid for I remember riding it home unhingedly on a dark winter evening; I remember I was skipping over the rough paving slabs and

my heart was racing as I tried to speed up and down kerbs without yet being able to ollie. I knew Fairfields was the most complete and busy London skate spot after Southbank and Rom. I have memories of going there and being the first one there and then by midday on some weekends there would be maybe a hundred people.

At first I would skate every school day evening in Sutton with a varying crowd. We would have long often manic sessions where we would skate around Sutton like there was no tomorrow; jump ramps were the thing but we rarely had them so we would skate things like a piece of wood propped up by a shopping trolley. Also wall rides were the thing and we were so up for it we would sporadically skate scrappy brick walls and smash boards... in the early days gluing boards felt like a weekly occurrence!

Fairfields was the most complete and busy London skate spot after Southbank and Rom, it had a stellar cast of characters. I have memories of me often being the first one there, and then by midday on some weekends there would be loads of us jamming... It's a bit of a blur, but I think I first went to Fairfields for a Mud Machine jam in '87. There were skaters, scooters, and BMX freestylers there. If I remember rightly, there was just one ramp there that was more like a whippy quarterpipe with coping than a jump ramp... we were going off the side all day! I think I'd just seen the Powell Peralta video 'Animal Chin' where jump ramps were kicking off. In terms of tricks, in those days it was about ollies and bonelesses on those crazy-shaped boards. The older, stronger kids were doing amazing street plants on the flat... I remember I would arrive at Fairfields proud of my little entry line, which was an acid drop off the block that led on to the Fairfields 'plaza'... If I remember rightly, the drop was as tall as a 13-year-old me! ●

M-ZONE
Charlie 'Chuckie' / 'Dave'
Burrows

When I started Mud Machine, we were doing BMX bikes and they were selling great. The unfortunate thing was... You know how skateboarding was massive in the '70s and then it died out? BMX went through that same phase. Every kid wanted a BMX bike. The ET movie came out and everybody wanted the Kuwahara ET bike. Sales went through the roof, then just like that, it fizzled out and all the kids were asking if we could get skateboards.

I got skateboards, but I didn't really want to mix the skateboards and the BMX together. Mud Machine was based on the fact that you race a BMX bike on the mud.

Peter Tarry

That summer of '87 was brilliant because we just had so much fun, and there was no one telling you you'd done it wrong. We got so little hassle, as well. Nowadays, let's face it, if you even want to take a picture on private land in London and got a tripod out, someone's going to ask you what you're doing or tell you to stop.

Fashions change and people change but for that summer, it was perfect.

What we did, and I'm not saying we claim anything beyond that particular place and that particular moment, was something quite unique. Certainly in British skating, and I think in the fashion side of it as well. I mean Chuckie would pay you, but he would pay you in clothes.

London in the mid- to late '80s was a brilliant place to be but we still had the IRA and things in London. Obviously there was a lot of ill feeling with Thatcher in power and all the rest of it, and the yuppie was on the rise, but you had *i-D* magazine, you had *The Face*; *Absolute Beginners* had just been made so there was the vibe around the young actors.

I don't like to use the word 'scene' because it wasn't a scene, it was a life, it was what we did, but we were part of something that we shared with other people and they were the best of times. Innocent times, very very fun times. Nobody was into drinking, nobody was into drugs, it was just a bunch of mates going out and doing what they did

I wouldn't say we changed anything or anybody but we had an incredibly good time. You know how they talk about how the '60s were such a great time, but only if you were one of those hundred or so people like the David Baileys and the Terence Stamps and people like that, but for that microsecond you felt like you were part of something that was just incredibly good.

Looking back now – and the timing had a lot to do with it, because it would be totally different now – but what we did was special, and we felt it as well. I truly, truly class those as some of the happiest days of my life, doing those pictures we did. It felt like we were recording something that was special. Even if it was a tiny special, it was still special.

SLAM CITY SKATES
Rob Dukes

I started working for Paul Sunman on Saturdays in Slam City in the basement of Talbot Road, the first proper Slam City shop. My main recollection is how much skaters wanted the equipment they saw in the magazines ridden by their heroes. The magazines had huge influence. The whole sponsorship thing really worked in terms of marketing.

When the first wave of young skaters appeared around 1987, they were very into Powell Peralta because of the way the Bones Brigade were marketed to them, as opposed to, say, Santa Cruz, whose adverts were more 'adult'.

I was always surprised that people would buy Vision Street Wear clothes. I thought they were rank. But non-skaters thought the brand was cool, and I suppose for younger skaters it was a kind of uniform to be identified in.

Skateboards, in real terms, were very expensive in the late '80s and I suppose that partly explains the popularity of stickers. We sold piles of stickers; a cheap way of changing the 'look' of your board. ●

LEFT TO RIGHT
[1] M-Zone ads by Charlie Burrows, photos by Peter Tarry
[2] Slam City Skates flyer from the Wind and Surf Show, Bod Boyle, by Tim Leighton-Boyce
[3] Rob Dukes, Slam City Skates, Talbot Road, by Mark Gonzales

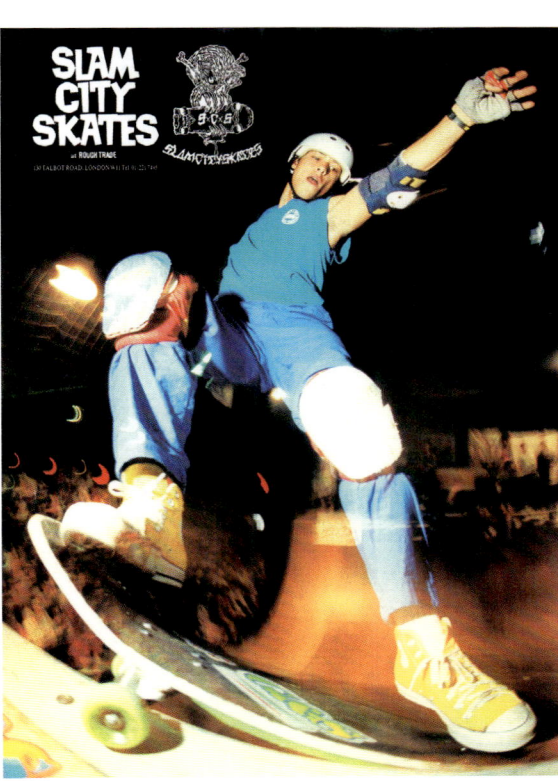

1987

    Elsewhere

CLOCKWISE FROM TOP LEFT
[1] Slam City Skates sticker, by Edwin 'Savage Pencil' Pouncey
[2] Mark Gonzales with a Slam sticker, Kennington, by Rob Dukes
[3] Slam artwork by Edwin Pouncey and Chris Long, London artwork by Mark Gonzales

Smell of Death

Lee Yau

They were just complete chaos. It was Steve Wilshire through and through. He did not care, and he does not care. He'd be there with his little dope pipe, puffing away before, not during because he's shouting at everyone, and after.

For a long time I didn't think that he could actually skate because he was just stood around, smoking away, and then one time I saw him skate, and he definitely could skate.

It wasn't a great place, around Meanwhile 2. You wouldn't go down there by choice, and it was unlit because all the lights had been smashed out. At the contest the light was fading, and for a while the only lights you had was flashes going off, then it got dark and the contest was over. It was just one of those things.

Steve Wilshire

I never really fitted in with anyone, I was just 'American Steve'. When I went to Banbury, to Mon's for an ESA comp, Derry Thompson was always telling me to do things. 'Don't smoke there!', 'Don't be there!', 'Don't do this, don't do that!', and it was kinda like, 'Fuck, why? Leave me alone.' So when I went home I said to myself, 'Well, I'm doing nothing else, so let's do a comp'. People were real serious but nobody was doing anything, so let's do something.

The Meanwhile comp was part of the Skate Drunk Series, where your entry fee was two beers but you had to drink the two beers before your run. The general theme was drugs and alcohol. And friends, and having fun. There was no money taken from people, it felt wrong. ●

CLOCKWISE FROM TOP
[1] Ricky Plante, Smell of Death Meanwhile 2 comp, by Lee Yau
[2] Crispin Robinson, Smell of Death Meanwhile 2 comp, by Lee Yau
[3] Contest placings, letter to *RAD*, from Steve Wilshire

Well any ways the Final standings for the CIRCLE A comp at meanwhile on May 31ST are:

1ST. PHIL - DEATH BOX - MILTON KEYNS
2ND WORZEL - DEATH BOX - MILTON KEYNS
3RD JAKE - SMELL OF DEATH, LONDON
4RTH CHRIS C - UN-SPON, LONDON
5TH STEVE - SMELL OF DEATH, LONDON
6TH ChrisPN - MADRID, LONDON
7TH NUT SACK - SMELL OF DEATH, LONDON
8TH DAVROSS-Scurvey Scumboards, KENYA
9TH Don BRIDER- BRAND X, FARNBOURGH

NO FIRE or petrol Bombs this comp, NEXT TIME. THE SPONSOTES WERE: DEATH BOX, ROUGH TRADE, Stupids: PUNK ROCK BAND, Edge Magazine. THE SMELL OF DEATH are NON PROFIT on the meanwhile comp I'll loose about £30 and Jim about the same, BELIVE me there is NO PROFIT in this, but at warrington they charge you to get in so they are making money - DONT LET THIS FUCKING HAPPEN - - Dont go to warrington -

CLOCKWISE FROM TOP LEFT
[1] Wurzel ad, *RAD*
[2] Pete Dossett, Crouch End, by Dave Hopkins
[3] Wind and Surf Show coverage in *RAD*, designed by Nick Philip
[4] Death Box teapot logo, by Graham 'Mac' McEachran
[5] Graham 'Mac' McEachran, Kennington, from *RAD*, by Tim Leighton-Boyce

Ian Deacon

In '87 there was a trade show in London, the Wind and Surf Show,[3] and there was a vert ramp there. Jeremy Fox was there with Wurzel and they were telling me they were launching this company called Death Box. There was a bunch of us from Brighton there and we're watching Dan-Z skate the ramp, and Sean Goff, and then it stopped. They pulled everyone off the ramp and then they put these dancers on the ramp, so we just started throwing shit at the dancers.

Duncan 'Wurzel' Houlton

At the Wind and Surf Show, everyone was completely ignoring us. The rest of the skate world were like, 'What? Doing your own company, in England? You can't do that.' We didn't have anybody on our side at all. No one.

The actual start of Death Box was in an East End pub with Mac. Jeremy was talking about it, and Mac just said, 'Well fucking hell, we should start a company'. Mac was never one to mince words. We just thought that Mac would have the first pro board, but he was quite an unassuming character, so it was quite embarrassing for him to have a pro board. But who else was doing McTwists on banks in '87? He just didn't like having attention.

Mac came up with the name Death Box, and all the names that came before that were X-rated because we'd drunk quite a lot. Mac was coming out with all the ideas, so we said he'd have the first pro model,

and he was like, 'Nah, fuck off, Wurzel's going to be the first'. There was no way he was going to do it. I'd been sponsored for a year and I was doing OK in contests, but I was forced to turn pro, basically.

We were in a situation where we'd assumed Mac would be the thing, and he refused to do it, and if Mac refuses to do something you're not going to get him to do it. I was feeling very nervous about it, and being down at Southbank going, 'I'm getting a pro board'. Shane O'Brien was like, 'Pro, man, you can't turn pro!', because this American hero-worship was still there. It wasn't really like turning pro, it was just the only way to promote the company. If you do a blank board and try to promote it, it's not going to work. You need someone behind it with a face, even if he's not doing good in contests.

A lot of people were down on it because at the time you had to be American to be pro. I was the first pro in England since Benjyboards in the '70s, and a street skater as well, and the boards weren't selling. At all.

We had an advert[1] in *RAD* for a few months for free. It was just my board, and a telephone number for Dee See Supplies. It ran for nothing because they'd turned it round the wrong way. We said, 'The board's upside-down!', and they said we didn't have to pay for it, so Jeremy said, 'Well leave it upside-down then'. That went on for a few months, and that was them trying to help us out, of course.

There was a lot of hype, but the actual amount of people skating wasn't that much, it was still building. We didn't have a video together – it took us ages to get a video together – so it was quite frustrating that the boards weren't selling.

That was the time when street skating was the big thing. There were a few old crusty skateparks, that no one was really interested in, and street skating was the only thing that was really accessible by that point. Accessibility was the thing, you could buy a cheapo board and go street skating anywhere, and there was bonelesses and jumping off things. Everybody could learn that, you could just throw yourself off something and try to land on the board. Then later you had the ollie coming in, which completely opened everything up.

Sean Goff

I was on the dole at the time. Everyone was. There's this weird conception that people made lots of money out of skateboarding in the '80s, but you never. There was fuck-all. The romanticised version was that you'd pack boxes in a warehouse, but that only happened for guys that went out to the States to stay. That was the time there was massive unemployment. I was on the dole because I couldn't get a job, it was that simple. ●

There was always a strong drive on the Island to innovate, I guess because of the lack of good street terrain. I can't say that this didn't happen everywhere because clearly it did, but I think being starved of good terrain is a driver for innovation.
GED WELLS

Ramps

FROM TOP
[1] Shide ramp, Isle of Wight, by Nick Herbert
[2] Scott Carroll's ramp, Broughty Ferry, by Nick Johnston

Elsewhere

Elsewhere

→ SHIDE
Ian Read

It's next to an old railway line.[1] We knew a guy who had a field we could rent. It cost nothing, it was so cheap, like old-school, medieval cost. Half a shilling for ten years or something. The pallets were the first thing to go down, to try to get a flat base. Steve Pannell's dad used to run a cash and carry, so he got loads of pallets delivered to us. A lot of it was begged, borrowed and stolen, literally.

→ MON'S RAMP
Mon Barbour

That ramp[2] morphed so many times, every time I resurfaced it. Once I put two foot of vert on it, which was a bit much and I cut it down. There were no handrails on the platforms, and how that thing held up, I do not know. My granny's greenhouse is there, and it was a miracle it never got hit by a skateboard, ever.

Every weekend there was 20, 30, 100 people turning up. I remember a whole load of guys turning up from Scotland one summer, and staying for a week. It got a bit full-on for my folks at times, but they were pretty understanding, considering. Everyone would camp out, it was a very loose affair.

→ KINGS CROSS
Arron Bleasdale

We knew that ramp[5] from going there on our BMXs. It was one quarterpipe the first time we went there. There was a stretch of tarmac up to it, which was probably just an 8-foot-wide quarterpipe with pretty tight transition, and then another quarterpipe came up and I think we helped a little bit, building that. It wasn't our idea to build another one but we were there and these people were building another

one so we helped. Simon Batten got really into it, and I think he ended up getting his hands on the Thrasher ramp-building plans and that all evolved into putting the two quarterpipes together at some point and making it wider, and we built the halfpipe that went to vert. It was 16 feet wide, and probably about 7 feet high.

We all helped, and we stole so much wood from building sites around Camden and – god bless my mum – stored it in my house. That lasted for a couple of months, just storing that wood, and then my mum's friend had a van and he helped us move all that wood in two trips down to Calthorpe Gardens. It was brilliant; it was really hard to skate because it was so tight and went to vert but we all learnt a bunch of stuff on it.

That jump ramp[4] was from my street – we took it down there when we were transporting all the wood to build the vert ramp. I would have been dropping in from the quarterpipe to hit the jump ramp.

Simon Evans

When Kings Cross was a vert ramp I remember going there and trying to drop in and just falling to the bottom on my hip and having to roll home on my skateboard because I couldn't walk. Vert was just so beyond; I'm so fortunate that it came around to miniramps and street, and that became more accessible.

→ WALKER WHEELS
Mike O'Brien

We built this funny ramp[3] with elliptical transition, concrete coping and a channel, and we'd go there all the time. It was super dangerous because to get to it you had to drive under this railway bridge and people used to chuck shopping trolleys

and paving slabs off the bridge to try and hit your car. People would shoot at you with air rifles, and the chip shop was just a slot in the wall. You didn't go in, they'd just pass your fish supper out because they didn't even want to let people in the door.

One night we're skating our ramp in this terribly rough area, and it's beautiful sunshine, and this guy strolls up to the ramp with a leather coat down to his knees, a quiff, and cowboy boots on. He looks really cool, and we're going, 'That looks like Steve Olson!',[3] but it can't be because this is Walker in Newcastle and he lives in California. We thought we recognised him, but out of context your brain just doesn't compute it. You'd only seen these people in magazines so it was like they were from outer space. So we're like, 'Alright mate? Are you Steve Olson?', and he goes, 'Yeah man'. He says he's come to skate and he asks to borrow a pair of shoes and a board.

And he's fucking gnarly; doing slash grinds and ollieing the channel. We ask him what he's doing here and he goes, 'My girlfriend's in a film'. So he just skates with us, and he's good fun. There's all these little Geordie kids going, 'Howay mate, give us a tab!', and he's asking us what they're talking about, so he ends up having to give cigarettes to all these little hard kids.

The next night this Mercedes taxi thing pulls up, and we're like, 'Alright, Steve's come back!', but then this drop-dead gorgeous woman gets out, in this white fur coat, and it's Melanie Griffiths who had previously been married to Don Johnson from *Miami Vice*. So skate-punk Steve Olson has kind of pinched Don Johnson's girl and brought her to a ramp in Walker. →

CLOCKWISE FROM TOP LEFT
[1] Ian Read, Shide, by Nick Herbert
[2] Mini Mansell, Mon's, by Sam Scott-Hunter
[3] Steve Olson, Walker Wheels, by David Duff
[4] Arron Bleasdale, Kings Cross, by Simon Batten
[5] Arron Bleasdale, Kings Cross, by Simon Batten
NEXT PAGE
[1] Arbroath ramp, by Scott Malcolm

Elsewhere

1987

LATIMER ROAD
Matt Sherman

Oh, goodness that place was sketchy.[1] It was so fucking sketchy. Not only was it quite a rough area of London, it had what I think was Europe's largest gypsy camp. I'm not sure I ever went there without there being trouble. Once we got stuck on the platform when a bunch of gypsies wouldn't let us come down and we had to wait them out for fucking hours. Mental. Terribly, terribly sketchy. I was always terrified of going there, but the Slam warehouse was near there, so I'd go there quite a lot to get shit off Paul Sunman.

Ian Roxburgh

We were there midweek, all skating away on the ramp, and all of a sudden these kids just swarm on to the flat bottom and stand in the way. They won't move, and we're like, 'Er, excuse me? Will you fuck off please?' Some of the older kids had bandanas covering their faces so you couldn't see who they were, and they had big sticks, rocks, bottles and shit like that. The kids' ages ranged from about six or seven up to about sixteen. We're all up on the platforms and they start chucking the rocks at us.

Then Shane O'Brien and Gavin Hills got in amongst them, they went to the biggest kids there and went face to face with them, and Gavin and Shane were telling them to get out of here, now! When you saw Shane, with his front four teeth missing, you'd be like, 'Oh, fuck', and when Gavin wanted to be, he could be intimidating, and he'd also spent a bit of time at borstal when he was younger and he had these tattoos on his arms – he explained to me once what they meant and they signify whether you're a sergeant or a corporal or whatever – and this kid saw his tattoos and basically went, 'Alright, we're going, see you later', and they all just scarpered. While chucking more stones and bottles at us as they left.

Paul Sunman

The Latimer Road ramp was owned and maintained by the Westway Sports Centre as part of the North Kensington Amenity Trust, which is the charity that supports the area created underneath the Westway overhead motorway that cuts through west London. Slam funded some of the material costs and Dan Adams planned and co-ordinated with Simon Chambers from the sports centre to build it. I assisted in the construction when I could spare the time and then helped to promote it, and we got to put our logo on the platform. I do remember getting the worst skate-related injury during construction when I fell through the ramp supports before it was surfaced. Thought my ankle was broken and I wasn't even on a board.

Dan Adams

Latimer Road came through Paul. There was this really fantastic guy at the sports centre at Latimer Road called Simon, who was a youth worker at the BMX track there. I think that he, and maybe some of his colleagues, had got in touch with Slam – because it was nearby – and had said that they were thinking about building a halfpipe, because some of the BMXers wanted it, and asked Paul for advice.

Paul said that he knew people, and he could help with this, and he called me. I was more a designer and an engineer of that thing than I was a constructor. I had a GCSE in Technical Drawing, but I just loved all that stuff. It was Amateur Hour, but that's the beauty of skateboarding, it allows you to take your amateur enthusiasms and progress them. I was a completely untrained carpenter, a completely untrained technical drawer, but I just liked it and skateboarding allowed me to build on those amateur skills. This for me has always been the beauty of skateboarding; there's never been anybody looking over your shoulder going, 'Now come on son, that's not right', which I fucking hated at school. Being told that you weren't doing it properly, or you weren't good enough, all that sort of stuff.

I specified a ten-foot transition, which was becoming the optimum thing very quickly. The Warrington ramp had been nine-and-a-half, and then suddenly we were reading that everyone was going to ten, so we knew it had to be ten. I went there and Simon had cut all of the transitions out, and I was like, 'Wow, they look huge!', and he smiled, said, 'Yeah, I might have done them twelve foot...', and then he laughed. It did feel fucking big, it really did. When you were standing on top of it you were very high off the ground. I think that has become part of legend; it was just fucking big.

It was very challenging to build it, having your extension cable cut through while you're working, by six-year-olds. Looking around everywhere for your hammer, then hearing this incredible clanking sound, this really aggressive beating of metal on metal, then you look to where you think that sound's coming from and you can see one of these kids up a railway embankment, up a pillar, smashing out the railway signal lights with your hammer.

Shane O'Brien

My first awakening to that was when I was asked by Slam City and the local council to do a skate school there, in '87. It was summer '87, they wanted me as a skate counsellor, because the kids were out for six weeks. So I went to see the local council and the people from the sports centre next to it that was running it all, and they wanted to run as many weeks as they could, getting young skaters coming into the whole scene, and they wanted me to teach them how to skate the ramp.

There was about fifteen kids on the first day that showed up, and they had no idea what a ramp was whatsoever. So it was teaching the basics; teaching them to run up, pump, fakie, frontside, backside, frontside, backside, see how high they could get up. Just the coaching thing. Some of them took to it, and some of them was like,

'No, this thing is ridiculous'. It was twelve foot high, it was red – which is scary – it was made of metal – which is scary – and there was the gypsy camp within fifty metres of it.

I'd have to go down to the Latimer Road train station, meet the bulk of the kids and skate up with them to the ramp or else they would get robbed. Then when it was finishing time we used to take them to the train station and back to the tube station so they would get back on the train and get home with their board and their pads and their Vans. It wasn't a good area, it was one of the worst areas to have a ramp. It was terrible.

We'd skate the ramp and the local travellers would be drunk and they'd come on the ramp and throw bottles at us, throw bottles of drink all over the flat bottom, smashing the glass everywhere. They would piss on the ramp in front of you. The only thing they didn't really want to do was they wouldn't risk fighting because we was old enough to fight and we had boards and stuff. It would have been a bit of a massacre if they'd have started on us. They never went over the top with the fighting thing because we wouldn't have tolerated that. But they did smash things and they did abuse it and they did foul on it and throw furniture all over it.

I was there one day when a young lad, about 15 – and I think he was drunk – was saying he was going to come up and fight us. So he's trying to run up the ramp to get to the deck, and he's running up and grabbing the top, and he's sliding back in. Running up and sliding down, and then he left his finger on the top of the ramp. He'd caught his ring on a screw.

The next thing you know the kid has gone running into the camp and about 50 of them come out, and they're all going to kill us, obviously. 'You've cut my son's finger off!' Then the police arrived, and we had to be put in police cars and they had to lock the police cars. The travellers were rocking the police cars trying to get us out. They just blamed us for it, and it was nothing to do with us. That was kind of the beginning of the end of that ramp. Skaters that went after that unfortunately took their backlash from that and the whole reputation of that ramp went completely downhill... it was a bad place to go and if you was there on your own, because of that major incident, you took a big chance.

FAWR RAMP
Greg Fabb

'Fawr'[4] means big. The surfers built it and the skaters adapted it. It was higher, so they cut it along and made a lower section so there's a tombstone.

SAM'S RAMP
Sam Scott-Hunter

This is my home ramp[3], the very first time we tried to build a ramp, and it was unbelievably bad. Fuck knows what the neighbours thought. No platform to drop in on, and every time you skate up it, it's just going to push backwards like a see-saw. I don't know how many weeks that lasted, but skate that was all I did every day from the moment I got home. ●

1987

SKETCHY
Dan Adams

Sketchy zine was a funny thing, because it just used to appear at events. They're hilarious. They're really, really bitchy, but they absolutely nailed the people that they were talking about, albeit in a fairly cruel way, but the scene was cruel, in a jocular way, with everyone taking the mickey out of each other, or criticising each other's shoes or clothes or haircuts.

Sean Goff

It got to about ten issues before people figured out who it was. The first ever issue appeared off the top of the bridge where the Crystal Palace ramp was, just dropped off the top. Everyone was like, 'What the fuck is this?'

Shane O'Brien

I used to live in the same street as Paul Browne; we lived across the road from each other so we went skating quite a lot together. He was a graphic artist, and he said he wanted to do a skate zine. He said he wanted to do real stories – comical stories – on real skaters, and maybe cover a contest and make it comical. He said he didn't know anyone, and that I knew everyone so I could tell him what was going on and he could come up with stories.

He'd do all the artwork and produce it, and then we'd go to a contest and he would hide them all underneath the ramp and there would be a big surge of, '*Sketchy*'s out!', and there would be mayhem. When people read it they'd be like, 'Who's actually behind this?'. Because there was way too much information about people in there. Someone knew about their lives in America. Which was me, because I used to go and live with them.

BOMBER
Vernon Adams

There was that transition year where Gavin Hills was doing his last year of art college and I was doing nothing apart from going skating, and once he'd finished we started to do *Bomber*, since we were both into writing. We started doing that because we wanted to write and you need an outlet

to do it, don't you? It was just something to do, I suppose. So we just started doing it.

We were quite lucky that Mike John let us have some photos for it but we quickly learned that taking skate photos with a little snappy camera is always a bit hit and miss. One way to get around that was to take photos where we would zoom in on parts of it. Like a close-up of someone doing a Smith grind or whatever, rather than try to do the classic skate shot. More of a zine skate shot in a way. But we did have good photos from Mike. He was very kind to let us have those.

We'd have to find somewhere that would let you photocopy on double-sided A3, which was always a bit of a nightmare because the machine would always jam. Or bits would fall off and get stuck to the photocopier.

We would come up with a flatplan, like you would for a professional magazine, work out how many pages we could afford to do, then we would work out how we would construct it. You'd get a piece of cardboard and literally glue all the pieces on to it.

If you create a spread for the centre spread, you'd have to work out the imposition, much like you would for a professional magazine or a book – what page has to go on the back of each other one – then you go to the photocopy shop with all your boards with all your bits stuck on. We did a deal with the local photocopier place up the road, because it's really expensive to do and we never had any money. I'm pretty sure they regretted that because obviously we just fucked their machine.

There were free bags in Safeways that were just the right size for it, so we used to seal our zine up with those.

It just sort of came together and people seemed to like it, and through that is how we met Ged Wells and Tim Leighton-Boyce, but there was also a journalist called Cynthia Rose who did a little feature in a Sunday magazine that featured a load of zines, including ours. That's how Tim came across it.

FLORIAN BOHM AND THE CROSSED OUT CONVERSE
Scott Wilson

When Converse were the de rigueur skate shoe, we all wore them and we used to always cross out the logo. I don't even know why we did. You'd get a marker pen and just put a big X through it. Someone saw a picture of Florian Böhm – probably doing a frontside boneless on vert – in a pair and we thought it would be a good name for a little magazine.

Ged came on board after the second issue. He was five years older and he was pretty influential to us, because that's a massive age gap at that point, so getting him on board was pretty nice.

Ged Wells

By networking *FBCC* to other zine makers and contributing to other zines, we all became connected to wider UK skate and creative scenes.

Because I was sending zines to Tim, he responded by asking whether I could contribute to *RAD* at the start of its transition from *BMX Action Bike*. I got to do a few comp write-ups and contributed some illustrations; TLB had to do a heavy grammar edit, my spelling was appalling. Come to think of it, so was Gav Hills', but Tim didn't judge, he still gave opportunities regardless.

I'd started making Insane back while studying on foundation, mainly hand painting t-shirts and shoes, then screen printing a little later. Insane got great support from Southsea Skatepark and South Coast stores in the early days. My mum started making garments and we had a good printing set-up at home.

Things really took off with the skate shorts and trousers; Insane Jim Jams were mainly sold mail order but also got stocked within the UK independents. Insane really started to work for me as a creative outlet, because I could do a lot of drawing focused towards this Insane world. ●

Zines

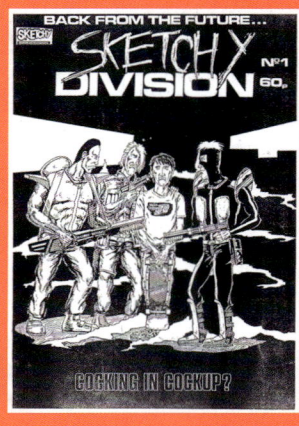

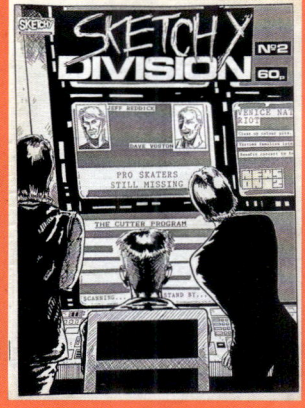

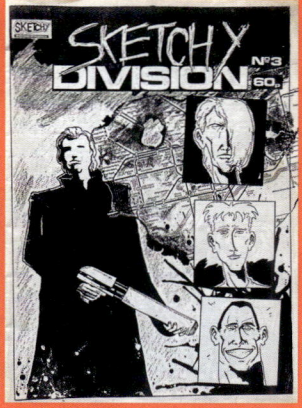

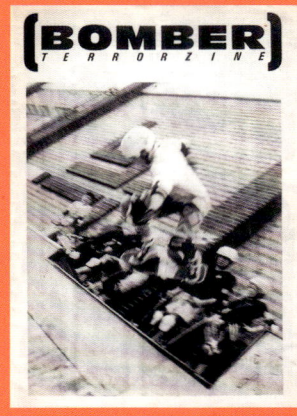

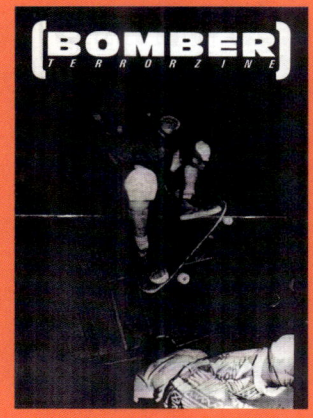

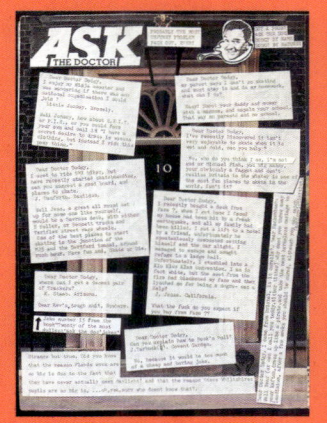

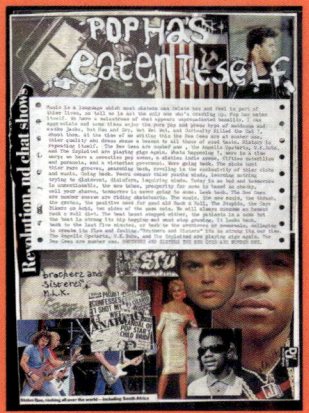

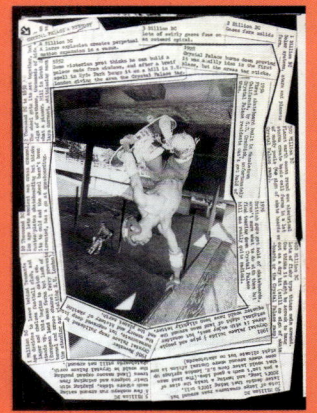

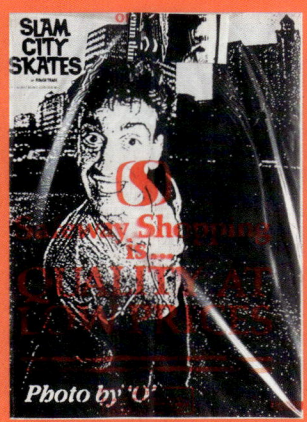

1987

Elsewhere

1987

198
8

Matt Keeble, Downderry, by Alex Cock

There was bugger-all money to be made. I kept accounts of all the money I got out of all my skateboarding thing back in those days and it's nothing. It really is nothing. You'd get £100 for a demo if you're lucky, and you had to get there yourself, and eat, and come back. It's not like it was easy money in skateboarding back then, we just skated, and it'd be like, 'Oh cool, they're going to give me £100 towards petrol money. OK, I'll go there'.

SEAN GOFF

Richard Williams, Southbank, by Lee Yau

CLOCKWISE FROM TOP LEFT
[1] Rob Dukes, by Lee Yau
[2] Ian 'Davross' Scudds, by Lee Yau
[3] Tommy Guerrero, by Lee Yau
[4] Paul Davidson, by Lee Yau
[5] Boma Jaja and Robbie Newell, by Lee Yau

Reuben Goodyear

The security guards were always trying to kick us off or stop us from skating there, and incredibly, whatever they did to stop us from skating, none of it was that effective and we'd always find a way to make good of a bad situation. Turning the lights off and throwing the stones down on the ground was probably the worst of it, but taking the paving slabs out? That was genius. We'd never thought of doing that, then all of a sudden we've got these wedged slabs and we're making ramps out of them.

Matt Dawson

Some of the tramps used to go really fucking mental, and didn't want us there, but some were really cool. Some would just get off their head on whatever they were taking and start being really aggro with everybody, but there was enough of us there to back each other up and there was quite a lot of skateboards getting hit round people's heads. Some of it was quite gruesome really, but it had to happen at that time, I suppose.

There we'd a phase at Southbank when we used to have a lot of roughnecks coming down and robbing people and nicking boards. We didn't have any money, so they're nicking boards, because boards were £120. They'd nick them then sell them, I'd imagine.

Simon Evans

I started skating Southbank back when Matt McMullan and Morbid and those guys ruled that place. I don't know what it was but I just loved Southbank. You could always skate it, it was like a dream. It was so smooth and beautiful. I used to go up there by myself, and when you're a kid you start making friends and then before you know it you're part of it, you're like a local.

At first it was really intimidating, just being there. Showing up and getting shouted at and laughed at, and then after a while you fit in. It was like that. I don't remember it changing really, but that was how that started.

Matt Stuart

Southbank was like Neverland; it was basically a bunch of kids flying about on skateboards doing what the fuck they liked with complete freedom, but also with an absolute democracy of people, with only an interest in whether you fucking make a trick or not and not interested in whether you're black, white, fat, thin, girl, boy... It absolutely didn't matter.

Matt Gold

It did feel like London, in parts, still had remnants of the Victorian era. The old docks and horse-drawn carts. Even around Waterloo, around Bankside where the Tate is now, that was really ancient, rundown, and almost prehistoric. That bullring down where the IMAX is now was almost a no-go area. It was like *Mad Max* going through there. London's unrecognisable since then.

There was the homeless guy that used to jump off Waterloo Bridge for money, and he got stuck in the silt one time. I thought he was going to die but he managed to get out.

We used to forge travel cards, we used to cut out a date and stick it on, so it would look like today's date, and from a distance you would just wave it. So many graphic artists came out of that crew, people like Will Bankhead and Ben Drury, endless people. So many of the scene are designers now, in some way.

Mike Manzoori

It wasn't all jazzy and developed like it is now. I was this little kid in no-man's land, and behind the big skate area it was just full of homeless people and you walked through a lot of homeless camps to get there, via Waterloo Station, through the underpass.

The first time I went it was scary; I felt like I was in *A Clockwork Orange* or something like that, and it reeked of piss, but it was unreal. It was unreal that I was at Southbank. It's changed so much over the years but there's still that same vibe when I go there. It's the most iconic, 'Oh shit, this is it' place. ●

M-ZONE
Charlie 'Dave' Burrows

We never had a computer in M-Zone. All the ads were done by my hand. Peter Tarry would take a photograph, I had a box of liquid dyes and I would drip the dyes on to the 35mm slide. Once it had dried off I would get my scalpel out and do the scratching stuff and then I would technically compose a small advert.

A lot of the people who did the scanning – so that it can be reproduced in a magazine – refused to work with me because they'd never seen anything like it. I found this one guy that thought I was hilarious as long as I got the maths right. Because I'm working with 35mm slides and I'm working with A4 magazine format, if you don't get the maths right it's either going to be too small or too big. That was the challenge because maths is not my best subject.

I did the artwork and Peter Tarry took the pictures. Twice a week, depending on how many people came round the shop, we'd get in my Range Rover and just go around and take photographs. Malarkey. Take a day trip to London and buy everyone a beer. And we just kept on doing it like that.

When I opened Carnaby Street, and had Stüssy, it attracted all the stylists. So the stylists came in and said they'd never seen anything like this before, and I didn't even know what a stylist was. They would ask if they could borrow clothes and I'd tell them they had to buy them.

Then once it started appearing in photoshoots in *The Face* and in *i-D*, everything just went through the roof. It had *The Face* and *i-D* stamp of approval, and that crowd is obviously not 12 years old. Twelve-year-olds were not reading *i-D* and *The Face*, but 18-year-olds were.

And then we couldn't even keep it on the shelves. We would receive a shipment and there would be other store buyers literally standing outside our store to get as much product as they could, for their store. One of our biggest customers was American Classics, and they're still in business. Stüssy didn't have that much

product for export, but because of it being in *i-D* and *The Face*, all of a sudden Australia wanted it, Germany wanted it... They didn't have enough product for everybody who wanted it. So we would place an order and probably get 30–40% of that order, because they were trying to please Titus in Dortmund, Germany, and the Hill brothers in Australia. There were too many people wanting the product and there wasn't enough product to go round.

We had ads in *i-D* and *The Face*. I was very lucky because my dad's best friend was the advertising director for both magazines. He would offer us the back page of *The Face* at cost, so we ended up advertising a lot with them and also *i-D*, basically because I was paying nothing for the ads. I wasn't paying face value, but that definitely added to people thinking, 'Wow, this company must be massive!', but it was literally because of my dad's dirt bike buddy who was the advertising director for *The Face* and for *i-D*.

Paul Mittleman

Stüssy, to me, was definitely more of a London thing. It went up north a little later when stores started buying it, but London was looking to America for sneakers and whatnot, the north was still a bit of a terrace thing.

Ray Calthorpe

Seal came in, just as they'd released 'Killer', and he goes, 'Alright? I'm going to be at number one next week, can you give me some free clothes?' Dave was just, 'No. Fuck off' and turfed him out. In hindsight, it wasn't really his style, was it? Jesus Jones maybe, but not Seal in his bondage gear.

Once we had Robert Smith from The Cure come in, and he said, 'Hello, have you got any large trainers?' So I showed him some Airwalk 720, or Inferno, and he sort of paused for a bit, looked at them, went 'Nah' and walked out. Not large enough. I think that was just before the 'Why Can't I Be You?'-era Cure, when he was wearing massive boots and baggy clothes.

I used to see Dave giving stuff away to people, and I thought, 'Well, if Dave's giving stuff away...', so I used to sell my

friends Vision shoes for £30 when they were retailing at £65, and stuff like that. That's the kind of behaviour that got me sacked, in fact.

Curtis McCann

Dave – or Charlie – was so good to me, he got me making funny, or maybe, stupid faces and put me in some of the M-Zone ads. If it wasn't for him I don't know how I would have had my skate career, I certainly couldn't have afforded to get to the level I reached without sponsorship. I didn't even have to pay full price for my second board, and soon after that I was getting stuff for free... I was this mad little 13-year-old from Sutton and next I'm hanging out with this fun 'grown-up' who had his own shop with his dad. From time to time we would go on photoshoots and drive around in a Range Rover... I was already partial to a drink so we would skate, have a laugh, and I would nearly always find myself at the pub eating a slap-up meal.

We had a lot of really fun times; the most memorable was a fashion show that the M-Zone skaters were part of. I remember jumping onto my board... so scared, however I didn't realise the catwalk had soft lino on it! So I ended up feeling like I was tik-tacking on mud in front of all these people for a very long time... my heart was racing! Later behind the scenes, in the alleyway, some of the fit 'grown-up' models were stripping and flashing before going into the changing rooms... Dave told me that I could go in but I was too shy! I was only about 13 or 14... Being sponsored by Mud Machine/M-Zone was a big deal to me because I was getting fashionable, and for what it's worth, expensive clothes... I was getting enough so that I could sell bits to fund day-to-day skating – just! And the way I remember it, it was like Christmas day came around every few weeks... at that time all I really wanted was to skate, get free stuff, get clean, drink some alcohol, and 'get off' with girls. To me skating itself was the extended energy of what I was feeling in '84 around graffiti art, electro, body-popping and breakdancing. →

Shops

Elsewhere

M-Zone ads, artwork by Charles Burrows, photos by Peter Tarry and Charles Burrows

M ZONE

TRUCKS

→ **CLAN SKATES**
Jamie Blair

With Pig City, I knew that if they had a skateboard shop, I could have a skateboard shop.

Davie Philip, his girlfriend at the time, his mum, and a couple of friends from Grangemouth were making skateboard shorts. Cutting the cotton to a basic design and sewing them up on sewing machines, but they had Velcro, and Velcro was seen as a new thing. Shorts that you didn't need to button up, with no belt loops or anything, and they were flying out the door.

He would have a bag of Poizone clothing with him at every skateboard comp he went to. People would want to buy it, so it would always sell out. Davie was such a good skateboarder; he had such distinctive style and he was right up there with all the best British and European skateboarders, and they wanted Poizone clothing as well, so the guys that you wanted to wear the stuff were already wearing it, so kids obviously wanted it as well. He had a good cottage industry going, so we thought that we could set up the shop and sell Poizone through that.

I went to the Prince's Trust, which at that time was a funding programme that would lend you interest-free money.

We also had the Enterprise Allowance Scheme which was a government scheme. Thatcher's children, really, so either you could sign on, or you could sign on and work and they paid you a wage for the first year.

They gave you a business manager too, so a business guy would come and ask us loads of questions, and we had to have a business plan. I sat for days and days writing out a business plan... What products we were going to stock, unit costs, all that. We had about a £3,000 initial order, which was ten skateboard decks, twelve pairs of Pacer Hogs shoes, some clothing and whatever else. Death Box gave us SOR – sale or return, which I'd never heard of before – so Jeremy Fox basically gave us a bunch of decks and said, 'Sell them and pay for them when they're sold', which was a help.

We'd have what looked like a cinema queue outside the door every Saturday and we used to have to fight our way to the front to open the door. Inside the shop was like a sea of people, and if you had to go and get a product you had to literally climb over people. And you'd have ten kids sitting on their knees watching a video while we're trying to step round them. We loved it though. Setting up boards all day long on Saturdays.

→ **SLAM CITY SKATES**
Rob Dukes

I first met Iain Baker in 1988, he was brought in as manager of Talbot Road and I was his second in command. Which was great fun, he was a really nice guy and easy to get along with. The only problem was, his band Jesus Jones were just taking off, and Iain was taking an alarming number of days off 'sick'. In the end he realised he had to make a decision, and left the shop.

Lots of bands came to either play live or just do meet and greet stuff at the Neal's Yard Rough Trade, and they had to walk through Slam to get there. I remember seeing Björk before she was Björk; the Sugarcubes visited the record shop and they were all upstairs looking at Lance Mountain t-shirts or whatever.

Katharine Hamnett was so humourless. Another – surprisingly – humourless one was Mike Leigh. He came in with his kids and asked to look at some stupid board game that we sold – it was like Monopoly or something, but rubbish. He asked me about it and I told him it was boring, and he got really shirty. I thought, 'Would you rather I told you it was good, and you waste your money?'

Russell Waterman

I started working in Slam City in 1988, and I drifted between Talbot Road and Covent Garden. My first job was to build some of the key clamping just before Covent Garden opened.

Paul Sunman was really good at taking chances and bringing people in. He didn't go to the obvious place for any of the stuff that he did, and I really admire him for that. I realised much later that he took chances and went with stuff that was really forward-thinking, and some of the stuff he's done has been hugely influential, and not just in skateboarding but in other cultures. A lot of what he did doesn't get the recognition it deserves, and he put some interesting people together.

There was some attitude towards Slam City to start with, especially from some of the older skaters, because it was a much slicker set-up than what they'd been used to. Skaters at that time were pretty moody with anything that smacked of organisation, or if there was any hint than somebody might be making money out of doing skateboarding, then there was a massive distrust. It's different now because a lot of people in skateboarding are quite rich, but at the time everyone was just trying to pay their way and make it work.

All of the Southbank kids were coming in, and I was often picking them up and throwing them out because they were so fucking annoying. There were people that I naively trusted at times, both at Neal's Yard and Talbot Road, and they stole stuff. After that, as far as I was concerned, if I was in the shop they couldn't come in. That's what a lot of the skaters were like, and I kind of get it, but also don't get it because the stuff we had going on there was very real. It was trying to keep something going and hold on to it, and some of these people rinsed it.

Paul Sunman

We were incredibly fortunate to have a circle of people who were invested in wanting to be involved and support the brand and ethos that we had created. Some of those people were supporters and customers and a few became employees, both part time and full time. Once it had become a business as well as a passion it required management, and then it requires a structure and someone to take responsibility for that. Most of that fell on my shoulders, and everyone looks to you for the answer to every question and to be the source of all knowledge. Google was not my friend; in fact, the closest we got to the internet was a plug-in telephone, a photocopier and a giant fax machine that was bigger than a fridge.

So the choice of people who became employees was always one of the hardest processes, and I'm always amazingly grateful to all the people who worked at Slam and Rough Trade for believing in what we did and were confident enough to entrust their livelihoods to us. It's not fair to consider any of them as somehow not relevant because someone defines them as a non-skater. Everyone who became an employee was there on their own merit and reflected who we were as a brand.

There was a lot of creative people who gravitated towards both Rough Trade and Slam City. We were very fortunate that there was a pool of talent that would want to be involved in what we were trying to do. Instead of us asking people to create anything to a brief, it was often an offer to create something they wanted to do based on their ideas, and not ours. Edwin Pouncey did several designs which he thought fitted with our image and ethos with no direction, other than 'Edwin, can you do a t-shirt design?' →

FROM TOP LEFT
[1] Clan Skates artwork and ads by Jim Rusk, Malcolm Hay and Jamie Blair in the shop
[2] Slam City Skates logos and ads by Edwin 'Savage Pencil' Pouncey; Russell Waterman, Southbank

DB &
SLAM CITY SKATES

VISION STREET WEAR ™

present

THE NIGHT OF THE

LIVING SKATE ZOMBIES

at

LIMELIGHT

136 Shaftesbury Avenue
On American Independence Day
Monday 4th July 1988
Doors Open 9:30 p.m.

Complimentary Admission For You & Your Stick
With This Ticket £5 without

This invitation cannot be sold or transferred
Right of Admission Reserved/Capacity is Limited
Proof of Age May Be Required

Surprise Demo's from
U.S. & U.K. Skaters

Mini Ramp

Videos

Hot Dogs

Pop Corn

Plus Music from D.B.

"Don't

Die

Wondering"

IN THE YEAR of our Lord 1988 AD, a strange phenomenon has begun. Certain planets in the heavens are moving towards an alignment, whilst in the homes of a city called London, unknown to the innocent inhabitants, high tensile steel ball bearings have begun to vibrate, and even now are being magnetically drawn towards a nineteenth century church at the very centre of the city. T
The church was said to have been built on the edge of an ancient circle used for mysterious and not so holy rituals. The cult was lost in the folds of time, or was it? For on July 4th when the planets and circle hit perfect alignment, the age old cosmic peace will be shattered and mayhem will ensue, for it will be.....

THE NIGHT OF THE

LIVING SKATE ZOMBIES

...GOD HELP US ALL!

Dan Adams

The Limelight night was through Slam, and it was all because the kooks were getting excited about skateboarding. Skateboarding was blowing up and everybody was realising how cool it is. Looking back it looks naff as hell, but Limelight was the super-trendy West End club in an old church on Shaftesbury Avenue. It was the London outpost of a famous New York club.

I went to have a beer, and because we'd been involved in building it we had VIP bar passes for the bar upstairs, and Michael Hutchence was there. It was very much the case that skateboarding had arrived, and we were in the room with everybody else now.

→ **SS20**

Mon Barbour

I smashed my knee up in the summer of '88, and I was in a plaster cast, and because I couldn't do anything else I actually got my shit together, went and did some business courses and opened the shop December the 1st, '88, with Dave Furneau.

At the time I was 19 years old, and Dave was probably 24. I persuaded him to remortgage his house to raise 15 grand, and then we borrowed 15 grand off the bank and we used that money to set up the shop. I asked Sean Goff if he wanted to work for us, so he was employed by me and Dave, and then ten months later he bought into the partnership at a bargain rate. I'm not very sure why, but he only put five grand in.

Our first stop was Shiner, because I was sponsored by Shiner, but it was quite a weird sponsorship for me because I was a vert roller skater, and no one did that kind of stuff but they just flowed me all sorts of stuff, and there was always skateboard equipment. But I do remember being really gutted that my first step into business involved money, because I just thought I was going to get credit straight away. I remember Michael, who ran Shiner, when I'd gone down there to pick up stuff – £1,800, £1,900 worth of stuff – being like, 'So, can I get a cheque then?', and me saying, 'Oh, I thought I was getting it on credit!' 'Not the first lot, Mon.' So I wrote out a cheque and had to very quickly put some money into the account to clear that, but Shiner were so supportive throughout the whole time with SS20. They were brilliant.

Alex Moul

I was on the doorstep the morning they opened, and I immediately started to bug Mon and Sean by asking about everything that was in the shop, which I'm sure was annoying. My mum actually told them that if I was bothering them, to tell me to fuck off.

That's someone's ramp [2] in Abingdon, and Tom Penny's in the background with a Mac board with an SS20 sticker on it.

Mon Barbour

It just took off, and it took off really, really well. I'd already done loads of publicity, so I'd already made up shitloads of stickers and they'd been stuck on ramps everywhere, so in the first issue of the magazine that we had an ad, there were already four or five photos where you could see SS20 stickers on the tops of halfpipes.

When I had the ramps on the farm, my mum and dad had a 55-foot diameter CND symbol painted on one of our barn roofs. My mum was one of the Greenham Common protestors, and my dad was a very leftwing Labour councillor, and in this area of Oxfordshire, it's just stinking rich with loads of Tories, so we were the black sheep of North Oxfordshire by a long way. So I already had that political leftwing affiliation through all that, and yeah, SS20 was a Russian nuclear warhead that was decommissioned in 1988, so that had a large bearing on the name. What I loved was that little Johnny, some 12- or 13-year-old kid, isn't going to know what SS20 is, but the mum and dad are going to.

So when little Johnny goes to mum and dad to say that he wants to buy a skateboard from a shop called SS20, mum and dad are gonna be horrified and they're gonna go, 'Don't go there, it's a leftwing communist threat!', or they're gonna tell him it's a military threat, but either way, little Johnny's gonna want to go, isn't he? It was a bit of reverse psychology but nobody really got it. It was just a little poke to the establishment, really. ●

CLOCKWISE FROM TOP LEFT
[1] Limelight club, including Phil Chapman, Richard Williams, Mac, Crispin Robinson and Warren Angell, by Lee Yau
[2] Alex Moul and Tom Penny, Abingdon, by Mon Barbour
[3] First SS20 ad, *RAD*, December
[4] Limelight overview by Lee Yau
[5] Limelight event flyer

Sean Goff

Pacer Hogs shoes were probably some off-the-shelf thing they got, whacked on an ollie patch, and then got a team together. It's basically a Vision canvas high-top, cheaper than Vision. People were wearing Converse high-tops, then Vision came out with theirs, then Pacer did the same thing.

They got the team together, and we had photo incentive so we'd have stickers and wear the t-shirts as much as possible, so they did a really good job of promoting it. A Pacer Hogs photo incentive was £25, £50 if it was full-page, but you'd get the photo incentive even if you weren't showing the shoes. It was the case that if you were in a magazine, they would give you the photo incentive.

You'd have two pairs of shoes and that was it. When one was worn out you sent them back to them, and they sent you a replacement. They told us that was so they could see how the shoes wore out.

With Death Box you'd get a deck maybe every two months, sometimes every three or four months. Probably four sets of wheels in a year. It's the stuff that you need; it's not like you had excess amounts of stuff, you just got what you needed. You just skated, but you were in a position where you were lucky enough that you'd get given a bit of free product and you're more likely to be able to crash at someone's house

because somebody knows who you are because you're in the magazines.

There was bugger-all money to be made. I kept accounts of all the money I got out of all my skateboarding things back in those days and it's nothing. It really is nothing. You'd get £100 for a demo if you're lucky, and you had to get there yourself, and eat, and come back. It's not like it was easy money in skateboarding back then, we just skated, and it'd be like, 'Oh cool, they're going to give me £100 towards petrol money. OK, I'll go there.' No one was making a wage. No one could quit skateboarding and have money.

I'd be really surprised if there was more than 200 of each of my models made.

I did the shape for my board, but we never had any say in the graphics and to be honest, I didn't care. I really didn't care about any of that stuff. If it looked really bad I'd have said something, but it was a Mac graphic, it was alright, it was on a skateboard and I like skateboarding and I ride skateboards. I've never chosen a graphic in my life. It's not that important to me, 'cause I'm not looking at it. I don't care what's on the bottom of my skateboard, I'm just going to skate it.

I really didn't care about any of that stuff at all; the only time I cared about Death Box stuff was when they came out with that shit V-tail. When that came out

it was terrible, so I had to pack it out with griptape. I told Jeremy how bad it was and eventually he got rid of it because it was just uncomfortable and unskateable.

Paul 'Rocker' Robson

It was funny, the day before was the B-comp, in the Livingston halfpipe, and just before I was going to do my run, my back truck snapped. Andy Lincoln said I could just use his board, so I did the contest on his board, and had a good time chatting with everybody that was there, then somebody shouts, 'Rocker, you've won', and I was quite overwhelmed.

Sean said he wanted to introduce me to somebody, and he introduced me to Jeremy Fox. Jeremy asked me a little bit about myself, asked if I was a street skater, a vert skater or a miniramp skater, and I just said, 'All of the above'. He asked for my phone number and said he wanted to flow me some stuff, and that was it. From that point on there was a contest every weekend. And that went on for about four years.

Pete Dossett

My first board was a Mac-shaped board, with no graphics on it, just a teapot, and it said 'Pete Dossett Experimental Model'. It was slightly shorter to make it different from the Mac, in case people thought it was too much like it. It looked like Tony Hawk's shape, but it's from a Lester Kasai board that was out at the same time. ●

SKATEBOARD! MAGAZINE
Ian Lawton

A mate of a mate, Andy Darling, who wasn't really a skater, had got drawn in – somehow – to work on *Skateboard!* magazine. Steve Kane had pitched this idea to the publishers and it was going to go ahead, but he hadn't worked out who was going to take photos or write it. Paul Duffy was the main photographer who got brought onboard, and someone got in touch with me, so I said I was connected to these guys in Liverpool so I could hook them up with Dan-Z and Dave Davies, and Steve Kane obviously had the connection with the Bristol scene. That's how the first issue of *Skateboard!* magazine ended up having stuff about Liverpool and Bristol in it.

It seemed pretty obvious at the time that the northern skate scene needed a bit more coverage so one of the first things we did was we went up to Livi and did an interview with Davie Philip, and I went up to the north east, to the fullpipes in Redcar. Mini Mansell took me there.

You'd just make connections. There seemed to be certain people in skateboarding then who'd take it upon themselves to be the kind of 'scene leader', and they knew everything that's going on. People were just very keen to get some coverage. The same with the Scottish lot, they'd bend over backwards to help you and take you to the places.

RAD MAGAZINE
Vernon Adams

Gavin Hills and I basically worked together as a team. When we were writing we'd write the features together, even before we worked for *RAD*. We'd get commissioned to do a feature and we'd both write the feature, I'd read his and he'd read mine, and then we'd sort of merge them together. It'd be like, 'Your beginning's good, your ending's good, we need to rework the middle' and we'd just work together like that.

We'd be responsible for certain sections of the magazine so we'd write those, but about '88 we got commissioned to do a book called *Skateboarding Is Not A Book*, and then we ended up doing quite a lot more stuff.

We got an advance to do the book and that was just great timing because there was the Euroskate '88 competition in Czechoslovakia, then Shut Up And Skate was happening in America, so with the money we got for the book we decided to go to Euroskate, come back for a week, and then go to America for Shut Up And Skate, and travel round.

I used some of the money to buy a lens, and a flash, to use on a camera body my dad had. My dad had a camera but he didn't have a fisheye or a flash, so I thought if I had those I could maybe shoot a few shots on a trip, if there was something we were at and there were no photographers. I thought I could maybe learn to take some better snaps, or whatever.

So we went to the comp, but then realised that if we were going to write about the comp we'd need some photos, so Gav suggested that I start taking some photos, but I really didn't know what I was doing, and when we got them back from the printers, that was clear.

I was writing under my own name but when I started doing photography I didn't want my pictures to be judged by my writing, or my writing to be judged by my pictures, so that's where the name Jay Podesta came from. And also, we didn't have many people on the magazine so it made it look like there were more people working on the magazine than there really were.

Steve Douglas

In the States I was such a skate rat that I wanted to find out what was going on, and Tim knew that he could rely on me, so my page was the last page done every issue.

I would make notes during the month, and at the end of the month I would scribble them down and fax them to him, and he would have to retype it and the magazine would go to print. The good thing about it was that the UK – and every other region that was getting that magazine – were getting the news way before *Transworld* and *Thrasher*. Those magazines had the news way, way later than *RAD*. ●

CLOCKWISE FROM TOP LEFT
[1] Ian 'Lecky' Leck, Thornaby, by Ian 'Meany' Lawton
[2] Davie Philip, Livingston, by Ian 'Meany' Lawton
[3] Steve Douglas page, *RAD*, December
[4] *Skateboarding Is Not A Book*, by Vernon Adams and Gavin Hills
[5] Rob Dukes, Kings Cross, by Vernon Jay Podesta' Adams
[6] *RAD*, November, Paul 'Rocker' Robson, by TLB
[7] *Skateboard!* issue 1, by Paul Duffy

CLOCKWISE FROM TOP LEFT
[1] Main Redcar pipe, by Ian 'Meany' Lawton
[2] Darlo, Redcar pipe, by Ian 'Meany' Lawton
[3] Pete Dossett, Morfa, by Ian 'Meany' Lawton
[4] Neil Danns, Morfa, by Ian 'Meany' Lawton
[5] British Steel, Redcar, by Andy Lincoln
NEXT PAGE
[6] Martin Bernstein, Broadmarsh, Nottingham, by James Hudson

Elsewhere

→ **REDCAR PIPES**
Andy Lincoln

What a weird place Redcar fullpipes was. You'd drive along the seafront and you had all the sand dunes on the right-hand side, then there was a big fence on the left. There was a hole in the fence, then you'd walk about 400 metres, then up a bank, then you could look down on the full site – this is all British Steel, this is supposed to be security patrolled and what have you – then you'd just wander down to the fullpipes and crack on.

Al Morrison

I worked at British Steel, where the fullpipes were. Redcar had the biggest blast furnace in Europe, and when they were buying it they got enough parts so they could build a second one, and they never built the second one. There was a compound where they stored all the metal that was meant to be for the second blast furnace, and amongst it there was three fullpipes.[1]

If the security guards found you they would escort you out and ask your name, and you'd always say it was Tony Alva or something, but we went there for years. I think they'd been there since the early '70s.

Paul Robson

It was really bizarre because it was high above the ground, so if you were up there you could be spotted very easily. We got in a few times and were able to ride it, and some of the big skateboard people – Jamie Blair and Davie Philip – came down and rode it with us a few times.

→ **MORFA**
Skin Phillips

I built the Morfa ramp, because I'd built the ramps before. That ramp[3] was constructed with probably twice as much wood as it really needed, and it was built on Fallbrook dimensions. It was big, and at the time possibly the best ramp in Europe. In all honesty only two local guys could skate it. It weren't for kids, really.

Greg Fabb

The council gave us proper money – I think it was 30 grand – and the council chippies cut the transition panels, and it was like a work of art – everything was done perfectly. The ground wasn't flat, so it was built on plinths of concrete paving slabs.

That ramp coincides with the death of vert anyway. We'd built a ramp that was hard to ride.

→ **BROADMARSH**
Carl Shipman

Me and my brother used to go to Nottingham every single weekend to skate Broadmarsh[6]. That's where we were skating street all the time. Broadmarsh were sick. Rough as hell, crappy ground, but such a good place and good people came through there. Alan Rushbrooke were always there, and Dino Squillino from Sheffield, he were sick as anything at Broadmarsh.

Then you had the inside of the bus station as well, which you could skate at any time and not get kicked out. ●

Elsewhere

1988

Elsewhere

THE SMELL O' DEATH LIKES SKINHEADS

COMP. NO. 7

SKATE COMP AT SOUTHBANK
SAT. MARCH 19TH STARTS AT 5.00PM
MARCH 19TH
NO ENTRY FEE•NO BIG EGOS+HARD DRUGS ONLY

'HOLESHOT WAS THE BIGGEST FUCKING JOKE EVER

→ **AMERICAN VISITORS**
Darren Howman
We went to Bedminster the day Natas and Jesse Martinez were doing a demo there. That was insane. We get there, they don't show up for ages, and the park's fucking chocka. Jesse Martinez showed up first and we didn't really know who he was, so everyone's just like, 'Where's Natas?' Then out of nowhere this golden-tanned, blonde-haired big dude rolls in. Natas was doing massive frontside airs in the snake-run[1], and I'd never seen anyone go that high on a skateboard in my life.

Lee Yau
That's one of my favourite photos[6] because it's got an architectural slant to it, and I'm an architect now anyway. The other flash going off is just an amazing coincidence. I did some LSD fly poster things, and on that little light, at the top, there's one of those on there and it stayed up there for decades afterwards. It only got taken down in the late '90s, when they boarded it all up.

→ **SMELL OF DEATH SOUTHBANK**
Lee Yau
The event had been mentioned in *RAD*, so all these little kids turned up with their mums and dads, expecting to see a competition, and Steve Wilshire was pissed out of his head, shouting into this loudhailer, chucking cans at everybody and telling everybody to fuck off. The comp lasted maybe four or five minutes before he started throwing cans at everyone.

He worked for the London Underground, and at the Southbank event he took us through a network of tunnels – he had a pass key or something – under the ground, and there's a room under Waterloo Station somewhere, and he had his bottle of vodka in there. There were a couple of bin bags full of empty cans, and a bottle of vodka. The bags of empty cans were to chuck at people afterwards.

Steve Wilshire
If you got a sticker, you had to throw it back up straight away, you could not keep shit. Who wants a fucking sticker? Throw it back up. And the guy that's going for the stickers? Fuckin' jump on his back and ride him around for a while. Sticker tosses[3] were the best part because there was a little bit of anarchy for a minute. ●

CLOCKWISE FROM TOP LEFT
[1] Natas Kaupas at Dean Lane, Bedminster, by Darren Howman
[2] Flyer for Smell of Death contest at Southbank by Steve Wilshire
[3] Smell of Death sticker toss, Southbank, by Lee Yau
[4] Will Bankhead shoots Natas Kaupas, Southbank, by Ed Gill
[5] Natas Kaupas, Split Skates ramp, Manchester, via Ross Milne
[6] Steve Caballero, Southbank, by Lee Yau

1989

Simon Evans, by Tim Leighton-Boyce

It was the last flickers of vert skateboarding, the last glow of a dying section of skateboarding, as it transitioned into street skating, but underground street skating. A lot of people fell off the vert thing and stopped skateboarding, and a bunch of new bloods took skateboarding somewhere new.
It was a generational thing too, because as vert skaters we were all in our mid-'20s, early-'30s, and then the new guys were 15, 16, 17... They saw the drop-off of vert and it just became stale, somehow, and street skating became really exciting.

JAMIE BLAIR

Jonathon Trenter, Preston, by Sean Keef

Elsewhere

CLOCKWISE FROM TOP LEFT
[1] Ben Wheeler, Telford, by Tim Leighton-Boyce
[2] Ian Roxburgh, Boston Manor, by Tim Leighton-Boyce
[3] Alex Moul (extract), *RAD*, March, by Tim Leighton-Boyce
[4] Ian Roxburgh layouts, *RAD*
[5] Ian Roxburgh, Cromer pool, by Tim Leighton-Boyce

→ *RAD MAGAZINE*
Reuben Goodyear

Telford[1] was a rad trip, that was one that sticks in my memory. I have no idea whether there was an angle on it, if there was a pre-conceived idea of a story or if it was just something we'd do and see what comes out of the other end. It was a loose arrangement, as everything was back then.

Ben Wheeler

Tim Leighton-Boyce took me and Reuben Goodyear to Telford because he basically wanted to do an article about the new towns and empty spaces. I grew up in Stockwell, so that was a random thing.

It was staged in a way, Tim deciding to take a couple of London skaters that he knew from Southbank somewhere else. But I think that was part of the point, taking these Londoners and seeing what they want to do in a new town that they've never been to. See what they find. That's the more romantic view of it.

Tim Leighton-Boyce

There was nearly always at least one person with me, which was done for a couple of reasons. One of them was from needing people around who could actually see what was going on with a skater's eye, and draw my attention to that person there in whatever shirt, because he's good and he's doing something that I should be photographing. Because I didn't have that instinct, and besides, there was too much else to be concentrating on. The other reason was, as a sort of insurance policy. To go somewhere, it's always a good idea to make sure there's somebody around who'll produce interesting stuff.

Alex Moul

Sean asked me to go skating with him one Saturday, and when he saw that I was doing jump-on handrails he said he wanted to get TLB up to shoot photographs. I didn't know what that meant, and I didn't know what sponsorship meant or what free anything meant, or what was going on.

He came up from *RAD* magazine, and we shot a bunch of stuff. I guess the handrail was pretty inspirational to a lot of young people, like, 'If that little kid's doing it, surely I can do it too'. I liked that about the whole thing. My mum got my 'Spike the Skate Animal' sweatshirt from Texas.

I got the next issue of *RAD* magazine from WHSmith and of course I wasn't in it. I was like, 'Ah, I knew it. That's alright.' Next month I got *RAD* magazine and opened it up and there was 12 pages of me[3], and that blew me head off. Jeremy called SS20 and asked if I'd like to ride for Death Box, and I said yes. I didn't know what that meant but all this free stuff started showing up at the house, and my dad was like, 'Where the hell did you get all the money for this? What have you been doing?', and I was like, 'I don't know, I guess I'm sponsored now?'

Ian Roxburgh

Tim would teach you things like how it's not good to have someone's face in the centre gutter or having their back to you on the cover. They should always be looking towards the open side of the mag. Little things like that. Occasionally, we'd get told at the last minute that there was going to be a sticker on the cover, and it's like, 'The fucking artwork for the cover's already gone off to print!' Sometimes we'd know it was going to be on there; you can tell the ones where we knew and the ones we didn't. Sometimes they'd put the sticker somewhere different to where it was supposed to be because they didn't give a shit.

By accident or design, we'd become the group of skaters that got together to ride any pools/ponds that came on to our radar. When we were driving up to Norfolk[5] the weather was getting worse and the rain was pouring when we arrived.

There was about eight feet of transition, with four feet of vert, which was covered with zinc metal sheets. We didn't think riding in the rain could be fun, but it was.

Sean Goff

I was one of TLB's go-tos, like, 'Call Sean up, he'll go anywhere', and he told me about this backyard pool, and I was just like, 'Yep!' Tim drove us there and when we turned up it was raining and there was water in the bottom, but it was like, 'Well we might as well have a go'.

This is the crap we have to deal with in the UK. Places like that, when you go with TLB, local skaters would come to skate with you because they'd found the spot. You don't wanna just turn up and be like, 'Nah, it's wet'. You want kids to be stoked because they've made an effort to tell people there's a spot. →

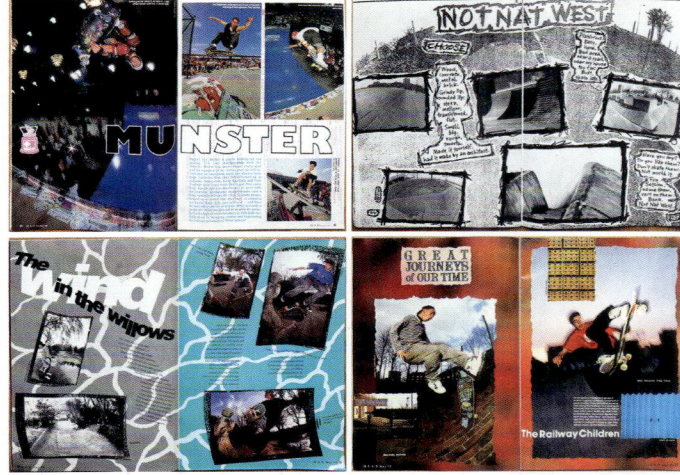

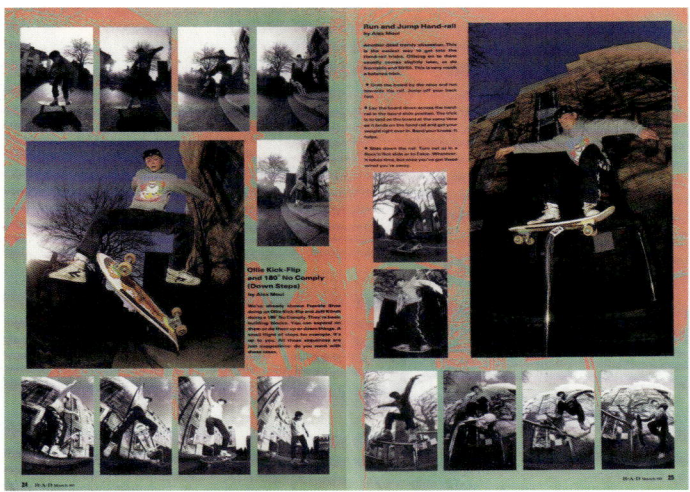

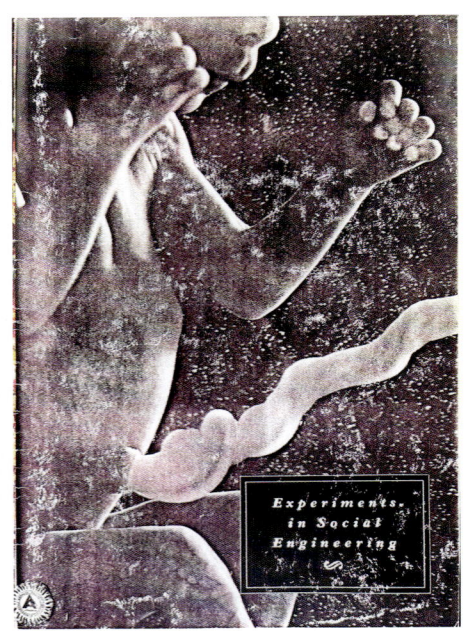

Nik Taylor

Buster, a skater from Cromer, said they'd found a pool in a hotel that was being pulled down; one of the other skaters lived opposite and had clocked that there was a pool, so we all went over and drained it and cleared it out, with the classic dustbins-on-ropes, all that kinda shit.

Thomas Bell from Sheringham phoned up TLB and told him about the pool, and he told us they were going to come down on this one particular day. After really hassling them, my parents said I could have the day off school, so we went there on the day and it was pissing it down with rain. We waited all morning, sitting in cars, and then my mum said I was going to have to go back to school after lunch and then – classic – they show up after lunch, so I missed it all.

Ged Wells

It was like a totally ironic fantasy skate, certainly the expectation of my dreams reading US skate mags since the '70s. Then it was this harsh bank-to-wall pool with massive vert and it was raining. I'm surprised that nobody got badly hurt.

It all goes back to the Island days; we were obsessed with innovation but had shit terrain. I never wanted to perfect a trick and have great style, my thing was more about adapting to difficult shapes in the street and doing something unexpected[4]. Of course I love all forms of skating but I reacted more when I saw things being done differently in mags and videos. In terms of street skating, being playful can be very internal and empowering. Especially lone street skating, where you can cruise along doing minor tricks like slides and nollies, what people might see as some absolute freak, but you don't care because you're on your way somewhere.

Arron Bleasdale

We went to Romford[1] that day and Bod Boyle was there, Steve Douglas was there, and some other pros that I don't honestly remember were there. They were fully padded-up, skating the pool, and I was just... I dunno, cocky as fuck! I was just really excited that all these pros were skating the pool, I wasn't even thinking that I was just in shorts and a t-shirt with my hat backwards. I think they were a little bit shocked that I was doing frontside 5.0s and stuff in the pool.

→ FREESTYLE/INVERT
Mark Noble

I'd been going to contests and taking pictures, so it came about that I could contribute to *Freestyle BMX* magazine, and then the ownership of that magazine came up for grabs. The publishers, Martin and Neil Higginson, ran a publishing company that did some regional magazines, and they did some of the early BMX magazines. Then they got into the premium-phone-line-competition thing, and because they were making so much money through those, they lost interest in the publishing company, and that was how the BMX magazine became available.

The Freestyle Association took it on, and because I'd been taking pictures and writing for it, I kind of became editor of that mag. It felt super important at the time, but looking back, it was little more than a zine, and I wasn't an experienced journalist at all. We were just putting a mag out and making it up as we were going along, working with distributors and advertisers to make it all commercially real, and learning the whole process of making magazines and growing a publishing company as we went on. It was pre-desktop publishing, and we were making some expensive mistakes and learning.

It had been my decision to introduce skateboarding into it, and we relaunched it as *Invert*[2] because that title could span both BMX and skateboarding. That was the reason behind the title, and the design behind it. Some of the diehard BMXers would complain, but we were just too into it to reject skateboarding.

Tom Hodgkinson

Gavin Hills did *Experiments In Social Engineering*[3] [5], which was a brilliant fanzine which was situationist philosophy mixed up with skateboarding. It was really creative and it came in a pizza box. ●

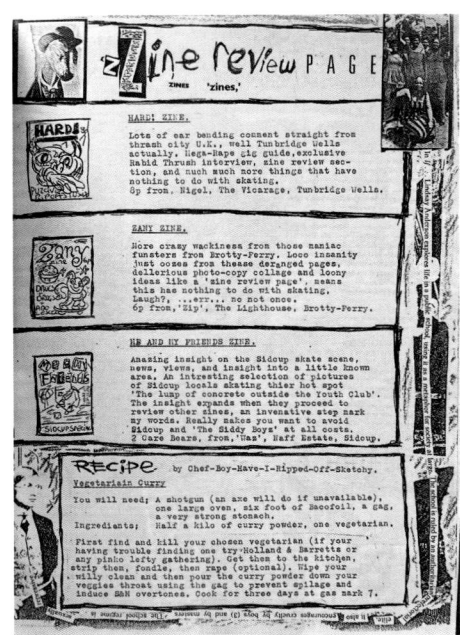

If you can't hack it, shove it

Tom Hodgkinson, Cambridge student success turned skateboard salesman, says he's happiest where it's hip

I HAD everything to look forward to. A Cambridge degree under my belt, all I had to do was wait for a "Yes we want you" from one of the journalists' training courses I had applied for. Then, after a summer in the sun, the transition from student life to real life would be effortless.

Of course, I only got rejections. And five letters from the bank made me realise that I wasn't going to get a holiday and would have to get a job. Fast. A vacancy in my local record shop awakened an adolescent fantasy — was the ultimate cool job in my reach?

I took in my CV and was eventually told they had found someone else — but would I be interested in working in their skateboard shop? How could I refuse — surely this was even more hip?

On my first day I sold £800 worth of gear and assembled two skateboards, a scary task considering some poor kid has spent £120 on the piece of wood into which you are nonchalantly drilling holes. Still, I thought this was pretty good going. But I was not so happy with the assumption customers make that you are invested with a boundless knowledge about the goods on sale: "What's faster — Powell minirats or OJ II Teamriders?"

"What's better for the street, the new Jason Jessee or the Jim Thiebaud?" Sorry mate — haven't got a clue. I think the pink wheels are quite fast . . .

And it isn't just skateboards, not by a long shot. There's shoes, clothes, videos, watches, hats, sunglasses and a million and one fiddly skateboard components. This means that as well as dealing with 15 screaming kids talking incomprehensible jargon (Has the Kendall mini got Hell concave? How much is Madrid Fly paper? Have you got any Indy hangers? Grindkings? Street razors in 95A? You have? Oh rad, I'm stoked now, those wheels are doin' it, man, those wheels are bad!"), as well as demanding free stickers and trying to pinch things, you have to spend hours with a hardened clubland trendy while he/she decides which brand of chunky trainers to go for.

Hassles apart, though, it's fun. Skateboarding attracts a stunningly wide variety of people, from 15-year-old South London hip-hop fans to serious artists (and other aesthetes), and from gifted and original designers and writers to hard-headed businessmen.

I'd never have met any of these people if I had been accepted on a journalist training course. Instead of learning shorthand, court law and sub-editing conventions, I have been transformed from a clueless skateboard ingenue into a breezy, confident salesperson, who can rattle on about the pros and cons of T-Bones and Toxic Wastes.

My lexicon of skate terms has improved dramatically. Do you know what an ollie to frontside 50/50 is? A stale-grab Madonna? A smith-grind to revert? An alley-oop lipslide? A rock 'n' roll to fakie? (They are all gravity- or death-defying tricks.) Even my own skating abilities (still severely limited) have improved — the other day I successfully completed a shove-it!

Among the more imaginative regulars, skateboarding is a creative act with the power of transforming an ugly piece of concrete into an object of beauty and promise. A kerb exists to be "grinded", the sloping banks outside a corporate headquarters exist for practising ollie blunts and nose-picks, car parks for no-complies and 360-degree slides. Modernist architectural nightmares are a skater's paradise.

All this plus discount clothes and shoes. And I sometimes get to work in the record department downstairs.

Perfection? Almost, but I've realised that all jobs are jobs, no matter how much fun they might appear to be. They all involve going to work every day, and £125 per week won't stretch to a mortgage. But hey, money isn't everything, and I'd hate to waste my youthful days planning my retirement.

Tom Hodgkinson . . . rad roller   PHOTOGRAPH: E. HAMILTON WEST

→ *SLAM CITY SKATES*
   Tom Hodgkinson

My mum just said, 'Look, you've got four weeks to get out and get a job'. She had a flat in Ladbroke Grove at the time, and I'd always wanted to work at Rough Trade, so I just walked in and applied, and they rang back and said no, but that they'd got me a job at the skateboarding shop. So I was thrown into that world.

They didn't want someone who was too involved in the skateboarding scene because all the young kids would have loved to have worked there, but they were too close to their friends and they would flow them free stickers and stuff like that.

It was good because all my mates – all the posh Oxbridge-y people – all became great friends with Ged, Gavin Hills, Vernon and even some of the boys, like Will Bankhead – there were some real characters among the 15-year-olds – and they all took the piss out of me non-stop. I was shit at skateboarding, but luckily Gavin was also shit at skateboarding, so we formed the Crap Crew and went around with a gang of the older ones so I didn't feel so intimidated at skateparks.

For me it was incredibly inspiring, and it helped sow the seeds of doing *The Idler* magazine because everyone in there was so entrepreneurial and it opened my eyes to a world where you didn't have to have a full-time job, in a sense. I mean, Gavin was never going to have a job. Or Ged. They're completely unsuited to the nine-to-five, but they were doing amazing things and even then I thought about how they didn't even have to work at Slam.

It's such a brilliant scene in skateboarding. All these brilliant, talented, 15 and 16-year-olds doing their own thing. This anarchist philosophy and anti-wage-slave ideas. It was a huge inspiration to see this way of life, where you lived by your wits – lived by your creativity – rather than get a job.

There was a definite feeling of being quite cool and being at the centre of things. I was the posh one, but it was a very middle-class scene. Most of them were actually very, very middle-class, and their parents were architects, and they lived in Camden, and they're arty people but they're London-y and quite street-y.

Ged Wells

I moved to London after meeting Gav Hills at the Prague Euros, and collaborating with Paul Browne's *Sketchy* zine. So I dossed at their places a bit, worked more at *RAD* and kept making Insane with my mum on the Island. *RAD* had given Insane quite a lot of exposure so sales were good.

I was approached by the then Slam/Rough Trade partners, and they wanted to start a wholesale operation and thought Insane would be a good starting position. I signed a piece-of-paper contract, and it was the same contract that The Smiths and other bands had signed with Rough Trade in the early '80s.

From the outset, my mum and I still produced Insane from the Island, so Slam stocked products like Jim Jams, then as the Slam operation kicked in, we transitioned everything.

Insane was very lucky because of my friends network. Tom Hodgkinson, Gav Hills and Cynthia Rose all helped tremendously in gaining Insane a wider profile in the *Guardian*, *Observer*, *The Face*, etcetera. So once my partnership with Slam geared up with products in the Covent Garden store, things grew very quickly.

Gareth Skewis

To me, what Ged Wells was doing with Insane was as important as Stüssy. Shawn Stüssy and Paul Mittleman were all aware of it. Things like Insane and Anarchic Adjustment, and Poizone, and Fergus Purcell, were this real avant-garde, forward-thinking thing. It was all on this same wavelength and it was all really important. →

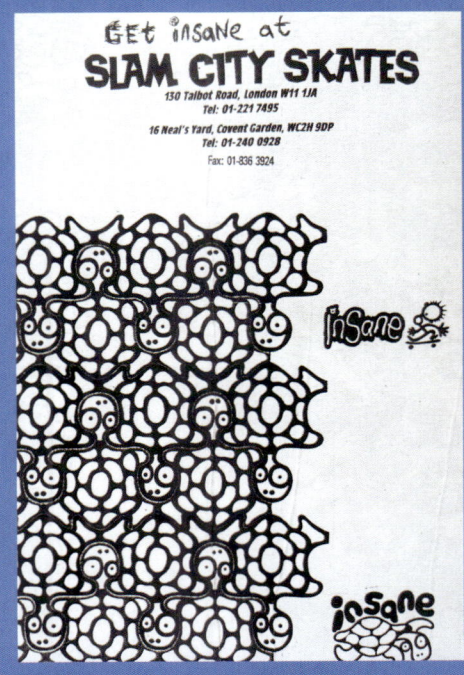

→ **M-ZONE**
Charlie Burrows

We outgrew our space on Lower Addiscombe Road, and the city had made parking a nightmare, although we were very close to East Croydon railway station. At that time Carnaby Street was in dismay. It was just a shithole; nothing was really going on there apart from the fancy pubs. Because there was nothing going on there, the rents at the time were super cheap. I managed to secure a spot there that worked out fine as M-Zone.

After M-Zone was open, Carnaby Street got better. Boots the Chemist opened up and the rents started to go up, too. We were making money, but it was not sustainable. I guess I'm not very good at reading small print, because then the rents just kept going up.

London burnt me out. 24-7 drinking and partying as well as working at the store... My girlfriend left me because she couldn't handle my lifestyle, and one by one all the old-school BMXers and skateboarders were all moving to America, so I was thinking to myself, 'London? California? London? California?', and I decided I was done. Bugger it. And also the rent was going through the roof so we probably wouldn't have been able to stay there another year anyway. I just needed a break, and working with your family is challenging.

So I moved to America and within six months I met a girl and we've been married now for over 30 years.

Alex Brindle

I worked in M-Zone from '89 to '91. I was 17 when I started. I was closer to Charlie's younger brother Mark who worked in there, who was a complete lunatic. I was this young impressionable teen and I would meet Mark at East Croydon station, we'd get the 8.20 train in the morning, and it would be Stellas in the buffet car on the train to Victoria, and then at 11 o'clock in the morning the White Horse pub in Newburgh Street round the corner opened and we'd be straight in for pints, and it would be pints all day until we shut at 5.30, then it'd be in the pub until 11 o'clock. I ended up living in the basement of M-Zone.

We'd spend our day answering the phone and every other call was a major magazine or a stylist wanting to come in and borrow stuff for photoshoots. It was pop stars coming in, actors, stylists and skateboarders.

One of the stylists that used to come into M-Zone was a guy called Miles Siggins, and he was always borrowing stuff for *i-D* magazine, or *The Face*, for all the different shoots, and he became friendly with Charlie, and Charlie employed him to do the Stüssy distro from downstairs in the basement. So Miles got in with Shawn Stüssy, and then Miles went away and went to Michael Kopelman and they started Gimme 5 together, and they took the Stüssy account, and that was that. I know the M-Zone family felt a little bit betrayed by Miles, but to be honest M-Zone fucked itself up. If we ain't got the money to buy the gear, then let someone else do it. Gimme 5 did it professionally and they're still going.

Charlie just went, he fucked off to America. Then the shop continued, but pretty badly. I was left in control of the shop, which was a very stupid thing to do, as a fucking 18-year-old alcoholic. I think I ran the shop for about six months or something. Over that period the whole of the Southbank would just come to the shop at lunchtime and we'd drink beer all day. We didn't really have any stock to sell so it just became a party shop. Then Charlie came back, like the prodigal son, and he brought Craig Campbell back with him. The shop didn't last much longer after that and then Craig and Charlie ended up almost like squatting on the premises, and they turned the downstairs into a club night. It was a fitting end. M-Zone was crazy, and it imploded.

Mike Manzoori

Jason Lunn convinced Charlie from M-Zone to send us to the contest in Birmingham. He even convinced him to send us to Glasgow to skate the Church ramp a week before the contest because it was winter. He basically said, 'It's winter, we haven't been able to skate. We need to train. There's this ramp in a church', and they sent us up there. Jason was there before me, and I went with my friend Ben, and I left my glasses on the coach so I was basically blind for the whole weekend that I was up there.

The next weekend was that NEC contest in Birmingham, and M-Zone sent us there as well. If it wasn't for them I wouldn't have been there, and I wouldn't have been able to skate for weeks.

After the contest Frank Messman told me they were doing a Powell Europe thing, and asked if I'd like to jump in. Right away I was like, 'You should get this kid Curtis... I mean I'm down, but this guy over here?!'

Then they sent me and Curtis to Italy to do our first demo ever. We had to skate this sketchy vert ramp on a beach that was downhill so one side was over-vert and one side was under-vert. It was horrible.

I threw away my return ticket because I thought they'd give me another one for the flight home. It was the first time I'd ever been on a flight and I got to the airport like, 'Where's my ticket?', and they said they'd given it to me, so I realised it was in the bin at the hotel. The distributor lost his shit, and he was just some party guy.

Basically it put you on some kind of pedestal. If there were photographers around, they'd probably want to shoot you more because you rode for somebody. It's as stupid and as simple as that. There were obligations, but it was more opportunity than anything else.

→ **SKATER-OWNED SHOPS**
Mon Barbour

All the shops had been taking these poxy little eighth-page adverts that cost X-amount, whereas you could get a full page a lot cheaper if we all clubbed together and booked out a page together[1]. It was just a practical thing. And also, for me, it just seems like the whole ethos is, 'We are skateboarding, we love skateboarding', so why don't we work together? We're not competitors, we're massive distances apart from each other and we're all part of this ecosystem so why don't we work together? We're all mates and it's better to work together than to be in competition with each other. Paul Sunman at Slam didn't want to do it because he didn't want to be associated with Pig City, but it was only awkward for about six months because Pig City went bust because they were a bunch of incompetent stoners.

It became a defining thing, buying from a real skater in a shop that was actually owned 100% by a bunch of skateboarders. Then the Age of Internet became the age of no one giving a fuck and there was no allegiance.

→ **OFF THE WALL**
Neil Danns

I had this little business called Rocket Productions – which is why on the Pacer board you had the rocket on it – to do the tours, and it all sort of fell away at the end. It came to its natural end, and everybody was starting up shops, all these skater-owned shops like SS20 and Clan, so I had to jump on the bandwagon like everybody else.

I had a friend from Surrey called Stuart Barton, who was a surfer, and he said, 'Let's get a skate shop together'. I wasn't really the brains, I was the front; I was the face of skateboarding. I think we had £500 each, so we went to Quiggins, which was a big building with little stalls everywhere, and they said we could have it for a hundred quid a week. We had this little unit at the top of the building and rung all the different suppliers: Shiner, Faze 7, anybody we could ring on the back of my reputation. 'Neil Danns here! How much credit can you give me?', sort of thing, but I was really conscious not to take too much stuff on, so when we opened I think we had nine boards and four sets of trucks and three sets of wheels, and some griptape and maybe 20 t-shirts.

Within six weeks we went from the smallest unit in that building to having the car park downstairs at the back and a massive unit. We got the loading bay, and they painted the floor for us, and I got given the old Docklands contest ramp, the vert ramp, and I cut it down. ●

CLOCKWISE FROM TOP LEFT
[1] Skater Owned Shops ad
[2] M-Zone ad, by Charles Burrows, photography by Peter Tarry
[3] Mike Manzoori, by Sean Keef
[4] Off The Wall ad
[5] M-Zone ads, by Charles Burrows, photography by Peter Tarry

Mike Manzoori

M-Zone would have been my first sponsor that people know about. I looked up to Curtis, Paul Wright and Jason Lunn so much. To be lined up with those guys, I was just like 'What the fuck?! Curtis McCann?!' To this day he's still the gnarliest dude. The sickest dude. Not just with skating, he was just a really rad cat. An interesting dude. He was light-years ahead of his time, for his age, for the era. His skating, the way he thought and the way he saw the world. As a little kid he was really influential to me.

We were talking about how to learn tricks one time, and he told me he'd think about a trick going to bed and play out every scenario, every slam, basically just think about it until he dreamed it, then he'd wake up and go and try it and it would feel like he'd already practised it. What other 14-year-old thinks like that? He would do it in his mind, basically meditate through the whole thing. That was some next-level shit.

Skating was a game to him. When miniramps were a new thing he would just play, like, 'What about this trick? I could do this, so I can do that', and we're thinking, 'Of course you can, because you're you', because none of us could.

Curtis McCann

As soon as I started skating, people were often giving me praise about my style and cuteness, so I did run with the idea that I had a good style! It was a plus when I sometimes felt threatened and snubbed by the American competition, and how hard skating sometimes was... I usually just tried to make tricks I wanted and then enjoy them as much as possible; even if I had a trick locked, I would do it over and over for the sheer fun of it... I guess that added to *my* style.

Simon Evans

Curtis lived really close to me, and he was just *famous*. He was a big deal. I remember one time me and my friend Chris went to Southsea skatepark – someone took us there, a parent or something – and Curtis came with us, and it was intimidating even being in the car with him. We went to Southsea and just watched him skateboard, and then we were aggressively interrogating him so it didn't seem like we were shy or nervous, but it was just amazing. He was so fucking good. He was so special. He looked great, he did great stuff. It was just like, 'Woah, I can't believe I went to Southsea with Curtis McCann'. It was really unfortunate that he broke his ankle. That's like Natas Kaupas or somebody breaking their ankle. He was so special. ●

LEFT TO RIGHT
[1] Curtis McCann, Kings Cross, by Arron Bleasdale
[2] Leon Parr and Curtis McCann, Southsea
[3] Curtis McCann, Shell Centre, by Peter Tarry

1989

Death Box & Bash

CLOCKWISE FROM TOP LEFT
[1] Pete Dossett, Knebworth, by Ian Lawton
[2] Sean Goff, Hurworth, by Sean Keef
[3] Mac ad, *Skate Action*, March
[4] Mac, Meanwhile 2, by Ian Lawton
[5] Duncan 'Wurzel' Houlton, Caldecotte, by Ian Lawton

Duncan 'Wurzel' Houlton

For the next Mac board, everybody looked at the shape and went, 'Oh no, fucking hell, what's going on, Mac?', and Mac just said it was to be like that or nothing. And of course there was the graphic[3]. I don't know how we allowed that, but if Mac wants to do something, he will. The t-shirts of that went into production as well...

We were starting to export to Europe by then, and who was the big distributor in Europe? Titus, in Germany. He was the big distributor for everything, and the world championships had already been held in Germany for the last 12 or 13 years.

We weren't even thinking about the fact that it had a fucking swastika on it. They opened the package, looked at the boards, sent them straight back, and we had to pay for them coming back. They didn't even say anything at all, they were so deeply offended. I live in Germany now and I can completely understand that. There is absolutely no excuse for it whatsoever. Mac wasn't racist or anything, it was just something we thought was cool at the time because we didn't think about it as much as you would nowadays.

Danny Calow

We would get the bus up to Washington, head-to-toe in Rocker stuff, and Rocker would be there. And we've got Rocker boards, Rocker t-shirts, Rocker hats and a Rocker hoody... Fuck. So we'd hide round the back of the vert ramp trying street tricks.

Paul 'Rocker' Robson

Seeing people riding my board or wearing a shirt of it felt great. I'm not going to lie, it felt really good.

I've always been very approachable and I always try to speak to people equally and on their terms. If somebody comes up to me, I don't know how much pressure they've put on themselves to speak to me, so I'll speak to them. I've always liked speaking to people. I'm just a person who was OK on a skateboard; it doesn't mean I'm a better person than you. I always had time to speak to people. If you're a good skateboarder you've got to be a good person as well.

I did Anti-Geordie Mafia, that was solely me. I cut all those little letters out of magazines, like a ransom note, and my friend screened a couple of stickers for me, then he got some screen prints on cloth, and a friend made some shorts for me, with inserts for hip pads. It lasted a little moment but obviously disappeared when Death Box came around. It was something that I did because everywhere that I went, people would go, 'Oh, you're from Newcastle!', and it used to tick us off. I'm from Sunderland, and Sunderland is totally not Newcastle, and I used to get quite a lot of gyp. Being called a Geordie when you're from Sunderland is quite a big insult... I used to encounter people thinking I was a Geordie.

My very first trip to the States, in '89, I flew to Houston, Texas, and Danny

Webster was there. I think he'd just been released by G&S. We got there on the Monday, and on the Saturday of that week there was a big vert contest in Austin, Texas, and we got the Greyhound up to there. The guy who had the skatepark there let us stay in the skatepark, because we didn't have any lodgings.

I'd told Jeremy from Death Box where I was going to be at certain times, because he wanted to check in with us and see how I was and stuff. There's an announcement over the loudhailer that I need to go to the desk because I've got a phone call, and it's Jeremy asking how I'm doing and what's happening. I tell him Danny Webster's there, and Jeremy goes, 'No way! Put him on!', so I give the phone to Danny and go back to skating.

Now, apparently, they were on the phone for a good couple of hours, because they hadn't spoken to each other for years. Danny came and thanked me for telling Jeremy he was there, and said he might be getting on Death Box.

I saw Danny quite a bit at contests, King of Vert and all that, but I never really saw him to speak to. I don't know if Danny was an early casualty of the 'vert's out and street's in' thing that was gathering momentum, because Danny was only a vert skater. I was OK on a miniramp and I was OK on street too, so I was always used for contests, whereas Danny just did what he did and he did it very well. →

→ **BASH**
Ian Deacon

When I was in the States from November '88 to April '89, I was hanging out with the photographer O a lot because when I was staying with my friend Nick in Huntington Beach, O used to stay over a lot. We knew O from before anyway, so we used to hang around with him a lot, just driving around in his pick-up truck. O used to go up to Steve Rocco's a lot, when he was still first getting going. When I first went there John Lucero had just bailed on Rocco.

Homeboy magazine was going, so we'd go to *Homeboy* magazine and that was when Spike Jonze was working there, and Megan Baltimore was working there, and when we used to go to Rocco's. Megan was there because she used to work for Rocco super early on. Ann was there too – who was Jason Lee's girlfriend but then became Mike Vallely's girlfriend and wife – because she was working at Rocco's as well. It was a really small little thing.

I remember the humbling experience of going street skating with Jason Lee, and just being like, 'OK, I'm fucking shit'. That was an eye-opener. I didn't know what was going on, and he wasn't pro or anything at that time. People had heard of him a little bit, it's not like he was super famous or anything, but he was better than everyone. His style was just perfect as well. It was like, 'Well if that's the way it's going, I'm dust', basically.

From being with Rocco, because we hung out with Rocco a lot, it just seemed really easy to start a company. Before, it was the Big Four or whatever. I used to go to Vision and there was an 80,000-square-foot warehouse just with Vision shoes in it, so that was what you thought a skateboard company was. Then you go to Rocco's and it's a tiny little place with people making Ghetto Wear clothing and a few stacks of boards. It was the polar opposite, and obviously Rocco was just using credit cards to make it happen. It was almost like a DIY punk rock kind of thing. You go and see the Sex Pistols in Manchester and it's, 'Oh, I can play guitar like that as well', and you go and see what Rocco's doing and that's not an impossible thing to do, you can actually do it. No one had really done it like that. In the '80s it was locked down, there was no new people, it was just big brands that brought in subdivisions.

That kind of opened my eyes, so I thought maybe I could do a little brand or something. It was like my Sex Pistols moment. I'd met Jeremy at one of the Smell of Death comps at Meanwhile, so I hit him up, and then went to Wellingborough to see him and he said he'd back it.

Merlin Nation

Bash, for me, was about two things – a local skate crew and art. I'd known Luke McKirdy since primary school in a village just outside Brighton. We used to skate to a DIY ramp on the beach near there one particular summer – maybe 1985/86. We'd get there for like 6am so we'd have the ramp to ourselves for a few hours. That ramp was great, 8 foot high and the first proper halfpipe I'd skated. We were the little groms bottom dwelling into backside grinds before we'd learnt to even drop in. I think that ramp only lasted for a summer so we'd go to the Level skatepark in Brighton and got to know all the skaters there.

A crew of us would go on missions to Southbank, Southsea, Meanwhile, Kennington, Hastings in the back of Steve Brooker's butchers van with no windows. And a load of us camped for a week at the Isle of Wight ramp one summer after our GCSEs in 1989 – loved that ramp and the local crew there were really cool. ●

CLOCKWISE FROM LEFT
[1] Mac, Kettering, by Ian Lawton
[2–4] Bash graphics, by Merlin Nation and Dylan Whickham

1989

Ian Gunner

It was Grover who brought Ray Muchmore, and Ray's nephew – which was Marc Ball – down to the park, and they were just skateboarding. Just having fun, doing this new thing. Ray's best mate was Gary Nardelli – they were plasterers together – and randomly, they just said they were going to open a skate shop.

They wanted to do it, they'd had enough of plastering, and they opened a skate shop in this place called In Shops, which was an indoor market in Harrow. It was one of these indoor shopping centres, with really random shops and market stalls, and it was just down the road from the skatepark. It was amazing because we didn't need to go to Buddies all the time, because that was our local.

They called it New Deal Skates, and then Steve Douglas came along a bit later and said, 'I want to call my brand New Deal. You be the distributor.' Nick Zorlac was in one of the first adverts doing a frontside ollie off the little quarterpipe, and that became our world. It was all there, and as it grew – and because of Steve they suddenly had these connections, so they had to grow quite quickly – the first thing they did was put a Portakabin on the skatepark, and moved the shop there.

They were literally the typical kind of plasterer, that was them, but they really embraced it. They got boards themselves, they were trying to learn to skate, they were making ramps, they were doing everything that they needed to do – in the right way – and it was cool.

Steve Douglas

When my wife and I turned up in London in 1989 for my brother's wedding I had six bags full of skate product. I had 30,000 stickers, I had boards, I had wheels, I had t-shirts, I had everything, and I still managed to come through Nothing to Declare.

I went to Harrow, and they're telling me I've got to meet these guys, Ray and Gary at the In Shops. I see Ray and he goes, 'I heard you've got some product', and I said I did, and he goes, 'I'll buy all of it', and I said, 'You don't know how much I've got'. And he turned up at my sister's house, sees it, and he's like, 'Alright we can't take all of this, but we'll take some stuff every week'. And that's how the relationship started. He would come over to my sister's house and buy stuff every week, and that's how we met and how I lived.

I had so much stuff that when I went to contests I actually sold to distributors. I met distributors because I was selling them fucking stickers because I had £30,000 worth of stickers, and stickers were fucking hot. I remember Rodga Harvey being really pissed off with me when he was selling stickers and I did a sticker toss right next to him. It was a lame thing to do but I remember giving him stuff, and then him selling it, which was not cool.

So in the summer of '89 we're doing this photo annual at *RAD*, and Paul Schmitt says he'll pay for an ad if I make the ad happen. So I went to Surrey Skates to get a board, and that was a trip down memory lane because my dad used to take me to Surrey Skates. I had happy memories of it, so I walked in that day and I said, 'Hey, my name's Steve Douglas, I used to be Steve Reid when I came in here and I used to buy my boards here, and now I'm a pro, I have a column in *RAD*. You're the distributor for Schmitt Stix, and Paul Schmitt has said that if I can make an ad, he'll pay for it. I just need another one of my boards.' The guy goes, 'Ooh, no, we gave Danny Webster a board and we never got it back'. I told them I was going to make an ad, that they weren't going to need to pay for, and it would sell more of my model for them. I said, 'Are you seriously fucking telling me that I have to get my wallet out to pay for my board to make an ad that you're going to benefit from?!' And I walked away thinking, 'Fuck this, skateboarding's got to change'.

At the 1989 September ASR trade show, Bob Denike from NHS came up to me and said, 'Whenever you guys want to get out of Vision, we'll take care of you', and I literally ran to Paul – this was probably two months after the conversation with Surrey Skates – and said, 'Paul, NHS will back us!', and Paul said, 'Steve, I've known that for ages. Rocco will too.' And right then, I said, 'We're getting fucking out'. ●

CLOCKWISE FROM BOTTOM LEFT
[1] Steve Douglas, Harrow, by Tim Leighton-Boyce, and Schmitt Stix ad
[2] Steve Douglas, Neasden, by Mike John
[3] New Deal Skates ad, *Skateboard!*

1989

Jimmy Boyes

I remember arriving in Liverpool for the first time to see a band, and there was a couple of hours until the band was going to start. I remember seeing this guy sitting outside the record shop on a skateboard, and we made eye contact, and this dude turned out to be Fez. He's like, 'Follow me!', and I remember pushing through the city of Liverpool with him, super fast, and he had the best style. It was like skating with someone from California. He had long black flowing hair like Scott Oster, and he would do these backside power slides round the corners of streets and do slappy grinds. I'm following this guy for about an hour and a half, blasting around town and the university, and then we got back to where we started. I remember him saying, 'There's a spare room, come down anytime'.

When I returned back to Durham, I was like, 'I'm fucking moving to Liverpool'. My friend Baz Scott and me hitch-hiked down, we got to the house and we just skated every day. Baz would do early-grab 360s down the Law Court steps, and I remember all the locals thinking, 'Who's this fucking guy?', and everyone enjoyed the energy from Baz. He was fucking fire.

Andrew 'Fez' Warrington

Jimmy used to stay at mine on various weekends, then one day he never went home. Moved in for a bloody year. If ever there was a real bona-fide skater it was him. I always said a true skater did so on his own as with others too. He did and still does. Mostly because his feet stink. I would put his boots outside the back door. He didn't care if his wheels were different sizes or brands, or if he had different trucks on a splintered deck. He still skated his heart out. He has one over me by being killed in a motorbike crash – and then resuscitated. A serious man of adventure and independence.

Stephen 'Kingy' King

The guy from Carcass who lived in 154 Poulton Road was from the North East, and that brought that crew over. Jimmy and his friend Barry came down and they turned up at the Courts. They'd got on the ferry, they'd skated through the Tiles, and it was the first time that Jimmy had been to the Courts. He'd never been to the Courts, never seen the Courts, and he went up to the handrail there and just fucking boardslid it without looking at it and he still had a fucking backpack on. To boardslide a handrail that high and long in '89 was just ridiculous. Everyone's face just melted. Straight after it, Barry kicks his board up into his hand and does a caveman down it. They were just fucking insane, next level. Jimmy Boyes and Barry were unbelievable, more than what we were seeing in *RAD*. ●

CLOCKWISE FROM BOTTOM LEFT
[1+2] Jimmy Boyes, Liverpool, by Kevin Banks
[3] Andrew 'Fez' Warrington, Edge Lane, Liverpool, by Ian Lawton
[4] Robbie Reid, Llandudno, by Ian Lawton
[5] Crosby crew, by Kevin Banks

1989

→ **ROLLERSNAKES**
Paul Haynes

Bill Danforth liked a drink, and a smoke. That kind of got him going; he couldn't really do much without a drink down him. Heady days.

Alan Rushbrooke

It was raw. They rocked up like a punk band, like a bunch of rock stars in leather jackets. Jef Hartsel the rasta dude, then Danforth in Doc Martens, Jesse Martinez... They all looked like rock stars, and they absolutely shredded that ramp to pieces. I was too shy to speak to them.

Mark 'Fos' Foster

That demo was unbelievable, and that was the day that I became a skateboarder. I was a little kid fucking around on skateboards before, but after that I was like, 'Nah, this is what I want to do'.

→ **BIRMINGHAM NEC**
Sibs Roberts

Neil Blender suggested – he thought it'd be a rad idea – to have the platforms sunk below the coping, so one side was just a regular platform, and the other side had the coping, and then the platform was about three feet below the coping [p.88[3]]. He was like, 'It'll be so fucking rad, people will hit it and there'll be no platform there, they'll have to just hang on it', and we're like,

'Fuck yeah!', because if Neil Blender says it, it's got to be fucking good. So of course we built it like that and all the guys came along and they're like, 'What the fuck is this?!' So we ended up having to build a little moveable bit so we could butt it up against the coping so you could actually skate it like a proper vert ramp with a platform on it.

→ **ISLE OF WIGHT**
Scott Wilson

Mac came down and painted the teapot. Jeremy organised the comp, and the ramp at the time was definitely unusual [p.91 [4]]. There wasn't many ramps like that around in the country. At that point we were watching a lot of *Fawlty Towers*, and we all really liked John Cleese, so we strung up a load of paper doilies all over the ramp which we felt was absolutely hilarious. The teapot kind of tied in with that as well, in a weird way.

→ **WIGAN 7 SPORT**
Jimmy Boyes

I got joint-first in the street contest with Alex Moul, and I remember leaving the place to skate street with him. Skating that car was fucking awesome. I remember having flashbacks of the Gonz doing a boardslide on the back of that car [p.88[2]], and thinking, 'Yeah, let's fucking do this!', as I approached it. →

"It was raw. They rocked up like a punk band, like a bunch of rock stars in leather jackets."
ALAN RUSHBROOKE

Demos & Contests

Bill Danforth, Rollersnakes Nottingham, by Ian Lawton
NEXT PAGE
Newtown comp, by Sam Scott-Hunter

Elsewhere

Elsewhere

1989

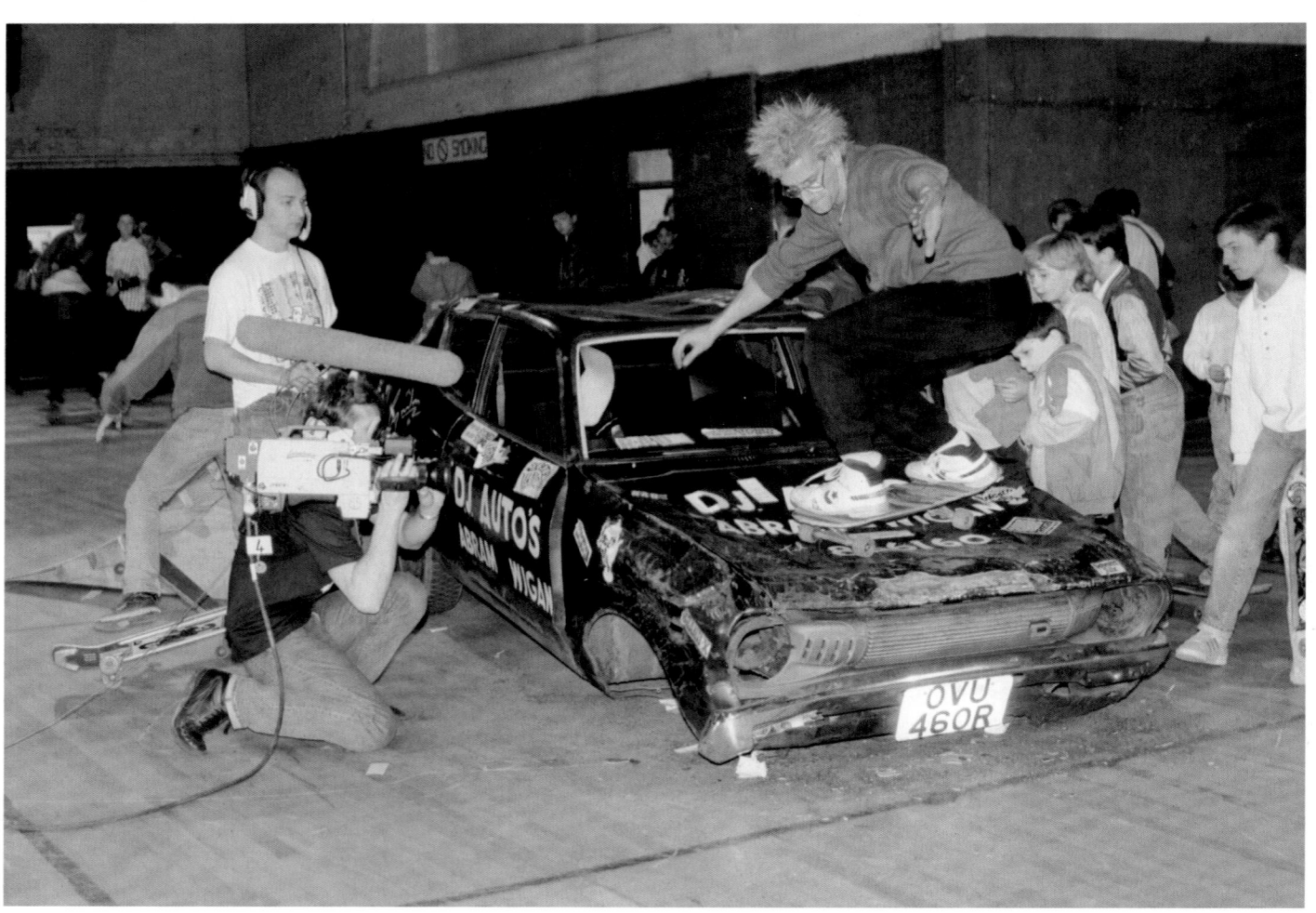

CLOCKWISE FROM LEFT
[1]   7 Sport contest, Wigan, by Sam Scott-Hunter
[2]   Jimmy Boyes, 7 Sport contest, Wigan, by Tim Leighton-Boyce
[3]   Birmingham NEC contest vert ramp with no platform, by Sean Keef

I was so pissed off with the way the whole Angel Lights thing went, although I loved it. I had constant arguments with the 'committee' on the run-up to it opening because the numbers didn't crunch, in my opinion. The overheads were too high and they were going to need hundreds of people coming in on a daily basis, and they've all got to pay £10 – or £8 or whatever it was – for it to work. They just pretended that twice as many people were going to use it, to get the money to build the ramp and open the park.

Colin McInnes

I loved it, but not as far as the madness of the running of it. I think my discomfort with the size of that place was like, 'How is this happening? How is this sustainable?'

Wingy

It was fucking scary there. It was rough as shit and we were only young. We used to sleep in there and they would lock us in at night, and just tell us not to leave until they came back in the morning. You couldn't go out round there at night.

Colin Kennedy

You'd go up there on a Saturday morning and do some manual labour, digging trenches for sanitation or something, and then you'd be allowed to skate for half an hour with your shoes all caked in mud, because this was all the way through a Glasgow winter. It was basically child labour to get the place built but that didn't matter because where else was there a ramp in Glasgow? And it's indoors.

→ **JOE MILLSON'S RAMP**
Joe Millson

That's me[6] on a Sean Goff that wasn't mine. It's a borrowed board, but I wonder now if I stole it, because I used to 'borrow' things from people who weren't really using them. If people have only got a board for show and they said I could borrow it, I'd wait until they'd asked me ten times to give it back.

This quarterpipe[5] was in Newbury, eight miles from where it ended up. The guy's dad had said that it had to go, so it was up for sale, and word got around that he was asking for £400 for this quarterpipe. I said we'd take it, and god bless my dad, because I took him to look at it because he had a flatbed truck that he'd borrowed from a mate or something, and we paid not a penny. They were on holiday so we just put it on the flatbed truck and drove it eight miles back and put it there. I do still owe Grant that £400. I built, with my mates, the other terrible end of this halfpipe, and we made it skateable somehow and we had such good times on this ramp. It was basically, 'Survive the drop in, do something on the good side'.

→ **DONCASTER**
Ben Powell

There was a roller rink[3] in Doncaster where it was a rollerdisco that had burnt down and the roof had caved in, so the rain had got in and warped the parquet flooring so there was all bumps and shit in it. So we went and found that, with no directions or anything, we just went to Doncaster on the bus and somehow found this burnt-down roller rink, and skated it. That was kind of our first experience of the idea of going on a mission based on something you'd seen in a magazine. ●

1990

Alex Moul, Meanwhile Gardens, by Ian Lawton

That freedom of London, of feeling like you could go anywhere and do anything, particularly at the weekend when most of London was shut. You could literally skate round The City – around the Square Mile and St Paul's – and you wouldn't see a person. It was amazing. It was a dream, really. *BEN WHEELER*

LEFT TO RIGHT
[1] Will Bankhead, Peckham, by Tim Leighton-Boyce
[2] Mon Barbour: Burning my ramps down... I was told I'd never skate again. I'd never run again... I was in a bad place and I torched them. I was already living in Oxford then, and the ramps were not in a fit state to ride, and I'd torn my ACL and had it replaced, so I thought I had to get rid of the ramps and that was the easiest way to do it. I got a block of hash and a crate of beer, and poured two gallons of petrol over the ramp and funeral-pyred it.

Simon Evans

Elsewhere

CLOCKWISE FROM TOP LEFT
[1] Simon Evans, Harrow, by James Hudson
[2] Matt Stuart, Harrow, by James Hudson
[3] Simon Evans, Jubilee Gardens, by TLB
[4] Simon Evans, Rollersnakes Nottingham, by James Hudson

Simon Evans

I met Matt Stuart and we were like best friends. You know when you're kids you just meet people and you're like, 'You wanna stay at my house?' 'Alright!' I thought he was super cool, really stylish, a really good skateboarder, but as soon as I met him we just clicked. He lived in Harrow-on-the-Hill, so we would just stay at his house, and he would go down to Harrow skatepark because that was his local because he grew up skateboarding round there.

The first time I met Ray [Muchmore] and Gary [Nardelli] was at Romford, and I thought they were nice. I was a kid and they were men, and Ray was skating the miniramp. I think Marc Ball was there too, and I thought it was really cool that they were older and they were skating.

That was another thing where I was in the right place at the right time. I think I was unofficially on New Deal but they were really making an effort to do something special, and it was a really big deal to me to be part of that.

I know that they were thinking about sponsoring Matt Sherman too, at one point, but I think they chose me because of my connection with *RAD*. At the time, that was a bit of an Achilles' heel because I wanted to be known as a good skateboarder and not as someone that just worked at the magazine. I kind of had a chip on my shoulder about that.

I left school at 16, because I wanted to skateboard. I was just going up to Southbank. I was basically getting pound coins out my dad's coin jar to go up there, but at the same time I started working for *RAD*, so I would basically work for Tim and then skateboard. I didn't even realise how lucky I was.

Then I went back to college, but I was writing for *RAD* so at the weekends I'd be going all over the country with Tim.

I look at a lot of things now and I feel like you can kind of see how things happened, but doing the art thing now, I wish I had the luck I had when I was a kid. I was just this skateboarder at Southbank and then one time Vernon talked to me, and I was doing writing, because I thought I was going to be a writer, so I said that to him and just offhandedly he said I should write for the magazine.

I would see TLB around, but I'd never talk to him or anything because he was sort of like local royalty, but then one day Tim came up to me and said he'd heard I wanted to write something for the magazine, and I said yeah, and that was how it happened.

I didn't even think about the stuff I was writing. I just treated it like a school project. I didn't even try that hard with writing and I didn't even think about my writing in a magazine. I was just doing it and I wanted to be a skateboarder more than a writer. When I didn't have the hang-ups and anxiety I didn't think I was doing anything important. Tim would ask me to do stuff and I would do it. I wasn't like Gavin, Gavin was a proper writer and I was

just a kid that was allowed to write for the magazine. I wish I could still think like that; now I'm just hung up about trying to make something good and I can't do it a lot of the time. But back then I didn't even think about it at all, really.

I remember going up to Sheffield and seeing Carl Shipman skate for the first time, and Cookie. Oh my god. That was amazing. I remember going up to Barrow-in-Furness and seeing Wurzel. We would just go all over the place. It was a dream, going to all these amazing places. Going up to Manchester or somewhere like that and seeing the ability and the quality of some of these skateboarders and thinking how good they were and feeling a bit weird that I was in the magazine. Rik Cooper and Femi, fucking hell. Those guys were amazing.

The first free stuff I got was from *RAD*. They would get stuff, the skateboard companies would send them stuff, and they let me have it if I wrote a review of it. I remember that was the first time I got free stuff and all I had to do was write about it and I'd get a skateboard or something. It was mad, it was so fucking cool.

Back then, being into The Beatles was the weirdest thing that you could do, when I was at school. I used to play the blue Beatles album all the time, the one with all the later hits on it. It was like, 'Why aren't you watching *Top of the Pops* and being into Spandau Ballet, what is wrong with you, you're mad!', and it made me feel so special that I was into The Beatles, and that's so stupid. Now it's like, 'Oh my fucking god'. It's just unbelievable. Now when I see someone wearing a Beatles t-shirt, I don't even see anything. It's funny when you're a kid and you really define yourself by the things you're into.

The first music where I really understood what the message was behind something, was when I listened to Pixies, to 'Debaser' and that album *Doolittle*. That was the first time when I kind of awakened to art, it was that more than The Beatles. The Beatles were like a comfort thing but it was Pixies and early Dinosaur Jr.

Tim Leighton-Boyce

The first thing Simon sent, or brought in – which turns out to be prescient – was an illustration, a pencil-and-crayon drawing. I don't know whether he sent that to us by post or brought it in, but it was something interesting. Nothing to do with skateboarding, by my recollection, and not the type of thing you could put in the magazine.

I think he was regarded as a slightly weird person. He's got an astonishing imagination, and mind, and a very good turn of phrase, so he was absolutely made for the magazine. Occasionally there are people who just really, really gel, like Gavin did. And Simon did, he completely fitted right in, and I shifted direction to accommodate that, I suppose.

Matt Stuart

James Hudson was like Tim, just super generous. Probably caned gazillions of pounds worth of film trying to get us

mugs looking good. He took Simon and I out for a *Skate Action* profile or something, and at that time we were both being given – Simon more than me, Simon was definitely better than me – New Deal stuff, so we were encouraged to go out and wear New Deal tops and be in magazines.

New Deal were actually incredibly generous because skating at Harrow skatepark is like skating on sandpaper. Your board just got annihilated within a week or two. It was literally like taking your board and sanding it down, so they used to give us quite a lot of boards because we were busy trying to learn all these new tricks, or in Simon and Alex's case, invent new tricks. It was extremely exciting. They were the innovators.

Marc Bultitude

When Simon got sponsored by New Deal, and he got that front cover doing the bluntslide, he had a big Death Box Rocker sticker on his board, and Gary from New Deal went absolutely mental at him. 'How dare you have that!' He really did give Simon a bollocking for that, and I think from that moment onwards Simon was just like, 'You know what, fuck you', and he had that attitude that he was going to ride whatever he wanted and wear whatever he wanted. He wouldn't wear their t-shirts anymore. That was a really weird moment.

Gary was looking at it from the sponsors' position of 'Why are you not wearing a New Deal t-shirt?' Simon got to the point where he'd get his package and give it all away to people, or he'd swap his boards. He was riding Alex Moul boards for a little while because he just didn't like the New Deal boards. ●

New Deal

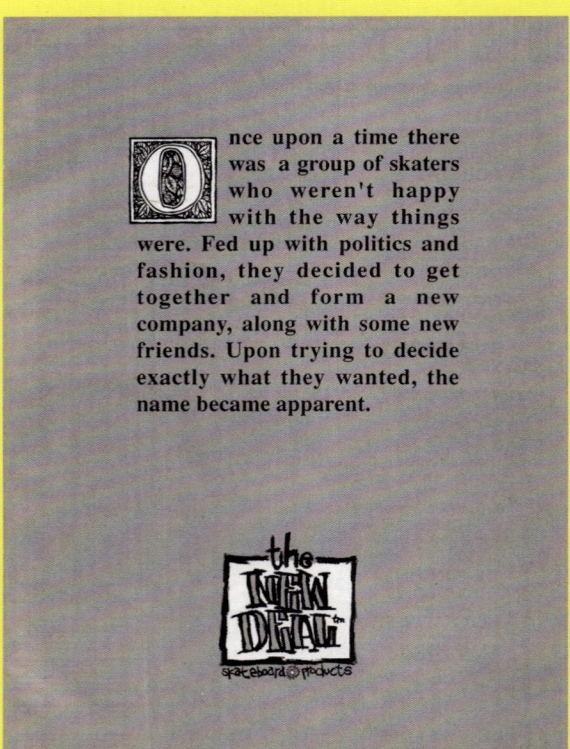

Once upon a time there was a group of skaters who weren't happy with the way things were. Fed up with politics and fashion, they decided to get together and form a new company, along with some new friends. Upon trying to decide exactly what they wanted, the name became apparent.

as long as we're not a rock-n-roll band and we don't make coffee...

san jose warehouse, alleyoop nose grind.
foto luke ogden.

STEVE DOUGLAS NEW DEAL

Please send any and all useful information to the NEW DEAL humane society.
p.o. box 3757, costa mesa, ca. 92628 tel. (714)546-DEAL

Distributed in UK by: New Deal Skates UK Ltd, 18 Greenhunt, Woodside Park, London, N12 8AS. Tel: 081 427 2812 Fax: 081 903 8765

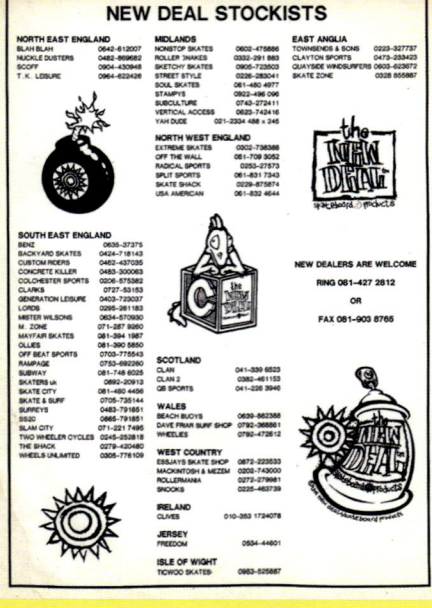

NEW DEAL STOCKISTS

NORTH EAST ENGLAND
BLAH BLAH 0642-612007
NUCKLE DUSTERS 0482-869682
SCOFF 0904-430948
T. K. LEISURE 0964-622426

MIDLANDS
NONSTOP SKATES 0602-476886
ROLLER SNAKES 0332-291 883
SKETCHY SKATES 0905-723503
STREET STYLE 0226-283041
SOUL SKATES 061-480 4977
STAMPYS 0923-496 096
SUBCULTURE 0740-272411
VERTICAL ACCESS 0623-742416
YAH DUDE 021-2334 488 x 245

EAST ANGLIA
TOWNSENDS & SONS 0223-327737
CLAYTON SPORTS 0473-233423
QUAYSIDE WINDSURFERS 0603-629872
SKATE ZONE 0328 855887

NORTH WEST ENGLAND
EXTREME SKATES 0902-736388
OFF THE WALL 051-709 3052
RADICAL SPORTS 0253-27573
SPLIT SPORTS 061-831 7343
SKATE SHACK 0229-875874
USA AMERICAN 061-832 4644

SOUTH EAST ENGLAND
BENZ 0635-37375
BACKYARD SKATES 0424-7 18143
CUSTOM RIDERS 0462-437035
CONCRETE KILLER 0483-300063
COLCHESTER SPORTS 0206-575382
CLARKS 0727-53153
GENERATION LEISURE 0403-723037
LORDS 0295-381183
MISTER WILSONS 0634-570930
M. ZONE 071-287 9360
MAYFAIR SKATES 081-384 1987
OLLIES 081-390 5850
OFF BEAT SPORTS 0703-775543
RAMPAGE 0753-692260
SUBWAY 081-748 6025
SKATERS IA 0892-20913
SKATE CITY 081-480 4456
SKATE & SURF 0705-735144
SURREYS 0483-791851
SS20 0865-791851
SLAM CITY 071-221 7495
TWO WHEELER CYCLES 0245-252818
THE SHACK 0279-420480
WHEELS UNLIMITED 0305-776109

NEW DEALERS ARE WELCOME
RING 081-427 2812
OR
FAX 081-903 8765

SCOTLAND
CLAN 041-339 6523
CLAN 2 0382-461153
QB SPORTS 041-226 3946

WALES
BEACH BUOYS 0639-862388
DAVE FRIAR SURF SHOP 0792-368861
WHEELIES 0792-472812

WEST COUNTRY
ESSJAYS SKATE SHOP 0872-223533
MACKINTOSH & MEZEM 0202-743000
ROLLERMANIA 0272-279981
SNOOKS 0225-463739

IRELAND
CLIVES 010-353 1724078

JERSEY
FREEDOM 0534-44601

ISLE OF WIGHT
TICWOD SKATES 0983-525887

NEW DEAL SKATE SHOP
HARROW SKATE PARK
CHRISTCHURCH AVE
HARROW
RING MATT ON :-
081-427-2812

MATT AT WORK
MATT AT PLAY

WE STOCK :- NEW DEAL, REAL, BLACK LABEL, SANTA CRUZ, SMA, PLANET EARTH, BLIND, POWELL ETC.

CLOTHING :- INSANE, PUZONE, THRASHER, STUBBY, SHOES :- VANS, VISION, AIR WALKS.

SNOWBOARDS :- WE HAVE A FULL RANGE OF NITRO BOARDS FOR SALE OR FOR HIRE.

OPEN 7 DAYS A WEEK
XMAS OPENING TIMES 10TH DEC ONWARDS 9am - 5pm (MON - SUN) XMAS DAY CLOSED BOXING DAY OPEN AS USUAL.

Steve Douglas

In early 1990 I turned up at the San Diego contest, and I was wearing a New Deal Skates shirt, and I had New Deal Skates on the bottom of my board. We knew that Chris Miller was on his way out, and then we found out he was out, he was leaving Schmitt Stix.

We went over to a Denny's and I said to Paul Schmitt, 'We're going to start a new company. It's called The New Deal, and if you don't back it, we're all quitting.' It was take-it-or-leave-it, it was non-negotiable.

So Paul went to check things, and we're all in the hotel room, and then he walked in and he said, 'As long as we're not a rock n' roll band and we don't make coffee, we're OK', and that became the slogan on the first ad, that Andy Howell drew on a napkin.

The funny thing about it was that we'd had a conversation about it as a group, that we had to keep this quiet. As we had decided we were going to do it we walked out, and John Lucero and Jeff Grosso were in the room next door, and Lucero came up to me and he's like, 'You guys are way too happy Miller just left... You guys are going to leave Vision and you're going to start a new company called The New Deal, aren't you?' I swear to God. I go, 'No way, New Deal is my friend's skate shop in the UK. You know Paul, he's the biggest fucking pussy, there's no way he's going to leave Brad Dorfman.' I couldn't believe it...

One of my goals was that New Deal was not only a new deal for a company, it was a new deal to change distribution. So one of the things I'm most proud of in my professional life is one of the least talked about because it's not really that sexy, but I changed the global distribution of the skateboarding world. I said to Paul that we have to change distribution, because no one in Europe gave a fuck. Shiner only put money in when there was money there. I thought, why not save money when you don't need to promote it so that you've got money to do tours when you need it,

because it's an up-and-down industry. I felt like all the big guys, the big distributors, had already made money, so we should give it to skateboarders and they'll look after skateboarding long-term.

Ray and Gary were there, I'm a proud Harrow boy, so I called them up and said I'd like to use the name for distribution, and they said that they would like to do distribution. We picked up Andrew Morrison to do distribution in New Zealand, Hazze Lindgren was starting Red Hot Sports in Denmark and Jean-Marc Vaissette was doing Tracker in France so we got him. Then I asked Paul what he'd think if I was a partner in this. He said that if I was a partner, I could do whatever I want, so I called up Ray and Gary and said, 'Look, Paul's down, if I'm a part of it', and they said they'd love to, and we started the company up. We all took £5,000 loans out with my brother who worked at NatWest. I said I was going to buy a car for mine, and Ray wrote a letter saying he was some big building company, because they were plasterers.

So how we launched New Deal in the UK was, we sent out the New Deal promo video to them and they duplicated 400, 500 copies, and they just sent them out to everybody. They'd turn up at skate spots and give the video out. In 1990 skateboarding was dead but our biggest customer was New Deal UK, because New Deal skateboards just went straight into being a big thing.

Ian Gunner

Matt Bain started working in the shop, Ray and Gary started working out the distribution model which became NDUK, Steve had the contacts in the US and they put another Portakabin on the side and Andy Vost became the sales guy. Ray and Gary literally filled their long-wheelbase Mercedes Sprinter with boards and everything, and had the mobile distribution unit and used to drive all around the country as sales reps, basically. So we had New Deal.

What we also had, which was really, really important, was we had security at

the skatepark, because the legends and the myths of Ray and Gary are kind of all true. They could look after themselves. They were karate sensei and they could defuse a situation and handle themselves, basically. The council appreciated it that there was someone there, and Ray and Gary were hands-on so they'd build quarterpipes, the funbox, all kinds of stuff. The pool got dug out while a driving school was being made in the car park. Ray and Gary said to them, 'If we give you some cash after work can you come and dig the pool out, cash in hand?' So that happened and it got renovated. They even put the new coping in themselves. Them two guys being there and us having a base meant that we'd get loads of people there, and it was more of a safe space, because like anywhere early-'90s, it was rough.

Not only did we have a safe space, and all this new stuff to skate, we had all these new skaters showing up, because the likes of Simon Evans and the Kings Cross/Camden guys would come down because New Deal was there. Harrow was back on the map, when it had been a bit of a void.

Andy Howell

At the moment we decided to split from Vision and start our own company, Steve Douglas offered the name New Deal, from a friend's skate shop in the UK. While he called his friend and got permission to use the name, Ed and Deanna Templeton – teenagers, not yet married – and I went to the grocery store to get some drinks and snacks. While there, I saw a box of crayons and drawing pad, and the idea that the New Deal logo should appear to be drawn by skaters, even children, crystallised into an image in my mind. A company created by skaters and for skaters should be branded to feel exactly that way. I imagined what a child would draw when asked to make a logo for a company offering a new deal to skaters everywhere. The logo drew itself in my mind, along with the icon of a newly risen sun, a new day, a new way forward. ●

CLOCKWISE FROM TOP LEFT
[1+2] New Deal Skateboards introductory ad, by Andy Howell
[3] NDUK business card
[4] Matt Bain, NDUK ad, *Skate Action*, January 1991
[5] New Deal stockists ad, *Skate Action*, November 1990
[6] New Deal Steve Douglas ad by Andy Howell, *Skate Action*, December 1990

New Deal Skates UK Ltd

Gary , Ray & Steve

18 Greenbank
Woodside park
North Finchley
N12 8AS

Tel: 081-427 2812   Fax: 081-903 8765

I can't wait to skate...

escape by Simon Evans

16 R·A·D Issue 91

R·A·D Issue 91 17

Take down these lines

I can't wait to skate... shit; that rhymes. The only thing to stop my shitty existence being well-shitty at college is the fact that I'll skate the weekend. I sip another plastic luke-warm chocolate. I fade from a smoke-filled refectory to a shiny masonite sea, I look down at the board beneath my feet, and it gives a sly wink from its rough back. Everything's going to be cool... I feel alive... stand up grind... the crowd go wild... I melt into the smooth transitions and appear on the other side... 'bic': Ollie tail-grab — smile.

I choke and land with a dull thud once more in education. I look down to my side, but only see cigarette butts and empty Malteser packets. Something is definitely missing — Starsky and em... Bonnie and uh em... knife and oh um... me and my...

I blink. The longest curb painted red without even a chip. I start to push, or do I? A slappy appears in my head, it feels so killer... a fakie Ollie nose-grind, I didn't know I could do them like that... blunt slide, first go! My head's so clear: no alphabet, no numbers, no question marks, full stop.

I turn to the drinks machine. I beg for a hot chocolate, but I know I will receive only warm chocolate. While I wait for my liquid refreshment, my fingers make funny movements on the side of the machine! I Ollie the 'enjoy CocaCola' sign and do a push-it on the coin slot, manual roll down to the warm chocolate and pick it up. Nobody appreciates my run, but that's not why I do it.

Life, Liberty, and the pursuit of happiness.

I slap my rucksack onto my back, I take me, myself and my warm chocolate outside. It's pretty cold, but I guess I'm used to that — I'd probably be wearing shorts if I was skating right now. I slide my free hand down the hand-rail and exit it to fakie. I look at the benches which haven't been slid — shame, nice ones as well, not too high, not too sticky and an OK run up. I watch my fellow students enter the college. I look at their feet, hoping to see some Vans or Airwalk. Instead I only see Kickers and DMs.

I think once more of my skate under my non-marking soles, rumbling along with my friends. We see a small wall, I push ahead and nose bump it "Yeah, Steve" "Yeah, Mike". We look back in pleasure at the object we have just conquered. We arrive at the skate shop, bounce on the chair, look at some boards, talk to Rob, watch a video — buy something maybe?

I click my head back to school, feeling as if I had been asleep. Or am I asleep now? Pretty deep man. I blink, and blink once more. I watch my watch: it's time to enter education and time to learn. Man, I can't wait to skate... shit; that rhymes. Shame it's only Monday.

Freedom to bump your nose, thats what its all about

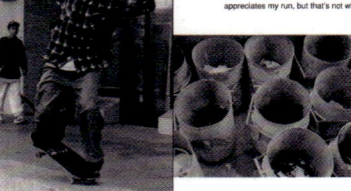

Free at last, free at last, thank god free at last

R·A·D Issue 91 19

20 R·A·D Issue 91

Mike John

I lost touch when *RAD* went out of business, basically. We'd been taken over by another publisher. Robert Maxwell, who owned the *Daily Mirror*, took over *RAD* and then the scandal came out about him stealing pension funds and he killed himself – jumped off the boat – and we went into liquidation. *RAD* went down owing us money; I was owed money, Tim was owed loads of money, and my son was due so I just kinda dropped out.

Ian Roxburgh

I'd been at *RAD* for about two years and the magazine was doing really well – the print run was about 100,000 copies per issue. Although, I don't know if it was selling that many, maybe 75% of that – and they hadn't put my money up. The magazine was holding up the other mags within the publishing house – we were making a profit, and the other mags weren't so much, especially the two games magazines – and I was being paid peanuts. I stopped because I'd been there for about two years and I think it was Dan Adams that said that I'd designed more issues than anyone else. I think I did 22 actual issues, plus the two photo annuals.

When Maxwell bought the publishers, I thought maybe they could finally put everyone's wages up a bit, but they said no, so I decided to leave. I went freelance straight away, with the other magazines in the building that were part of the old Croftward Publishing.

Dan Adams

I had always wanted to be involved in a skate mag, because I *loved* skate mags. It was very exciting for me that Tim was doing one, and although I was at art college from late '87 to 1990, I always kept in touch, and was able to do little bits of news, and those ramp plans and things like that.

At that point I was more in the orbit of Slam than I was in the orbit of *RAD*, and

by the time Ian Roxburgh had to leave the magazine, Tim was asking around. I told him I didn't have the skills but I would love to do it, and I was willing to accept what was essentially a very low fee from the publisher – because they didn't want to invest – and I was willing to do it as a freelancer. Tim had lost his office and what the publisher was offering at that point wouldn't keep anyone there full-time. So I took it, very willingly.

I didn't have the level of skill as a graphic designer to be able to do that properly, and what I ended up doing was a slightly halfway-house between the free-range, looser approach of Nick and Ian, and then this slightly more controlled graphic style, trying to be a bit more like *The Face*.

There was a slight disappointment for me when I realised that we were entering this 'street phase', and that kind of skateboarding was becoming a dominating aspect of the magazine content, and that wasn't where my deeper interests lay. I was very much a vert guy, and that's my first love – and it still is – but I grew to appreciate that you could still get beautiful photographs out of street skateboarding.

Tim Leighton-Boyce

Every photo that wasn't by me cost me money. I was the person who paid for those. So during the selection process I'd be sitting there biting my tongue thinking, 'Nooo... Another one!', because I paid for them all. I just got a flat budget to produce the content and the more other people write things and the more other people photograph things, the less I take home. But that was OK. I was using those words and those pictures because I thought they were great, and they made it all better.

I never said to anyone that I wanted one of mine in, which was ironic because there were a lot of people around who wanted 'that one in because it's got a bloody great sticker on it', or 'that one because he's a mate', or whatever.

It was a very dynamic process, and there was a huge amount of input from everyone else, because I knew that I didn't actually know. One of the advantages of being slightly older than people, and also such a bad skateboarder that it wasn't worth even thinking about, is that I knew it wasn't me who knew. It was the other people who knew, not me. I had opinions, but when it comes to the nuances, especially when you get into the technical era of street skating, I was absolutely clueless. I couldn't choose between four pictures of somebody doing whatever. Shane was the chooser-in-chief for quite a long time, and Simon and people jumped into that role. I don't actually appreciate the differences sometimes. I'm photographing shapes, and patterns, and movement and colours and swirls, but I don't really have an appreciation of the skating technicalities of it.

At university my favourite film director was a guy called Nicolas Roeg, who made *Walkabout, Performance, Don't Look Now* and *The Man Who Fell to Earth*. I wrote a thesis at university about him; I was obsessed with him, and *RAD* is absolutely full of jokey references to his films. Quite extensively *The Man Who Fell to Earth*. The line, 'Visitors, there have always been visitors. I've seen their marks and I've seen their places' is a line from the film where he's talking about previous alien visitors, and I'm seeing wallride marks on the car park next to the 'Visitors' sign. Another Nick Roeg line we used was, 'Nothing is true, everything is permitted'. That was a very *RAD*-type thing, and that's out of *Performance*.

Once we ran a caption that said, 'The captions are just a trick to get people to look at the picture', which is a Brian Eno line about lyrics: 'They're just a trick to get people to listen to the music'. His stuff was another influence. ●

LEFT TO RIGHT
[1+2] *RAD* spreads, by Dan Adams
[3] Jason Maldini, Boo, Ben Wheeler and Simon Casey with *RAD*, June, at the Casey brothers' flat, by Corin Casey

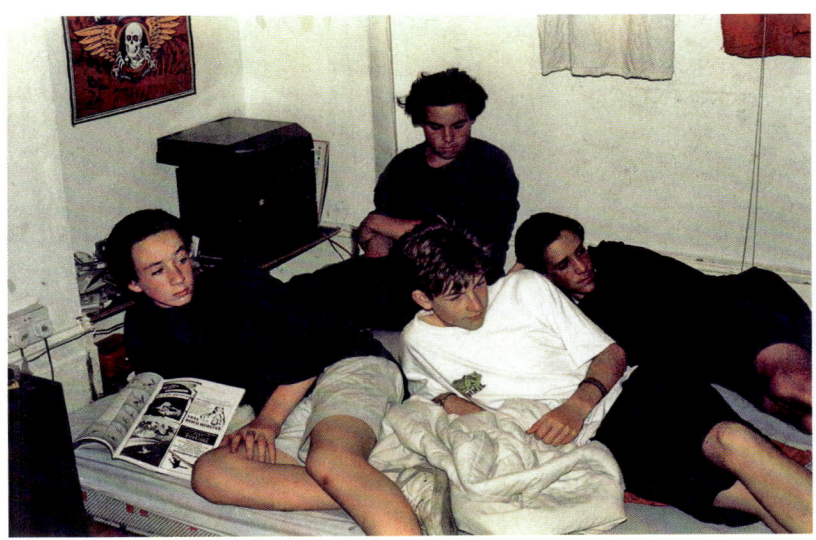

1990

James Hudson

So I've had work published in *RAD*, and Martin Higginson, the publisher of *Skate Action,* asks me if I want to work for their magazine. I don't have to think about that for very long because of course I'm gonna do it.

I did one issue with Sean Keef with me as the assistant editor, or chief contributor or something, where I basically give them some of the American stuff that I'd just got and some contests I'd shot. Then Martin just said he'd sacked Sean and I was to clear his desk and I'm the new editor. He told me the budget and told me to make the magazine. I seem to remember the budget was £1,000 a month... That was for everything. That was for my 'salary', all the film and processing, all the travel, contributors, everything.

The freestyle skater / photographer Shane Rouse had a deal to supply a certain amount of pages of content. It had been set up previously by Sean or Martin. It was nice for Shane because although it was only a few hundred quid, it was regular income. Of course the first thing I had to do was tell Shane that I can't even afford that now because that's a huge chunk of my budget. I seem to remember he was – understandably – pissed off.

Shane Rouse

I wanted to see my work get out there, and I always wanted to work for *RAD*, but freestylers were outcasts of an outcast society, in public perception, and I always tried to fit in but I'd never fit in. I was a socially inept late developer and I suffered from foot-in-mouth, so I can understand it.

With *Skate Action*, I could get my material in there because it wasn't a group of people that really knew skating. They were clueless and they had very little input from cool skaters, or top-level skaters, so I just tried my best to get my photos out there through that and make sure it was as good as I could do it.

When I was helping out with the magazines, I wanted pictures of myself in the beginning. I got a camera and got people to take pictures of me with my camera, and then I took pictures of other people, and that's how I got into photography.

Skateboarders are very creative and have an alternative way of looking at life and of seeing things, so I was quite lucky that I had a reasonable eye for taking pictures, with a little bit of guidance from Dobie.

I had no idea how big street was going to become. I just thought it was a marketing thing, in the beginning. ●

LEFT TO RIGHT
[1] *Skate Action*, January 1991, first issue with James Hudson as editor, Rik Cooper, by James Hudson
[2] Ian Deacon, Brighton, by Shane Rouse

THE SLACK HACKS ARE BACK - WITH A VENGEANCE

SKATEBOARD!

£1.50 / dm9.00
Feb / Mar 1990

WILD STORY:
EPISODE 1

BRUM
EL GATO
SCOUSE & MANC

Mark Noble

Noble Moore Publishing was my dad, Peter, and his business partner. They wanted to produce a publishing company, and took on these titles, and *Skateboard!* was taken on with warts and all – with Steve Kane – as an opportunity. Steve was the editor, we did the design in-house, and Meany – Ian Lawton – was shooting photos.

Steve's very set in his ways, very diehard skateboarding, and anything else didn't really matter. Which is fair play, and credit to him, but I guess that rubbed up against the commercial reality of trying to run a publishing company so there was a falling-out, and I ended up taking it on and editing it.

Ian Lawton

Officially I was the deputy editor. When Steve Kane left, Mark Noble was the editor but essentially it was me that was coming up with all the copy and finding out the news and all that.

It was on such a shoestring then, compared to what it was. The days after *Skateboard!* magazine was sold, and in particular after Steve left, it took a budget cut and we were running it on a shoestring. It was very hard for me to come up with enough content on the amount of money they had to give me, each month. Some issues ended up being just too thin on content, I felt, as it went on. I didn't feel particularly proud of it as it started to thin out. ●

TOP TO BOTTOM
[1] *Skateboard!*, Feb/March, first issue under Noble Moore,
     Andrew 'Fez' Warrington, by Ian Lawton
[2] Ged Wells, Meanwhile Gardens, by Ian Lawton

103

Ian Lawton

Matt Hensley was over and I managed to hook up with him, so we went to the Southbank, then Hyde Park. It was just me and Matt Hensley wandering around, basically. It seemed ordinary at the time, just wandering around London with a skateboarding legend.

Paul Haynes

Mark Gonzales stayed at my house in Derby for about a week, and he got friendly with some girls around here. We did a lot of filming at the ramp in Nottingham and took some photos. One of the clips was in 'Video Days', at the end. It was a tricky ramp to skate, but to watch Gonz and Ron Chatman skate it was fantastic to see.

Rob Dukes

We were walking through Nottingham and there was a lady dressed up as a witch, and Mark exclaimed 'Oh look, a witch' as though he thought that's normal for England, and then he remembered it was Halloween. ●

CLOCKWISE FROM LEFT
[1+2] Matt Hensley, Southbank, by Ian Lawton
[3+4] Mark Gonzales, Rollersnakes Nottingham, by Donovan Pennant

1990

Geoff Rowley

We were one of the main skate crews that were in the city all the time and lived there. We were going into the city all the time. Dave Mackey was coming from the north, with the Southport crew, then there were the Crosby guys, like Kevin Banks, Andrew McDonald, Nicky Ryan and all the rest of it, then all the Liscard guys coming through the tunnel or on the ferry across to skate. They were living in Wallasey, so we all had slightly different upbringings, and yet once we all found each other, it was epic because you never knew who was going to show up in town. You never knew which crew was going to be at the spot.

The music heads were older than me and they liked different skaters. They liked more of your punk skater, and I was more into progressive skaters, but once that barrier was broken, there was no punk, there was no metal, there was no hip-hop, we were all just in it for the same reasons. I can't tell you how much love was around there, between all those crews. It was fucking immense.

Fez was always in the city centre because he didn't have a job, so in the middle of the day when everyone was at school, Fez and Jimmy Boyes were ripping around the city, and I'm only getting into the city on Saturdays and Sundays. My main influence came more from seeing Fez and Jimmy and catching glimpses of them skating fast through the city like shadows.

In Liverpool growing up, all the ramps we had, had no flat bottom. Edge Lane had no flat bottom, and then when Neil Danns put his ramp [p.108[3]] into the back of Quiggins, there was no flat bottom! I was a street skater, and I'd never skated ramps, so I didn't know how to do a grind, frontside or backside. I didn't know how to carve, and I still can't carve the way I want to.

I had access to Edge Lane but if I'd go there I could get glassed, or I'd go to Bootle with John Dalton because if I didn't go with John Dalton I was going to get beaten up. Bootle had a metal Rareunit ramp, which was eventually burnt down. A metal ramp that got burnt down.

Kevin Banks

It wasn't really until Dan-Z's ramp that everyone started really getting to know each other. Conversations on top of the ramp and stuff like that; rather than just skating round everywhere it forced everyone to speak to each other. That ramp and the shop really brought the scene together. It got us all talking. We'd end up sharing trains together on the way back so a lot of friendships were formed through that.

Neil Danns

One Saturday I opened my shop and some kids come down and said they'd been to the new skate shop up the road. Everyone's got a right to business, I didn't have no ownership over Liverpool, but if you're working with someone like that and you've got a good relationship with them,

you'd think they would give you notice, you'd think they would say, 'We're opening in Liverpool because we think we can do better than you'.

Then suddenly, they just went. As quick as they'd come. I don't know if it was a business scam or what, but when they come in they just tore the city up, really. They were just interested in making a buck, but it wasn't done well. But maybe I was being a bit naive, doing it for the love of skateboarding and a love of the people in my city, so maybe sometimes I should have been a bit more ruthless.

Tim Bladon

Split Skates in Manchester wanted to branch out to Liverpool because they would see this constant stream of kids coming down from Liverpool and the surrounding areas to buy stuff. Because of our trips there, we got to know the guys that would skate Manchester, guys like Chopper and Femi and Rik Cooper, and because of skating with them we got to know the guys in the shop, so Robbie and Fez started working in Split Skates over the Christmas holidays when they needed. When they wanted to open a shop in Liverpool, they called Robbie, and told him they needed two people to run the shop, so Robbie called me and asked if I wanted to run Split Skates in Liverpool with him, and of course I did. →

Geoff Rowley

When Split Skates opened, Tim was the connection. He was nice to me, he was nice to us all and made us all feel welcome in the skate shop. You don't want to go in a skate shop and feel you're not cool enough to walk in the door when you're 14 years old and you don't even have hair on your balls and you don't even have a scumtache – but you wish you had one – and you've just been beaten up the day before. You don't want to be rejected when you're going somewhere where it's the only thing that you like. Tim was so open and welcoming.

Tim bridged that gap between these little shits that were 12 and these guys that were men. Robbie and Adam Cooke and that were men, and they were doing men things, like having girlfriends and all that stuff. Tim was a pleasure. I always remember Tim saying, 'How rad?', 'How rad is that?', that's all he would say.

I'd go into the city and I'd see this whirlwind, this flash of lightning and thunderbolt skate past me, and it wouldn't stop. I kept seeing it at all the best spots, and as he was going through he'd do a trick – and the trick would be outrageous, it would be something gnarly like sliding an eight or nine-stair handrail – and he'd carry on pushing down the street.

I would see this guy around and I didn't know who he was but he had great style, he skated fast and he had no fear, and he had the best attitude. That was Jimmy. We didn't know each other that well, but I was influenced by him and his style of skating.

I wanted to be Jimmy Boyes; I wanted to skate through the city and lipslide the biggest rail in the city and just skate away. I wanted to be an enigma.

I remember sitting down and talking to Fez and realising he was a sponsored skater, and he knew what was going on. He was a man, and he skates like a man, and he skates like nobody else – he had a long ponytail and a purple headband and high-top Converse and Z-Rollers on a Z-Pig board, so it's nine inches wide and he's doing G-turns like I've never seen before and he's the nicest guy and he's smoking Consulates.

Fez is such a lovely man that he gave this little kid the time of day, and Fez made me feel like part of that group of older guys. They knew what good music was, they knew about skating, they knew what *Thrasher* mag was. I didn't know that stuff. I wanted to skate with Robbie Reid and those guys but I didn't know them like that; I was the little grommy kid.

Fez introduced me to the outdoors, Fez introduced me to a style of skating and to an attitude that I didn't know existed. I've been skating my whole life and I've never slowed down, and I'm the same fucking kid. I was put on Earth to go balls to the wall, and Fez gave me that feeling inside, and Jimmy gave me that feeling inside, that made my heart grow two times and it made me feel invincible once I started to get good at skating.

Jimmy Boyes

I lived at 154 Poulton Road for about three or four months, and then everyone ended up getting evicted. I remember being on my own there, squatting. Going there alone in the evenings with no electricity on, and just drinking cold soup. I was thinking about moving back home to Durham, but I stayed, and I would just skate. Most of the kids I skated with in Liverpool were still at school so I would skate in the daytime, go into museums and kill time. I'd run into kids on the street, like Rowley and Ocean, and Barry Wong, and we'd always be stoked to see each other.

I remember seeing Chester for the first time and thinking, 'Wow!' It was so gnarly. It was like going into a scrapyard skatepark. There was loads of big slabs of concrete in the way of certain runs, but I remember being stoked.

When I rode down from that frontside wallride – almost a grind – I had to pretty much jump off straight away because there was not that much to ride out on. I would have loved to have returned there, but that place was fuckin' raw. It was all broken up but it must have been from the '70s. I'm stoked I was there with Dave Davies, Tim Bladon, Fez and Meany. ●

CLOCKWISE FROM TOP LEFT
[1] Neil Danns, Irby, by Ian Lawton
[2] Jimmy Boyes, Chester, by Ian Lawton
[3+4] Nicky Ryan, Off The Wall ramp, Quiggins, Liverpool, by Kevin Banks

Elsewhere

"There was the phone box at Southbank, and that was like my first mobile phone, because my mum used to call it. It would happen a lot, people's mums would call..."
RICH FILE

Mike Manzoori

It did get weird really quickly. We did the Powell tour around the UK, and that was terrifying. At the first demo in Bracknell, my leg was trembling as I was dropping in after Tony Hawk. Everyone takes their run, then I guess it's my turn now... And I skated Bracknell! I grew up on that ramp, so I should know it, and I just remember fucking falling on axle stalls and shit. All my mates shouting for me, 'Have it! Have it!', and I'm just going, 'Fuuuuuuck... don't know what I'm doing!' I was fucking terrified. After that demo we went to fucking George Harrison's house because his son Dhani skated, and I remember thinking that I was in another world. I didn't know what I was doing there.

It was fun and everything but when I came back home I sent them a letter to say that I didn't think I was cut out for this. I did a couple of tours and I was just scared so I thought they should get somebody else. I was pretty overwhelmed.

Curtis McCann

To me, the idea of being sponsored by Powell Peralta, pre-World Industries, was like the equivalent of being part of the Harlem Globetrotters. In my experience, watching Bones Brigade videos was a fun, almost religious, daily activity. When I think back to my going to the Powell Peralta European base, I can't remember if I even considered the chance to be sponsored by them, I just thought I was going on to a competition in Copenhagen... Anyway, it turned out like a dream... before I knew it I was sponsored by Powell Peralta, and for that long weekend I was rarely 'teetotal', and skated the 'best' street course all day... Soon after, I started travelling quite regularly to competitions and demos around Europe... I travelled to Holland, Denmark, Germany, Italy, Belgium, Poland, France, Czechoslovakia, and Switzerland. A few years later there was talk of me turning pro and having a 'Euro model'... I was glad that I didn't turn pro because I knew I wasn't good enough. When I think back to that time, I would have been happy if they just paid for my daily travel card and some fast food, but being the way I was, I didn't think to ask!

I liked most contests because in those days you would see big American contests with amazing street courses, but rarely get to skate something close... at Euro comps you usually had better-than-average things to skate!... things like crazy fun boxes with overly steep foot-high 'handrails'! I had high hopes so contests often depressed me when I knew my runs should have been better. My favourite contest has to be my first Copenhagen contest. I flew out to Amsterdam – and I'd never been on an aeroplane – I turned up at a decent indoor mini ramp, and the next thing I knew I was sponsored by Powell Peralta. We then drove to Copenhagen in a new team bus picking up team members along the way. At Copenhagen I placed third in my first pro-am competition! (With Americans!) I remember that because I was pretty much shop-sponsored as a 'model', I had a strange hang-up about how good and deserving I was as a skater... so in my early teens that trip meant a lot to me. ●

'All my mates shouting for me, 'Have it! Have it!', and I'm just going, 'Fuuuuuuuck... I don't know what I'm doing!' I was fucking terrified.'
MIKE MANZOORI

Sponsorship

Elsewhere

CLOCKWISE FROM TOP LEFT
[1] Mike Manzoori, Bracknell, by James Hudson
[2] Mike Manzoori, Morfa, by Ian Lawton

1990

→ **DEATH BOX**
Andy Scott

I'm not too sure how I got on Death Box; I think Rocker probably mentioned me to Jeremy Fox because I was skating with him quite a lot. It was a bit weird, because I was getting decent packages off Joe Burlo, so I was torn between the two, because Death Box was only quite small back then and I don't think it was ever credible. Death Box was a little bit childish with the graphics and things, and H-Street was American and it was cool. I was torn between the two but I'm pretty glad I did go to Death Box. At the time it was stressful, wondering what to do.

→ **BASH**
Ian Deacon

Bash started in '89, and didn't have boards until '90. I was doing it on a Prince of Wales scheme, where if you were unemployed you could get money to try to do a business, so I had that for a year or so. It was like getting unemployment money, and I think Jeremy did that when he started Death Box as well, because he was making helmets before that.

Jeremy had the Death Box warehouse in Wellingborough, in this rundown building, and he could get boards from this guy Paige Hearn in Little Rock, Arkansas. He'd been through a couple, he tried to get boards from Madrid but they just sent him shitty boards, and then he settled with this Paige Hearn guy who did a pretty good job. There were crazy concaves but the boards were generally pretty good. The original three was Luke McKirdy, Neil Fry, Merlin Nation. Then Jeremy got Pike and Chris Lonergan on.

Merlin Nation

We grew up skating everything. There's always been a culture of transition skating in Brighton, but we were constantly exploring town for spots at the same time. Neil Fry and Colin Pope and the Worthing crew were coming into Brighton to skate at the Level and we'd be learning flip tricks and stuff at the bottom of the vert ramp transition. We'd still be skating the ramp too though. And we'd always be rolling around town finding new things to skate.

I met Deacon at the Level too, so the crew happened really naturally. We were getting some Death Box stuff flowed before Bash products existed, some Dodo wheels and those gigantic rails. We'd still be skating around local spots – me, Luke, Neil and Deacon and the rest of the crew as usual – then photographers from magazines started showing up a bit. It was all very easy going, no pressure and felt very spontaneous. It was just fun skating, learning new tricks and messing about with your mates. The best way.

Then the art side led to me designing an early Bash logo and Deacon's pro board. I'd been drawing some magazine ads for the Pig City shop, and me and Dylan Whickham, who did the amazing graphics for Deacon's mini mode, made a zine called *Rub A Dub* – just repping the Brighton scene – making home-made stickers all that stuff. Just a DIY attitude. I have hippy parents so at the time I was into Grateful Dead artwork, Rick Griffin, Kelley and Mouse. All that West Coast US psych stuff seeped into the designs I did for Bash. ●

LEFT TO RIGHT
[1] Death Box graphics, by Mace
[2] Bash graphics and catalogue, by Merlin Nation and Ian Deacon

LEFT TO RIGHT
[1] Poizone garments and labels
[2] Anarchic Adjustment t-shirt prints, by Nick Philip

→ ***POIZONE***
Jamie Blair

Poizone grew pretty rapidly. Our initial stock of it was still made in the old Davie Philip fashion, cottage-industry style, mostly in Grangemouth but the Shetland wool stuff was done in Dundee. We pretty quickly realised we couldn't manufacture the quantities we needed, and the quality was still quite rudimentary because we didn't have double stitching or anything like that. It was all done on sewing machines.

So we started scouting around and we found a manufacturer in Glasgow, David Roberts, who had a place over in Templeton Business Centre, and they had about 20 machinists. Davie had a basic pattern for the trousers but we just started designing clothes, basically.

We were being quite creative with it, and asking for stuff they hadn't done before. At that point there were no skate clothing brands in Britain; we were the first and we were trying to break the mould. We did the shorts, and then stack hats, then skateboard bags, moleskin trousers, then jackets and shirts, then the Harris Tweed stuff. And part of the idea was to keep it at a price that kids could afford.

I wanted the Harris Tweed label on every garment, but you only get one Harris Tweed label with every metre of fabric that you buy. I came up with a cotton shirt that had a panel of Harris Tweed, and that top section was only half a metre. I contacted the guy at Harris Tweed and sent him photos of the garment and asked if we could use the Harris Tweed label on it, and he thought about it and said, 'Ach, OK then, aye', so I managed to get extra labels to authenticate it. We used the Harris Tweed and the Shetland wool and wherever we could we used Scottish suppliers.

→ ***ANARCHIC ADJUSTMENT***
Nick Philip

When I made that Heroin Satan Fuck t-shirt I thought, 'OK, what is the Christian right in America most scared that their children are into?', and that's why I put that on it. There was the whole thing about hidden messages when you played an Iron Maiden record or a Judas Priest record backwards, so the message was that the Christian right were paranoid that their children were getting brainwashed by pop culture.

The first version was just black ink on the black shirt. When you print black plastisol on a 100%-cotton black t-shirt, depending on the pigment dye of the shirt, you see it. Especially in bright sunlight. That was the first iteration of it, then we did a reflective version where we used reflective ink, which was a little bit more visible when you wore it normally. If you were in a club and the lights flashed, or if you were walking down the street and a car light hit it, it really came up. ●

Elsewhere

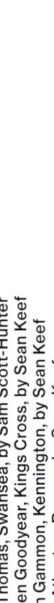

1991

Tom Penny, Cowley Road, Oxford, by Tim Leighton-Boyce

It felt like life couldn't get any better. Like you were on the cutting edge of life. I don't think I ever made that statement in my mind at the time, but looking back, I felt the excitement. We were witnessing the creation of something, as it was unfolding we were right there.

RICH FILE

Jimmy Boyes, Queen's Bank, Newcastle, by James Hudson

Tom Penny

We had a tiny little ramp round the back of the house, that Dougie built. Dougie's the same person that built the Cowley Road ramps opposite SS20. It was only about two foot high, there was a long bit of roof in the room it was in so we had to make it really small, but it was there for a year or so, in Jericho.

Botley was my first contest, and it was my first ever photo[2]. I managed to get first place, so I was quite lucky that day. I won a Death Box board, before I was sponsored by them. I had a photo doing a backside tailgrab one-foot on the subscribe page in *RAD* at that contest.

There were some photos on the Cowley Road ramps that Dougie built, there was a melanchollie to fakie, and a few different photos from that ramp at the same time. It wasn't the best thing in the world to skate, to be perfectly honest, but we always had enough things here and there. Enough to keep us going, and motivated to skate.

Davy Van Laere

They gave me the pro model around '91, and of course as a young kid you say yes, but I think there was pressure of being sponsored. Some people can handle it, some aren't made for this. I got my board, and within a half year I stopped skating. I was realistic. You skate with Alex Moul or some guy like that who has mega talent, you know that you don't have their talent.

Pete Dossett

When I was at school I'd tried to draw a cigarette packet graphic. So when Jeremy said he had an idea for my graphic, I said I'd had ideas for graphics, and I told him about the cigarette packet, and he said that he thought it was 'a bit too soon'. Mac had already done the Punch and Judy one at the same time as he did the first one, the Cherub one, so Jeremy said he wanted to go with that because it was a bit gnarlier.

At the time I was thinking of JPS – John Player Special – but instead of JPS I'd have 'PJD', my initials. Jeremy didn't smoke, but eventually he started smoking and he smoked JPS, but he went with the Marlboro packet because it was a bit more international. JPS works in England, but Jeremy was trying to capture the European or the American market. That graphic worked better than any of the others.

Ian Deacon

Death Box was doing really good for a while, and then obviously skateboarding crashed and then Jeremy had this massive flood in '91; the place above him flooded and all the boards got screwed and it was the usual insurance nightmare where you couldn't get any money from the insurance company. That screwed Death Box pretty badly.

Harry Bastard

I got Bash boards, which turned out just to be Death Box boards. That's my first ever sponsor. I was 13 or 14, so I was starting to work then, and I had a shitty job in Tesco's stacking the freezers. I went to Copenhagen with Rocker, Mouly, Geoff, all of that lot, when I was a kid. I said to Tesco's that I'd been offered this opportunity to go to Copenhagen to a skateboard competition, and skateboarding to them, back then, was a pile of shit so I just sacked my job off. My parents hated me, but I was out there for about two weeks, in the back of the van with Andy Scott, everyone chain-smoking fags, yellow nicotine stains everywhere and getting out the van and having to walk across borders instead of being in the van because we weren't all allowed in the van.

Sean Goff

I told Jeremy to cut my sponsorship. It was the Southsea pool comp, and we'd had Otis by then so I had a young child so I wasn't gonna spend as much time skating, trying to promote myself. At the Southsea pool comp street skating was coming in, vert skating was dying, and I wanted to go out winning the contest, but I didn't. Davie Philip beat me, but that's just the way it goes.

I remember telling Jeremy beforehand, 'Yeah, don't bother making my board anymore. It's not really selling as much as it should, and it's all about street skating now and vert is dying', and he went, 'I'm glad you said that, because I don't think we can do it anymore anyway'. And in the end that was it. I was pretty much on my way out then anyway. The *Spirit of the Blitz* video was all Pete Dossett, Alex Moul, all the young kids; that's what that video was promoting. Those guys went out and they filmed proper long sections.

Paul 'Rocker' Robson

We were told we were filming for something, and I remember we tried to do a lot of it around the contests. There's some footage from Dundee, and some stuff at Barrow-in-Furness, but the lighting wasn't too good. The guy that did most of the video was a guy that used to work at the BBC, who was a good friend of Jeremy's. He had access to some really high-end equipment but he just couldn't get the lighting done. We got a little bit of stuff from Bury and Goshen, and some stuff from Wigan and Preston, but most of it couldn't be used. The stuff you see of Andy Scott and Jocke Olsson at these ramps, it's just one trick at a time because you couldn't video the other side because it was just too dark. That video didn't have the budget Powell had.

Alex Moul

I love this photo[3] because it's an ode to Matt Hensley, doing a tailgrab noseslide. It's such a shit rail but it looks quite good.

Me and Matt McMullan were always talking about 'popcorn'[1] back then, and popcorn meant you were doing tech tricks, like three flips and impossibles, but down stairs. 'That guy's well popcorn.' That was before people were saying, 'That guy's got mad pop', for ollie height. →

Death Box

CLOCKWISE FROM TOP LEFT
[1] Alex Moul, Harrow, by James Hudson
[2] Tom Penny, RAD subscriptions ad, by Tim Leighton-Boyce
[3] Alex Moul, Nottingham, by James Hudson
[4] Davy Van Laere, Washington, by James Hudson
[5] Davy Van Laere, Washington, by James Hudson

　　　　　　　　　　1991

Ben Wheeler

The Children's Film Unit was a film workshop in Battersea that I used to go to on a Saturday morning. It was an amazing, brilliant place. We used to pay ten pounds a year and one pound a week to go to this workshop and we'd do 10am 'til 4pm on a Saturday and you'd get into pairs and you'd write a short film and you'd star in it and shoot it on 16mm film. Once a year Channel 4 gave them the money to make a feature film that was by kids, for kids. So we had an adult producer and an adult director – Colin Finbow, that started the whole thing – and a director of photography. We'd go away and stay in a school down in Seaford near Brighton, this boarding school that was closed for the summer, for two or three weeks and then we'd go and shoot a feature film. It was incredible, it was properly structured filmmaking with everyone working in different departments, so you had proper roles exactly like a film shoot is now.

I was there from age 13 to 17, and towards the end video was starting to be a big thing, and they had this funny old Video8 camera, so I borrowed that from them, and me and Simon and Corin would go to Southbank and shoot as much as we could with that camera. We'd tape the fisheye lenses that they had from their stills cameras on there and skate around with it, with the recorder pack in a backpack, and shoot everything we could, and then we decided to make our own skate video. Then we spent ages editing it on VHS, on an editing suite in Brixton. It had very crude editing equipment but we'd spend days there. I think we had to pay twenty quid a week to be there.

It was great fun and I'm still really proud of that video. I'm a professional cinematographer now, it's what I do for a living, and I'm still really proud of that video and how we cut it and how we put it to music, as young kids. We were aping what we'd seen in American skate videos, obviously, but we had good ideas and I think we carried it off quite well, and I think it's a brilliant bit of archive of what Southbank was.

At the time we didn't think it was worth anything, it was just a document of our mates and we were making it for us, with no commercial interest whatsoever. Looking back now, that's madness, but those guys have got the one VHS hard copy that existed.

Simon Casey

The security guard in the start of the video is saying on his radio, 'We've got some right hard nutters down here'. That's kinda what we called the video, but it never really came across.

Corin was better at photography than me but I kinda got into films, into filmmaking in a very amateur way, so I think I was filming a bit more, and it led into filming skateboarding when I was about 16 maybe, so about '89 or '90 we were filming skating, because why not?

Ben Wheeler has a massive part to play in how the video came about. He was connected to the Children's Film Unit, so got a camera to use. We had a friend called Bridget – who passed away a few years ago, unfortunately – she worked at the London Institute, and she got us an edit suite.

I carried on filming, and I'm sure I filmed some stuff at Southbank with the *411* camera when that was passed around. I filmed Curtis at Liverpool Street, at that double set round the back, and I don't even know where that footage is

Curtis McCann

As per usual, I wasn't impressed with my skating in *The Southbank Video*, but if I remember rightly it might have played a part in getting a few skaters sponsored. When I look back at it, I'm amazed at what some of them were doing – it's so easy to watch skaters, especially in videos, and forget just how hard skateboarding actually is. That video had things like late grabs to fakies on the tiny steep bank near the National Film Theatre or nose bumps on the 'stop bars' at the Shell Centre... those tricks freak me out to this day!

Corin Casey

We'd just film everyone, and kind of put it together. Each person skating, you'd snip that out and put it in their section when we were doing the editing. We'd film sessions; it wouldn't just be us and one person. We'd all go skating as a group, whoever was at Southbank. Whatever session was going on, we'd just be videoing stuff. It was quite organic how it happened. We were just poor kids and everything was borrowed.

We didn't do it to sell a video or anything. In hindsight we were just dumb little kids with no aspirations. We were just doing it as something we enjoyed doing. →

1991

The Southbank Video

CLOCKWISE FROM TOP LEFT
[1] Simon Casey (front) and Tony Luckhurst (skating),
     Shell Centre, by Corin Casey
[2] Ben Wheeler, Southbank, by Corin Casey
[3] Tony Luckhurst, Festival Hall, by Corin Casey
[4] Ben Wheeler, St John's Church, by Corin Casey
[5] Tony Luckhurst, Southbank, by Corin Casey
NEXT PAGE
[1] Rachid Lamgyntaz, by Corin Casey

Elsewhere

1991

Ewer Street

Winstan Whitter

It was '91 that the bars at Southbank came in, and there was a huge lull when that happened. You'd have 200 skaters at Southbank on a busy day, then it went down to much less than it is now on a quiet day. It went down to about 20 people, and we'd be some of those 20 people, still trying to skate, but it was a bit like just having our heads in our hands, wondering what we do now. We heard that Dave Duncan, the ramp builder from the States, had come over to build a skatepark called London Bridge, and that was a godsend.

Arron Bleasdale

We – the Camden bunch – and Corin and Simon Casey, and a few people from Southbank, all helped clean that place out. It was just full of garbage and trash, and it was an old props warehouse, so cleaning it out was pretty gross and hard work, and then we were part of helping to build it as well.

Curtis McCann

I think I skated Ewer Street every day for the summer it was there, and as usual it felt like a very long summer. That place was so good to me and enabled one of what I call my skate 'primes'; around that time injuries were starting to affect my ability to do a lot of the latest street tricks, but thankfully the transitions at Ewer Street were easier on my knees and ankles. I'm so glad that I was able to film my 'Celebrity Tropical Fish' part there… at the time I thought it was a bit shit but now I like it!

Tom Penny

He's one of my favourite all-time skaters, Curtis. When I was younger, Carl Shipman and Curtis McCann were always my two favourite skaters from the UK. I remember seeing Curtis at Southbank and at London Bridge, one of the first times I

was down in London, when he was filming for the Powell video. I was around for those sessions, I saw some of those tricks in real life. He was so far ahead of his time it was ridiculous. It was bonkers what he was doing.

Paul Stylianou

Danny was a bit of a geezer, and he used to be a ticket tout – he was a Del Boy – and Kai was just hilarious, he was very camp and he just wanted to be part of the scene. My uncle John said, 'Yeah, my best mate Danny is building a skatepark up in London Bridge, I'll introduce you'. So off we went up there, and they were literally just laying down the first foundations for the miniramp and the vert. Without hesitation Danny went, 'Right, you're on my team', and he said he wanted me to take care of all the affairs because I knew all the skaters. He didn't know anybody and he was doing it purely as a financial thing, because at that time it was the beginning of private raves, the whole rave scene came along at that time. That was his main intention, and the raves that were held there were just off the charts, and I can safely say he was making a fair few pennies out of them.

I vividly remember the last rave they did was a Friday into the Saturday, and on the Sunday we opened the park and I said to the guys we could have a session, and I closed the shutters. About three o'clock in the morning we could just hear the shutters getting broken into, so we're all freaking out, and as the shutters went up there's a dozen policemen, some officials and bailiffs, and they had a writ. They told us to grab our shit and go otherwise they were going to arrest us for illegal trespassing.

In the back room, outside in the courtyard, was the skate shop, and luckily that had a padlock on there so they couldn't

get in. It was a full-blown skate shop with decks and trucks and wheels and shoes and everything in there. So they just kicked us out, they didn't even enter the premises, and they just shut the shutters and put a massive padlock on, and that was it. And there was a bailiff's letter on the shutters, with a writ.

So I called up Danny from the nearest pay phone and said what had happened, and he didn't seem too fussed, which was kind of alarming because I'd woken him up. He's going, 'Yeah, OK, I'll be down tomorrow', then the penny dropped and he goes, 'Shit, all the money from the rave is in the shop!' So I had to sneak in round the back and jump walls, and back in them days there was glass in the concrete on top of the walls so it was full-on SAS stealth-mode and I managed to get into the shop and lo and behold there was the basket and there must have been thousands of pounds in that thing.

I managed to grab it for Danny, and then he said that whatever I could take from the shop, I could keep it, but unbeknown to me he hadn't paid for the stock. We're all robbing this equipment and it hadn't been paid for, but back in them days it wasn't our problem.

I met Danny round the corner – he pulled up in his Porsche – because he couldn't be seen in that area because he had this illegal arch, basically, and I gave him the big bag of money.

It still got skated for a while after that, because it was a perfect ramp for Central London. They were going in, I think through the back entrance, but they weren't taking the piss. I think eventually the contractors went in and knocked everything down and it was done. →

Elsewhere

1991

Simon Evans

I wasn't there that much, I guess because of the arrogance of being a purist street skater, I think. It was amazing though, wasn't it? The first time I kissed a girl was there, and I remember Mike Manzoori going off on the miniramp.

Rob Dukes

I was there that night, it was a kind of a party as well as a skate session, Simon was sat on top of the ramp talking to this girl he'd just met and he told me later that he'd told her that he didn't know how to talk to girls, and she was really nice about it.

Ben Wheeler

I was there more for the parties and less for the skating, by that point. Everyone was skating that a lot but I'd got into girls and raving, and kind of stopped a little bit, but I remember going to a couple of parties there that were really good. It'd be half skaters, half ravers, which was a nice combination.

Shane O'Brien

The tail-slapping phenomenon started pretty much in that period in that warehouse. I'd seen it at Stevenage about a year before; Dave Allen was whacking his tail and whacking his truck on the coping, making loud noise. Then in the warehouse it seemed to be 30 or 40 people at one time doing it. The whole thing transcended into a place of massive noise, massive echoing, screaming and shouting. It was crazy.

Mike Manzoori

It was so good at the time. It was the first indoor place we had in forever and it was the best summer, but we were all indoors and we missed all the sunshine, but we didn't give a shit because it was such a well-made set-up for how compact the space was. We took advantage of as much of it as possible.

What I heard was that they didn't pay a single penny of rent or bills for the whole time they were there. They just ran it until they got kicked out. They'd paid for Tim Payne to build the skatepark in there obviously, and they were taking money at the door, so they'd charge people to come in for the most part – although we were always trying to wing it, just paying a quid rather than three quid or whatever – so they made a bit of money off of the skating but they didn't pay any rent.

I heard they'd even tapped the electricity, they'd wired it to the train tracks above so they weren't even paying any electricity bills. It used to be full of theatre stuff, and when they cleared it out they kept some of it so that's where those cherubs and the big curtains came from.

Matt Dawson

As a skatepark, it was brilliant. That's when everyone kinda left Southbank, and it was kinda left alone for a bit, because of the bars.

Reuben Goodyear

At the end of '91 London Bridge got taken down, and I never really found a footing back at Southbank. I don't know what changed, whether it was the new generation coming in or if I'd just been there and done that and saw that there was other things out there.

Ryan Mills

When Ewer Street opened it became a bit more social. Everyone started hanging out and smoking, drinking. The early '90s saw a bit of a boom in skateboarding, before it died a death again. We were getting invited to clubs, and fashion shoots, and all sorts.

Matt Gold

It was amazing but in some ways it was kind of the death of skateboarding for me. Towards the end of London Bridge it got pretty ravey, and the gangsters who ran the place were just doing raves because it was a way of making money. We got the taste for raving and its associated substances.

There was the fallout of all of us going raving around that time, and the summer of love got a bit darker. When the drugs changed and people started doing more crack and more smack, some people got themselves in a bit of a pickle with it.

Luke Davidson

Ewer Street was there at a time when skating in London had switched from parks and ramps to real street skating. UK skateboarders realised they actually were as good as the Americans, to a point. There was a confidence. It felt like a changing of the guard, and the level of skating in Ewer Street was just insane. People were getting really good really quickly. ●

CLOCKWISE FROM LEFT
[1] Midi ramp overview, by Wig Worland
[2] Exterior, by Wig Worland
[3] Lee Stewart, by Ian Lawton
[4] Mike Manzoori, by Wig Worland

1991

Jay Doherty

There wasn't much coverage of Ireland during the era of The Troubles. Who the fuck would want to come over here to skate around really shit spots and risk getting shot?

We were in County Derry, over on the north west. Ballykelly, our village, was fairly stuck in the past; the men go to the bookies, most folk you know are on the dole, the women worked in the factories, Catholics and Protestants are fighting, cricket for Protestants, Gaelic football for the Catholics. The culture was fairly bigoted, divided, close minded, with IRA murals and 12th of July parades.

In no way was there any forward-thinking culture at all, but there was about ten skateboarders for about a year. The town beside us had a good scene and there was various good scenes around.

The Troubles didn't affect your daily life when you were in the thick of it, only looking back do you realise what a mental time that was to live in. There was always bomb scares and there was always bombs. There was army on the streets, all the time, and anywhere you went – especially in and around Derry, or crossing over the border – there would be a heavy British Army presence everywhere. It was all you knew, growing up.

Jimmy Boyes

I got a little bit ill at that Dublin contest, and it was years later I found out what made me ill. The contest[3] was sponsored by an orange juice company and I remember just fucking drinking litres of it. A couple of years later I discovered with an allergy test that I was allergic to red wine and orange juice. During my run I felt so heavy and lethargic, and I remember not having that good a run.

The day before the contest everyone was flying around, buzzing, just skating, but I think the next day I was ill and I didn't do that well. I remember getting my arm branded on the ferry, and I still have the scar. There was this one dude that as soon as Snoz branded him he passed out, on the dance floor.

Simon Evans

That was probably the biggest one for me, because I went over there with New Deal. I went over there quite a few times, to Clive's Skates. His son, or his younger brother, was in the Commitments. That was amazing that year, meeting Jonno and Rosie and Simon. I loved going to Ireland.

It was a little scary when I was in Northern Ireland one time, being English at the time was a bit dodgy, but I just really connected with the Irish guys. It was a really fun time.

Kevin Banks

That ferry ride was nuts. Especially the ferry back. It was Snoz's twenty-somethingth birthday and I had some footage of him getting the bumps and he gets thrown up and his head goes through the roof, into this false ceiling, and the fucking ceiling falls down. He ended up on the deck with this false ceiling on top of him, laughing his head off. Everyone was a bit drunk. And on the way back it was carnage.

We were all sat on top of the ferry chatting, and then someone would go off and do a wallride on the funnel or something, or try to slide the benches we were sitting on or something.

That was a great comp. It ended with about thirty of us in a hotel room in Dublin, and I think Arron Bleasdale paid for it, like, 'Yeah, whoever wants to stay in here'. Me and Ocean went out on the town, we went out drinking with the Death Box lot like Jeremy and Rocker and Jocke, and we ended up drinking with Rick Charnoski, the American. We went on the piss round Dublin with him so we didn't get back until about two o'clock in the morning, and there was literally nowhere to sleep in the room, it was just bodies everywhere. Ocean ended up sleeping underneath this cupboard, and I had to sleep on top of it. It was only about a foot wide so I could only just get one shoulder on it, and I couldn't get the window shut. So I woke up quite early, and I was reading RAD magazine, and literally everyone in the room was in it apart from me and my mate.

We just went down to the comp, at the Point Depot – I think it was Wingy who took us down – so we just went in and pretended we were building the street course, and ended up helping out, building the course, and we kipped in there that night. That was on the Friday. Snoz built a ramp off his own back. It was like a session, really. Curtis McCann was there, Jimmy was skating, Simon Evans, Manzoori, all just skating it as it's being built, a closed-doors session. That was pretty cool.

The next day was the comp, and it was a strange one because the people that were organising it, I don't think they knew what they were expecting because the security were a bit heavy from what I remember. I didn't have many issues with them but I know people got thrown out and manhandled a bit.

There was an orange juice fight in the green room afterwards. It was sponsored by Sqeez orange juice, so the green room was just full of orange juice on the Sunday after comp, and there was just litres of orange juice getting lobbed everywhere, it was carnage. People getting hit on the head with cartons of orange, and pools of orange juice everywhere. ●

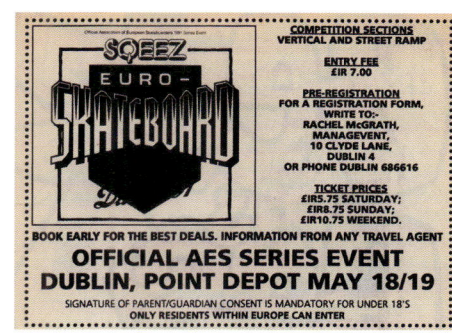

CLOCKWISE FROM LEFT
[1] Greenisland skatepark via Jay Doherty
[2] Patrick Deroulede, Sqeez contest, by Kevin Banks
[3] Jimmy Boyes, Sqeez contest, by Sam Scott-Hunter
[4] Ad for Sqeez contest
[5] Antrim ramps via Jay Doherty

Tom Penny

For a youngster in Oxford, in that area, Alex Moul was the biggest thing on the planet when it came to skateboarding. Any time you saw Alex Moul when you were a kid was the best. I remember getting the bus to Abingdon to go to his dad's house because he had a miniramp in the garden and we'd be so nervous walking up to ring the bell. We're just little kids and Alex Moul was already a superstar back then.

We'd skate that ramp with him, then we'd skate the BMX track in Abingdon. It was fun, those days. Of course there'd always be the option of skating Oxford, so I'd see him in Oxford too. I always had a lot of respect for Alex, he was far ahead of his time.

Mon Barbour

Sean did the Stüssy rip-off logo[3]. He just drew it up one day and we looked at it and were like, 'Fucking hell, that's great, Sean'. We first did it on these really heavy-duty Fruit of the Loom t-shirts that were just unbreakable. It had the Devil Bomb on the back on the very bottom, in a colour fade.

There's a really famous picture[2] of Tom Penny doing a melon to fakie on the Manzil Way ramp wearing that t-shirt, and after that came out he got a box from Stüssy, with a note saying, 'Thanks for repping us'. Even Stüssy didn't realise that that was our logo.

Danny Wainwright

SS20 was more of a scene going on; I was good friends with Tom and Scamp and I used to go and stay at their houses all the time. Me and Joe Habgood would hitch-hike up to Oxford a lot of the time. I used to hitch every day from where I lived into Stroud, and back, to go skating, and then we started hitching to Oxford, to London, just stood at the side of the road hitch-hiking. We never had any money, me and Joe grew up poor kids, so we couldn't get money for the train and all this so we used to disappear for days and hitch-hike around.

Tom lived in Jericho, and he never had a door key. There was the front door, and then to the left was the bay window, and that was his bedroom in there. He'd just jimmy the window up and climb in, then he'd open the door and let you in. We were always there, smoking hash and hanging out. Tom's room was bare, no carpets, nothing. Just floorboards, a mattress and a little cupboard for hanging up his stuff. I was sponsored by SS20, but Sean Goff would make me pay trade price for stuff, and then I'd just get boards on tick and never pay for them because I never had money. I never had a job or any of that stuff. ●

LEFT TO RIGHT
[1] Tom Penny, Cowley Road, Oxford, by Tim Leighton-Boyce
[2] RAD, November, Tom Penny by Tim Leighton-Boyce
[3] SS20 logo by Sean Goff
[4] SS20 interior, by Mon Barbour
[5] Alex Moul, Abingdon, by James Hudson

1991

Insane

Sofia Prantera

I was at St Martin's – I studied fashion – and Ged Wells was going out with one of my friends, Claire Corrigan. I'm Italian so I have a passion for sportswear, although I wasn't necessarily interested in skateboarding as a subculture, but Claire introduced me to him because he was looking for a sportswear designer.

I went in to meet Russell Waterman and Paul Sunman, and I didn't have a job, so it seemed like a good thing to do. I was really into Stone Island, CP... I was really into Casual culture, and my degree show was based on that. I was really into technical fabrics. I wasn't into football at all, but I was into the way football hooligans dressed. A lot of friends from the north of England had introduced me to the way that Italian fashion was being reinterpreted by football hooligans, and I really loved that, so that's how I ended up doing it, really.

I started working there straight away; I don't think they'd lined up a lot of people for the job, the interview was very much, 'OK, you'll do'. I started when they were still in Talbot Road, and the week I started they had this massive Insane delivery, which was going to Japan, so the boxes were going through the Rough Trade store, downstairs into Slam City.

The crossover between skate fashion and terrace fashion was nowhere near as intertwined as it is now, and I tried to make Insane into this slightly technical thing, when I think I just should have been way more what Ged wanted, which was illustrations on the clothes, but illustration is quite hard to design with, because I liked more technical styles. Applying illustrations to the actual clothes, not t-shirts and sweatshirts, was maybe not completely my taste, but it was his brand and not mine.

Ged Wells

The video was a major collaboration of content, both film and music. The whole experience was very playful and I don't think anybody cared that this was not a cutting-edge skate video. David Slade and I were mates through making zines and we always shared ideas. We edited the vid at Sheffield art college and film cooperative.

David has a mad energy and loads of technical skills. He was totally open to very oblique ideas because he is also very experimental. The Super8 time-lapse aspects of the video worked very well, got screened at the London Film Festival. All the fast-edit sections were time-consuming to edit on Umatic tape, think we did a couple of all-night edit sessions.

Ed Gill

So me and Will Bankhead stayed the night at Ged's house and then we got up at five in the morning and we skated non-stop from wherever the fuck we were in west London to Buckingham Palace. Ged was filming us on a Super8, shooting intermittent frames, and that's Chapter 7 in the video. That's why we look so dozy and sleepy at Buckingham Palace – because we'd been awake for four hours and had hardly slept.

I love 'Mouse Is Pulling the Key.' It's really nice, the enchanting music in our bit. It's really emotional and really sad, with that black-and-white Super8. I find it really sad to watch because it's like a memory.

Rob Dukes

The video annoyed nearly everybody when it came out. Skaters can be just as rigid in their thinking as 'normal' people. They were expecting a video full of skateboarding. ●

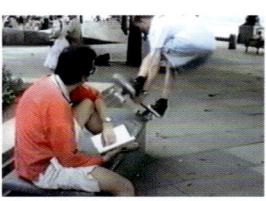
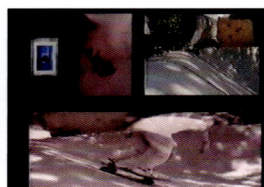

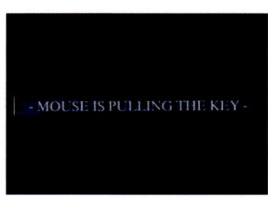

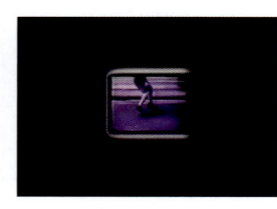

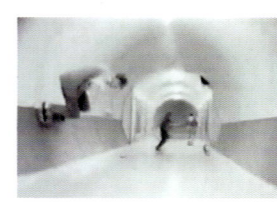

CLOCKWISE FROM LEFT
[1] Stills from *Mouse Is Pulling The Key*
[2] Insane stickers, video, by Ged Wells
[3] Alex Craig, Aberdeen, by Scott Malcolm
[4] Insane catalogue and boards, by Ged Wells

insane fountain

© insane 91

insane

Presents

"Mouse is Pulling the Key"

by Ged Wells

Standing watching
Fight of Circles
and Lines, the
Circle Smiles
as it rolls and
Chases the Line, and
Again Falling, and
Again dreaming,
Shapes reoccuring.
If the key fits,
then Wear it. Look
back at time, Look
back at what is
coming, the Circle
and the Line are
still running.
hide in a Sad Story,
wake in its Happy
ending, haunted
by its Sense.
Circle and Line
trip in time.

thank you for the music OJ, Simon
THULE courtesy WIIIJA records.
thank you Dave Slade. All Who
skated ALL who Helped.

"MOUSE IS PULLING THE KEY"
28 MINS.
COPYRIGHT 1991
SLAM CITY SKATES/INSANE

VTS/TDK HQ TAPE

"Mouse is
Pulling
the Key" by
Ged Wells

New Deal Distribution

Simon Evans

Leaving New Deal was the biggest mistake I made. This is a lesson to myself: Don't quit a company because of the team manager. That's what I want to say about that. I was just a kid and everything came so easy, and I just figured it would always be like that.

They got this new team manager in and he didn't like me, and he didn't even know me, it was just what I represented. He was an older guy, and I didn't like him, and I quit New Deal because of the fucking team manager. That was all it was about and I was just an idiot and I really regretted doing that. Then I was basically on Think flow. I was really on to a good thing with New Deal. Never quit a company because of the team manager, because they come and go, but I just focused on this guy and I just didn't like him and I was young and arrogant and I was like, 'Fuck this, I'm out'. I didn't really think it through, I just really didn't get along with the guy. He was playing these little power games with me and stuff.

Steve Douglas

Competitors were laughing at us because we didn't have a database, and we didn't even know what a database was, but what they underestimated was the hard graft that those guys were doing. We got the Transit van, and they fitted it out so we had this van that would travel round the country and it would be all visual, so you'd walk in and you'd see rows of decks and rows of t-shirts. Everyone would go in there and overbuy because you could see it all, and it wasn't just a bunch of boxes. ●

LEFT TO RIGHT
[1] Simon Evans, Southbank, by Corin Casey
[2] NDUK Transit van interior, by Steve Douglas
[3] Carl Shipman, Nottingham, by James Hudson
[4] Skate Action, June, Alex Moul, the last issue, by James Hudson

"After six months of *Skate Action* I was basically scraping a living. Occasionally I'd sell a picture to someone else..."

JAMES HUDSON

James Hudson

I was criticised about my 'relationship' with Death Box, and the amount of Carl Shipman pics I ran later on, but when you've got £1,500 to make a magazine and pay your mortgage and Carl Shipman is one of your mates, or Pete Dossett lives round the corner, what's going to happen?! I guess it was similar in London for Tim. Simon Evans is a really interesting guy, his skating was kicking off and he was keen and available, why on Earth would you not shoot him?

After six months of *Skate Action* I was basically scraping a living. Occasionally I'd sell a picture to someone else... I think there was one point when I was doing *Skate Action* but I really wanted to sell a picture to *RAD* because I knew I'd definitely get paid 50 quid, whereas if I worked out what I was taking home per page in *Skate Action* – after I deducted all the fuel and processing costs – it was probably about five quid a page. There were definitely points towards the end where I thought, 'I've got this cracking shot, maybe I can sell it to Tim and he can publish it with someone else's name on?'

Martin Higginson took me into the office one day and said that although *Skate Action* wasn't losing any money, it wasn't making any money and it was just still a liability for him. He wasn't into it so he was going to close it down. ●

1991

Elsewhere

Dave Mackey

We would get to Liverpool early, we would be at Southport train station at 8.30am. You'd be there with your bacon butty and your huge bottle of Coke that you're gonna carry around all day, so we'd get to the Law Courts by 9.30am, and Geoff would already be there, skating. This little kid with blonde hair flying about, and he was just gifted. He could do all the tricks that everyone was trying to do. Not in a showing-off way, he was just skating. It wasn't in the way where you'd think he was going to become the best skater in the world at a point, because Nicky Ryan and John Newby were phenomenally talented skateboarders. There was a reason you'd go anywhere in town and it'd be 'the Newby stairs', 'the Newby ledge', all these spots in town were John's. He conquered them.

Kevin Banks

You knew when you went out with Geoff you'd get photos. He was just on a different level, from the first time I met him, which was at Dan-Z's ramp, and he was tiny and he was doing these massive ollies to nose-slap to fakie, and grabbing all different ways, like a tailgrab to nose-slap. But he'd just go backwards and forwards; he couldn't grind and he couldn't do an axle stall. He'd just drop in and do a fucking massive ollie. He wasn't carving, or using the ramp, but it was just like, 'Jesus Christ, this kid's fucking mad'.

Geoff Rowley

I was obsessed. I wanted to visualise tricks and figure out how to do them. My drive to progress has been there since I was a little kid, it's the only way I know how to skate. I wasn't the only one that was obsessed and learning tricks every day, John Newby was so good at skateboarding and Martin Wainwright could ollie like I've never seen. Barry Wong had style and the trick selection and he skated so fast. There were a load of skaters with

different styles coming out from Liverpool. There could have been 30 pros come out of our scene, and that's because of all the influences, I think.

We knew what was going on because we'd been through it all our whole lives, having stuff stolen from us and being in fights, because Liverpool was rough. We knew that the older dudes from the housing estate nearby would send their kids or their little brothers to case us, to check out if we were hard or not and if they could rob us. This happened every fucking second in the city, so if you don't react with, 'I don't give a fuck and I'm going to smack you in the face', you're gonna get hurt and you're gonna get picked on and it's gonna happen faster than if you just try to get out of there. If you can't leave immediately, you have to defend yourself in these situations because people take advantage of you. Even if you're not a strong person or don't like fighting, which is totally fine, you still have to engage or you're going to be in a worse place.

I was from Aigburth and a lot of people would say that was quite nice, and it is, but it's in the city just the same, when you're four-foot-five and you look like you're eight years old. That's part of childhood, and growing up, and I'm thankful I had good people around me, older guys, to introduce me to drinking and smoking and drugs, all in the right way. Whether I did them or not I was around the right group of people to experiment and figure out who I was. All of my growing-up experiences and all of my life experiences have come from all different people in the Liverpool skate scene. To this day I call up those skaters every day because we love and support each other.

James Hudson came to Liverpool for the day and John Dalton and I just went skating all day with him, and shot an article for *Skate Action* on Liverpool. I had a 'First Impressions' in that, and those were some

of the first photos of me, John Newby and John Dalton. That was the start of it. Once I saw that, it was like, 'Shit, I can skate and get put in the mag? What the fuck?!', and I didn't know what that meant, but I wanted to get gnarlier.

I shot with Meany for *Skateboard!* mag, I shot with James Hudson for *Skate Action*, but I didn't really shoot for *RAD* because that was more southern and they didn't really come up north. Not intentionally, they only didn't come up because they didn't have a photographer up there. *RAD* was really good. Shooting photos was part of doing that stuff, but Meany was the one who bent over backwards. Meany was the one that made an effort to shoot these photos of this little shit of a kid, and James Hudson made the effort to come all the way to Liverpool and spent the day shooting us. Thank you, James.

Percy Dean

The Police Bank was in the middle of an estate. Even though it was next to a police station, it didn't make any odds. People would come out and they'd be chucking stuff. You'd be skating and hearing bottles whizzing past and smashing, so you'd be skating on broken glass 99% of the time.

The Police Bank was a spot, and it changed everyone's lives. It changed the way you skated, and it changed how you felt when you did something. It was something that no one else could skate; no one that came to Liverpool could skate the Police Bank, so if you put the time in there yourself it'd give you something that no one else had. It was something to be proud of, and everyone from Liverpool could skate it and no one from out of Liverpool could.

Greg Fabb

Percy got called Billy Bison because he looked like a bison. He was enormous. He would barge stuff. ●

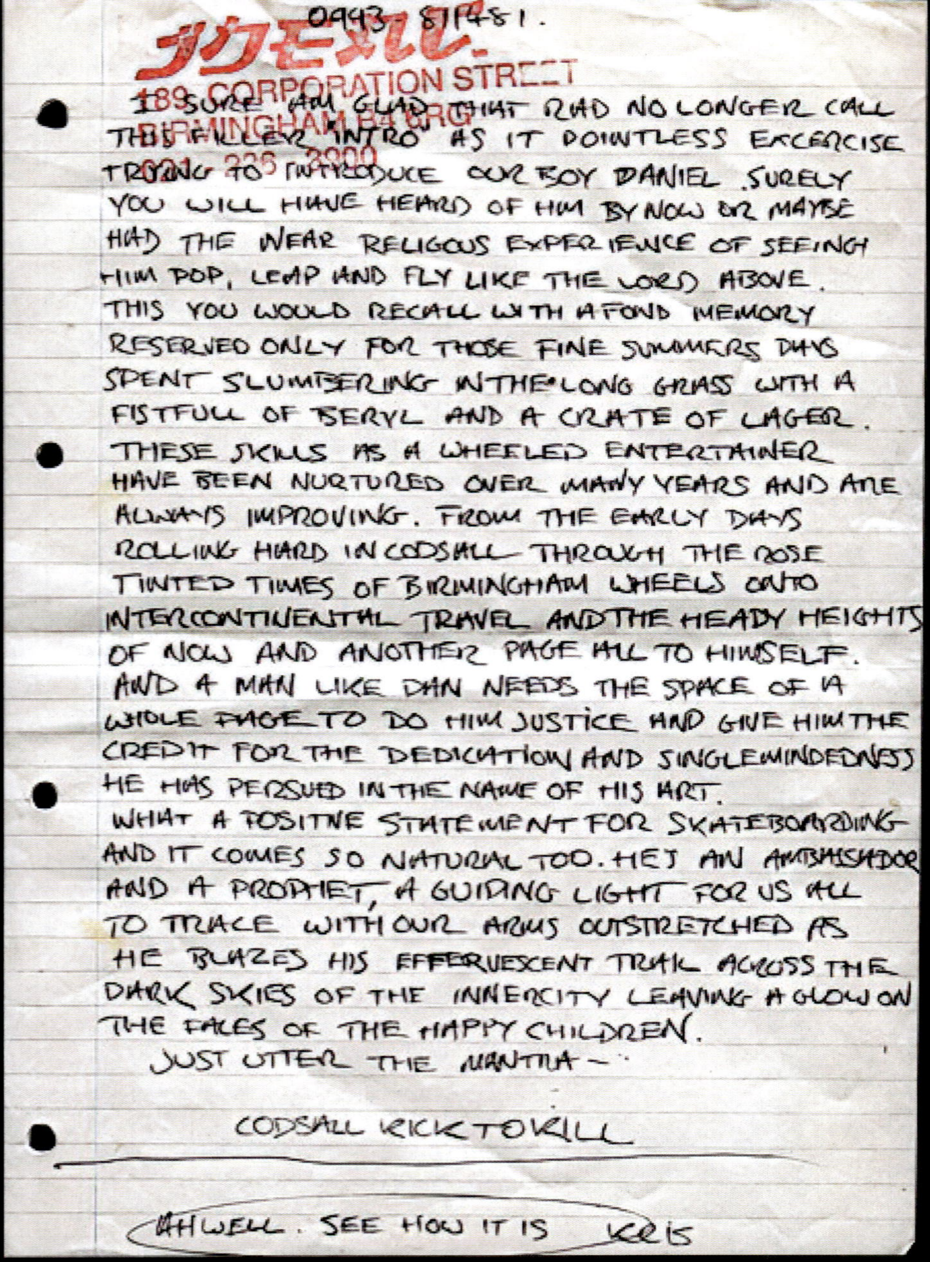

0943 871481.

IDEAL.

189 CORPORATION STREET
BIRMINGHAM B4 6RG
021 236 2000

SURE AM GLAD THAT RAD NO LONGER CALL
THIS ALLEY INTRO AS IT DOUTLESS EXCERCISE
TRYING TO INTRODUCE OUR BOY DANIEL. SURELY
YOU WILL HAVE HEARD OF HIM BY NOW OR MAYBE
HAD THE NEAR RELIGOUS EXPERIENCE OF SEEING
HIM POP, LEAP AND FLY LIKE THE LORD ABOVE.
THIS YOU WOULD RECALL WITH A FOND MEMORY
RESERVED ONLY FOR THOSE FINE SUMMERS DAYS
SPENT SLUMBERING IN THE LONG GRASS WITH A
FISTFULL OF BERYL AND A CRATE OF LAGER.
THESE SKILLS AS A WHEELED ENTERTAINER
HAVE BEEN NURTURED OVER MANY YEARS AND ARE
ALWAYS IMPROVING. FROM THE EARLY DAYS
ROLLING HARD IN CODSALL THROUGH THE ROSE
TINTED TIMES OF BIRMINGHAM WHEELS ONTO
INTERCONTINENTAL TRAVEL AND THE HEADY HEIGHTS
OF NOW AND ANOTHER PAGE ALL TO HIMSELF.
AND A MAN LIKE DAN NEEDS THE SPACE OF A
WHOLE PAGE TO DO HIM JUSTICE AND GIVE HIM THE
CREDIT FOR THE DEDICATION AND SINGLEMINDEDNESS
HE HAS PERSUED IN THE NAME OF HIS ART.
WHAT A POSITVE STATEMENT FOR SKATEBOARDING
AND IT COMES SO NATURAL TOO. HE'S AN AMBASSADOR
AND A PROPHET, A GUIDING LIGHT FOR US ALL
TO TRACE WITH OUR ARMS OUTSTRETCHED AS
HE BLAZES HIS EFFERVESCENT TRAIL ACROSS THE
DARK SKIES OF THE INNERCITY LEAVING A GLOW ON
THE FACES OF THE HAPPY CHILDREN.
JUST UTTER THE MANTRA —

CODSALL KICK TO KILL

AH WELL. SEE HOW IT IS   Kris

Kris Ludford
We've known Dan since we were super young, and he was always a thorn in our side because he was always skint and always needed boards. He could break a board in a day. In twenty minutes. He had tick with us, and he'd pay us on dole day, but he could break two or three boards in a fortnight. He was always gifted, and he left for Chicago when the shop really started picking up a bit of momentum. It was great when Dan returned, even though he'd beaten himself up and pretty much retired himself through injury.
LEFT TO RIGHT
[1] Kris Ludford, on Dan 'Jagger' Ball, [2] Dan 'Jagger' Ball, *RAD* intro, by Tim Leighton-Boyce.

I went up to Livingston on my own. I'd saw pics of the Livi Fun Day, and I just thought that I had to go to it the next year. It said in *RAD* when it was, and I booked a National Express. I was 15, I had a shaved head, and I told my mum I was going to stay at a mate's for the weekend.

I got the National Express up to Edinburgh, and then another bus from Livingston, and turned up the day before the Fun thing. Nowhere to sleep, no sleeping bag, nothing. On the Fun Day there were punk rock bands playing at the top of the halfpipe, and a fight suddenly broke out, of epic proportions. I remember seeing someone's head kicked in, properly, for the first time in my life.
JOE MILLSON

1992

Elsewhere

FROM THE TOP
[1] Dan McCaulay, Ipswich, by Andrew Stark
[2] Carl Shipman, Worksop, by James Hudson

Vert had died on its arse completely by '92, when it was little wheels, baggy trousers and hip-hop, and the whole culture of skateboarding changed. Music, clothing... It flipped completely from what it was.
SKIN PHILLIPS

1992

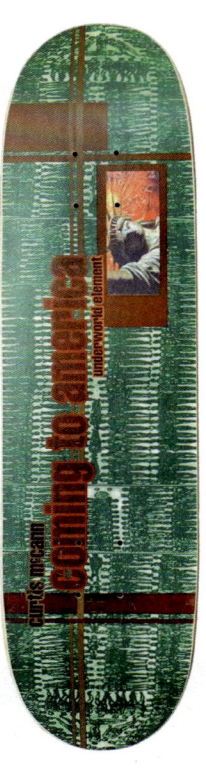

Ian Gunner

Because of NDUK's links to Deluxe, suddenly you've got Cardiel and Gonz there. It was a very quick transition from this little market stall in In Shops to having probably the best skateboarders in the world staying in a bed and breakfast in Harrow and skating the park.

Skin Phillips

Cardiel was 18, nobody had seen Gonz for maybe a year and a half – he'd been in New York doing art – and he made an appearance. I knew Karma and Alan Petersen really well from my days in Visalia and I'd already shot those guys so I had a really good relationship with them, and Karma was really good friends with Cardiel.

I remember going to the off-licence with Cardiel and getting him cider, and going shopping for adidas Gazelles.

Nothing went wrong, it was all good – although there was a glassing in a pub we were at in Scotland – but it wasn't a tour per se. Nobody knew who Cardiel was – he was still on Black Label – Mark has been MIA but he was still incredible. There would only be 10 or 15 people at the demos.

I saw Penny on that Harrow trip, and I was like, 'Who the fuck is that?', and Tim said, 'It's this kid Tom Penny', and he looked like he was fucking 12. I asked where he lived and Tim said he lived in Oxford, and I was like, 'Where's his parents?', and Tim went, 'I don't know, he just comes down and he does mushrooms.'

Tom Penny

Pretty much one of my first real sponsors was New Deal. Steve Douglas set me up with New Deal when I was a little kid, and I have quite fond memories of going up to Harrow for the first time, to get my package. Curtis was skating for Underworld Element at the same time and he'd gone down to get his package the same day. It was like a childhood dream, Curtis was there and I couldn't believe it.

We got the train back into London together, and I was trading my New Deal stickers for his Underworld Element stickers. I'll always remember that, trading stickers on the train with Curtis.

Curtis McCann

I think I was on Vans in 1991 through the New Deal skate shop in Harrow... one thing led to another with the New Deal/

Underworld Element connection and I joined their team... it's a bit of a blur but I remember meeting a tall Andy Howell for the first time. I was a bit in awe because I was starting to get into hip-hop and it was the first time I saw someone wearing large ear-cup headphones... he was looking a bit punk with cut-off shorts and bleached low-top Airwalks... when I got home I copied them right away! To me being sponsored by UE really felt on trend, and the minute I met him I felt the overwhelming urge to tell him I didn't think I was a very good skater anymore, and as I was babbling trying to get the words out, he just said words to the effect of, 'Don't worry, some days I skate like shit!'

I liked the *Skypager* video, but at the time I wasn't hyped about my part ... it mostly just fell into place with some old TLB footage... at that time I was thinking more about the fact that I had just had surgery on my ankle and had just turned pro, which was my childhood dream! I was more concerned with healing so I could go back to New York and maybe get my skating level up! ●

1992

Duncan 'Wurzel' Houlton

Vert skating was just not interesting at the time. There wasn't much going on there, and you had a bit of a disinterest, and with street skating it was like a double-whammy. And it happened so quickly. I didn't realise what was going on, but Jeremy was saying that he couldn't sell boards that were big, and anything that's not a street shape, just forget it.

Paul 'Rocker' Robson

To be honest, I didn't see the end of Death Box coming. The last contest that we did for Death Box was the Spitalfields contest; Mark and Peter Noble put a contest on in Spitalfields Market, a street contest and a vert contest. I won the vert contest and I think I got second in the street contest. That was the last contest I did with Death Box, August 1992.

It was apparent at the time that street was in, and I was predominantly a vert skater and a miniramp skater. I could hold my own on street at the time, but this new wave of street was coming through, and I don't think I had a place in that, or in the ideals of what Jeremy was doing with the company.

All the established vert places in the UK were gone, or going, and I felt like the scene was fragmented. Contests didn't draw people in anymore. I noticed that massively because I wouldn't see people that I used to see very frequently. I remember how different it was. I absolutely loved the time I spent on Death Box, so this was really different. I used to travel every weekend, and now I was probably travelling once a month.

I had eight boards altogether, but one board never made it for sale, which was the Rocker Mars Bar graphic[2]. We actually got told to cease and desist, from Mars.

Andy Scott

I was riding for Death Box, with all the older guys. We'd just been on a trip to Hamburg, and we were at Harrow skatepark, and there had been word that all the old riders were gonna get kicked off. I was with Rocker, and he told me, 'I don't know if you know, but all the riders are gonna get kicked off. He's starting a new company.' So I just immediately felt I was gone, I was over.

Pete Dossett

I was working at Death Box, screenprinting, doing cuts of artwork, walking the dog, doing everything Jeremy couldn't do, so I wasn't too bothered when they stopped my board. I knew what was happening with changing the team and moving things forward. Fresh blood on the team and stuff like that, so I wasn't bothered about not having a board. There was a new generation coming through.

Ian Deacon

Death Box changed to db. Jeremy and I went to see this lawyer in Aldwych in London, and we were talking about going to America, potentially. He told us that there was no way we'd want to use the name Death Box in America because as soon as any kid gets hurt we were going to get sued, because we're saying that the skateboard itself is a death box. We told him it was the thing in a pool, but he said it sounded like a coffin. So we were advised not to use the name Death Box at all.

Street skating completely took over, and that wasn't really Bash. Bash was kind of like a bit of a hybrid, so Jeremy said I could still do a company, but we'd stop Bash and do something else. I'm pretty sure it was his idea.

We got Christian Heitzmann, who was pretty much the best street skater in Germany at the time, and we were trying to get Curtis McCann. It was supposed to be Curtis and Christian, and with Luke McKirdy on as well. There was talk about Tony Luckhurst but he wasn't going to quit Santa Cruz so that never happened. He was never really in the picture I don't think, there was just kind of loose talk, and everyone was uncomfortable trying to nick him off Shane O'Brien as well, so it wasn't really going to happen. Tony would have been cool to get because Tony was amazing, rest in peace, but it would have been lame on Shane.

We tried to get Curtis in '91, and he came up with the name 'Flip'. We had a name, like 'The Mob' or 'The Mafia', a gangster-ish kind of name. 'Gang Skateboards' or something like that was being thrown around, and then Curtis came up with the name Flip, so we went with that.

We thought he was going to do it, and then Powell just clamped down on the whole thing. Jeremy and I actually met George Powell in '92. We got invited to →

LEFT TO RIGHT
[1] Alex Moul, Shell Centre, by Tim Leighton-Boyce
[2] Unreleased Death Box Rocker board
[3] Death Box Alex Moul Bazooka Joe board
[4] Death Box Alex Moul Cockpit board
[5] Tom Penny, Cowley Road, Oxford, by Ben Gregson

1992

Powell at the trade show, George invited us to his office in Santa Barbara, so we went there and we got a full dressing-down from him. Like, 'Who do you think you are, trying to steal my rider?', it was pretty funny. He was kind of cool, and then he was like, 'Who the fuck do you think you are?' So Curtis was going to quit and then didn't quit, he got sucked back into Powell.

At first there was the Jensen twins, Ivan and Christian, from Copenhagen. These little twins, they were super rad, then one of them got cancer. He lived but he got cancer super young. One was more street and one was more vert, I think, and they were at that Eindhoven contest where Mouly was wearing these big Bench cargo shorts, and that's when Jeremy got them on Flip, because we talked to their mum. Right around that time is when Jérémie Daclin was riding for Death Box as well, after he won the Eindhoven contest in '92, then he quit and started Cliché. Christian had bad ankles, basically. He kept getting hurt all the time. He could skate but he couldn't skate at the level he wanted to.

We kept the name Flip because we didn't know how the whole Death Box / db thing was going to work out if we did go to America, so we thought we'd just make it all Flip and merge everyone together.

Tom Penny

Jeremy used to travel round England when he was younger, looking for various different skateboard talents. He came across me at one of the contests at Cowley Road that SS20 and Dougie had organised. I think I got first place at that contest and he thought that I skated quite well and asked if I wanted to be sponsored. I was skating for New Deal at the time and because it was an English company and New Deal was an American company, I decided to go with the English company.

I remember calling Steve Douglas very nervously and telling him that I was going to decide to ride for the English company and not for New Deal anymore. He was fine about it and he said he could understand and it was no problem. He said that if that was what I wanted to do, then all the best. I had no idea back in the day that Flip was going to turn into what it ended up turning into. I wasn't 100% on New Deal anyway, it's not like I was on the American team or anything, it was just a distribution thing from London. I had various different reasons.

It was just as Death Box was coming to an end and turning into Flip, and I think they got me on the team thinking that the future team might be based around solely the new riders that he was getting as he was travelling round looking for talent.

I think we knew they were going to do Flip. Death Box was more of an '80s sort of thing, an old-school vision of skateboarding, and the new style was getting quite popular at that time. Jeremy wanted to do something that was more with the times and more modern. Around the time he was looking for new talent here and there, I think he already knew that in the future he would be doing what he did. He knew what he was doing the whole time and we were just unaware of the whole thing, we were just little kids that skateboarded.

One of my fondest memories of that time is of Mike Manzoori, when I used to go up to London when I was a little kid, and sometimes we'd go down to Uxbridge. That was pretty much the best miniramp in England at the time, and everyone used to go down there. Mike Manzoori would be down there, Matt Dawson would be down there, the generation before the generation I knew who lived there. They'd all been skating the London Bridge ramp, and you could see at the Uxbridge one that they were absolutely incredible.

I remember Mike doing waist-high ollies pretty much the whole width of the ramp, and going to backside disaster so fast, and then into the ramp. He's so nice, and when you talk to him you forget how good he is at skateboarding. He's a really good skateboarder. You hang out with him and talk to him and you don't think about how he's absolutely ridiculous at skateboarding.

Geoff Rowley

I liked Alex Moul's skating but I wanted to see him skate, because the pictures I saw in the mag made him look like he was as good as American skaters. I wanted to see what he looked like in person, and he was as good as American skaters. He was the reason why I felt like, 'Shit, rad! I'm going to ride this board and keep riding this board'. When I went skating with Alex, Alex was lovely, and every bit a great skater.

The first day I went skating with Alex he did a backside nosebluntslide bigspin out along a six-foot-long kerb [p.156]. I had no idea that anyone could do backside nosebluntslides like that. I could do them and poke into them and come out, Alex locked in for six feet and bigspinned out the end. ●

techno king alex?

new deathbox concave on all new models & slicks now[ish]

contact distributors: leisurescope tel 081 309 5144 fax 081 309 5145

LEFT T TO RIGHT
[1]   Mike Manzoori, Uxbridge, by Tim Leighton-Boyce
[2]   Death Box Alex Moul ad, photo by Paul Duffy
[3+4] Mark Foster's scientific rat and bird illustrations

Fos

"Blackpool accepted me on to Scientific Illustration, which is really gnarly, detailed illustration... This dissected rat took about two months of my life to draw."

FOS

Mark 'Fos' Foster

I was at Burnley college with my friend Mark Newton, and we loved it. We were having the time of our lives, it was the best thing in the world. We had two years where we just fucked around and went to art college and went on trips to London and watched VHS tapes and read comics and learnt how to talk to girls – the whole thing.

We were doing shitty jobs – I was working in a pizza factory – to get money to buy boards and shoes, and then we started applying for universities, and I applied to all the places that had good skateparks. I wanted to go to Bristol, I wanted to go to Harrow, all these places that had legendary skateparks, and I didn't get into any of them.

I wanted to do illustration and I ended up having to do a foundation course, so I went to Blackburn for a couple of weeks before this one art college in Blackpool accepted me on to Scientific Illustration, which is really gnarly, detailed illustration. So I ended up doing that for eight months because you could get a grant. I lived five days a week in a B&B and came home at weekends, because the skate scene in Blackpool in '92 fucking sucked and it felt like it was raining all the time and I was the only person skating because loads of people had given up.

I could draw really fucking good after college. It's got to be better than a photograph, otherwise people would use a photograph. Photographs are imperfect because they have flare on them, or they can be out of focus. This dissected rat took about two months of my life to draw. So I applied everything I learned there to everything I did after that. ●

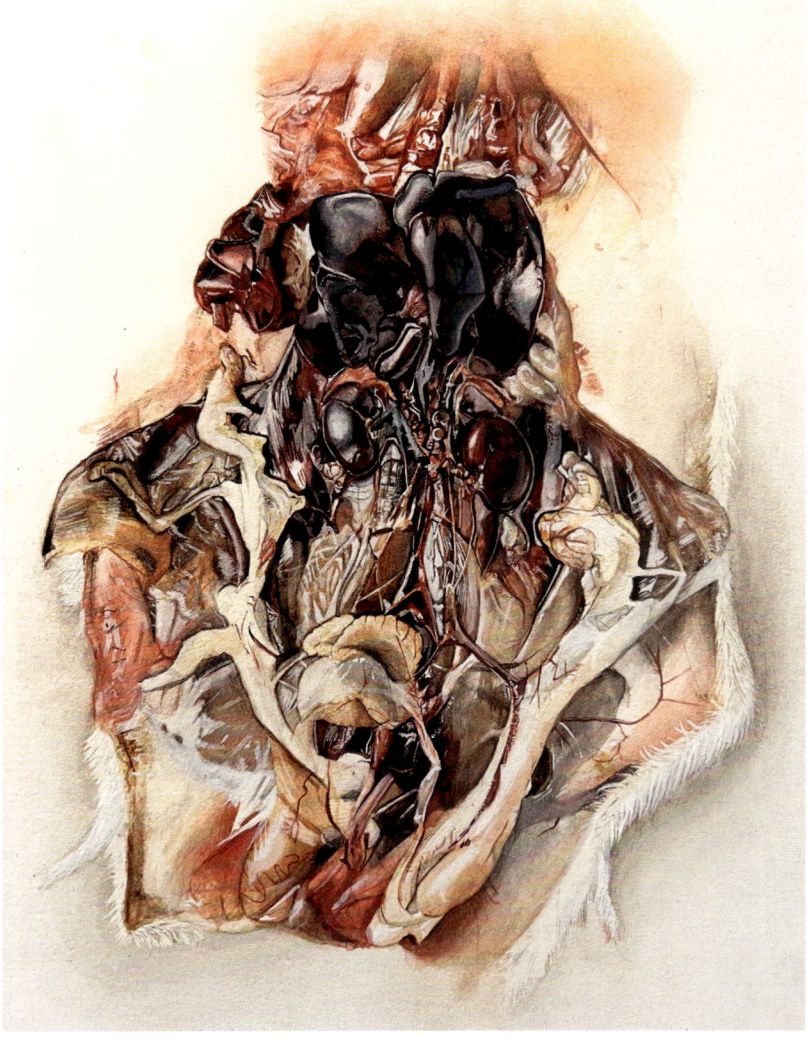

1992

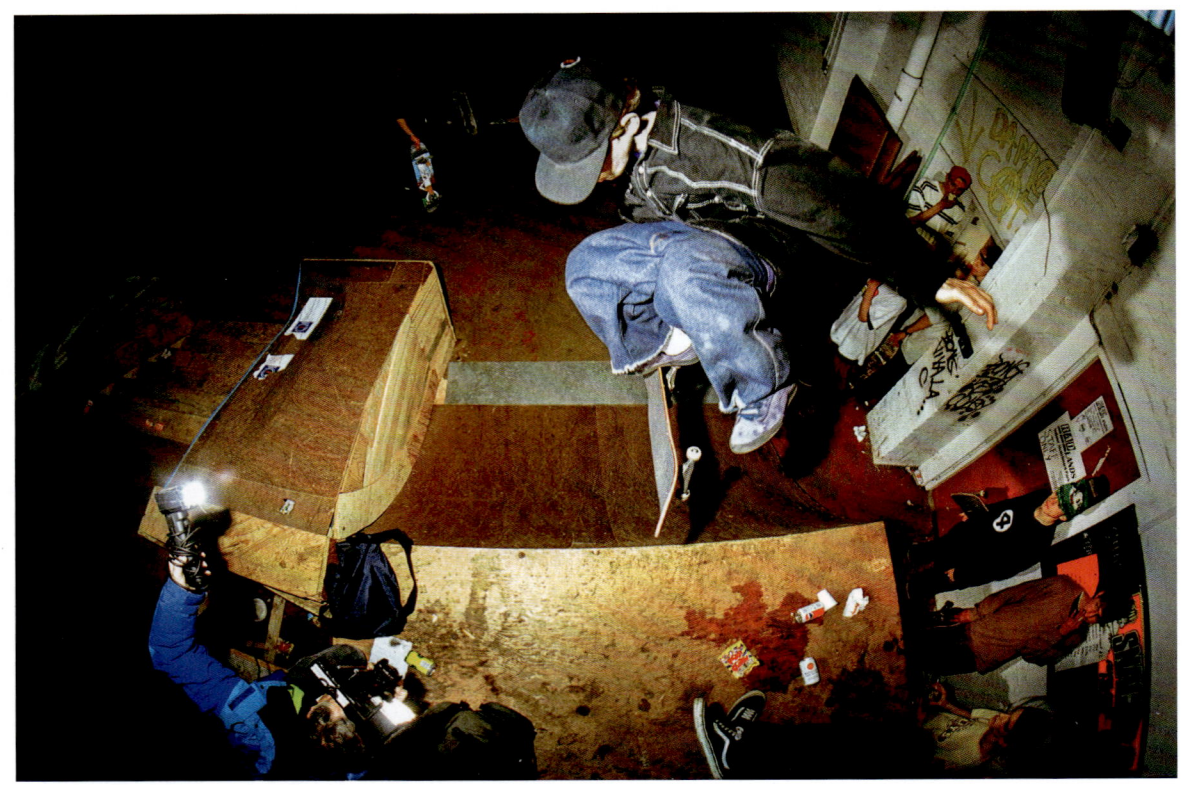

Elsewhere

Damian Ince

When Milton Keynes was first built they built this brand-new bus station with tons of marble everywhere, and my dad had a cafe there.

Me and my brother skated, and there was no real skate shops where you could get stuff from. There was a little store in a rollerskating rink that sold some stuff, but not a great deal of stuff. So my dad basically phoned up Jeremy Fox because he ran Death Box in Wellingborough and we lived in Northampton. He got his number out of a magazine and said he wanted to start selling boards. We went over to the factory where he was painting the boards and everything, and it was absolutely amazing. It blew our minds.

We started off with a couple of boards and that, and it grew a bit from there. The cafe had two sides, one side into the bus station cafe bit where all the chairs and tables were, and then through to the back was into another little sort of entrance bit. The back used to be all sweets and cigarettes and stuff like that, and that's what turned into the skate shop. Loads of people skated the bus station at the weekend. It was quite big.

We started getting stuff from New Deal as well, and it built up into quite a big shop. We did a leisure trade show at Willen Lake in Milton Keynes, where Caldecotte ditch is. My dad said we should get a stall at the trade show, and basically bought a miniramp. In *RAD* they used to have the classifieds, didn't they? There was a miniramp for sale and it was eight foot wide and five foot high, it weren't a lot of money, and it was collection-only. So we got a ramp, and it ended up in our garden.

In April '92, there was a contest at the bus station and we'd built up quite a relationship with Jeremy by then. We'd kept going to see him and he'd seen the business grow, and by word-of-mouth this comp got quite big – people from all over the country came. Flynn Trotman came, Jagger came from Birmingham, the London boys, Alex Moul turned up. Rob Selley had some ramps that he skated by his house, that his dad made, so we had them and we had some quarters and a manual pad box as well. This was on top of the blocks that were there anyway. I think about 200 people showed up.

My dad had quite a long lease left on the cafe, but he was speaking with Jeremy about it, and Jeremy was saying to my dad that he should do a skatepark as well. Obviously you've got Tom in Oxford, Geoff's in Liverpool and there was Andy Scott and Alex Moul at the time as well, so I guess Jeremy wanted somewhere for his skaters to skate. If there's a big pro skatepark there, his skaters will get more exposure and stuff like that. So my dad just went for it.

When we were looking for premises, we met up with Alex Moul and Jeremy Fox to go and have a look at this building to see if it was good or not. The floor was red and it was so pristine and nice, and Alex Moul was doing these pressure flip late flips, over knee high. I just thought it was fucking amazing that we were looking at a building to see if it'd be any good for a skatepark and Alex Moul is there, testing the floor. It should have just been me and our kid, but Alex Moul was there, and he'd beat Ed Templeton at Eindhoven! He was one of my heroes but he was normal. He was just a lad who treated me like another lad and he was super cool. That first experience with a pro skater, someone who'd won a comp in Europe and he's my hero, for him to just be a normal person, I didn't get fanned out or nothing like that.

So Tim Payne was over, there was Chilly – Dave Childs, the BMXer from Kettering – and Snoz as well. Mark Snowball. Originally me and my brother just wanted some real street obstacles, and not the crazy big ramps that actually got built in the end. We wanted some small obstacles that everyone could skate.

After the first week of opening, Keith Hufnagel and Coco Santiago came over. Those two stayed at our house and they were the most humble, nicest people you could ever meet in your life. None of the Yank big-headedness at all. I'd never seen Hilfiger before, and Huf was the first person that I saw Hilfiger on. He actually left his boxer shorts at our house. A big 'Tommy Hilfiger' written across the waistband. I'd never seen pants like this before. They were boxer shorts and they were down to your knees, like shorts that boxers wear. I wasn't going to phone him up and say, 'You've left your pants here mate, do you want them back?' My mum washed them, and maybe they helped me do tre flips because not long after I had a full-page in *RAD* doing a tre flip wearing them.

Chris Atherton

Everybody got to know each other better through Radlands. We threw ourselves about, and we didn't realise that skateboarding had a degree of finesse. Tom Penny turned up and showed pretty much everybody that you can skate without falling off. There's a finesse that you can achieve when you're skating if you just calm down a little bit, focus, and you can just land everything smooth.

Toby Shuall

A few times I bunked off school to go to Radlands, and the only person that was there was Penny, and I just watched Penny get good by the hour. He'd just get left there, and he was good anyway but that's why he got so good, because all he'd do is skate. He was always there.

Alex Moul

That was where Tom really started to shut things down. I'd be skating with him and all of a sudden everybody in the park would just stop and watch. Then he'd be like, 'Hey Mouly, why is everyone looking at me?', and I'd be like, 'Because you just did a one-man demo of tricks you didn't even know you could do yet'. Then he'd be like, 'Let's go and smoke a spliff at the pool table because everyone's looking at me and it's weird'.

Everything was possible with him. Even skating the vert ramp. He'd gone from being a sketchy kid to the most natural fella on a skateboard. ●

CLOCKWISE FROM TOP LEFT
[1] Tim Leighton-Boyce shooting Tom Penny, by James Hudson
[2] Radlands original hand-drawn logo, stickers and membership application
[3] Tom Penny, by Jono Atkinson
[4] Tom Penny, by James Hudson

Geoff Rowley

The Law Courts were kind of the centre, and the black marble block there was where we'd all learn our ledge tricks. Liverpool had no other ledges, the rest of it was banks and stairs and rails and nasty shit, so we hung out there because we weren't really messed with and we never got kicked out. There was also a section undercover with lights for those rainy Saturdays – or weekend nights.

There was a phone box that was about 50 feet from the ledge, and everybody had the phone number memorised. You could just call that phone at any time, and if anybody picked it up, it was probably a skater and you could just ask, 'Who the fuck's there right now? Who's skating?', and you could just go there knowing who'd be there because you'd called the phone box. Or I'd wait until I went into the city, then I'd call everyone on their home phone numbers from that phone box. You always knew you could get into the city and call a couple of guys from that phone box.

We had that clusterfuck of 'I have no idea who's going to be in town today, but I left my house because I was having a rough day at home', and you'd find someone always, and life would be a little bit easier. It was fucking amazing.

Sponsorship came from Kevin Banks saying I was a really good skater. He kept saying I was good enough to be sponsored, but I kept saying, 'What are you talking about?' Yeah I wanted to be sponsored, yeah I wanted a free board, I wanted to know if I was good enough, and it took Kevin Banks making an edit of all the tricks he filmed of me on a tape and sending it to somebody before I was sponsored. It was Kevin.

When I went to London, Matt McMullan accepted me. I was a little shit from Liverpool, and at that time in London you weren't really spoken to nicely if you were a Scouser, and when I opened my mouth I was Scouser all the way through. I just kept my head down; I didn't really enjoy sleeping on the floors in sleeping bags. I had good times with the London skaters, but as far as progressing my skating by going down to London, nah. My progression came in Liverpool.

I was schooled very early on like, 'Look at the form, look at the style, look at the way he's looking back after he's done a trick'. Then the indie influence, Dinosaur Jr and Sonic Youth and all of that, was Kevin Banks and Ocean and then you had Percy Dean and Adam and Howard Cooke and Robbie Reid liking more hardcore music, and then the hip-hop influence from John Newby. Then as they were getting older they started smoking weed and drinking and I'm sitting there, along for the ride.

Barry Wong has transcended generations in the Liverpool skate scene, he skated all the way through. Since the day that he started skating, Barry's skated regularly, progressively and hard. And by himself because he loves it, or with somebody else because he likes skating with other people as well. He's been there for every generation, right through to Charlie Birch and the next generation. Dave Mackey, Barry and John Dalton have been the most communicative and connective.

Percy Dean

Geoff basically tore through skateboarding all over the world, and became one of the biggest deals in skateboarding worldwide, and just to know that he was one of us and he'd come from where we were and he'd been part of our lives, we were proud of him. In Liverpool you're there for each other, but you're there for each other in a really brutal way, so if anyone does anything good, the first thing in Liverpool is to shout them down, or not support them. The support is there, probably more than in other communities, but you have to be told, 'Who the fuck do you think you are?', more than, 'Well, done, that's really good, I'm really proud of you'. The shit comes first, and you have to understand that everyone's proud of you but that doesn't come gushing out of people from Liverpool. If you think you're the shit, the admonishment will come gushing out pretty fast. Real pride is always there, but it's inside rather than shown, in Liverpool, I think. ●

Liverpool

Elsewhere

Ian Roxburgh

They were between designers when Tim asked if I'd like to come back to design a few issues, so I came back and designed those last three issues, numbers 107, 108 and 109. Issue 109 was the last one I was ever going to do, so I made sure I got a few friends on the cover. My mate Andy Humphries is on there and I'm doing a boardslide in an underground car park which was about 200 metres away from the *RAD* office.

Steve Hicks

When I interviewed for the job with the publisher, they said I could do the skateboard magazine, and that was the thing that made me lean into it.

What comes to mind very clearly is the first conversation I had with Tim, and him sort of saying that they'd had a guy who did really cool graphics and who did stuff on the photocopier, and then how they got put on to this other guy who didn't seem to care and wasn't really into it. I remember being really excited by that, and thinking he was really cool. There was a point where Tim said, 'We've never printed anything from the screen before, but let's see what happens', and the main thing for him was as long as you could see the pictures.

The thought was pretty linear; at that time I wasn't having a lot of rational, deliberate thinking, you just did things that were interesting. There was a brief moment of careful thought of, 'These guys were fucking around with the photocopier, and abusing the photocopier, how can I abuse this Photoshop? What would they not want me to do?', and I found the colour halftone picture where you could set the dots to 12 pixels, to make a lot of those gradients with the massive fat dots. If you look at them they all have nasty, crispy edges because it would generate you a two-bit image and it didn't have aliased edge and stuff like that.

Very frequently what appeared in the magazine was quite different from what was on my screen, and it took me years to learn how to really emulate it. There's a huge difference between a thing that is emitting light and a thing that is reflecting, and a magazine page is reflecting light and a screen is emitting light. I became aware of the fact that there was a preciousness when something starts to reflect light rather than emit light.

There was a big cultural thing at the time where people with success and money who are winning are not the most interesting people, it's the people who are struggling and who don't have anything who are the most interesting.

There was something like that going on with the content of the magazine, where it was, 'Let's stop shooting guys that are sponsored, on ramps, and let's find some kids who you've never heard of who are hanging out in a car park in Birmingham, and let's find out what they're wearing and what they're doing'.

Really cool magazines – places that have a staff – were doing these really cool things with graphic design, and computer effects were starting to come in, and it was like, 'Wait, I have a computer!' I felt spiritually akin to those 15-year-old kids in the car park in fucking Birmingham. They would see a rail they could skate and I would see a filter I could use. Taking that stuff and playing with it and seeing what would come out.

David Carson's stuff is aggressive but it's still quite restrained, and I just wanted stuff to be a fuckin' mess. Just to jam it all in, and see if I can use a hundred fonts. You almost get to a point where there's so many fonts that there's only one font, because it's like the wood for the trees when it's that kind of density.

There's a sense of rebellion, and it was useless wooden toys and rails, and Photoshop 1.5 and filters. It was, 'How can we say "Fuck you" in our own way with this stuff that we have access to?' There was a little bit of, 'Fuck you, I'm not going to have one font, I've got Fontographer so I'm going to have 50 fonts', going on. And that's not something to be proud of, but that's kids.

Vernon Adams

Tim needed people he could rely on to do different bits of it that needed doing, so doing the product page was one of the things I took care of.

So we'd photograph it and send it back, and sometimes we'd test stuff, but testing, it's really just 'using', isn't it? Just riding it. Some magazines tried to turn it into a science and went a bit overboard on it, but unless you're Paul Schmitt it's just bullshit really.

At the end of the day, people want to know what boards are out and what companies are happening. People are interested in that, and it is interesting.

Tim Leighton-Boyce

We didn't do product reviews because I didn't want to do product reviews. The whole bit in the magazine that Vernon did, was very much a bit like other elements in that we felt like we ought to have it so we should do it. I know *Skateboard!* magazine had gone into extensive detail, but that was one of the key things about *RAD* as I saw it: most other consumer magazines at that time were about selling a product so they're full of product adverts and they do product reviews and product tests – that extends to bicycle magazines, camera magazines, hi-fi magazines, whatever – and what I wanted to do with *RAD*, and what I think we did do with *RAD*, was make it a magazine about doing the thing, and not having lots of product reviews.

Because I'd been involved in skateboarding fairly early on, I was extremely cynical about product testing, as if there's differences between these things. At Alpine we had a durometer gauge, so you could sit there with a box of wheels and you would get multiple readings off the same wheel, let alone two different wheels. I felt like I didn't want to go there.

Back in those days, before everything moved to China, they were pressing multiple boards at a time, so according to where it was in that stack, the concave would be different anyway. There was so much like that.

The gear that we got sent mostly went back. It's true that sometimes somebody would ask if they could keep one and most of the suppliers would say yes, but most of that stuff went back, and quite often they'd send round a courier to pick it up. We didn't have delivery carrier contracts, but they did.

Curtis McCann

I wrote a few things for *RAD* magazine… I remember they were honest, I thought, unambiguous, and a bit cringy to a confused me! I tried it because other skaters had done it; however, I wasn't a very creative person outside of skating at that time… but it was money per word, which went away for the odd beer at Southbank or wherever. I didn't have a computer then so I just winged it with a pen and pencil.

It was always exciting and fun shooting photos for TLB and the *RAD* guys, but it was a stress because most of it was shot before video capture… therefore, it was important to get a trick as 'down' as possible even though they were often your latest! It's funny, at that time tricks were changing so fast that I would be bothered that I would have to wait a month or so for my tricks to appear in the magazine. ●

"I just wanted stuff to be a fuckin' mess. Just to jam it all in, and see if I can use a hundred fonts. You almost get to a point where there's so many fonts that there's only one font…"

STEVE HICKS

1992

Tony Luckhurst was an amazing skater. He was fearless beyond belief. I saw him do things and hurt himself in ways that I wouldn't have got up from. I was such a flipper, but he wanted to do stuff down 17 stairs. He could skate transitions as well as street – I think he just preferred to be up in the air.
ELTON WHYBROW

Tony Luckhurst (and Dan 'Jagger' Ball), St Albans, by Corin Casey

Six Pack & London

Elsewhere

CLOCKWISE FROM TOP
[1] Sam Silverstone, Matt Stuart, Simon Evans and Marc Bultitude, by Tim
      Leighton-Boyce
[2] Simon Evans and Winstan Whitter, by Tim Leighton-Boyce
[3] Jonny Wilson, White Hart roundabout, by Tim Leighton-Boyce

Tim Leighton-Boyce

One thing about the Six Pack is that I don't even know who the Six Pack were. That was a very negative phrase, and I know that people like Simon got very hurt by it. I was annoyed by it but just knew that it was bound to happen because they were perceived as a homogenous group of 'the new style of street skating', so there's always going to be people who are pissed off with that, miffed by it.

Shane O'Brien

Tim was constantly with them, they was in the magazine every month and Tim was taking them around on the weekends. They went for the full-blown fashion thing, the baggy-this and the small-that, which is all fine, and that was the whole movement, and they could see that being the beginning of the future.

They were the modern thing, they were the new thing, they were happening, they were trendy, and the rest of us had to get used to it. We just had to accept that this is the next phase in skating. We didn't know how long it was going to last but we had to wait and see.

Matt Stuart

We were the Six Pack. It was Sam Silverstone, Simon Evans, Marc Bultitude, myself, Ed Loftus and the other two are interchangeable, depending on whether they were in the car or not, and that's Jonny Wilson and Winstan Whitter.

Shane O'Brien came up with the term; he's a nice guy but he was from the generation before and maybe there was a bit of resentment that these kids are getting all this coverage and hanging out with TLB. So 'Six Pack' was kind of a cuss.

We were all pretty insecure kids, but the nice thing was that Tim took Simon, specifically, under his wing and would drive him around anywhere and everywhere, and whoever Simon was with would jump in the car as well and that was either Sam, Marc, myself, Ed, Jonny or Winstan. Sometimes someone would turn up by train or something because you can't get six people and a driver in a car.

The Six Pack didn't travel as one, obviously we would split up in case there was a terrorist attack. You can't have the whole Six Pack being taken out at the same time.

Simon was the poster boy for modern, technical skateboarding at that time and so he was disliked by the old guard, and younger people were jealous of him. He got a lot of shit along the way, but Tim took him under his wing and totally looked after him.

Simon Evans

Tim hates to hear this but I feel like he was the dad I chose. He was so welcoming and so lovely, and interested. He got me into all this music and everything, he got me into The Kinks, Jack Kerouac, all that stuff. I love him. I love him beyond.

There was some weird stuff said, like, 'What's the man doing hanging out with all these kids?', some of that crap going around. It makes me sad that there's any of that. He was the most wonderful person; I owe him everything and he just opened up the world to me.

I thought Tim just liked us. I didn't think it was anything to do with ability or anything like that. It's weird.

I was really self-conscious about being in the magazine. I'll be really honest – I felt really persecuted. It really got to me. I felt really bad because I kind of escaped from my life into skateboarding and then it got weird for me, because I was in the magazine a lot, and the Six Pack stuff. It really hurt my feelings and was part of why I never came back to England. I know it sounds really stupid but I thought that everyone hated me, and I had a lot of issues with that. A lot of the time I thought everyone was talking shit about me, so I had that going on and I had a chip on my shoulder about that.

There was hate-mail going to *RAD*, and that's kind of why I dropped out of writing for the magazine too. I didn't want it to seem like a total nepotism thing, I wanted it to be from the point of being a good skateboarder and not just because of my connection to the magazine.

I was confused and I was very wary of people because I thought everyone hated me. I was really paranoid, and that kind of developed as I travelled around England as well. It was like, 'Simon Evans? I've seen him with a book in his back pocket. He ain't all that.' There was a lot of that, but it's just kids. I don't know if it's generalising but it's so English to have a moan about that sort of thing, but I really got upset about it.

I might have delusions of grandeur but there wasn't that many skateboarders around and I felt like I was part of some weird thing and I just couldn't handle it. I couldn't handle the negativity of it.

Death Box was weird at the time; not that there was any kind of competition, but they definitely won. Jeremy Fox was very toxic at that time as well but I understand he was trying to do something big.

They made these Simon Evans backpacks, they mocked me like that, because we all had backpacks. Just making fun of our style. Stupid shit, but I couldn't handle it. Matt McMullan had one and he wrote me an apology letter afterwards. It just felt really toxic there for a minute and that really hurt my feelings. I just wanted to escape from my life into skateboarding and it just became this horrible thing.

When I think about it now I really feel bad about being so fashion-y and stuff.

My *RAD* interview didn't change anything for me. It's really stupid but I just felt more insecure. It was like a George Costanza moment and it didn't change anything for me but it makes me happy that anybody got anything out of it.

It was those difficult years when you're transitioning from a child into a slightly older child... There were power dynamics going on; my dad was a very dominating man and that was our culture clash. My mum, bless her, was just embarrassed to see me. If she was walking down the street she would cross over if she saw me, because of the way I looked. It was just a rough time, but it wasn't as rough as some people had it. I mean, my parents loved me. We just went through that turbulence. Some people's parents don't give a shit about them.

Ed Loftus

I never considered myself part of it. I was with those guys, but I wasn't as good as them. Shane and a lot of those guys had been around, and I think they all just saw through it, and saw the fashion part as being a bit silly. But the skateboarding, as far as the shit Simon was doing, was really innovative.

Jonny Wilson

There was a period of time when we were in *RAD* magazine quite a lot... People weren't happy with the flippy tricks. Obviously we felt very connected but I always felt there was some disconnect there.

Matt Dawson

Tim Leighton-Boyce would ring me in the morning and ask where we were going skating that day, and then the magazine would turn up, we'd skate, and get a load of pictures taken and it was great.

Then it all changed, and the Six Pack got involved, and a lot of people were bitter. I couldn't give a shit, I just wanted to skateboard so I didn't really care, but a lot of people got bitter and thought they was taking over what we were doing, and then they got involved in *RAD*. It was a real funny time, looking back on it now.

Andy Humphries

They had this reputation outside London that you couldn't skate with them because they were cunts, but it was complete bloody nonsense.

Matt Sherman

Tim used to sometimes drive us around places. Looking back we were little punks, little brats. He was so generous, did so much for us, but I just never, ever recognised that at all. When people were giving me all this free shit, which was such a nice thing to do, I just thought that was what happened.

I didn't understand the reason that they were giving me free shit was to promote their company. I honestly didn't realise that and nobody explained it to me. Probably because it shouldn't need explaining. So I never really bothered; I always did that cool thing in skating where if there was a photographer I was always of the opinion that you just sit down because you don't want to be showing off in front of the photographer. If someone explained to me that they gave you the t-shirt so you get in the magazine, I would have skated much more in front of the cameras, but I would always just sit down. I look back and think, 'What a dick, how did you not realise that's why they were giving you that shit?'. →

[1–4] Simon Evans, 'The Land that Time Reshot'
This work recreates a popular skatepark in Southbank, London, which Evans, one half of the artist duo Simon Evans and Sarah Lannan, frequented in his youth. The artists meticulously mapped out the park as it existed in the 1990's, inspired by the theory of Psychogeography, which focuses on the psychological experience of the urban environment. At once personal and public, the work illustrates a particular nostalgia for Evans, who was a professional skateboarder before he was a professional artist. Hands and disembodied

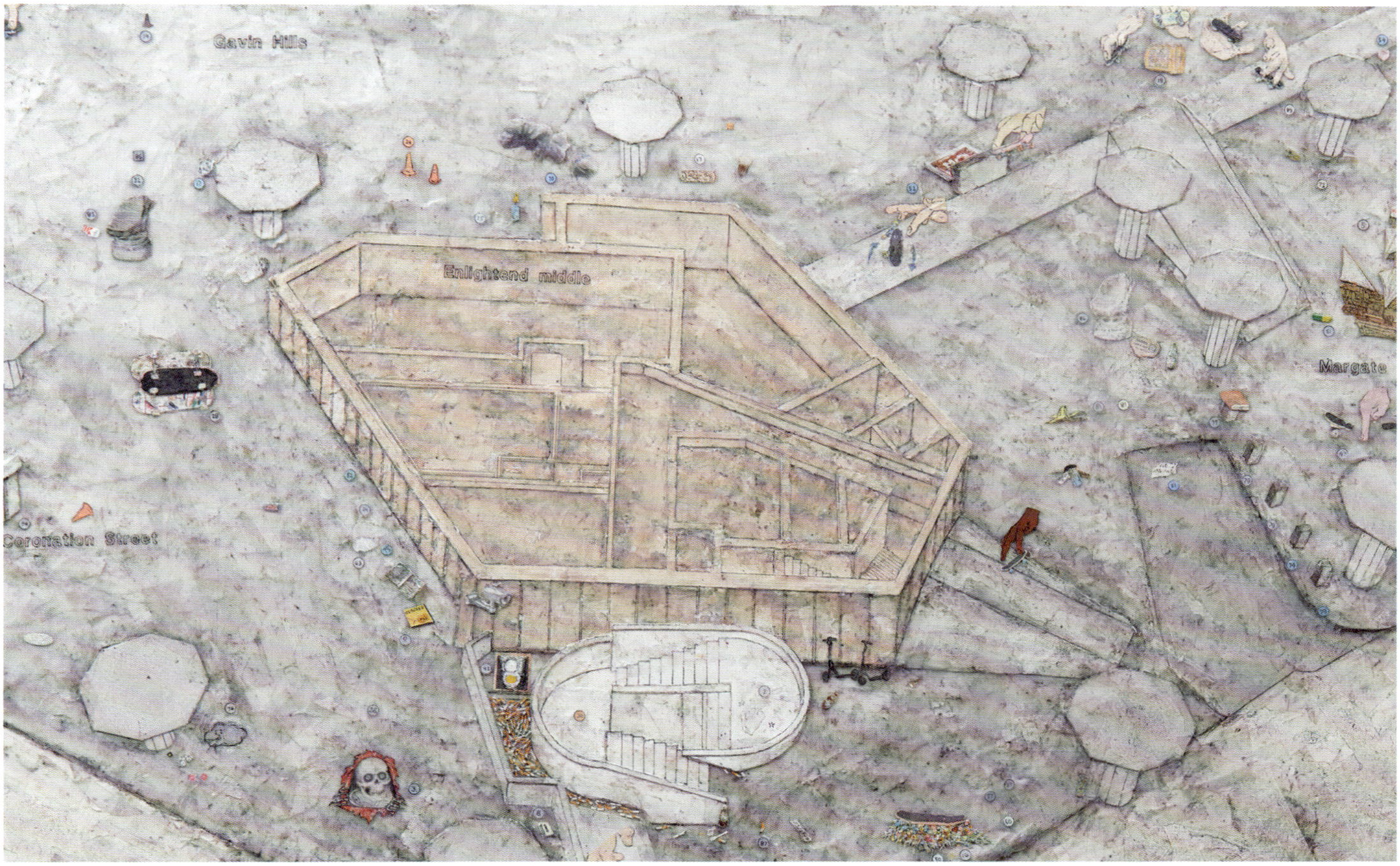

fingers fingerboard across the park's geography, playfully imitating the moves of skateboarders on a small scale. The park is dotted with imagery from Evans' childhood and British history – notably, a depiction of the *Golden Hind*, once helmed by Francis Drake, and a Brontosaurus, whose validity has been called into question since its discovery by British scientists in the 19th century – as well as nods to the present day through imagery of discarded medical gloves. The work explores the blurred relationship between toys, games and the real-life counterparts they seek to imitate, and the interplay between past and present on one's experience of space.

1992

They just felt so good to skate in, and it was just cool that it wasn't Vans, because Vans hurt. I just remember seeing them somewhere and I couldn't believe how cheap they were.
SIMON EVANS

Footwear

1992

PREVIOUS PAGE
Simon Evans, Jubilee Gardens, by Jay Podesta
CLOCKWISE FROM TOP LEFT
[1]   Simon Evans contact sheet frame, by Tim Leighton-Boyce
[2]   Tom Penny, Simon's Skatepark, Dublin, by Skin Phillips
[3]   Danny Wainwright, Radlands, by Skin Phillips
NEXTY PAGE
Simon Evans, Kennington, by Tim Leighton-Boyce

Russell Waterman

I certainly hadn't seen anyone wear those shoes before Simon. Simon Evans is a unique individual; he's a brilliant, brilliant person.

Ben Wheeler

The fashion thing is one of the biggest things that came out of all of it. Skating is a massive industry now, but it's the fashion and the way that streetwear has become such a big thing in the last 20 years or so that has come completely and utterly out of skateboarding, and nowhere else. It genuinely feels like what we were wearing in those days was literally the kernel of all of that. I find that really interesting – and galling at times – but I think that's one of the most prominent things to come out of skateboarding, really.

Ryan Mills

Macro, the cash and carry my mum and dad used, had an adidas shoe called the Tactic, which was basically a Dunlop Green Flash, with a weird little toecap around the front. A really basic looking shoe. I put wide purple laces in there, went to Southbank, and everyone's bugging out on these shoes.

Then I went to Slam, and I must have got stopped about six times by people asking about the shoes. I was sitting on that bungee seat that they used to have at the front of Slam City and this woman comes up to me and says, 'Excuse me, where did you get those shoes?', and as ever, I couldn't tell her. She's like, 'What do you mean? My son wants a pair', and her son was there and he was probably ten or eleven. She asked how she could get a pair and I told her to meet me there tomorrow. I asked what size she wanted and she said a size six, then she said she should get a pair for her other son who was there and looked like he was into it, so a size ten as well. So I'm talking to this lady and another guy walks in and says, 'Where did you get your shoes from?', and he said he needed them for his shop, which was Duffer of St George, round the corner. So I said to the lady that it'd be £50 a pair – these shoes were £2.95 a pair in Macro – and then I went to speak to the guy. He said he'd take whatever shoes I could get, so he asked for 15, 20 pairs all in different sizes.

I went back and got my dad to drive me to Macro because now I've got to buy as many shoes as I could take, and then I went up to Southbank on the train with three bin liners full of shoes. I used to go to Mash on Oxford Street, a hip-hop clothing store, to get different coloured laces. So I got the two pairs of laces and then went to go and meet the lady, who was Katharine Hamnett, the fashion designer, and her two sons, and she gave me a hundred pounds.

Then I went round Duffer of St George, and I hadn't agreed a price with him, so I said, 'You can have all of these here for £200', because I didn't want to carry them around. I think he got 11 pairs, and he just pulled four £50 notes out the till, like, 'There you go'. So I'm a little kid with £300 in my pocket, from spending less than 60 quid. Everyone at Southbank wanted them

but I never let anyone know where they was coming from so I never let anyone know how much profit I was making. People would ask me where I got them and I'd just say it was from a place by me. Then they'd ask where I lived and I'd tell them it didn't matter, and if they wanted them they could either pay me now or pay me tomorrow. I was literally just hustling shoes at that time.

You were finding other avenues to get your stuff, and no one was wearing skate labels anymore. It was cheap, functional shoes, Gap chinos, combat trousers, stripy t-shirts, so nothing really had blazing logos or screenprints. Then that era went into designer labels and no one's looking like a skateboarder. You'd be digging everywhere because wherever you go, you might find dynamite there. Just going to some random shop and hoping you could find something.

I'd clean my shoes, I'd clean my laces and bleach my laces and I'd iron them dry so they were super flat and I'd just weave them in so they looked good in the shoe. You couldn't run away from anyone because your shoes would just come off.

Russell Waterman

adidas and Puma were so far behind what was going on, that they'd missed what was happening. These kids could get three pairs of shelltoes for the cost of a pair of Airwalks, and it made sense to them. We were still selling Airwalks in Slam, still selling what we had, but what people really wanted was Puma Clydes or Gazelles or shelltoes, so we had a new challenge of finding those. And we did find a few occasionally, but on the whole we let other people deal with that stuff.

The sports companies were always behind. People on the street were appropriating stuff, whether it was Tommy Hilfiger or whether it was Ralph Lauren; they decided what they wanted to wear and they took it and wore it the way they wanted to wear it. Six months later the companies would go, 'Hang on, something's going on here', and by the time they caught up and decided they better cater to that, the people had moved on.

It was interesting because when we all came along, we threw a new thing in there because we were not just appropriating stuff but we were now owners of our own companies catering to our peers. But it did not take long for the sports companies to work it out and to make the jump.

Buggers like us would try and buy up the stock, so the price would double, and then the sports companies were looking at us like, 'Hang on, there's something going on here', and then they'd come back with a £60 shoe six months later. They went from £5 to £60 in the space of six months.

Jay Doherty

You would get chased through the streets and people would throw stones at you, because you dressed like a fucking eejit so you stood out a mile and you were

an easy target. All that's good for you, and it creates more character and resilience.

If you were a skater then, you were totally down. You weren't trying to get a ride or trying to be cool. It didn't offer anything apart from skateboarding.

Danny Wainwright

There was an old sports shop in Gloucester, and he had a back room full of Puma States, Puma Suedes and adidas Gazelles. The Puma were selling for £9, so we used to go every couple of weeks and get a pair, and to this day it's one of my favourite shoes. I think it's one of the best skate shoes, and I can't understand why Puma aren't running with that.

Chris Atherton

At school I looked like an alien, with a skinhead and massive baggy clothes. We was pioneering things and we didn't realise it. Nobody got it, and it's funny now, further down the line, everybody gets it. A lot was happening all at once but you don't really realise, you're just living it at the time.

Dave Mackey

No one else was wearing them. I remember my first day in college, in '92, turning up in cut-off jeans, big t-shirt, Puma Suede that were absolutely battered from skating in them, and people just laughed at me. I remember people laughing because no one wore that stuff. It was alien to people in Southport.

At that point in time the number of skateboarders had dwindled. Wheels were tiny, we were skating Tesco's kerbs, and we'd been skating in that style for probably a year. We'd found drink, we were going clubbing, so skateboarding started to become an afterthought, so the numbers of your mates that still skated dwindled. We'd had a 30-strong crew in Southport, and that had dwindled to six or seven, so the six or seven of us would go to Liverpool, and there would be six or seven from every other area going to Liverpool, so you'd be skating 40, 50, strong again.

Arron Bleasdale

There was Lilywhites in London, which is West End, but there was this sports shop in Kentish Town, in Camden, called Ace Sports, and they had Puma for £11. They had the Puma States; they had the suede ones and they had those white leather ones that I managed to come up on and I got every pair in my size. They had the Gazelles and Campus as well, they had a bunch.

All of Southbank got turned on to the Lilywhites thing, and they had nothing left. If you were a size eight, nine or ten, they'd be gone, and obviously I didn't tell anyone about the Kentish Town spot, that was my spot. Most of the skate shoe brands were sketchy at the time, I didn't like them, and I'm not about to try and get a pair of shoes for free and I don't even like the silhouette, or pay £60 or £70 for a pair of shoes that are butt-ugly when I can buy six or seven pairs of what are dope shoes. And they skated pretty good too, especially those leather Pumas. They actually lasted a while. →

Chris Hamer

I used to get a lot of Made in Europe adidas and Puma into Sheep, and sell them to Americans and Japanese. I did quite well with that. Once I bought 75 pairs of black and white shelltoes and sold them to the Japanese on the same day, tripled my money and sent them out the day after. I did quite a bit of that to keep the shop going, because I could get shelltoes for three or four quid back then – because we had the adidas factory down the road – and sell them for a tenner a pair in the shop. Selling chinos for a tenner, and Levi's. Skate shoes and skate clothes were coming in from distributors in London, and they were so expensive up here in Manchester.

A lot of trainers went to American shops because you couldn't get adidas or Puma in the States at the time, and we'd get Nike coming the other way. It was just swapping, because importing rules meant you couldn't get a lot of them here.

Marc Bultitude

The fashion of it then was that we wanted to wear something that was totally not skateboarding. Puma Clydes and adidas Gazelles. The Filas that Simon had on, kind of joked him into buying those. It was a joke that he bought them, and then that picture was in the magazine and everyone talks about them trainers in that shot in the interview.

We used to wear golfing jumpers, and Slazenger shirts, like what your grandad would wear. No one was wearing those. That started off a whole fashion thing. I really noticed how fashion took that '90s skating look and really ran with it.

When it was baggy pants and small wheels I think there was a whole load of skaters who thought, 'What the fuck is all this, they look stupid, they look like clowns', but they didn't get it.

Matt Stuart

How the hell could you skate in shelltoes?! But Simon did it. He was into the crazy colours and dying his hair. He was definitely a kind of fashion icon in skateboarding, in a weird way, at that time.

Reuben Goodyear

Skate shoes were so overpriced. They were £50, £60 even back then, and nobody had the money to spend, so everybody was looking for cheap options, so the adidas Gazelle was one of them, and the Puma States. It was always good if you could come to Southbank and go, 'Yo, I got these for a fiver!', or ten quid or whatever, and they were rad for skating in! They were the perfect alternative to a skate shoe.

Ben Allnutt

We were going to all sports shops, and the best would be Intersport. The types of shop where you knew they had stock that wasn't on the shelves and that couldn't be returned. They had bought that stock and they had to sit on it. There was a sports shop right in the centre of St Albans that we would go to, and they had stock of nubuck Puma States in all-mustard, all-olive and all-burgundy. They were awful, but like in all

these places, the supply got dried up really quickly. There were maybe 30 pairs, and within two weeks, done.

I remember the shop guys going, 'Where's this coming from? Why do you want these?' It's pre-internet so why did this happen? Nowadays if there's a trend coming through it's online, but there's just not even a version of that nowadays.

Colin Kennedy

You'd get Puma Clydes from Macro, and with pants, it was whatever you could get your hands on. There was a lot of mail-order business coming out of Manchester at that time, because there was so much demand for that product. There was no way you could own a pair of Fuct or Blind jeans, and I had these terrible jeans called 'League', and they were fucking horrible but they were the only thing I could get that recreated that look. Just following the lead of what we were being fed, basically.

Martin Kennelly

There was this sports shop in Chesterfield where you could buy Puma Clyde and Puma Suede, all those, for £9. So they were the shoes. We saw those shoes going from bargain basement to slowly appearing on the shelves in proper sports shops, where they were marketed and brought back.

Ray Calthorpe

Paul Shier had a Macro card, so he was allowed in there. I remember once I bought a pair of canvas low top adidas, with the adidas logo embroidered on the side, and they were £3.99.

Paul Shier

I went to Sacramento with Rayman when I was 18, so 1992, and stayed with his pen-pals, these girls. One of them was Nick Tershay's girlfriend, so I met Nick and we'd go to Nick's house and play pool with him and his uncle.

We hung out and skated, and we only went to SF one day, and Jovontae was at Embarcadero. I can remember I was wearing yellow Puma Clydes, with a black sole, and people were hyped on the shoes at that time.

So I went back to England, and I kept in touch with Nick on the phone, and he ended up asking if I could send some shoes to him, Mike Carroll and Rick Howard. I think it was adidas and Puma for Nick and Mike, and Dr.Js for Rick Howard. I would buy them at Macro, they had these rubber-toed canvas adidas, and Dr.Js, and I think I got the Pumas somewhere in Croydon, and they were all £9.99 or something.

I ended up sending the shoes, and Nick said he'd get me a box sent from World Industries. I just waited, and waited and waited and then just gave up. It was just, 'those boards are never coming'.

Then one day a box turned up at the door, that had been shipped by boat for however long. It had a letter in there written by Rick Howard, thanking me for the shoes, and in the box – I still have it at my mum's – was the 101 Natas Satan graphic, it had a Danny Way Exorcist board in it, a

Guy Mariano Mobster board, wheels, Fuct clothing, a Mike Carroll White Mafia board and a few other boards. I can remember just being tripping.

They asked for shoes, and I sent them, and I didn't think anything about it at the time, and then it was written about in the *FTC* book years down the line. Someone mentioned whether I played a part in the whole shoe-world of people wearing adidas and Puma and Converse and all this in skateboarding. Maybe I played some tiny part in it. They just wanted the shoes they couldn't get in the US, so they got them, and I got the boards, and now I work for adidas. At the time, we were buying those shoes because they were cheap.

Ryan Mills

Converse Dr. Js popped up. They were a white low top with the arrow and star on the side, and they were £12 a pair from Bon Marché in Brixton, and then they popped up in Macro, the cash and carry.

I was asked to go to SF by Simon Evans and Ed Loftus, because a guy out there had started a new company called Experience – Simon got his pro model on there and Ed was a paid amateur – and they said they needed someone to fly the flag in London. They said if I paid for the flight they would cover everything else, although it never really worked out that way. I'd already given Ed a pair of Dr. Js that were too big for me, and he'd said, 'By the way, bring some Dr. Js with you'.

So I went to Macro and bought eight pairs in different sizes. I got stopped by customs going out there, and they asked why I had all these shoes. I said they were gifts, because they had no shoeboxes – because you didn't get shoeboxes in the cash and carry – and I'd taken the price tags off, and they let me go. I turned up at EMB with a Thrasher board bag with my board on the bottom and it was just full of trainers, and minimal clothing.

I started a bidding war between Chico Brenes, Jovontae Turner, all those guys were just fighting over these shoes. I thought I was going to get robbed if I didn't close a deal soon. James Kelch was there, and he was just so vocal. I'd been looking up to these guys for the past year and a bit, and now they're just all shouting at me.

Then Jovontae's like, 'Just come to my car', and he walked me over to this frog-green 2002 BMW from '76 and he opened the trunk and he's like, 'Yo, homie, what do you want?', and he pulled a shoelace of wheels out and he put it round my neck, he gave me a pair of Blind jeans, he gave me three prototype Jovontae boards, and he goes, 'I just want a pair of size tens'. I went, 'I thought you was an eleven?', and he went, 'I don't even care, I'm gonna curl my toes up and make sure they fit'. So I was like, 'Alright, fine. Cool'. Then Chico took a pair and he gave me four boards and two sets of wheels for one pair. ●

1993

Elsewhere

Danny Barnett, Southbank, by Skin Phillips

For me it was tragic, as somebody who'd dedicated their working life to skateboarding, to have to walk away from that and hand it over to someone else.
TIM LEIGHTON-BOYCE

RAD / PHAT MAGAZINE
Tim Leighton-Boyce

I knew things were going to change. It was a really, really dark, dirty dreich day in February. We used to always all go to lunch together, at one of the cafes in Clapham or Streatham, but this time we'd gone all the way to Putney for some reason, and we were driving back from that and I got a call from the publisher, and she was saying that they'd decided to stop doing *RAD*.

At that point we had a big problem, but at some point they asked if we wanted to buy it, so we basically started putting together the funding. They offered to sell it for five thousand quid, and I foolishly – because I'm such a softie on most things – I thought, no, and I haggled over it because nobody else was going to want to buy it. So I did, I haggled, and that turned out to be a big mistake because they had got somebody else who was interested in buying it, so they sold it to him.

We put out a newspapery thing, to keep people interested, because we'd got some money lined up, but we didn't have distribution so we had to go through this business of trying to get a distribution deal, and that's what was our undoing.

We went back to Comag, and they said, 'There's no room in this market for two skateboard magazines. This isn't going to be a skateboard magazine, is it? It can't be a skateboard magazine', and that's where *Phat* came from. I think we would have made that work, if we'd been able to survive.

The first thing is, come up with this concept that isn't a skateboard mag but still can have skateboarding in it. So we came up with that. Then there was the second bit, which really turned out to be a death blow. They said: everybody that comes in and says they're a journalist says that they've got mates who are journalists who'll write about us, and that isn't good enough – we want to see a budget for PR and spend it with a pukka PR agency to do the launch. So we had to find a PR company who would do the launch for us, and we did, and they came up with the perfectly good strategy that we'd come up with a big story that

we could get some coverage around. And that's where the gun culture thing, about guns and rap music, came from. If you read it – and it's got several different aspects to it, because lots of people worked on that, not just Gavin – it's taking the line that this isn't glorious at all, and it ends up with people dead in real life.

The PR people got going on it, and I don't know if it had started to get any momentum when what happened, happened, but what happened was that this coincided with the James Bulger murder and so suddenly children being violent was hugely topical, and everyone just piled in. Really, really piled in. Everybody was all over us and it was absolutely horrendous being in the focus of a storm like that.

Thank God for Gavin, because Gavin basically became the person who fronted all of that. Having said that, he probably could have handled some of it better. He became a bit combative in a way, but why not? You're under this constant attack. But maybe it could have been possible to calm it down and get people to actually see that it doesn't say anything like that.

We survived for three issues with it getting worse and worse, but the irony was that the advertisers were beginning to come. Various music industry-type advertising agencies had liked what they'd seen, but what was really doing for us was the newsagents and distributor saying that they'd had people complaining that they had that terrible magazine, and having to take it off the shelves. It was big coverage, in the newspapers and on the radio and TV. The TV people were funny because they'd just come from interviewing the politician Rhodes Boyson about it and they said, 'His eyes aren't too good, he hasn't even read it'. Mothers Against Murder and Aggression, all manner of stuff just piling in on us.

They were right that we were just using it to get publicity, and unfortunately it doesn't show up too well that there's a daisy in the gun, which is a homage to Marcel Marceau. Or it might have been De La Soul.

An awful period, that was. And I spent ten years paying for it.

I regret stopping, because I feel like I was stopped, but I don't think I could maintain the level that I did for much longer. I don't know how I managed all those insane journeys, and the total absence of any type of life outside of that. It was all I did, and we had pulled off this trick of evolving and evolving, but there's a form of inertia that does set in at some point and we probably would have fallen into that and become too established.

For me it was tragic, as somebody who'd dedicated their working life to skateboarding, to have to walk away from that and hand it over to someone else while I deal with 'other stuff'. Dealing with the distributors, dealing with the printers, dealing with the people who were producing the magazine, all of it. I was running the magazine and there's a lot of stuff that goes into producing a magazine.

I was so, so hurt at the end of *Phat*, totally devastated by that. It really messed with my head and so I never looked at the *RAD* magazine that lingered on, and I still haven't. And I never really looked at *Sidewalk*, even though I was working at *New Deal UK*. I was very, very hurt.

Matt Stuart

It was a BB gun[1]. I shut the whole thing down! I remember Tim asking Sam to do it, Matt McMullan and Ed may have been asked to do it, but no one really wanted to do it that much, so I said I didn't mind. It was in a studio and it was all a bit different because we'd never been in a studio; with skateboarding we're always out and about.

The green jacket I'm wearing was a Stüssy moleskin jacket, and I'm wearing Plan B jeans too. I was as cool as I could fucking be and I was to hold a gun with a flower in the end... No problem.

And then the magazine came out and it was fly-posted, and I remember my mum saying, 'Matthew,' – and 'Matthew' is bad news – 'what is this? I don't think this is that cool, why did you do that?' And then of course there was the WHSmith backlash where they withdrew distribution. It's actually a pretty iconic cover. →

Magazines

Elsewhere

SUNDAY 18 JULY 1993 — THE OBSERVER — ENCOUNTERS 3/49

Phat chance of provoking teenage violence

Gavin Hills tells Andrew Davidson why it is ridiculous to ban his new skateboard magazine.

Would you want your teenager to read this comic?

by Christy Campbell

Media men hope to cash in on the basic instincts of streetwise young rebels

Fatal issue for trigger-happy teenagers

THE directors of W. H. Smith and similar organisations doubtless owe a responsibility to their shareholders, but surely not at the expense of our public safety and morals.

Making magazines such as *Phat* readily available throughout the country aggravate the already explosive growth of gratuitous violence and theft on our streets.

The feeble levels of retribution meted out to offenders mean that crime does pay, to the extent that such offences as car-radio theft and house burglary are now much time will pass before we take the same attitude to a rash of deaths caused by gangs of trigger-happy teenagers?

Bob Newman
Bath,
Avon.

tor of a new teenage magazine that glamorises violence. The ability to sidestep moral in earning their living be the root cause that is wrong with today.

M. Trott

Phat – ragga slang for 'hot' – is the latest magazine to hit the shops. Well, some shops. With a gun on the cover, distributors are running scared

Spat over Phat

183   1993

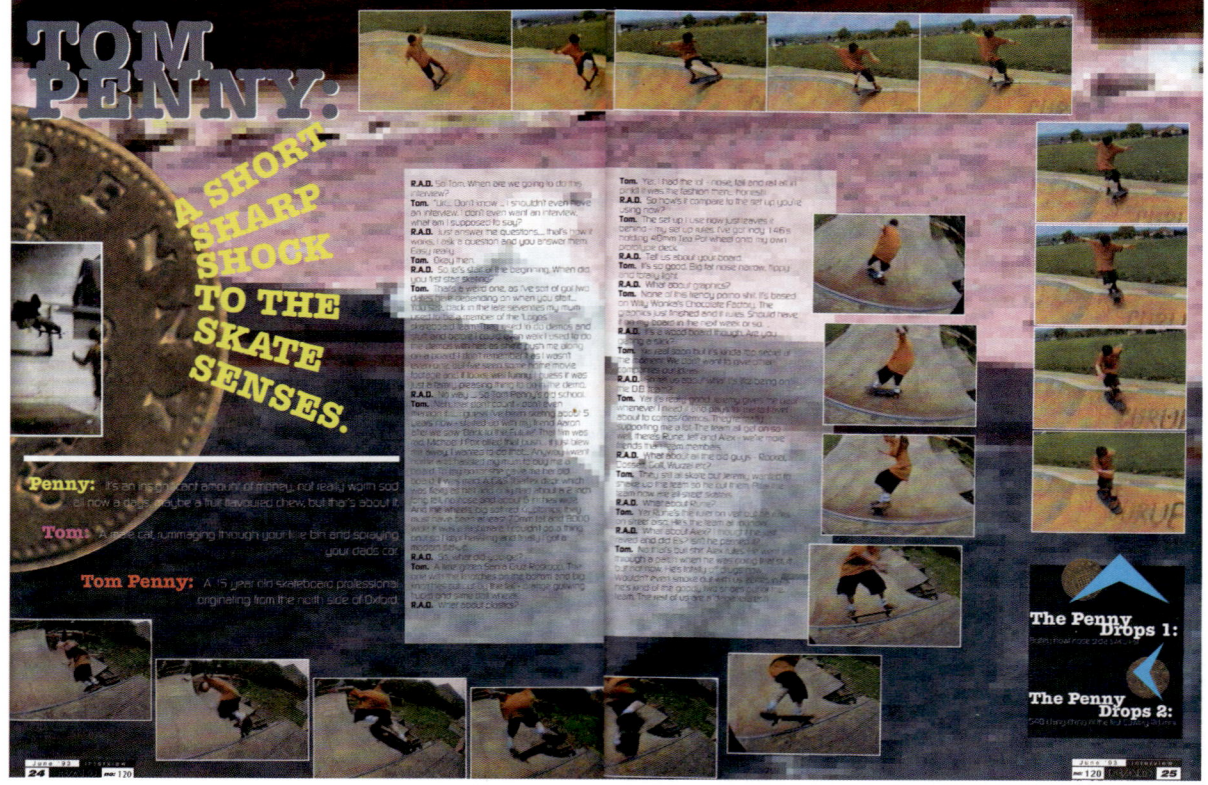

Sofia Prantera

That could have been a lot cooler [p.183[2]]. I think it did possibly undermine my position as a female creative in this business, not because I was in my knickers necessarily, but mainly because the art direction was quite shit; there was definitely no female empowerment there.

Being female in this very male-dominated business has been a difficult line to walk at times, it's one I've had to walk my entire career, and – although I've never felt discriminated against – you do realise that there's a different lens on you because you're not male and you have to choose to embrace that in whichever way you want.

In the naughties skateboarding became hyper-sexualised and commercialised, and I found that visually uninteresting and degrading to women, and it's a reason why I moved away and went back into fashion. The minute that 'look' got commercialised anything cool about it was eradicated. If you had Chloe Sevigny, Deanna Templeton, Kim Gordon, they were all doing really interesting female-skewed work within skateboarding in the mid-'90s, and that was very much what had attracted me to all of it, and what I felt a part of. Yes, it was sexualised at times but it wasn't exploitative. Subsequently it became this shrunken pink shit; when skateboarding became successful it was taken over by the big brands, and it was commercialised in this dull fast-fashion way.

Oliver Knight

I remember I got the cover gig [p.183[3]] as Jonny Wilson had pulled out of doing it, and it was a simple case of Tim saying to Ray, 'How about that kid?' Arriving at their office in Tooting, it was just a cool scene; a real punk do-it-yourself vibe. I didn't give it much thought about being on the cover, I just turned up in what I normally wore; plain tee from C&A, 40-inch-waist jeans and a pair of Stan Smiths found in a dusty sportswear shop for a fiver.

Looking back at it now, *Phat* magazine really encapsulated the energy of the UK scene, and it was so much more relatable than the US magazines with palm trees in the background of each shot. What was happening in the UK skate media was definitely a two-way thing; we were just as much creating the culture as we were consuming it.

Tom Hodgkinson

Gavin's got that laddish football hooligan, 'drink Tizer, fancy birds', thing. He basically invented *loaded*. Gavin was definitely a big influence on James Brown. Quite a few of the early *loaded*s were really, really good, and it was better than *Vice*.

I wrote loads of pieces for *Phat* under the byline of 'The Idler' because I was trying to get this Idler name out there, but I should have put my own name under those.

James Brown

I remember we had this magazine in the office, this very thin little skateboard mag, and I can remember my boss, Alan Lewis, had either found it and given it to me or I'd seen it somewhere and bought it. It was on glossy paper but it was designed like a fanzine and they had these little screengrabs of skateboarding.

Alan and I were looking at the screengrabs in it, which we hadn't seen before. We did a lot of stuff in *loaded* about things we'd seen on television, or moments in football matches, or scenes from films, and you couldn't get images for them, because if you went to a photo library for a film you'd probably get a promotional shot, or a shot of a famous scene that they'd used in the posters or something like that, so screengrabs were what we used in *loaded*.

Steve Hicks

I only met James Brown a couple of times, but he took a lot of things that I think were Gavin's instincts about journalism, which I don't think Gavin thought about very much – he was just like, 'This is cool', 'This is fun'. James was more articulate and corporate – and more power to him – to be able to sell that through. It seemed very clear that *loaded* took a lot out of that playbook.

I hate 'cyberpunk' as a phrase, but the whole thing about it was that it was only 20 minutes into the future. What William Gibson did was, he took the world and cranked the jog wheel and let it go, and thought, 'What does the world look like if it's what it's like now, but it just carries on like this?', and that was *The Sprawl* and *Neuromancer*. There was some of that going on with the design of *RAD* but by the time we got to *Phat* it was much more intentionally about culture. It was almost like an 'owning' of culture, like, 'This belongs to us too, Hollywood belongs to us too'.

In many ways *Phat* was a little bit too young. It was a little too naive, I think; it wore its teenage-dom too strongly, it didn't have any aspiration. What James did with *loaded* was to dial that down a little bit, and have more Hollywood content, more girls, and big pictures.

→ **RAD MAGAZINE**

Alvin Singfield

It was only at the demise of *Phat* that Joe – my boss – said, 'These guys are taking over the *RAD* name, and I think you should help them out because they don't know what the fuck they're doing'. It was almost an obligation to Joe, with him being an advertiser in the magazine and him wanting to have a skateboard magazine. You've got to remember that at that point, that was it! *Skate Action* had gone, *Skateboard!* had gone, and with *Phat* gone, these guys doing *RAD* was the only shot at there being a British skateboard magazine.

Joe asked me to be involved with it and I didn't like it because it wasn't the *RAD* that I'd grown up with and loved, but in my mind, it was that or nothing. I'm glad I kind of helped it stay afloat because if I hadn't, maybe Jim Peskett wouldn't have connected with Andy Horsley and those guys from *System* who managed to take it over and rebrand it to *Sidewalk*.

Obviously I was just shooting pictures of the Faze 7 riders for whatever we were doing so I would just give them stuff I didn't want, and more often than not they weren't very good but they'd end up in the magazine. I wouldn't speak ill of them as people, so I was happy to help because before there was *STM* and *System* and those guys got involved, what the hell was there going to be? In a world before the internet, how could there not be a British skateboard magazine? It kind of had to exist.

The few times I went up there – and I didn't go up there a lot because it was on the other side of Oxford in the middle of nowhere – it didn't seem like they knew much about what they were doing, and I think that was reflected in the magazine. Video grabs were fine when they were in *Phat* and it was a tiny little sequence, but the moment you start trying to blow that up it looks bloody awful. For the stick I got at the time for helping them, and for the fact that everybody thought the magazine was shit – which I would 100% agree with – it just seemed like the right thing to do at the time.

Sean Goff

RAD magazine was sold off to Arcwind, and no one wanted anything to do with it, so effectively the only skateboard magazine was going to die, unless someone came in.

Eddie and Stig took it over, because they were from the snowboard side of it, of the publishers, and because they knew me from the shop, they gave me a shout to see if I'd help out. Now, what you've got to remember is that I'm running a skateboard shop, and without having a skateboard magazine, how are you supposed to promote skateboarding? How is skateboarding supposed to live? So if a skateboard magazine dies, then skateboarding could potentially die, so I'm going to help out.

The way I saw it, was that I was gonna go in there and help out as much as I can until someone else comes along and does a better job. So it was kinda like triage. You help out, you keep it alive as long as you possibly can, until someone with more skill can bring it back to life. The publisher was about 15 minutes down the road from me. I ended up speaking to him, and he asked me to come on as Associate Editor. So I did that.

We wanted to do a Tom Penny interview. We had some photos, and it was mostly sorted, and I kept asking him to do the interview and he kept not doing it, so one time I asked him if we should just make it up, and he said that we should.

So the interview in *RAD* magazine with Tom Penny in 1993 is complete fiction, and the sister that is mentioned doesn't even exist. →

→ *SYSTEM MAGAZINE*
Wig Worland

The first time I met Andy Horsley, he came up to me at a Spitalfields contest and he said he was doing a magazine, and told me to send him pictures – he did the same to Tim Leighton-Boyce, I don't think he knew who Tim was – and he gave me a thing with his address on it. He seemed very nice. He was a kid from Nottingham who'd met a kid from somewhere else and they'd decided to put together a skateboard magazine straight out of university.

Paul Haynes, very sensibly, could see that the writing was on the wall for the other mags and he wouldn't have anywhere to advertise if there wasn't a magazine. He had a business to run.

Andy Horsley

I went up to TLB because I had no idea who he was. 'That guy's got a camera. Yes, he's got a ski jacket on, but he's got a camera as well.' I went up and said hello and told him we were starting a magazine up in Nottingham, and asked him if he was interested in sending us any photos and I think he actually said, 'I'm TLB, I work for *RAD*,' and I went, 'Oh shit, no way', and walked off and bumped into Wig. We were all just on the same vibe of having fun, and there was less pressure to do anything, really. Wig said he had a ton of stuff that hadn't been used and I think we used everything that he had in the first issue.

Ben Powell

Paul Haynes, who owned *Rollersnakes*, was really forward-thinking; basically if you worked there and you had any kind of creative brain, you could do a zine, or do whatever you wanted. Design some t-shirts, do skateboard graphics, make a video, whatever – get on with it.

Which is why *System* magazine proper started. *RAD* at the time was shit-*RAD*, and he's going, 'This is fucking terrible and I'm paying to put adverts in it! You can probably do better than this, right?' to Andy Horsley, who's like, 'Yeah, probably'.

Joyriders wasn't made as a *System* video. Jon Robson had the footage, they were doing a magazine, so it stood to reason that they would release a video because that's what proper magazines did. I think that was a bit of a statement of intent, because that was when *RAD* was run through *Arcwind* and it was shit. It was like, 'Here we are, three idiots who don't know what we're doing and we've made a video. Fuck you, give us a magazine', which was basically what happened because they got headhunted to do *RAD* quite soon after that.

Paul Haynes

RAD took a big dip when it changed hands. Andy Horsley and Chris Forder used to live in Nottingham, and they used to come to the shop, and we'd got friendly with them. Andy asked us if we'd back them to start a magazine, and I said yes, so we invested in an Apple Mac and they started taking photos and doing some editorial, and we produced the first magazine on the Apple Mac. We'd load an image, press a button on Photoshop, and it would take two hours to process the information. And it was in black and white.

For the first run we made 12,000 copies, totally too many, and we only sold a few thousand. We gave them away with orders, so we got rid of them in the end, and we carried on. ●

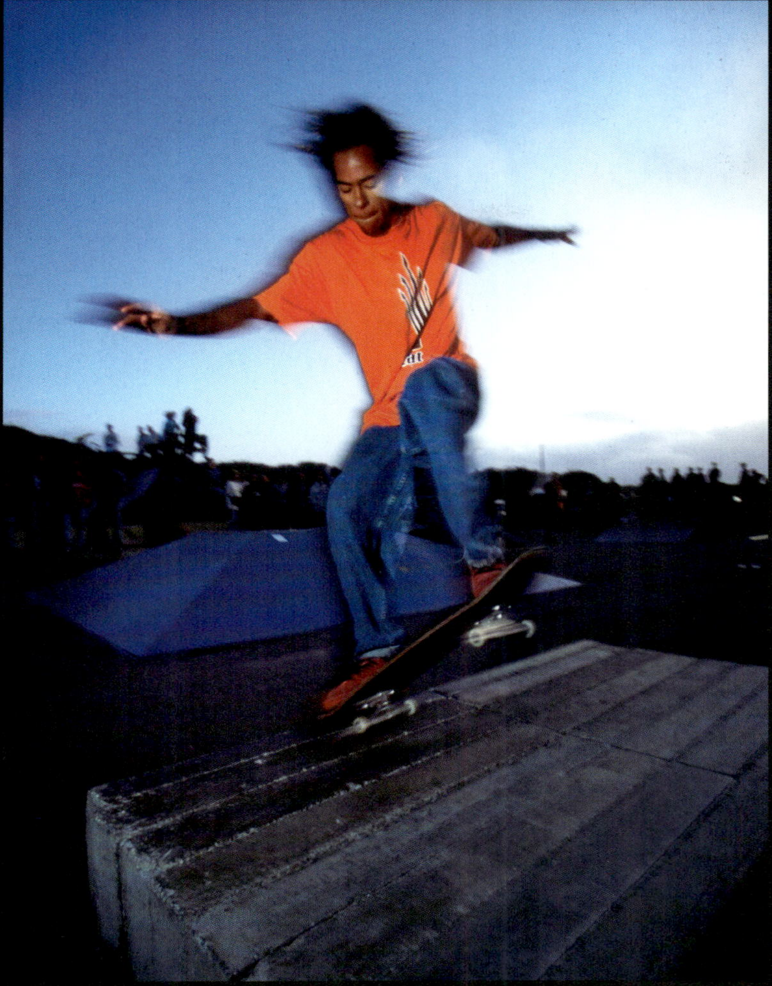

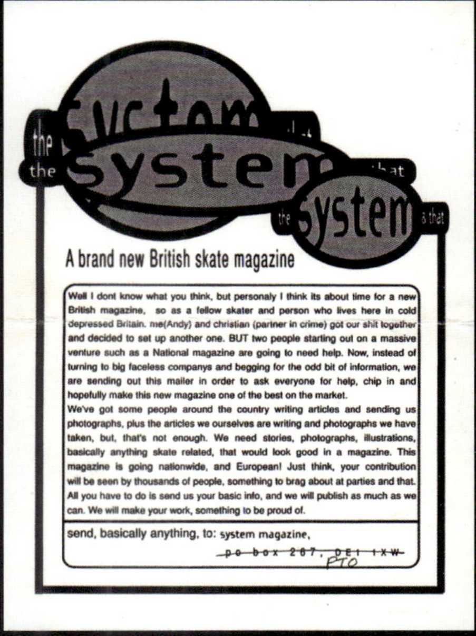

Well I dont know what you think, but personaly I think its about time for a new British magazine, so as a fellow skater and person who lives here in cold depressed Britain. me(Andy) and christian (partner in crime) got our shit together and decided to set up another one. BUT two people starting out on a massive venture such as a National magazine are going to need help. Now, instead of turning to big faceless companys and begging for the odd bit of information, we are sending out this mailer in order to ask everyone for help, chip in and hopefully make this new magazine one of the best on the market.

We've got some people around the country writing articles and sending us photographs, plus the articles we ourselves are writing and photographs we have taken, but, that's not enough. We need stories, photographs, illustrations, basically anything skate related, that would look good in a magazine. This magazine is going nationwide, and European! Just think, your contribution will be seen by thousands of people, something to brag about at parties and that. All you have to do is send us your basic info, and we will publish as much as we can. We will make your work, something to be proud of.

send, basically anything, to: system magazine,

po box 287, DE1 1XW. PTO

CLOCKWISE FROM TOP LEFT
[1–3] System covers, by Wig Worland
[4] Sal Barbier, Mount Hawke, by Wig Worland
[5] System announcement flyer
[6] Wig Worland shooting Sal Barbier, Mount Hawke, by Ben Gregson
NEXT PAGE
Carl Shipman, Broadmarsh Bus Station, Nottingham, by Wig Worland for the non-existent fourth issue of System

187   1993

Elsewhere

1993

sex, cannabis, alcohol, pear smoothies, Bruce Lee, cream slices, Linda Lovelace, Streetfighter 2, lsd, masturbation, Corner Shop, cars, fabric, X-large, punk rock, pancakes, spirit of '77, hip hop, mum, dad, television, Jagger, Ideal, dyed spikey hair, tattoos, dick piercing, pitbulls, bombing, hippies, sandals, oi, Kiss, riots, life, death, guns, the Beasties, bongs, shotgunning, slamming, Black Sabbath, Sid Vicious, Hustler, threats, DIY pornography, Clockwork Orange, Jamie Reid, Holmes, skunk, Buds, buds, Manga, Wire, burritos, drag racing, Buba, melon smoothies, vibrators, nurses, lace underwear, 40 ozs, drive bys, Deep, Glocks, bondage, fish tacos, hate, X-tra Fuct, anarchy, Sesame Street, the Anti-Christ, Minor Threat, situationism, Tipper Gore, Cypress, Fridgidaires, Repo Man, switchstance, Seditionaries, world domination, toys, and skateboards. We are

fuct

(+44) 071 221 7495   fax (+44) 071 221 2726

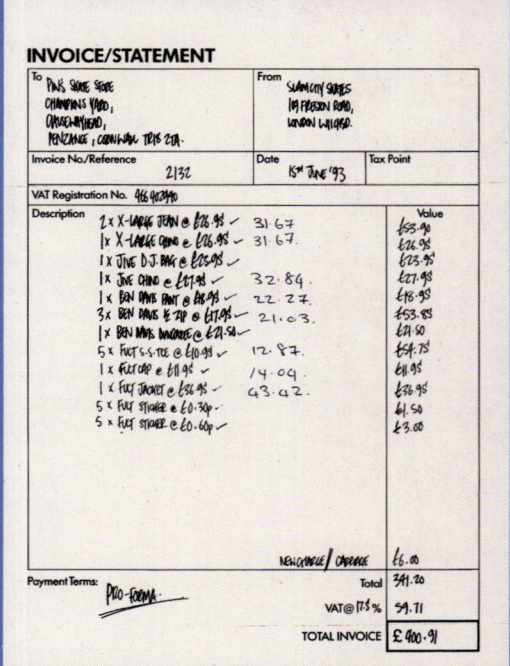

CLOCKWISE FROM TOP LEFT
[1] Chance Meeting on a Dissecting Table of a Sewing Machine and an Umbrella (sleeve) by Nurse With Wound, artwork Steven Stapleton (1979)
[2] Fuct ad by Russell Waterman
[3] Slam City Skates ad, Simon Evans and Marc Bultitude, photo by Will Bankhead
[4] Slam City Skates invoice

→ **SLAM CITY SKATES**
Russell Waterman

I was the one who went and got Fuct and X-Large. I knew that Fuct were trying to make more cut-and-sew stuff, whereas certain shops would come to us and all they wanted was the Ford Fuct t-shirt. They would have bought a hundred Ford Fuct t-shirts off us and not touched any of the other stuff because that's what they were about, selling massive numbers of the thing that sells. I understand that, but that wasn't what we were about; we were about trying to allow these labels to grow, trying to help them create scenes within certain cities and go forward. With people like Fuct that was impossible, because they were absolutely barmy.

Nurse With Wound put out a list of their influences on one of their early records[1]. Didn't say anything about it, just a massive list of bands and real obscure shit that no one knew about, and it became a kind of wants-list, with people pre-internet trying to hunt out all these bands. That kind of format, of just listing a whole bunch of stuff around your vibe was probably what I thought of when I did that[2].

There's some dodgy stuff on there, but it's quite a good list. A load of this stuff probably wasn't that well-known at the time. I don't know why I put 'drive-bys' in it, that's a bit sketchy. It's probably stuff that I thought I and they had in common, and stuff that was around that we thought was interesting.

Erik Brunetti did his own version later on, and he credited me for that, and Erik would always take the credit for whatever came his way. He'd take a graphic and take the credit for it, but he actually gave me credit for that one, which I was quite touched by. Like he is human after all.

Someone like Bond might go off to the States and buy a little bit of Fuct and put it in his shop, but no one was doing it seriously and no one had attempted to distribute it. Same with X-Large, no one had attempted to distribute it.

Ben Davis was a good one to get – just from following what was going on – and they were a brand that only did workwear.

Sharon Tomlin

I went to college in Surrey, then I went back home – near to where Dan Magee lived, in Bedford – and after a few weeks I gave Chris Turner from Slam a ride, because he was friends with my friend. I knew what Slam City was, because everyone did, and I made a joke like, 'Ha, can I get a job?', and he went, 'Well, actually...'

Paul Sunman's ex-girlfriend, Suzanne, worked at Slam but she was having a baby, so she was leaving and they wanted another woman to work there, to keep things chill. That was the idea.

Chris was the manager when I started, and I was given this little blue book of everyone who'd been shoplifting, and my job was to be 'security' or whatever. It was kind of a bullshit list; it was really

a list of people that they didn't like very much. At first, it was all cool. I had my little book of all the people that were supposedly shoplifting, and I'm a pretty good judge of character so I could tell the people who were only coming in to steal stuff, and so much stuff was being stolen when I first started working there. Chris at the time was this crusty-punk anarchist, and he didn't really care. He just sat there and people would literally come in, pull the tags off stuff and walk out with it. So they were losing tons of stuff, plus he wasn't nice to people. Mums would come in to buy shoes and stuff, and he was rude and stand-offish. He just wasn't into it.

Mike Manzoori

There was this idea that if a shop or brand or anyone was successful, skating back then was very much, 'Oh, you're doing well, I want a bit of that, I should have some of that'. Old dudes would come into Slam and expect a discount or free stuff, and then after being told not to hook people up, Sharon would be scolded for not hooking up these old dudes just because they did a layback grind in the '70s. How was she expected to give a fuck about those guys? Slashback Larry from Gillingham going, 'Don't you know who I am?'

Sharon Tomlin

The keyboardist from Jesus Jones had worked at Slam, and I didn't know this. He came in once and sat behind the counter, and we'd been told by the Rough Trade partners that there was to be no one behind the counter because they were super paranoid about us getting robbed. I told the keyboardist from Jesus Jones that he couldn't sit behind the counter and he had such a hissy fit, all, 'Don't you know who I am? Who the fuck are you?', and I'm just going, 'Why do you need to be behind the counter?'

I'm kind of obsessive-compulsive, and I have to fix things, so if I see something's not working, I'll fix it. So I just started organising, and tidying stuff up, and getting stuff sorted. Making sure we had all the stuff people were asking for. Within a few months there was a real rise in profits, and that's when the Rough Trade partners started to ask what was going on, I got promoted to manager, and Chris got sent to the warehouse to do sales.

Things were running smoothly, we weren't getting robbed as much, and the Rough Trade partners were like, 'We love you!' The Rough Trade partners were always allies. Jude and Nigel and Pete were my best friends. Paul and Russell not so much.

When I first started working there, everyone was friends. There was a handful of people who were stealing and didn't really want to hang out in the store, but then there was the Six Pack, like Simon and Matt Stuart and Ryan and Sam and Jonny and Winstan – and they were regulars, just hanging out. They didn't particularly buy anything, they'd get griptape and bits to get by on, but it was all chill and everyone was friends.

I was hanging out with those guys, going to clubs with them, or parties at Matt Stewart's house, and that's when Paul and Russell were like, 'You don't understand, they're just playing you, they're pretending to be your friends'. That was when the mindfuck started. I was like, 'Well, I don't think so, but whatever'. I didn't think that was the case.

We had all new stock of X-Large, and a skater came in, and while his friend was talking to me he put on a big pair of 40-inch-waist pants, he put on a jacket – put on a full new outfit – and shoved boards down his pants and walked out the shop and set the alarms off. That just fucked me up because I couldn't not tell the bosses we got robbed by a skater, and then of course they're like, 'Yeah, see? They're not your friends, they're just trying to rip you off.' That took away my credibility, and any leg I had to stand on.

I think a lot of people had a chip on their shoulder all of a sudden, that there was a woman there telling them what to do. It was the '90s, after all. People talk about 'incels' now, but that was what it was like. One-on-one everybody was cool. People would have arguments with their parents and they'd come and stay at my flat; I was friends one-on-one, but when it was a group it was almost like they had to be dicks to me. It was a weird dynamic.

Seb Palmer

Slam in the Covent Garden era, in the Sharon era, was just incredible. She was a really phenomenal connector; she'd be going for dinner with Chloë Sevigny and Harmony Korine one day, and hanging out with some young skater in town the next.

Marc Bultitude

Will Bankhead took that photo[3]. That was just one of them days hanging out in Slam. That was probably the start of streetwear getting big. Everybody would come into Slam, stylists would come in and say they were doing a shoot and ask to pick up a load of clothes. You'd see all the party people coming into Slam, and Barnzley from Stüssy, so you got to know that scene.

In such a short period of time it seems like we did so much. When I look back on it now it's only four or five years, but the friendships that formed in that small period of time were really powerful. →

SUMO
Seb Palmer

The first Sumo was upstairs at The Forum, and it was not boutique at all, it was just a good curated selection.

Martyn Lau was having a break before uni, Rhona Lord was at uni, so there was three of us, and Rhona's boyfriend put some money in. I barely put any money in, I was just the one who was driving the ideas. I think we started with five grand, but I was the one who called around the distributors, like, 'Hey, we're about to start a shop, take a risk on us!', and it was Russell Waterman at Slam who said he'd give us a chance. We rented a car, took the five grand in cash, filled up the back, came back and put it in the shop, which was just bare bones. Somebody made us a counter, and we hung boards off nails in a brick wall.

It had graffiti inside it, because Seth Curtis was into graffiti and we made friends with all the graffiti guys, and that kept the shoplifters at bay.

Fraser Cooke was distributor for Pervert, Subway, all of these weird little abstract brands that we'd get little bits from. We'd go to Gimme 5 and we eventually got Stüssy. We sold Supreme in the store. It was an eclectic mix of brands. Slam was amazing and Holmes was phenomenal.

The two influences for me were Ideal, because those were my guys as I was growing up skating, and then Sheep. Sheep was a kindred spirit.

At the start I didn't have any money, so I'd go to charity shops and buy the 40-inch-waist jeans and cut them down, so part of starting that shop was because I wanted that stuff and I didn't have the money.

The first shoes that we got was when we went to Debenhams and bought up all their Clydes. We put fat laces in them and flipped them, £15 to £30. Shoes weren't distributed then; Vans was through New Deal and it was sporadic, what you could

get. There was no pre-order culture. Simple we could get, and Airwalk we could get somehow – the Jason Lee and the Tony Hawk – and then the first DCs through Faze 7.

The shop was small, but it took off. You were picking things up like, 'Oh, so-and-so will like this, I'll get this in an XL', and that's the art of buying, although when you get into pre-ordering it becomes a serious business and it becomes different.

Sumo came before Supreme – we were '93 and Supreme's '94 – but as soon as Supreme came out we were like, 'We can't use the "Su-" anymore', so we focused on the O. At some point I sketched the SMO114 logo where the O was both an O and a 0.

Then the O became the logo, and we did the split-O on hoods across the zip; we did it as just the O in places, and it became a label design. We made our own font, and it's called Sumivers, because it's a version of Univers. It's slightly different, it's thicker and fatter. Ben Weaver did that.

We had a list of names of things we were going to call the shop, and 'Mischief' was one of them. 'Fusion' was one, and that's a terrible name, but 'Sumo' was there because it was like fat, X-large, bigger-than-life, but we never played on wrestling. We made one reference to it ever. It's a word that means more than the word means.

→ **ROLLERMANIA**
Patrick White

When I was working in Rollermania in '93, Tony Coffey had this idea that he'd buy loads of old-school boards, late-'80s boards, that Shiner had held on to but wanted to get rid of, and he'd cut them down into a popsicle shape. They'd have a shitty little nose and a ridiculous concave, of course, but he had this handyman guy outside the shop with a Black & Decker Workmate cutting these down, and he'd sell them as beginner boards. All I can think now is how much those boards would have been worth now. ●

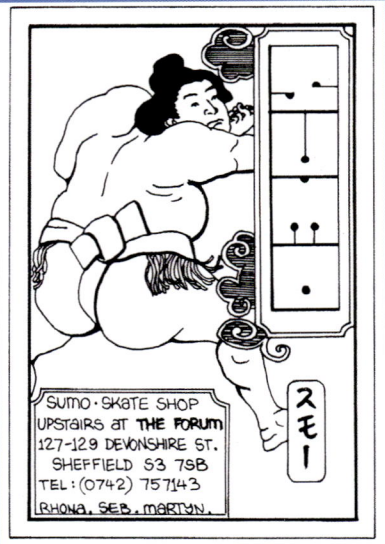

"I remember them sending us boxes of shit. I remember when it turned up at my mam's house I was thinking, 'Mint! Stuff for nothing!'"

NEIL URWIN

Neil Urwin

When I left school, going to London was consistent. I was back and forward to London all the time, I was skating every single day, and there were tours coming up to here.

I remember Ray from New Deal saying he'd sort me out with products, and I remember them sending us boxes of shit. I remember when it turned up at my mam's house I was thinking, 'Mint! Stuff for nothing!' Boards and t-shirts. The first package I got was all New Deal stuff, and I was bang into Underworld Element; Pepe Martinez was the man. Again, style. My favourite skateboarders were more about how they looked than how they actually skated.

So they started giving us boards and then Ray told us about Steve Douglas, and said New Deal were looking to make a flow team in the UK, so it was me, Mark Channer and Danny Barnett. And they told us that only one person is going to end up being on the proper team – on the actual US New Deal team – and I remember thinking how fucking sick both those guys were.

Douglas called one day – and I spoke to Douglas a lot because I was a flow rider – and he said I was going to ride for the proper team. I remember being in South Shields with my mam and my dad one time when Ray was up, and my dad going, 'Who's this Ray geezer? I should meet him or something.' My dad had never got anything for nothing in his life, and he was a bit, 'What's the fucking deal here? What's going on? So they send you free stuff, but what do you have to do in return?' It was a very different world for him.

At that point in time it just felt easy. I remember skating a kerb and doing fakie 5.0 kickflip out and I remember thinking how easy that was. I could never fucking do that four years later! It was not physically possible. I think I got a kind of sweet spot for two or three years where it just became easy. ●

liquidphoto

switchstance 180° nollie flip

big spin decks and wheels.......for those who live to skate but can't afford to live

LITTLE DICKS

BIG SPIN, 200 MAIN STREET SUITE 104 – 176
HUNTINGTON BEACH CA. 92648

☐	**KING DICKS**	KINGPIN AND	
☐	INDY/VENTURE	☐	VENTURE FEATHERL
☐	**RUBBER DICK**	TRUCK CUSHIONS	
☐	FIRM	☐	FIRMER
☐	**BENT DICKS**	ALLAN WRENCH	
☐	**SCREWY DISKS**	AXLE NUTS	
☐	**HOLEY DISKS**	TRUCK CUSHION WASHER	
☐	**LEAKY DISKS**	TRUCK AXLE WASHERS	
☐	**JIMMY HATS**	PIVOT CUPS INDY/VENTU	
☐		THUNDER TRUCKS	

FK YOU!!** I WON'T do what YOU tell m

BIG SPIN. 200 MAIN STREET SUITE 104 – 176
HUNTINGTON BEACH CA. 92648

you have the right to

Steve Rocco

We left it up to Faze 7 to decide who would get flowed boards. I remember Shiner being the sort of 'big guy', but we always liked to go with the other guys. That was how we'd do business. We never had contracts, we'd shake hands, and I think we would have got Faze 7 from a trade show.

Alvin Singfield

When the recession hit, we lost over half of the skate shops we had.

At that time people were sanding off their graphics to have them blank, and people were buying blanks because they were cheap. Skaters couldn't afford to spend 50 quid on a deck. We, as a distributor, had all the best shit. Shiner had all the old-school stuff but we had World Industries, Blind, 101, Plan B, Menace, and all those boards were just sitting in the warehouse. Stacks and stacks of them. It would never have been an issue to sell them before, but when that recession hit, it felt like almost overnight all of that went, and shops were shutting left, right and centre, and we had to combat that somehow. Joe Burlo knew we had to offer a product which was affordable. A cheap deck and a cheap wheel. But how could we make it cheap without it looking too cheap? And Joe was adamant that it wasn't a blank, because he believed that they weren't good for the industry. And it also had to have a team.

Shiner started to sell blanks and we've got piles of Plan B decks that people just didn't have the money for. I didn't like the idea of blanks, and Joe really didn't like the idea of blanks, but with Flip going to America I wanted to have a British brand, and Joe didn't believe that could happen because he didn't think there was a market for it. What he did allow me to do was create a blank brand, which was initially going to have a one-colour screen on it, but ended up with the logo burned into it. It was purely called Big Spin because I was trying to learn big spins at Leigh-on-Sea the day before. That's how shit I was at coming up with a name.

Joe decided we'd pretend it was American. We had a warehouse in San Francisco where our stuff would ship to Heathrow from, which was also the address of Screaming Squeegies, the screenprinting house. That was the address of many different skateboard brands, so we used that address.

Joe said we'd have a team, and I was to pick the boards to copy, so I went out to the warehouse and picked a 7.5 Daewon Song, a 7.6 Mike Carroll and a 7.75 Sean Sheffey. We sent those to the wood shop and had them copied, then every few months I'd go and pick another three shapes out and send them out and get new boards done. We gradually built up a really good team of street and ramp skaters on Big Spin, and we used to sell Big Spin boards like the olden days, in boxes of 10 or 20, and boxes of 100 wheels, because they were so cheap. We'd found a way of supporting the British skate market with affordable products because people simply couldn't afford Plan B or Blind or 101 anymore.

The first slicks we got done were shit; they bubbled up and the slick came off, but we sort of powered through it just because it seemed like such a revolutionary thing at the time.

Almost right out of the gate Big Spin sold like hot cakes. We put three decks out each time. There was always three shapes. Shops would be ordering 10 or 20 of each shape and 100 of each wheel. Because the wheels were cheap as well. I think we had 53mm, 55mm and 57mm wheels, and we were doing bolts. It went from five team riders to ten team riders and it just grew and grew.

And t-shirts, Jesus. The funniest one ever was the 'Fuck You I Won't Do What You Tell Me' one, where it was a picture of a balaclava-ed guy with his finger up with 'Big Spin' written on his knuckles and the LA skyline behind him. That was me. I thought about what I could do that was cool and was more hip-hop based, but with that message. I loved the cover of Ice Cube's *Amerikkka's Most Wanted*, with him in focus and a ton of guys behind him, so I asked Joe if he had any cool photos from when he'd been in LA – because he was always taking pictures – and he had a picture of the LA skyline so we literally just went outside and put a white sheet up and he shot me with a balaclava on and with 'Big Spin' written on my fingers, and we superimposed – not Photoshopped – that on to the background and it looked fairly realistic. We shoved that out and we fucking sold hundreds of them.

Dan was the only person that cottoned on that was me. I don't know why he noticed it or why he gave a shit about it, but after that people realised it was me, and that Faze 7 was Big Spin.

Dan Magee

Me and Piers Woodford were looking at the Big Spin ad in a magazine and we're like, 'Alvin, this is you in this advert, right?' It was so obviously Alvin's body shape, and his little hand. We're like, 'Alvin, this is you!', and he blustered out the whole plan of how Big Spin was meant to be an American company and how Joe tried to keep it a secret.

I'm still a bit mental about people taking loads of sponsors. It's one of those things where you're lying in bed thinking, 'Fuck, why did I say yes to riding for something like that?' I probably wasn't good enough, but one of my pet hates is people just taking any sponsor. Why would you take something shit? Big Spin was just blank boards! But when you're only getting two boards a year – one for Christmas and one for your birthday – you don't question it. And blank boards are not as bad as getting a board with a horrendous graphic on it.

Mark Baines

I was actually convinced it was an American brand, because Alvin had told me, 'Yeah, the guys in America want you on', and obviously that was bullshit. It was just their little blank board brand. The only way I found out was when the 'Fuck You I Won't Do What You Tell Me' advert came out, because that's Alvin on the advert. That's when I was, 'Oh, it's not an American brand', but I think it was all a joke by then, we were to keep it hush-hush, and it was kind of laughed off. I wasn't bothered by then, whatever. At the time, doing a UK brand is probably not gonna work so they need to do it as a US thing. Some years later it wouldn't matter because UK brands were popular, but at the time I think that was the reason.

Paul Shier

The funny thing is with Big Spin, I only ever got one board. That was it. Alvin rung me up and asked me if I'd like to ride for Big Spin, and obviously I said yes because I had nothing else going on at the time, and I'd bought Big Spin boards before because they were cheap.

I got this massive square, flat box, and I opened it and it had one board in it. At the time I was riding a 7.75, and they sent me an 8.25 which seemed massive, but I set it up anyway because it was a free board, and I just dealt with it. What am I going to do, complain about the free board I just got? ●

LEFT
Big Spin ads and product

Elsewhere

Brian Sumner

To me, what got me into it, was skating was a total way out from the system. Once you see an ollie, once you ride down the street, it just takes over. It's romantic. This is our thing. I just became obsessed with this.

I'm showing up trying to download everything, 'What's this trick? What's that?', and all these guys are all so nice and I love that they even looked at me like a little brother because I was so annoying, but it was just that I loved skating.

Everyone would go from the Courts, 50 or 60 of us from all these different towns, different cultures and ethnicities, to the Tiles, to the Cotton Exchange, to this spot and that spot. Someone wants to do this, someone wants to do that. You're pulling up to a ten-stair and someone wants to ollie it. So for me, I just wanted to be in the fight, doing this, and I would just obsess and think about it. To me it was just somewhere to aim.

I would go and do a nollie shove, and nollie shove the other way, a pop shove, a frontside shove, a kickflip, heelflip, nollie flip, backside flip, fakie flip, half-Cab flip, frontside flip, fakie heelflip, half-Cab heelflip. I've never said that to myself but I would do that until I did it without falling off, and that was just warming up. It wasn't because I wanted to get sponsored, I just wanted to skate. I just couldn't sit still.

Barry Wong

Brian was unusual – he was a very unique person – and you'd think he maybe had ADHD because he'd get into things intensely. One month he might listen to a load of Misfits, and then the next month it might be a rap artist, and as he was skating, he would recite the lyrics to songs and he would integrate that into his skateboarding.

Geoff Rowley

Brian had the John Dalton influence, the Howard Cooke influence, the Mackey influence and he had the Barry Wong influence, but he also had the Brian Sumner, West Derby, rough part of Liverpool, influence.

Brian brought another young generation to the city, and he was a little turd, probably like I was a little turd when I was going around with all these guys that were older than me. He was quite annoying, and I was quite annoying, so I related to him.

Ian Deacon

I think Geoff was always a bit underrated, at a certain time in England. Just maybe because he was in Liverpool. He had photos but I don't think people realised how good he was. Obviously Tom's got way more natural ability but Geoff's got that drive, he'll go for it, but you wouldn't really see that in a contest. If you saw a contest you'd think that Tom was way better because how Geoff skates doesn't really tend to come across as good in a contest. ●

CLOCKWISE FROM TOP LEFT
[1] Geoff Rowley, NHS building, by Kevin Banks
[2] Geoff Rowley, Mountford Hall, by Kevin Banks
[3] John Newby, Littlewoods, by Kevin Banks
[4] Brian Sumner, NCP car park, by Kevin Banks

CLOCKWISE FROM TOP LEFT
[1] Tom Penny, by Wig Worland
[2] Contest placings
[3] Contest ad
[4] Contest ticket
[5] Wallride wall, by Damian Ince
[6] Tom Penny, by Wig Worland
NEXT PAGE
Carl Shipman, Nottingham, by Skin Phillips

Steve Douglas

I'm a proud Englishman and I was just embarrassed that Germany were leading the way with contests. Titus used to buy his stuff from Surrey Skates, and now he had this massive contest which was amazing, but then there'd be contests in the Czech Republic, or in France, and I was going, 'Man, why the fuck can't the UK do an event as part of this?' Enough was enough and we, the distributors, had to do something here, so we all agreed to work together. We were all building our own businesses, but we all wanted the best for skateboarding so that we could all do better from it.

Münster was set in, and they deserve that, but I said that we should be the week before or the week after. We had a big meeting and it was as simple as that, and the Radlands contests started. We got together and we did it and it wasn't that hard, really.

Ian Deacon

The first big Radlands contest happened in '93, the proper big one with the Americans, and that happened because Steve Douglas came over and there was a meeting at a services on the M1 somewhere. I went and Jeremy went, for Death Box or Flip or whatever, Burlo was there, Steve was there, Richard Allen from Shiner was there, Chris Ince was there, and it was basically deciding to do this proper contest in England, and rather than everyone hating each other – which they kinda did at that time, because Steve had started New Deal and that pissed Shiner off because he was nicking brands or getting the new brands – we were all going to unite on this thing as an industry. That's where the idea that we'd all work together and support this Radlands contest came from.

This idea that we'd get this contest together and seven or eight people who were at that meeting all decided to work together to make this contest happen because Steve was saying that's what the UK needs to get skateboarding growing again. I don't know if anybody knows about that, but there was that meeting to promote skating in the UK again, and to do it with this contest at Radlands which Chris Ince had just opened, because it's the perfect venue.

Alvin Singfield

Joe had been doing this brand from San Francisco called Experience. The guy who owned Experience, Roger, had no fucking idea, although he was a nice enough guy and he had some money, and he did Pure Wheels too. Pure had Scott Johnston, Eric Koston and Tim Gavin on it, but Experience only really had Eben Jahnke and so he wanted to do something more with it. Simon was out in San Francisco, and Simon got on, and that all went well but where it went Pete Tong was when this guy Roger told me to get Tom Penny next.

I told him that wasn't going to happen because Tom was with Death Box and he was going out to America with Flip, but Joe said, 'You work for me, and I'm telling you you've got to go and ask Tom Penny'. It was a really bad idea and I didn't want to do it, and that's probably the only time Joe really made me do something I didn't want to do. Not that I thought I was going to anger Jeremy or Ian Deacon – which is what happened – but he told me I had to do it.

There was a miniramp just up the road from SS20 on Cowley Road in Oxford, and we were there with Tom

and Rune Glifberg, but we were going to Northampton and they asked if they could catch a ride. On the way there I'm thinking, 'Fuck, Joe needs me to ask Tom about this', so I just tell him the guy from Experience really loves how he skates and he wants me to offer him a deal to ride for them, although I know he's doing the Flip thing so it's probably a no.

Tom said it was really nice but he wanted to see how the Flip thing pans out, and I agreed. Tom, obviously doing the right thing, told Jeremy what had happened, and I ended up in a choke-hold from Ian at a St Albans comp, and Ian's a big fucking guy. At that age I think that was one of the most terrifying things I'd ever been through, I was scared he was going to kick the living shit out of me.

I remember going into work the next day, really fucking angry, and shouting at Joe for making me do that. It was degrading, embarrassing and horrible. That bothered me for a long while. A few days later Ian rang Faze 7 and apologised, because he's a businessman and he didn't want it to badly reflect on what they were doing as a company.

Ian Deacon

We'd all agreed to work together – a kind of truce, I guess – and then in October Alvin fucking tried to steal Tom... That's probably what set me off even worse; we'd done all this unity shit, we weren't nicking people, we're all good, then he goes fucking off-piste and tries to nick Tom. We'd already had Shipman nicked and what could we do about that? But we don't need some idiot in England trying to nick Tom for a company that we thought was a pile of shit. ●

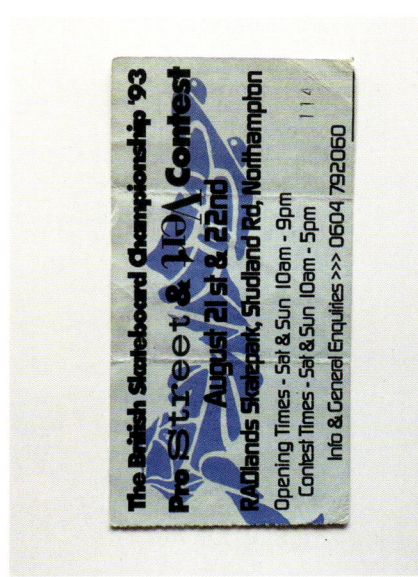

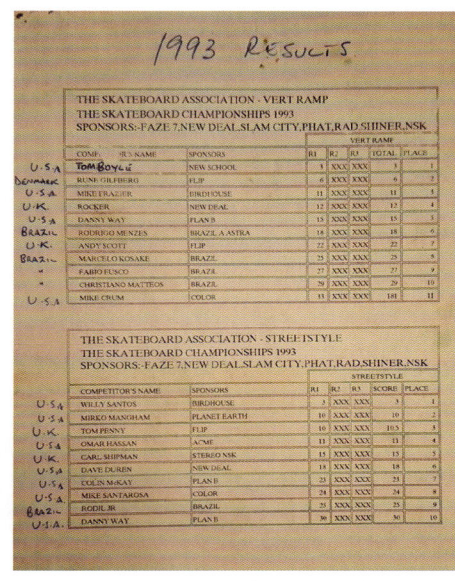

Elsewhere

1993

Sponsorship

Ian Deacon

We never made Carl Shipman boards. We had a Harlem Globetrotters graphic for Carl Shipman but we never sold Carl Shipman boards. Shipman was on Flip when there was still db, from what I remember. He was never on Death Box or db.

We had a little short time with Shipman and then we went to Münster in '93, and Jason Lee and Chris Pastras talked to Carl, and there was this sketchy guy called Yves from Switzerland, who was the distributor for Stereo there, who was doing a lot of the behind-the-scenes undercover work on that switch. It was a bit of an awkward situation because I knew Jason. It wasn't the best situation but the funny thing in hindsight was that Tom and Geoff were skating that same contest. Carl was obviously way more impressive in that contest than the other two, he was doing frontside Cab flips down the seven stairs, so they must have just gone for the glory rather than gone for the longterm – like, who's going to be better in potentially five years' time or whatever. Four or five years in Geoff's case anyway, and two or three years for Tom.

So we took Carl and his brother out, and then Carl went to Stereo, but we took them both back to England. It was kind of a weird situation but there was no other way for them to get home, so what can you do? Then they went to Switzerland, to Le Grand Bornand, then they came to Radlands and Carl was already on Stereo by that point.

Carl Shipman

I was skating Northampton a lot, with Tom and Geoff, who were literally sleeping in Jeremy Fox's warehouse, which stunk of paint fumes and all that.

I went over to Münster with Flip, and then I got on Stereo, and the best thing I remember was Deacon saying that you should do what makes you happy, and being really supportive. They brought me home as well. I was only 17, and they were so cool about it when I left. It worked out in the end. Obviously it worked out for them lads.

I was going to have a Harlem Globetrotter board. I don't know where that graphic come from, it was just so random. It ended up being Geoff Rowley's board, but it had my initials under the baseplate.

You know how you feel when you don't belong somewhere? That was how I felt about Flip. I felt like I didn't actually belong in that team. I didn't want to be in that team. They were skatepark skaters at that time, and I used to skate vert and street.

Tom were getting better, Geoff were getting better, and they just went over at the right time and it worked for them. I couldn't see myself wanting to ride for Flip, as good as they got and as good as a team they had. I just didn't feel like they were my bag. I felt like my skating were going to go in a different style to what Flip's were, and Stereo presented itself at the right time. When I were skating with the Stereo lads at Münster, it were like I could just slide in. It was so laid-back, and I never liked the pressures or stresses of skating. Flip were planning on going to America to dominate, and they did. I've got full respect for them.

Skin Phillips

Carl was *exceptionally* good when he was good. Carl was a working-class kid, he's from an estate. Skateboarding was a way out for him. I didn't ever see Carl drunk or belligerent, he was pretty fucking on-point.

I did Carl's Pro Spotlight for *Transworld* under a pseudonym. *Thrasher* and *Transworld* fucking hated each other back then, they were rivals. North and south rivals. Maybe the magazines liked each other early on, but it turned into having to pick one or the other and that was your side and never the twain should meet. It was like that back then because there was the north/south rivalry, straight up. I wasn't involved in the rivalry because I was from fucking Swansea, and I didn't really give a fuck.

Carl Shipman

We did that Pro Spotlight in about a week. We did some stuff round Worksop, then went to London, to Southbank. We did it super quick, and it was round about the time of first going out to the States.

It's easy to shoot with Skin Phillips, he's an absolute legend. He's one of the best photographers that's been out there, and one of the easiest photographers to take pictures with. He's a lovely bloke.

When you aren't filming tricks, people disbelieve you made them tricks. That's another side of skateboarding I couldn't bear. I remember going to Hubba[3] and they're like, 'You've got to do this!' Bear in mind you're on 40mm wheels, and that's a nasty, horrible ledge. The picture on the cover is not a make. I did go back and make it, but because you didn't get it on film, people discredit what you've done. →

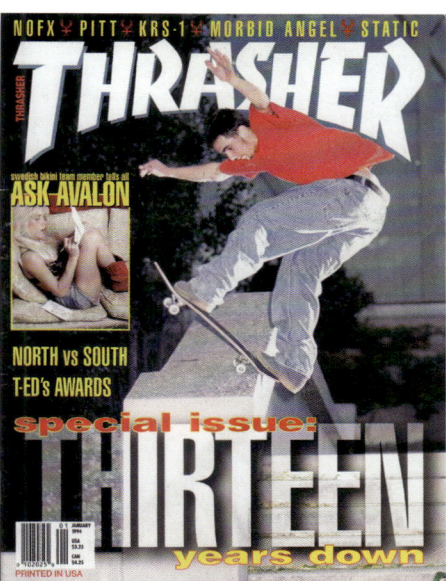

EXPERIENCE
SIMON EVANS

HARD DAYS NIGHT

415-861-0102

CLOCKWISE FROM TOP LEFT
[1] Mike Manzoori, Milton Keynes, by James Hudson
[2] Mike Manzoori, St Albans, by Skin Phillips
[3] Simon Evans Experience boards
[4] Simon Evans Experience ad, *Big Brother* issue 10
[5] Simon Evans, Southbank, by Skin Phillips
NEXT PAGE
Mike Manzoori, Harrow, by Wig Worland

A lot of skaters – vert skaters and park skaters – were disappearing. They weren't around no more. I said to Mike Manzoori, 'Look, the market's moving different places now. Fashions are changing, no one's skating with pads anymore.' There didn't seem to be any structure to that type of skating, so I said, 'If you're interested, get yourself to America quick. Get yourself to NHS, go speak to Bob Denike, go speak to Jeff Kendall, and ask them where you stand here. Ask if they want to turn you pro.'

Every trade show I went to in Europe, from '91 to '93, even distributors didn't know the way skating was going. They were lost. Everyone was lost, and I think they were nervous with vert and they wanted more street, street, street.

Mike Manzoori

I went to the States and stayed with Bod Boyle and travelled around. Shane was like, 'When you get there you've got to have a meeting with Jeff Kendall and Bob Denike and the NHS dudes, and see what's up with this board', and I'm like, 'Mate... I didn't ask for any of this, I'm not doing that'. He kept pushing me when I was on the trip, asking if I'd talked to them yet, but I didn't want to do it.

On one of the last days of the trip I went back to northern California to fly home, so I went, 'Fuck it' and set up a little chat with them and they basically laughed me out the room. All, 'Nah dude, that's not happening at all, dunno where you got that idea from'. They told me they'd tried Euro boards with Claus Grabke and Sören Aaby, and Claus had sold some boards but it was too much hassle and Europe wasn't really a market they cared about. I hadn't even wanted to ask!

That was immediately before a German contest, so I come back to Europe and tell Shane what happened and that I didn't think it was working out. Then I got a call from Kendall telling me they were going to have to cut my pay, and I just told him I didn't even know what was going on. So then Shane tells me we're going to Münster and when we get there I wasn't to tell anybody what was happening, but I should just skate real good and get a new sponsor. He was trying to manage me a lot.

So I get to Germany, get to the street course, and the first person I saw goes, 'Hey, I heard you quit Santa Cruz!' Super weird.

When the Santa Cruz thing went south I ended up getting hooked up with New School. The place that distributed that was Surrey Skates, and I went down there one time to pick up a couple of boards and I see ATM boards next to them. I'm like, 'Wait a minute, Ron Chatman...', so I called up the distributor in the States like, 'Hey, is there any chance I can get ATM boards instead of New School? I don't even know what New School is and ATM's pretty sick', so the person said they'd speak to Ron. Ron was there and he said he'd speak to Gonz and see what was going on, and call me the next week.

Next week this guy Ned Hadden from ATM calls me up like, 'You're on ATM!', and I'm like, 'Holy shit!'; little did I know that that was the week that the entire team left. Gonz, Ron Chatman and Steven Cales had all bounced and they were going to put together a new team with Mario Rubalcaba, Kip Sumpter, me and Jeff King. A bunch of randoms, basically... It was such a bait-and-switch and I didn't realise until way after. They're like, 'Come to the States and meet Mario', and I'm like, 'Who's Mario?' I didn't even meet the Gonz.

Simon Evans

After Think I got World Industries flow. Who wouldn't want to be on that? They were like the pinnacle of skateboarding back then. I got on flow for a little bit but then I thought I wanted to be a writer, and I thought I could apply the same kind of effort to becoming a writer, but it doesn't work like that. So I went back to school, and being young I was like, 'I'm gonna quit skateboarding now and become a writer', because it was something I could do for my whole entire life, and then what happened was Ed Loftus came back and he said there was this guy who had a new company called Experience in San Francisco, and that sounded like a path for me. I was going to go to university and study literature but there was this opportunity so I thought I might as well go and do that and then come back, because I was already over skateboarding by this point. But then I ended up just staying in San Francisco because I loved it so much.

San Francisco was such a beautiful city then, in the early/mid-'90s. It was fantastic. Culturally as well, discovering that there's all these writers and going to the City Lights bookshop was amazing. It was like an awakening for me, being there and being away from home. Being away from England and my parents. It was so beautiful and I loved it and I just wanted to stay. I met a girl and just decided to stay with her.

Carl Shipman was around too. You'd be at Wallenberg or something and all of a sudden you'd see Carl and he'd be like, 'Alright, Yeah?' He was amazing, fucking hell. That guy was a skateboarding titan. Him, Tom Penny and Geoff Rowley, those guys were so, so good. That was my Shane O'Brien moment, those guys were the next level. They were like gods. Carl gave me a belt back in San Francisco and I still wear it. I really, really loved Carl. I got my nickname from him – people call me 'Chevans' – when he was staying at my house. He said, 'Me and my brother think you're a bit cheesy, so we call you Chevans'.

Experience was a fucking nightmare, it was horrible. The guy was a weasel, he was awful. When I was in America, skateboarding wasn't like what it was when I was in England. It was never the same. I wasn't as into it and there's a whole different culture, those guys were jock-y. Skateboarding was changing too, we'd be down at Embarcadero and I felt like I was losing interest, and I was blinded in the heat and there was the smell of hamburgers everywhere. It's only looking back that I see when it was really special and when it just kinda fizzled out. ●

Elsewhere

1993

Clothing Companies

→ ***LORD***
Andy Coombes

I was skint, I had £8 to my name. Ridiculous baggy jeans like clown pants were the fashion and everybody wanted them but they were too expensive for me. At the time, there was a little store in Liverpool that used to make jeans. They were a jeans factory in their heyday, and it was run by an old lady I called Juicy Lucy. You could walk in with a pair of jeans and get them to copy them, so every skater in Liverpool was going there. The jeans cost £8, which was lucky for me.

I had a pair of jeans made and I got 'Lord' embroidered on them. The name Lord came about because it was my nickname. I trawled the internet, which was a new thing at the time, so I bought Lord Clothing.com and that was it, I was committed.

I took the jeans to Robbie Reid, an old school friend, at his skate shop The Fleapit, and Robbie said he'd sell them. He sold them that day, and he ordered more and that was the starting block.

→ ***SIESTA***
Alex Cock

Phil Penwarden had just moved from New Zealand and was starting to get into the scene, and his mum taught him how to make a copy of Skate Rags pants. They were £45 to buy, and at Trago Mills, which was this sort of everything-shop in Devon, you could buy fabric and he could make them for about £9. Nine quid's worth of

fabric and he would sell them to us for £11, making a whopping two quid profit.

I wasn't rich or anything but I had a couple of pairs of the Skate Rags pants that I'd got for birthdays or Christmas, and he just took them and copied them. Phil has an engineer's brain, so he went from his mum showing him how to do the pattern, to when he'd meet people he'd be like, 'Can I just take a look at your jacket?', and he'd start taking their jacket off and turning it inside out and looking at the inside and the person would be like, 'What the fuck are you doing?'

We'd done our GCSEs, neither of us thought we were clever enough to do our A-levels, so we went and did – for whatever fucking reason – Hotel Management at Plymouth College. Six months of that was living in France, so we were learning about food and the hospitality industry and all this boring bullshit which we hated, but we met these French skateboarders when we were there, so we would spend our days off going skating and smoking weed and hanging out.

When we got back we didn't want to be hotel managers, so we binned it off and borrowed five grand from the bank manager to start a business, and that was mega-money in 1993.

We were trying to think of something that was non-offensive, and we were coming up with all sorts of things, but we saw a dog basket with a sticker on it that said 'Siesta'. And we were into dogs. ●

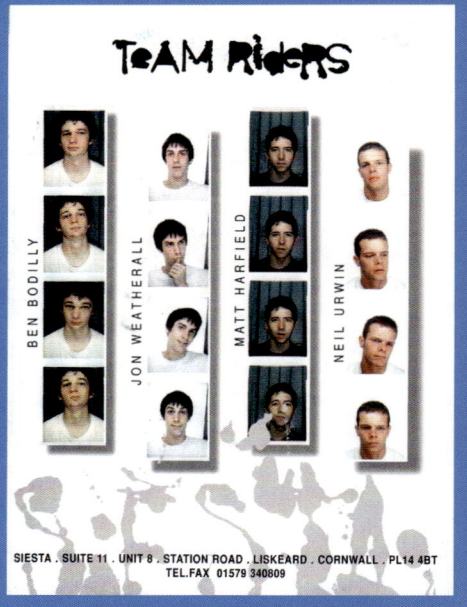

→ **411VM**
Arron Bleasdale

I had no idea what *411* was going to be. I think Steve Douglas told me what they were planning to do, but I didn't really think about it that much, or it didn't make sense. Like, 'What are you talking about? A video magazine?' So he asked me to film some stuff for this video magazine, and I think in my head I was thinking of video screengrab sequences in a magazine.

My friend Rob Ganly, his mum had an old, fat video camera, so we took that out to Cantelowes and did total dad-style filming. He just stood in one spot and panned around. Stood on top of that pyramid at Cantelowes, filming from there. We sent off the tape and totally forgot about it, and then that issue comes out and it got really popular. At the time I was thinking that if I'd known that's what it was going to be, I would have made a bit more effort.

→ **BUBBLEGUM WEEKEND**
Mike Manzoori

That was basically a stepping stone to my whole career, that video. We went to Amersham College, me, Mat Fowler and Mark Channer. Mat and Mark were a year ahead of me, and Mark was doing Media Studies so he had access to those VHS editing suites. With me and Mat's courses, for the first year you did a month in all these different subjects, and in the second year you focused on one, so he focused on Graphic Design for the second year.

He made 'Jello' the name of the brand for a skate company and he did all the stuff you would for a skate company: stickers, boards, shirts, hats, all that stuff.

At the time, Santa Cruz had sent me a VHS-C camera to get some footage of myself to send over to them for a video, so I figured that I had a camera, Mark had access to this editing thing, Mat's doing his thing... So for a joke we just thought, 'Let's be the team!'

But basically we thought we'd film a team video that would supplement Mat's presentation for his final major project, so went out for one weekend and filmed ourselves around Wycombe and Amersham and Harrow and wherever, and that's why it's called *Bubblegum Weekend*.

That was when I first thought, 'Holy shit, this is fun', when I was able to marry up music to skating, and time things slightly. We didn't have much control over it because I hadn't figured it out yet but it was a super engaging experience, and the guy who had control of the editing room was kind of frustrated that his students didn't use it anymore, so it was left empty a lot, which meant I could book it out whenever I wanted even though I wasn't in his class. It wasn't a masterplan, it just happened like that. ●

AGE - 21, YEARS SKATING - 6
SPONSORS - Stereo, Venture, Vans, XL

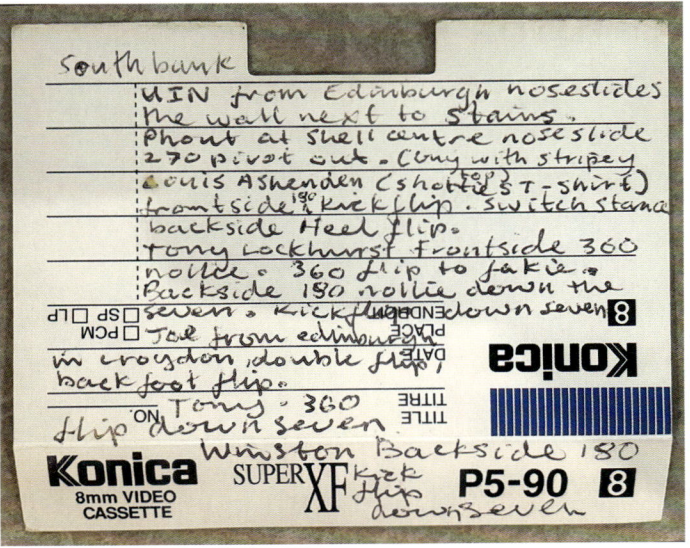

LEFT TO RIGHT
[1] Lord flyer [2] Siesta ad, *Phat* issue 2
[3] Siesta catalogue (extract) [4] Bubblegum Weekend back cover, by Mat Fowler
[5] Arron Bleasdale, Cantelowes, from *411VM* issue 1
[6] London Metrospective tape insert, filmed by Skin Phillips

1994

Elsewhere

Dan 'Jagger' Ball, Wolverhampton Civic Hall, by Wig Worland

Before Sunday trading it was like a ghost town, there was nothing going on. In any town centre you could skate anywhere, and then they kind of introduced it partially. It was still kind of chill and people weren't really coming out on a Sunday, so you could still skate, and then it suddenly exploded into being the same as a Saturday. That probably fucked up British skating. That probably put a big grinding halt on the evolution of British skating. It fucked up kids living in small towns.
DAN MAGEE

Elsewhere

→ **RAD MAGAZINE**
Jonny Robson

At the time, *RAD* magazine by Stig and Eddie was the worst. Not the worst skateboard magazine, but the worst magazine in the world. The writing was just astonishingly bad and the captions were off-the-charts shit. I honestly thought skateboarding was dying. Andy Horsley had been doing *System*, and he got a call from Mark Kasprowicz – who's the *Windsurf* publisher who had three mags on the go and was planning to bring in Tudor Thomas to do *White Lines*, the snowboard mag, who were inspired by *Loaded*, the lads' mag – who asked if they would want to come and do his magazine. He said he'd move them to Oxford, thinking there were two of them. It was Horsley and Chris that were doing it really, with Wig Worland as a photographer but Wig wasn't going to move from Stony Stratford anytime soon, but Horsley said, 'It's me, Chris, Harry, and this guy Jon Robson'.

Mark said he'd get a four-bedroom house in Oxford and sort out the deposit and the first month's rent or something, and that he'd pay two people £200 a week. He said he was going to relaunch *RAD*, and do *White Lines* and *Surfer's Path*, and he'd do his windsurfing one in the background, and Jim Peskett would be the ad manager.

They went there, and they went into work every day because you didn't have a computer with the internet at home in those days so they had to drive out to Wootton – which was about a 40-minute drive from where we were in central Oxford to his barn where the other magazines were being done – to press buttons on a Mac.

It was the first time we did a colour mag. *System* was a colour cover but it was all black and white. So Horsley and Chris felt their way through that, inspired by *Raygun* and *Club Homeboy* and things like that. Horsley loved The Orb as well, all that kind of design.

I was just on the dole, and by then I was smoking weed. I met a girl from Nottingham who happened to be a successful model in London so I used to go to London all the time to visit her, so I used to bum around basically – in brand-new skate clothes that I got from the product page – and hang about with her. I was living in Oxford but I was into going to London and going to clubs and stuff and Horsley and Chris would just doggedly do their work, Monday to Friday, nine to five. Harry just skated.

So it was me and Harry rattling around in the house, and Harry kind of keeps himself to himself. He reads a lot. And me, I'm just a twat, and everyone gets sick of me really, really quickly, so we used to separately do bongs in our own rooms and just listen to music and he would be dying to go skating.

Horsley would say, three days before it had to go to the repro house, 'Jon, have you done those wheel reviews yet? Have you done that Northampton contest yet?', and I wouldn't even have started it. Wouldn't even have any notes. Nothing. What a twat. I had no sense of responsibility at all. Horsley and Chris were so patient, until they weren't. Horsley would burst into my room and just go, 'You write that fucking article now!', and pull out a record and just slam it on to my lap and tell me to start, and I'd be all, 'Tom Penny did a kickflip and everyone cheered' and then eventually end up with 16 sheets of A4 and he'd be like, 'Is this everything? Has it got titles? Has it got headings? Have you done the captions? Yes? Right, now fuck off', and he'd give it to this woman to type up, then it would go to the repro house – I didn't even take an interest in how that worked – and then the magazine would come through and they'd be like, 'That picture's a bit dark... Didn't realise the type wouldn't show up there... Fuck it', and we'd be halfway to doing the next one anyway.

Mon Barbour

They moved to Oxford, next to SS20, and it was such a laugh. It was mutually beneficial too, they'd get sent all this product to put in the mag and they'd bring it in, like, 'What can we get for this?', and we'd be like, 'You can have an eighth for that, a quarter for that'. Nothing was ever bought with money, it was all just hash.

→ **STM MAGAZINE**
Ben Powell

I went into *Rollersnakes* one day and Rob Johnson said they were all leaving to go and do *RAD* and that I should ask to get a job there, at *Rollersnakes*. So I went and spoke to Leigh Haynes and he said I could have a job.

Because they weren't doing *System* anymore, because they'd left to do *RAD*, he got me and Johnny Morrow to do *STM*, the paper zine, as a sort of addendum to the mail-order catalogue. It was fun to do and we'd just fuck about. There's stuff in it that was just a case of, 'Right, it needs finished in half an hour, so let's spend half an hour on it'. That's just a traditional route into doing a magazine isn't it? Doing a fanzine. *System* turned into *STM*, because they didn't want to carry on calling it *System* because that was the name of the magazine but *STM* basically is *System*, isn't it? Just written a different way.

Paul Haynes

STM was a small venture, and it was just a case of printing a few things and doing a few t-shirts, so I headed that up. We had staff in the shop that would help out, so it wasn't a major thing. It was just an ancillary business just to keep things interesting. Boards were still very expensive so we could see a market there; Joe Burlo was bringing out Big Spin, and Panic, so we wanted to compete in that market, the £30 skateboard deck. We did it so it could be our brand and we'd control it and it wasn't a massive revenue earner but it kept us in that kind of area. →

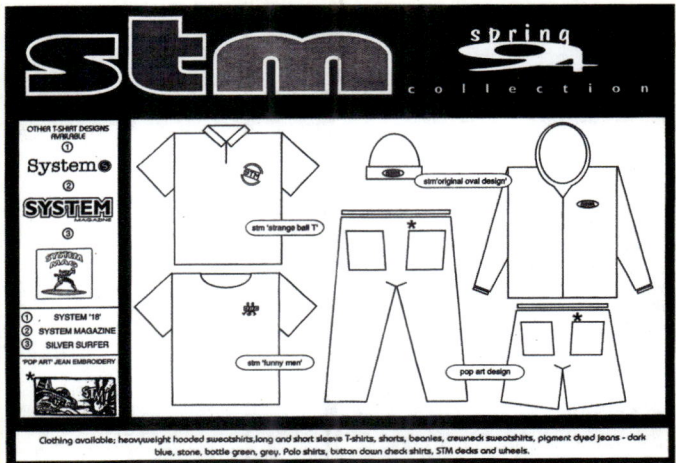

Panic

Alvin Singfield

I went to Joe with the idea for Panic. I said I wanted to do what Mike Ternasky did with Plan B and I wanted to get the best guys that we had on the other brands – be it the American brands or Big Spin – and start a British skateboard brand. It was very blatant with that first ad[2], and I'd asked Mike if I could do it and he'd laughed and said 'yeah'. It didn't quite have the same impact of having Tony Hawk and that on it, but I liked the idea. I liked the idea of having a team, and that was always what was important to me. To show them as a team. You had all these guys that were sponsored in Britain but none of them were a team. You had all these guys like Arron Bleasdale and Mike Manzoori who were super amazing but they all rode for American brands.

What I wanted to do with Panic was a truly British brand, and not just a brand from London, and the only skater that was on Panic from London was Paul Shier, and that's Croydon. My first pro was Matt Pritchard, who's Welsh, my second pro was Colin Kennedy, who's Scottish. That was always my thing about having a truly British brand and that's why when we did our demos and tours we went to skateparks that nobody else ever bothered going to because I felt that everybody was going to the same skateparks and doing the same demos. In my opinion, one of the downfalls of Blueprint, years later, was that they stopped doing demos and being out and about with the British skaters. Then when they brought in the American guys, it was alienating.

Matt Pritchard

I used to have a pager, I never used to have a phone in my house, and Alvin would page me and I'd give him a ring from a phone box outside my house. One time he

was telling me they wanted to start a British skate company, and it was going to be called Panic and I'd be the first pro. It was fucking insane because I never dreamed that I'd become pro.

I remember working in a factory at the time, and I used to fucking hate it, so I could leave my job and I just fucking skateboarded for a living, which is fucking ace.

Pieter Janssen

If it wasn't for Mike de Geus I probably never would have went to the UK, because my nature – and my nickname – is Parra, which is for 'paranoid', so I wouldn't dare to take that trip on my own, but he was more adventurous. He said he knew everybody, and I just believed him, but he didn't think it through at all because we were going on the Christmas holiday. We didn't realise that the UK takes Christmas pretty seriously.

We arrive and ended up at around Fairfield, freezing cold. Paul Shier was there and we asked him if we could stay with him, and he's like, 'No mate, it's Christmas. What are you thinking?' Then we went to Southbank, just to find people, and we ended up splitting up.

On the first day I was with a guy who lived in a council estate, and he didn't have any money so we would get sandwiches from Pret A Manger, because he knew that around 7pm they would throw all the stale sandwiches out from the day, and we grabbed that bag and that was our food for the night. I asked him how he paid the rent and my mind was blown when he told me the government pays the rent.

Dan Magee

Panic started with Matt Pritchard, Jon Hayward, Selley, me, Piers Woodford and John Cattle – and then I got Paul Shier on – that was all Alvin's original distributor

crew. Joe got John Rattray on, Joe was the one that wanted Rattray.

Milton Keynes became the meeting spot when Alvin started to do Panic. I don't know why it was never London.

It's very hard to not be critical of Alvin because at that time he had a fucking crazy reputation for being affiliated with Joe because people didn't like Joe as a distributor, and he was one of those guys that had a lot of bullshit chat. Even before I met him he had a rep.

His influence is very much prevalent and I wouldn't be here now if he hadn't given me the chance to run with what I did. He did give me my first hook-up too, even though it was the worst fucking shit. Faze were very forward-thinking and they would give free stuff to people even if it was just giving some people one or two World boards or whatever.

Clean skateboards had just come out and Joe was distributing them, and me and Rob Selley wanted to try to get those boards because Big Spin was shit. We asked Alvin and he went, 'What if... Imagine there was a company and it was all British riders. Would you be interested in that?' And we said yeah. That sounded pretty cool. I was genuinely stoked on that idea. And he mentioned Plan B because he was obsessed with Plan B. He pitched it like that, with it having all the best riders in the UK. I was into it because I didn't want to ride for Big Spin but it was a kind of sick idea.

Everyone was hyped on it but as soon as he told everyone the name, everyone was fucking bummed. I remember that was a big thing, but he was going, 'No, we can make it good!' That's why it was PNC. Like MNC. Everyone was kind of hustling to try and make it not 'Panic'. It was meant to be like, 'When you see this team coming you will Panic!' Fucking hell mate. →

FROM LEFT
[1] Dan Magee, Liverpool Street, by Nick Hamilton
[2] Panic announcement ad, RAD, November
[3] Matt Pritchard, Milton Keynes, by Wig Worland

SIX OF THESE SKATERS ARE GOING TO LEAVE THEIR CURRENT SPONSORS TO FORM A NEW COMPANY

MATT PRITCHARD   SEAN WARD

SAM SILVERSTONE   JOHN CATTLE

DAN MAGEE   COLIN KENNEDY

GREG NOWICK   PIERS WOODFORD

JOHN HAYWARD   ROB SELLEY

PAUL ROBSON   FLYNN TROTMAN

?

1994

No one was down for a British company, really, at all. Even with Death Box, people weren't all about it, were they? They did a really good job of what they did but it wasn't like everyone was all about Death Box and rode the boards. People would be like, 'Oh, Death Box have got Alex Moul, he's sick', but they wouldn't really be buying his boards. People wanted American stuff. Even when Flip started.

There was a bit of a weird Faze/Alvin stigma which all stemmed back to some age-old distributor beef with Brand-X or Jeremy Fox or something. I can understand it because it's Joe and he did kind of rub people up the wrong way in terms of distribution and stuff. I don't know what the beef was but somehow Alvin became part of that and was this Essex loudmouth. I did love Alvin – we used to hang out all the time – but it was a weird throwback and I'm sure Alvin didn't help it.

There was this thing where we were always fighting Joe's shit ideas, and fighting Alvin's ideas. Even if you had one good idea, they would always have another really crap idea that would cancel out the idea you had.

Even when we started Panic, production was fucking awful. We didn't have boards, so at one of the first Radlands comps, Alvin got Selley to hand-paint the boards, and Pritchard's idea was to turn up dressed as the Little Chef. Pritchard was the sickest rider at the time, but to me, that's anti-publicity. If everyone's kooking you, and Pritchard's dressed as the Little Chef in a comp run, that doesn't make the company cool. It might if you're Death or something but not when you're trying to do a different kind of brand.

So we turn up with our hand-painted boards and Pritchard dressed as the

Little Chef, and Don Brider had made a sick fucking screenprinted Panic board – because the name's got out because Alvin's got a big mouth or whatever – that was a hundred times better than any of the boards that we had. Sick shape, sick graphic, sick screenprinting. And as we walked in to Radlands, he's holding it up showing it to us, and we're just little kids wondering why this guy's being lame to us. I don't know the backstory but he was always quite gnarly to me because of my association with Alvin. They'd just be lame to me and vibe me out.

Starting a new UK company was tough enough, but walking in there with a bunch of fucking Tipp-Exed boards and Don Brider's there in the entrance laughing at us... I can remember feeling so shit when I saw that. It was full fucking hate-mode and I don't know if it had a lasting effect on me but if that stuff happened today you'd get cancelled for sure. It would be a massive thing. I was a quiet kid but so many things happened that made me go from being a quiet kid into just being a cunt.

Rob did the first Panic boards, and I guess they were supposed to be like World boards or whatever. So instead of the Chico Brenes Travelodge, you had the Little Chef. That's the reason why they had that. Experience had a Gap board and a Banana Republic board, so that's why you had the United Colors of Benetton. Rob used to always wear United Colors of Benetton tops for some reason, and that's why that board was so small because it was meant to be Rob's board. The Celtic Dragon must have been Alvin's, because he was always about seeing something and ripping it off. Finding some clip art and ripping it off and making it. There was another one with

a centurion's head on it, which is literally from the signs they had when you drive into Colchester saying that it's a Roman town or something like that. They were on clear wood and they were screened at Chicken's print shop, but the way they were made up was so bad. They were hand-drawn, and on United Colors of Benetton, the 'O' was like a potato-print 'O'. It was so bad. Another thing that Alvin and Joe fucked up, because they faxed over the shapes, is the Little Chef came out like a bent dagger. The shape was ridiculous. Now if you got that you'd fax them back and tell them that that isn't the shape, but what I was told was that because there was this beef with Death Box and they were good friends with Chicken's, Deacon and Fox went in there, saw the boards, fucked with the shit and got them to make the boards and send them back like that.

Ian Deacon

I was actually working at Chicken's. I could see us definitely fucking with the Panic boards, let's put it that way. I'm not saying we did it, I don't know if we did it, but I could see it. Just because of the whole Alvin thing with trying to steal Tom. It could have happened, it could have not happened, but I feel like if Jeremy was there and saw that, I could see him maybe putting a spanner in the works because he was really good friends with the main screenprint guy. It's definitely feasible. It wouldn't have been me but I wouldn't deny it. Alvin fucked that whole thing up.

We thought it was funny that as soon as we left England, Burlo started Panic. That's what it felt like. We didn't have a problem with Blueprint, it was just Panic, because as soon as we left, Burlo started Panic. It was like, 'So if we stayed, you wouldn't have started Panic? Is that how it works?' ●

FROM LEFT
[1] Ronny Calow with Panic Benetton board, by Richard Stainthorpe
[2] Panic Little Chef board, hand-painted by Rob Selley
[3] Dan Magee, Cantelowes, by Nick Hamilton
[4] Second Panic ad, RAD, December, photo by Alvin Singfield
[5] Pieter Janssen (bottom right) with London crew, by Mike de Geus

MATTPRITCHARDPETERSWOODFORDJOHNHAYWARDALVINSINGFIELD (TEAMMANAGER) DANMAGEEROBSELLEYJOHNCATTLE

PANIC

RAFE HALL · PEBMARSH · HALSTEAD · ESSEX CO9 2NS · TEL : 0787 269000 · FAX : 0787 269888

1994

Ian Deacon

Everyone knew db was Death Box, but it was kind of neutral. Jeremy was talking to people in America because it was supposed to move in '93, and it was going to be funded by Watson, but then Watson decided to do Maple instead. Beggars couldn't be choosers at that time, because skateboarding was pretty screwed. Per Welinder wanted to expand Birdhouse Distribution, and he started talking to Jeremy, so we went with Birdhouse, luckily, in '94.

Geoff came with Jeremy and myself. We arrived June 30th 1994, and I think I was there two or three weeks and then Radlands and Münster were happening, so I got sent back to meet up with Rune, Andy and Tom, to do Radlands and then we drove in Dennis Atherton's car to Münster, and Wingy took his van.

We went to Amsterdam and they had the Amsterdam vert thing, two days in between Radlands and Münster, and there was always a vert demo there. We slept behind a Heineken factory one night, in the cars, then we went to the demo the next day.

We went to Münster the next day and we parked in some field somewhere, on the way, and then in the morning someone – I don't know if they were Dutch or German because I didn't know where we were at that point – came out with a shotgun and chased us out the field. I think we just slept in the grass with sleeping bags.

We only had US work visas at this point. Jeremy and I got E2 visas – foreign investor's visas – and then Geoff and Tom, because they were 'essential employees' got E1s, because we were investing in America, basically. Fifty per cent of the company has to be owned by Americans or something, and the other half could be owned by whoever, and you have to invest. It wasn't like there was lots of money, but Per could show that he was going to buy all these skateboards and do all this stuff. The plan was sold, it wasn't like they said they were investing a hundred thousand dollars in Flip, it was that we were part of this business with Per Welinder and Tony Hawk originally. We were all 25% each. You had to present the business plan, basically.

When I went to the States in '94, I went to an early IASC-type meeting in that weird spaceship restaurant at LAX, and I fully got into an argument with John Falahee there. He was saying how brands weren't legitimate unless they had their own wood shop or something, and I wasn't having that at all. I'd just moved to America, I'm not having this guy try and fuck with my shit. My whole life is here, I've put every last penny into this, it was all or nothing and no one had done what we'd done before.

The quotes[1] were all real. *Transworld* and *Big Brother* knew we were doing that, because we were getting boards from Rocco, from Prime. We'd go to the *Big Brother* office a lot, because Per was good friends with Rocco, and Tom would shoot with Kosick a lot.

Ed Templeton laid some ads out for us as well, because Ed had a computer when no one had computers because Macs were super expensive. A Mac printer was like ten grand or something stupid and you had to get everything drum scanned.

Geoff had the *Transworld* cover in '94 but I don't think anyone realised who he was. It was weird, it was almost too soon. If Geoff had that cover a year later it probably would have made a lot more impact. It was so crazy what he did at that time, and doing it in three tries or whatever it was, that they just had to put it on the cover. He wasn't even riding a Flip board, he was riding a Hook Ups board with a Street Rod sticker on it. We didn't even have boards at that time.

Darren Howman

The Girl guys were ripping into Tom Penny's style at Radlands in '94. They were all in a little huddle, and definitely Chico, definitely Mike Carroll, and a couple of others, were really taking the piss out of his style, and Eric Koston was the fucking worst. Koston's a fucking knob, he was a fucking dickhead. They were basically standing at the side, mimicking Penny's stance, all bouncing off each other like stupid lemmings. It was like a high school clique of jocks.

Tom Penny

I don't really notice things like that, I don't really pay attention. I only look for the good things. I'm not the type of person to say anything bad about anyone, but I don't think they did, to be perfectly honest. I don't remember them saying anything to me. I didn't hear them say anything. I always got on with everyone from America that I met.

Pretty much every one of the skaters at that contest, I'm friends with them now and we all get on really well. I think that was just confusion. Plus, it's all fun and games; people make fun of each other all the time, if you're with your mates. It doesn't really make any difference and I don't really mind. ●

FROM LEFT
[1] Flip US introduction ad, *Big Brother* issue 13
[2] Tom Penny, Radlands, by Wig Worland
[3] Tom Penny ad, *Big Brother* issue 14
[4] *Transworld*, November, Geoff Rowley, by Dave Swift
NEXT PAGE
Danny Wainwright, College Green, Bristol, by Wig Worland

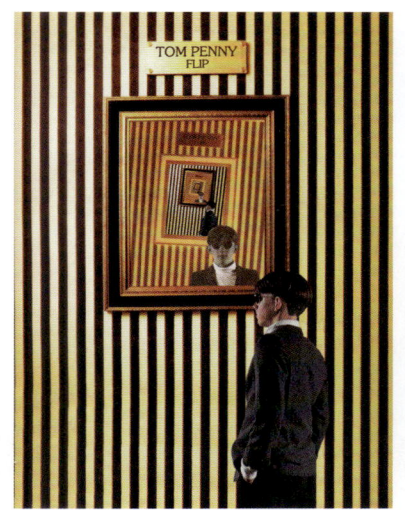

Elsewhere

Danny Wainwright

I called Shiner myself, and spoke to this bloke who dealt with sponsorships, because I needed stuff. He said he'd speak to somebody, and he called me back one day and he said I could get boards from Shuvit, this sister brand that Vision did at the time, or he could give me Powell stuff. Powell is not the coolest brand in the world, especially back then, but it's not like they were a fly-by-night brand that was going to disappear, so I was down to get some Powell stuff.

I started doing better, getting coverage in mags and doing well at contests and whatnot, and then Todd Hastings, the team manager at Powell, hit me up. I got a phone call from him in California and he said he wanted to bring me out, and check me out. So I was like, 'Fuck, OK. This is crazy', because I was about seventeen.

George Powell was an amazing bloke. His decisions about keeping me on Powell, and paying me, changed my life. I remember being at Powell one time, and going to his office and telling him I needed to make some money. I told him I was selling bits of weed back home to survive, and I wanted to do this skateboarding thing, but if I can't get paid I'm just going to go home and carry on selling weed. It was weird talking to George like that, but I was open and I just told him. In his office he'd have mellow jazz playing, and his Labrador, Bones, would be there. He said he'd sort me out and he'd give me a couple hundred bucks a month, just so I had a bit of money in my pocket. I wasn't pro and that was back in the day when amateurs didn't get paid.

I bypassed the whole Euro scene, I went straight into going to the States. It wasn't 'til later that I got more into going to the Europe scene.

We did an ad[4], and Cab weren't there for it at all, they Photoshopped him in. If you look at the jeans, both those pairs of jeans have the same creases. They just put him in by magic. I remember seeing that ad and being like, 'Wait a minute, Cab weren't there'.

There was the Mike Manzoori photo at Kennington, and it said it wasn't a make, and it said, 'We want to get Danny Wainwright down there', and that was like a red rag to a bull for me. I got there and I was like, 'Woah, fuck, this is gnarly'. Joe Habgood's like, 'Fuck off, just do it!', and I'm telling him there's no way I can do it. It was scary. We were stood there at the roll in, and I just pegged it at it, and flew over it and took a slam. Joe's like, 'Yeah, see, it's easy. Come on.' Joe used to egg me on to do shit like that. So then it was like, 'Right, fuck it, let's get it'.

Harry Bastard

I loved skateboarding and we did it all the time, but I never thought I was any good at it. Then I sort of realised, especially after we'd went to London quite a bit, that the people from the *RAD* days that you thought were amazing skaters, were actually pretty shit. People like Curtis McCann and Mike Manzoori were obviously amazing, but there were a few who I was just like, 'Really?', not to diss anyone. That was when I thought that I could actually make something out of skateboarding.

I had Tom's Super Nintendo and it got nicked. We got robbed one night when we lived in that house [in Oxford, working for *RAD*], and I was a computer game addict, so at that point I was like, 'You know what? Fuck this. I'm going to try and make something out of skateboarding.' I was already getting flowed little bits of stuff by god-knows-who back then, and that was when I could live off £100 a month, because I wouldn't pay rent and kip on people's floors.

Mark Channer

Ray really hated the blank boards and white shirts thing, and for that photo[5] I repped. New Deal shirt and New Deal hat. If someone's giving you free shit, you should put it on. Be savvy. I remember overhearing Ray once saying, 'If you scratch my back, I'll bend over backwards to scratch yours', and that really stuck in my head. The day that *RAD* came out, Ray took me to the product bit next door, at Harrow and just loaded me up with t-shirts and boards. He didn't take it lightly that I'd done that.

I saw Ray punch a guy in the face and throw his bike out the park once. I think the guy was graffitiing in there and the council were giving the shop heat about it. So I'm under no illusion of what they're capable of. ●

Curtis McCann

When I first started skating, I did find it easy because I wasn't really scared. After BMX and breakdancing, it was one of the first 'mainstream' things I wanted to do, so yeah, I did work hard at it. Obviously, after a few years of skating hard every day, injuries like a broken leg made things very difficult... however, I was definitely a 'gifted' skater in the sense that within a year of skating, I was sponsored by Mud Machine/M-Zone, which let me, and motivated me to keep skating, learn new tricks, get more sponsors, and go places... those were the days where we felt like just by being on the Greater London travel map, we felt safe, we could get home!

I broke my ankle at Wallenberg in San Francisco. It was my own fault cause I really was not in the zone. I was determined to ollie the stage steps even though the school gate was not open... because the gate wasn't open it meant getting speed, and foot placement in time was a real issue, plus I was wearing fresh day-old shoes. I tried it countless times and finally cracked my ankle; thankfully, my ankle didn't 'roll' and damage the ligaments and the crack was basically painless, but I couldn't walk on it. Luckily there was a hospital just across the road, so I sat on my board and was rolled over. There the hospital put my ankle in a plaster and told me not to put weight on it, and gave me some crutches and codeine... the following Monday I had three screws put in my ankle... that weekend I hopped around a rainy San Francisco in plaster without my crutches. That ankle injury was the real beginning of the end for my skateboarding... I struggled on and the following summer I went back to NY and within weeks decided to stop skating and hang out with kids!

I had a crazy time in New York! I was immature at 20 years old... and had so much fun. I'd had dreams of going to New York since being a *Sesame Street* fan as an infant... and soon after arriving I met the friendliest girls that let me stay with them while their mum was on holiday... it felt like being an alien on another planet and although I was painfully shy '40oz' bottles and the kids really made me feel wanted. I was getting over a broken ankle, so my focus was less on skating and more on drinking and smoking 'blunts'. I remember rough, London-like skate spots and beautiful parks, we were buzzing around the place with red eyes at all hours of the night... the days and nights were humid... and surreally electric. One of my funniest memories of the trip was going to Coney Island beach to swim and stay the night on the beach. I remember I was trying to talk to this insanely pretty girl who I couldn't take my eyes off, and to cut a very long story short, someone stole my drying shorts while I slept, so I had to spend the next day walking around Coney Island in some tacky-print open-front boxer shorts!

Although I then thought I would skate forever... when I gave up skateboarding it felt like the right time. Injuries and a type of mental fatigue were the reasons I stopped... I just skated too hard!

In my days I would twist an ankle and try to skate it off twenty minutes later... it might sound obvious now but my advice to myself then would be to take your time, rest properly, and then you might not need to stop at all!

Jeff Pang

Luckily we were on the same team, so that's how Curtis and I connected. He was the most genuine, sweet, loving, kind, supportive person that I've ever come across. When he came to New York, the rough New Yorker skate scene totally accepted him and embraced him and he won over all the skaters, everyone on the downtown scene. It was a tough shell to crack and Curtis just danced his way into everyone's hearts. It was a great time.

He was such a positive being and it shined through in his personality, his face and his skateboarding. Everything he did was just so cool and smooth and stylish. And beautiful. It was a beautiful thing to witness.

When he left New York it wasn't as if you thought that this person was not going to be a part of your life for the rest of your time on Earth. He left, and his body left but his energy stayed behind. It was around the time of the movie *Kids* being filmed and there was a lot of shit going down around Curtis, and he was just one of us. He was one of the people on the scene in New York from the jump.

Alex Moul

I was trying to have an actual teenage year, and be an actual boy. Every weekend I was at a demo or a contest, and all my mates at school were going out and meeting girls and I wanted a little bit of normality. Getting into DJing was access to that world, which was nice, and I got a job in a record store.

The magazines were slagging me off too, like the 'Abingdon's Techno King' thing, and there was bad rumours. I went to Southbank and some kid asked me if I had any pills. I was like, 'What, no!', and he went, 'Everybody knows you need two pills to even get up in the morning'. Scamp went to Northampton after I hadn't been for a month or something and someone went, 'Sorry to hear about Alex', because they thought I'd died of a heroin overdose.

There were all these rumours, and you had to wear the 'right' gear, and that wasn't skateboarding anymore, to me. So I'd just skate with my mates when I wanted to. Probably like how Tom felt, with all the pressure later on.

I started writing tunes, and DJing in clubs, and I started getting recognition for that, and I had a steady girlfriend and we had a house with a mortgage and all that stuff. Then, full-circle, I started to miss skateboarding. ●

FROM LEFT TO RIGHT
[1] Abingdon rave flyer featuring Alex Moul as Moul-E
[2] Moul-E and Lucida, Aquarius/Above the Clouds label, Code-001 records
[3] Alex Moul DJing, Oxford, by Andy Horsley

1994

Chris Hamer

What we were doing on Tib Street, this streetwear thing, nobody could get their head round it, and there weren't enough people buying it to keep us going, really, but it looked great and it was right. I remember getting Zoo York through Slam, when Slam first brought it in, and Supreme when Michael Kopelman got that, and Bathing Ape, plus I was bringing in stuff like Champion and Carhartt and Dickies and adidas and Nike and North Face and Ralph Lauren, all the hip-hop-led stuff, myself from the States.

I was grey importing most of it, unless a distributor ever got it. Russell at Slam, and Sofia and Paul, they had our back and they were really fucking cool. Joe Burlo and Faze 7 were pretty cool. New Deal were alright but in my eyes – they were rudeboy plasterers who got into making money from skateboarding. But Gimme 5 got it and Slam got it. There were very few people doing it back then, and it was really difficult to keep the business going, but what we were doing was bang on.

Manchester was rough, and I'm this little white guy with some proper heads stepping to me. I had one guy come in and say they wouldn't rob me if I gave them money, blah blah blah, and I told them to go fuck themselves, but we had guns pulled on us a couple of times in the shop. It was twice with guns, once with a machete, once with a baseball bat and numerous times just violence. I had a gun put to my head in my house, when they tried to raid my house because they thought I had all this money because the shop looked good. Rik Cooper opened the door to them, totally innocent. 'Chris, there's someone here asking for you!', and this guy balls in with his mates and pulls his gun out.

I came back from Chicago with a shitload of really good stuff, ready for Christmas, and guys came in with guns on the Saturday morning and took nearly everything I'd brought back, and ran off down the street with it. It fucked me, that one. I really struggled to bounce back from that because I'd borrowed the money off some dickheads to buy the stuff in the first place.

Rik Cooper

I ran the skate shop downstairs for a little bit. We had a pool table down there and there were some dodgy guys coming in and out. It didn't last that long because people just weren't ready for it. The two or three years later there were quite a lot of shops selling all that stuff, and they've all done really well, but sadly for Chris, it was just too soon. ●

"We had guns pulled on us a couple of times in the shop. It was twice with guns, once with a machete, once with a baseball bat and numerous times just violence."

CHRIS HAMER

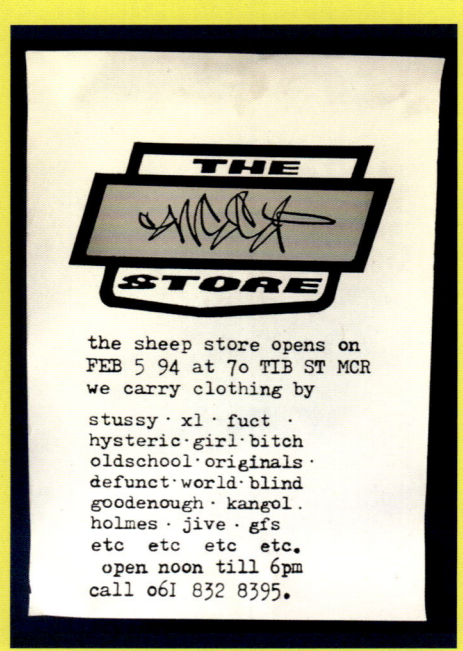

Fos

Superhero basically came from me not relating to anything that was in the shops at the time. I'd go to Slam, I'd look through all the t-shirts, and I wouldn't like any of them. None of them spoke to me, it was all very logo-heavy and there was no fun in it. None of them had what I wanted. I was into comic books, Japanese Manga – the weird monsters, not the girls and all that – and stuff that was outside of just skateboarding.

I met my friend Hiro Nakata and he gave me skate videos from Japan, and toys that he'd brought over, and he really opened my eyes to more things out there. I had my love of American comics and I'd grown up reading *2000AD*, and those were the things I was into, and not just whatever skateboard t-shirts were in at the time, so I started making my own t-shirts.

We were just having fun and we never ran one ad. It was word-of-mouth, it was literally people walking into a skateboard shop, looking through the t-shirt rack and going, 'Fuck, I like this one'. That was all we had going for us, so there had to be something that they related to, in order for them to want to buy it over the thousand other t-shirts. Something worked. We ran it for a good few years and we just had fun doing it.

It was in Slam at first, and they loved it and they sold a bunch of it, and then I made a t-shirt that said, 'If you don't skate, don't wear our fucking clothes', because everyone was wearing skate stuff and I just thought it was a funny statement t-shirt. And then I think a couple of people there who didn't skate took offence to that, and didn't order any more from then. But it was in Slam for a while and it was in other shops in London.

Oliver Payne

I was 14 or 15 and I read a thing in *i-D* magazine about a clothes shop in Soho called Acupuncture, and it looked amazing, so I went down there that weekend and pretty much immediately got myself a job as a Saturday boy. It was a punk secondhand clothes shop and people would just hang out there all day, it's where I met most of my formative friends. No one was from London; this was one of the first times I was meeting people from all over the country, and from other countries.

One dude that was hanging out was a skater from Rawtenstall, in Lancaster, and that was Mark Foster, or 'Fos' as he's known. With an 's' as opposed to a 'z'. You'd hear his friends from up north call him Fos, and not 'Foz' as everyone in London would call him.

He was basically just skating and being sober, and into milkshakes, junk food, horror films, comics and stuff of that nature, he was great. I used to skate a lot with him and he really encouraged my shit, weird, not-trying-to-be-cool-and-trendy skateboarding. He had his own little bedroom t-shirt company at a time when that was a really exciting thing to do. It was rarer than it is now, and it took a little bit more back then to be like, 'I'm going to make illustrations and graphics and buy t-shirts wholesale and find a screen printer and sell them to shops'. Obviously you can fucking do that in your lunch break now.

Hiro Nakata

It was our first week at Goldsmiths College in New Cross in 1993, and I was minding my own business, walking to my studio in a Blind hoodie. Suddenly, someone shouted from behind me, 'Hey, do you skate?!' This was when I first met Mark. He could spot the smallest Blind logo on my chest from a distance. The man is a true skateboarder. ●

1994

1995

Alan Rushbrooke, Beeston, by Wig Worland

There was never a moment in my whole youth where I wanted to be sponsored for skating. That was something that just didn't come into your head, you just skated.
 PAUL SHIER

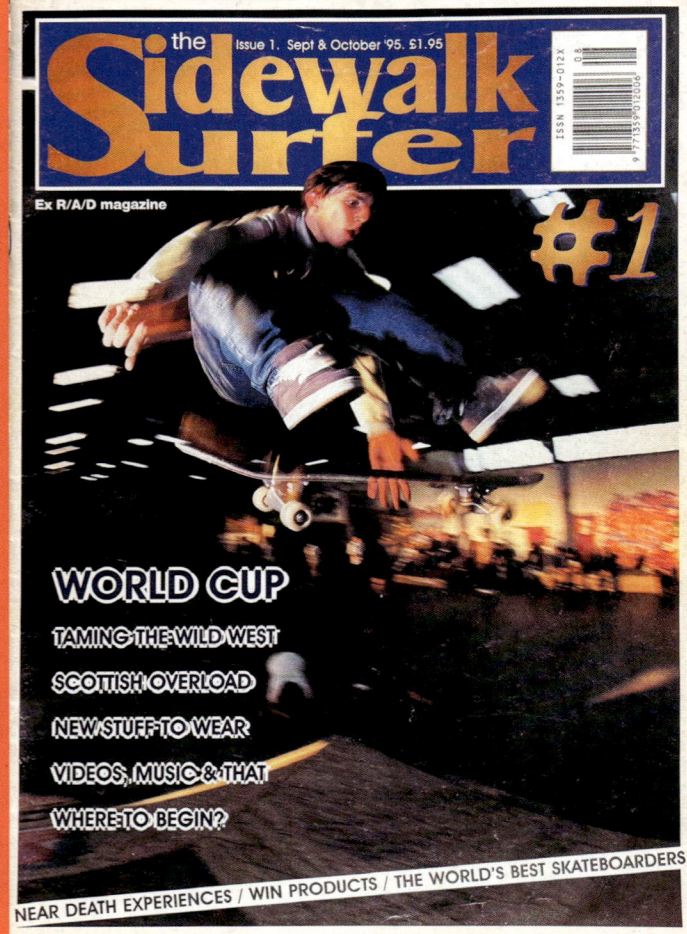

Elsewhere

FROM LEFT
[1] STM zine *Sidewalk* announcement cover, Simon Evans, by Wig Worland
[2] *Sidewalk Surfer* issue 1, Tom Penny, by Wig Worland
[3] Ben Powell and Alan Rushbrooke, Wakefield, by Wig Worland

SIDEWALK
Andy Horsley

We needed a new start, because it was a whole new thing. We had 'Ex *RAD* magazine on the first cover'. We sat around the kitchen table in the house that we all shared – me, Harry, Jonny Robbo, Chris – and we went through reams and reams of ideas for a name. It's weird because it's a shit name. 'Sidewalk Surfer' is fucking awful, but we came to the conclusion that if you're in Smith's and you see it, it's like skateboarding at its very beginning, harking back to its core. That phrase means skateboarding, full stop, nothing else. It can't be construed as anything else. It's not like 'Document', Document could be anything. This was before we had any competition or anything so it was like, 'Fuck it, let's just do it'. I messed about with that logo and it looked better than it sounded, because of that font, and it all fitted together with the 'S' so we just went with that.

It really was the wild west, we had no one checking it. When we got interviews faxed to us, and we had to type them up, we'd give them to the receptionist lady who was like 65 years old, and she would type it up but she would swap all the swear words out. She'd change stuff to 'bugger', or 'rotter', because she couldn't bring herself to type the words, so we'd have to go through it and change all the swear words back.

We weren't 'Fuck London', but we were definitely, 'London can chill because it's had its exposure for so many years so let's go elsewhere'. Jim Peskett bought us two Vauxhall Astras – Wig had one and I had one – and we had a credit card for petrol so we were instantly like, 'This is great, let's go!' During the time of the first five or six issues, we'd almost met everyone in the entire UK because it's not like we would be staying in hotels, we would sleep on everyone's floors. We'd get pissed with everyone and we were instantly mates. We'd go to Scotland, meet everyone, come back down and then the people from Scotland would come and stay with us in Oxford. It was somewhere else to stay. Whisking the soup, bringing everyone together. We weren't only going to do stuff with the 'cool' people.

We were living the dream as well as recording the dream, because we were just skaters too. We would go skating until three in the morning at a carpark just up from the house and the we would get up and go somewhere to shoot photos, then we would come back and go skating again.

Without Wig, *Sidewalk* would have just been *System*, in a way. He kind of made us grow up. I didn't shoot photos – and I wasn't even interested in that – until the end of *System*, really, because I was always with Wig. I thought it made sense for me to try to learn to shoot photos so I could help fill the mag.

When Ben came to work for us, he was the brain, he was the encyclopaedia that we needed. We were the ones who'd go out and skate and fuck around but he had the knowledge and he knew all the long words so it was like, 'OK, you do this'. If you look at the amount of words he wrote in the mags, as a designer it was a nightmare because everything had to be reduced in size. 6-point text. It was fucking mad.

Ben Powell

The reason I know Andy Horsley and all that is because I used to go into Non-Stop and into Rollersnakes because I lived in Nottingham, and I think me and Brad Garner ended up going to Radlands with Horsley, Harry, Oliver Bradley, Jon Robson and a bunch of other people, and Harry did a double heelflip over the hip at the pyramid which was pretty good because all I'd ever seen him do before was scream and snap boards. It was like, 'Oh, he's really good! He's not just a noisy bellend.'

From that I got friendly with Horsley and that, and I guess that's why they asked me to do stuff. I was the dude at Rollersnakes who they'd ring up when they had two blank pages and needed something doing.

The first thing I did for Horsley and Wig-era *RAD* was the thing about that skatepark in Bradford and that was them going, 'Fuck, there's half a page left', so I went to Bradford on the bus with a disposable camera and took some photographs of this tarmac thing and wrote some shit about it, so they had something to put in there.

Wig Worland – obviously, being Wig – had amazing contacts already in all parts of the country, because he was the guy who'd been shooting forever. Horsley's a really likeable dude, isn't he? I've never met anyone who doesn't like him; it's impossible to not like the dude. So he just got stuck in straight away, and when people meet him they want to hang around with him so it was maybe easier for them to approach people and get content because people liked Horsley because he was funny and everyone knew Wig, and he was a fantastically good photographer so people wanted him to shoot photos of them.

Sidewalk from the outset was financed by Jim Peskett. The publisher basically putting his house up as collateral. We did favours, like Rollersnakes got preferential rates because of the existing connection between everybody who went on to do the mag and because we'd only really been able to do it because of Paul Haynes, and he spent a lot of money as an advertiser anyway. Mon and Sean at SS20 got mates' rates because it was Oxford and that was our local shop and they were our friends.

It was kind of anarchic, but we'd all come from shitty jobs really. I was lucky, I worked in a skate shop, but I think the rest of them might have been on the dole or whatever, and then all of a sudden we're being paid to do a skate mag.

Apart from Wig we were all from shitty northern towns so the fact that somebody was paying us to do something that sick meant that we were really proactive. Yeah, it was disorganised and none of us knew what the fuck we were doing, but it was a big cultural responsibility. Perhaps more for me than anybody else because I was so into magazine culture, reading Steve Kane and TLB and Gavin Hills and all that.

It was just like, 'OK where's nobody been for ages? Nobody's been to Scotland. Let's go to Scotland.' There were no shoe companies funding anything and we didn't have an expenses budget for about the first 25 issues so we'd just get in someone's car, drive to Edinburgh, stay on someone's floor, go skating, come back and there you go. That was how you did it; it wasn't like it is now where you have to have 40 meetings with a load of knobheads who work for the shoe company before you're allowed to do anything, you just did whatever the fuck you wanted.

In terms of feature articles it wasn't consciously not-London but it was consciously going to places that it felt like didn't get a lot of coverage. That 'Joyriders' video is a good example of this; people were doing insane Simon Evans-level shit in somewhere like the Elswick council estate in Newcastle in '91 but they weren't getting any coverage. Or they were but it was in *Skate Action*, which hardly anyone saw, unfortunately.

I mean, I wrote letters to *RAD* and to *Skateboard!* as a kid going, 'Why the fuck is there never any coverage from Yorkshire?' just like people wrote in asking them why they didn't come to Ireland or the Isle of Wight or Glasgow or wherever. So because we had a magazine to fill every month we'd go to the fucking Isle of Wight or to Ireland or to Glasgow.

The other thing, from a magazine point of view, was that if you went to Southbank or wherever, the people there were used to getting coverage, whereas if you go to fucking Barnsley or Arbroath or wherever people go absolutely mental and destroy themselves because no one's ever gone there before. Which, cynically from the point of doing a magazine, makes it a piece of piss because you turn up and everyone in the scene comes out and does the best thing they've ever done because they want to be in a mag. That's how you fill a magazine. You open the opportunity book. 'Come on Tommy Ten-Balls, let's see what you've got'.

My approach to it was very much influenced by Steve Kane. He was preaching that kind of *Sniffin' Glue* ethos in skateboarding. Do it yourself, make your own shit, fuck everyone else... I think, culturally, we were a bit closer to that than to what Tim and Nick Philip were doing – and not that we didn't like that because we fucking loved it – but you can be interested in going to Barnsley without being anti-London.
→

We had a magazine to fill and if we go to London people maybe can't be arsed because they don't know who we are, but if we go to Plymouth people will end up in hospital, do you know what I mean?

Paul Silvester represented the reason why *Sidewalk* needed to exist. Some dude who didn't speak, who lived on 9p noodles and literally lived in a cupboard who doing switch 5.0s down handrails pretty much before anyone else but didn't have any sponsors.

I went to film him one time and he said he didn't have a job, so he didn't have money and he didn't have any shoes, so he couldn't come out his house. So I went home and got him a pair of shoes that didn't even fit him but he put them on and came out and did something bonkers.

There was maybe a class aspect to it too, which I didn't consciously see at the time, but that was there. Think about your Ben Leydens and your Stu Grahams, people like that, they're working class as fuck in an industry that's inward-looking and only looks at one place because that's where all the brands are and that's where everything's happening. Them people are never going to get a chance, are they? Fuck class prejudice, but those people's potential to shine is circumscribed by their class to a certain extent, and I was a little bit tinpot-Marxist at the time.

Horsley won't have conceived it like that, he'd have just thought, 'I'm a scruffy bastard from up north so let's give some other scruffy bastards a chance', which is essentially what it was.

And that's not anti-London because there were working class people in London; it was just easier to do it in other places because people were more keen because they'd not done it before. It's quite easy to get free stuff now, or cheap stuff or whatever, but there were people – like Paul Silvester – who literally could not afford to go skating when they were skating on

a level where people should be throwing free shit at them. But there was no industry.

I wrote stuff from the very start. I think I've got the first article in the first issue and then I had articles in every issue. When it started saying I was 'Assistant Editor', that's when Jim Peskett asked me to please send some fucking invoices in and I started getting paid. Because prior to that I just did it all and didn't think about invoicing because I was just stoked to do it and it didn't cross my mind that I didn't get paid for it.

The issue of *STM* with Simon Evans [p.236[1]] was a precursor to *Sidewalk*. The cover date is after the first issue of *Sidewalk*, but that's Horsley – there's three issue 64s or something – and I'm pretty sure that was created to say, 'This is what we're doing', and it was sent around to skate shops.

Mike Manzoori

There's something magical about Wig Worland. Every time we go out together, it's like a good curse. It's frickin' nice. I've never met anyone that makes you feel so chill. I know he wants to get something done, we all do; when you're out shooting with someone you want to come home with some goods, obviously, but he never makes you feel like it's a, 'I've come all this way, let's see what you've got', kind of thing. You just feel obliged because he's so chill. I think that's the most comfortable I've ever been with any photographer.

Some of the days out I've had with him are some of the most epic I've ever had. Like, 'Holy shit, I did all of those in one day?'

There was one day I met him at Harrow and we got that frontside pivot in the halfpipe; doubles with Matt Anderson over the hip; I got an ATM ad in the streets of Harrow ollieing off this little bank over this handrail/corner situation; we went into town and I got the front cover of *Sidewalk* front boarding at Southbank; I got a Sheep shoes ad ollieing over a Hubba at St Paul's;

and I got a contents page in *Transworld*, wallriding. All in the one day. I'd go out with him and be like, 'Damn, this guy makes it so fucking easy, and a good laugh'.

Pete Evans

One time in the *Sidewalk* office Ben was feeling a bit aggrieved, saying, 'Man, people are always writing in saying "Why do you always feature your friends, it's never anyone that you don't know".' And Ben just said something like, 'I would like to imagine that anyone could be my friend, so it's always going to be our friends. If we're not friends and we do an article on them, by the end of it they probably will be.' I remember thinking what a nice way that was of framing it, and what the scene was about.

i-D

Alex Cock

We were in that same magazine as the Panic guys. I always read *i-D* and *The Face*, because I was absorbing the music and the fashion shit, so it was rad being in that. That was our pinnacle, being in some non-skate media.

People definitely took us more seriously after that. We sold to people like Simon Porter, who had Fly on Kings Road. There was a couple of shops where they were the first true British skate/streetwear shops. This early photo-streetwear stuff that was coming through. Some towns we'd go to, there wouldn't be a proper skate shop there, so we'd try and find the shop selling hip-hop stuff, because there was Spliffy and Dready, and there was rave clothing.

Seb Palmer

That *i-D* was crucial, where they were all lined up. That photoshoot was great. They're pushing Droors big time, and they've all got the first DCs on, and they look like skaters. It's a really well-composed photo; there's a hat backwards on the left, a beanie, Magee's holding his hat and his eyes-to-camera is great there. Just all the details. ●

FROM LEFT
[1] Panic team, *i-D*, February, by Andrew Montgomery
[2] Alex Cock and Phil Penwarden of Siesta, *i-D*, February, by Donald Milne
[3] Mike Manzoori, Southbank, by Wig Worland
NEXT PAGE LEFT TO RIGHT
[1] Mike Manzoori, London Wall, by Wig Worland
[2] Matt Anderson and Mike Manzoori, Harrow, by Wig Worland

1995

Elsewhere

1995

Andy Coombes

The Fleapit used to print t-shirts, and Robbie Reid said I should do a t-shirt. So I copied the Blockhead 'Nothing Is Cool' t-shirt because I always wanted that shirt and I could never find it. I used that graphic and stuck Lord on it. It's a great graphic from Blockhead so not surprisingly, it sold well.

So I'd sold jeans and t-shirts in The Fleapit, and then my twin brother Nick said, 'You should do a t-shirt that says "Tiny Penis" on it.' I had a random call with Stu Dawkins who owned Backyard, the skate and BMX shop in Hastings, and he said he'd heard I'd been selling some bits in The Fleapit. I told him that Nick said I should do a t-shirt with 'Tiny Penis' on it, and he said, 'Cool, I'll have ten'. So I was like, 'Well, fuck it, I'll print it'.

It was just a copy of the 'Ravers Suck' shirt, which was pretty popular at the time. A week after I got them printed, I was doing an interview for *White Lines*, a snowboard magazine, with the Beastie Boys, and I happened to have the t-shirts with me so gifted them some Tiny Penis t-shirts.

Somehow, the Tiny Penis got featured in *i-D* magazine, which had nothing to do with skating and was very much fashion and trend driven. I called them and asked if I could get a credit for the t-shirt, and the guy went, 'Oh yeah, we've been wondering who you were', so I told them I had a picture of the Beastie Boys with it, and they asked me to send that in and that really was a turning point.

The band Green Day wore the Tiny Penis. Fatboy Slim called and ordered some jackets for Skint Records. The Beckhams were in *Hello!* magazine with Lord hats, it was all quite funny. Nowadays if that happens you've blown up, you'd be way bigger. You'd go viral. I never thought I was making a brand but that's what had happened. ●

"I never thought I was making a brand but that's what happened."

ANDY COOMBES

Seb Palmer

I always wanted Sumo to be the best-looking shop. I went to New York in '95, and Supreme had started but it was really basic. The only thing that inspired me from Supreme was the TVs in the window, and them being a brand. At first they were just a shop with a skate team, and everybody had skate teams; it wasn't a phenomenon but we all just loved the name and the cleanliness of the Kruger font.

Autechre have various sub-names, and they did a record as Gescom. On one side it says 'Go Sheep' and the other side says 'Go Sumo'. They were customers but they didn't even know us that well, they just made a love letter with that EP.

They had that record 'Bad Vilbel', and Bad Vilbel is the twin-town of Glossop. When you drive into Glossop you can see that, and they were driving between Manchester and Sheffield all the time. I went on to live with Rob, and became very good friends with them both.

Steve and Rob from Warp Records were phenomenal, and the guys that worked in the shop there were obviously customers. Until they moved to London, Warp were big supporters of us, and so were Designers Republic. The skate shop was in the centre of all those things.

We went to Warp and said we wanted to do a Sumo Warp t-shirt and gave them the sketch, and they said that Ian Anderson should do it, so Ian at Designers Republic did the graphic[2] for us and we made it reflective on a black t-shirt.

I was super into EPMD, and what's different about this[3] from other people who ripped off that logo, is that this works correctly because the U goes into the space, like the P drops into the space. We only ever did it in the colours that were on the records – we're purists in our detail –

but we also met Eric Haze and talked to him for a long time. I said we were going to rip off his EPMD logo and he said, 'Go for it. I ripped off Delicious Vinyl from Delicious Pizza, that's all part of what we do in our culture.' It was a super nice conversation. There was nothing legal, and he didn't own the thing, but it was the blessing of doing it right.

There were a lot of people whose first invoice was to Sumo. Ben Weaver, Sam Ashley, French did his first exhibition at Sumo... I like to think we were connecting people and giving people their break.

Someone once wrote on the front of Sumo, 'Feng Shui Knobheads'. I always wanted to do a t-shirt of it. There was a rival crew in Sheffield; they were the rockers and we were the hip-hop kids. That became the guys that did The House, and they've outlasted us all. It's like Nick Zorlac at Power – Nick's the rocker, and all respect to him and Cates and their crew, because he's outlasted everybody else.

Slam was pretty organised, even if some of the stuff was hard to get, but some of the skate stuff was really hard to get through Faze, and I think that's why they lost brands, but I've got a lot of time for Alvin Singfield. That's a good guy with a good heart. He wasn't the coolest, with his ponytail, but Alvin was on our side at the time. He knew what was up. Dan Magee was just like us, but everyone has somebody who supports them, and enables them to get to that situation, and that was Alvin to Magee. As much as he'll bemoan it, Alvin was probably driving him around and facilitating everything. Alvin had a heart, and a love for skateboarding and you've got to give him that respect.

Magee is clearly a genius. He was a fast talker and really good on a skateboard as well. ●

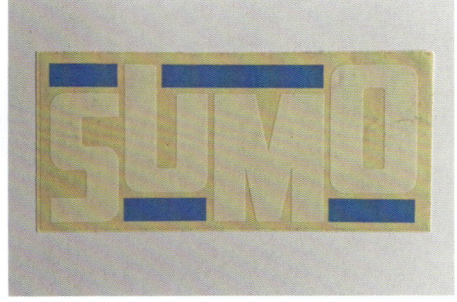

1995

Dan Magee

I can remember going into Slam and all those Panic boards were in the bargain bucket and this dude was taking the piss and laughing about them when I went in. He said he was sorry and he didn't mean me to hear all that stuff but it was like going to the skatepark and somebody slaying you. That kind of vibe. People thought it was a bit shit, especially people in London.

Blueprint came out of me kind of throwing my hands up and going, 'This is not going to happen, I can't change it and they don't want me to change it', and seeing if I could convince them to start a sub-company even though I wouldn't get anything financially out of it, but at least we'd have good boards to ride.

That was why we had to split it, because of all the fighting against other people's ideas. It's not because we hated Alvin, we loved Alvin, but we had to let him and Joe Burlo do their thing and if we had ideas to do another thing... That's why we needed to do Blueprint. I still had to ask Alvin, I still had to pitch it, and I was still at university, but Alvin convinced Joe to do it, which is kind of crazy that he did. Convincing him to set up a second company at the same time is kinda mad.

There was another breaking point as well, when he went to Clintons Cards and picked out some fucking greetings cards – one was jumping frogs, one was a dancing hamster, one was aardvarks – and just got someone to redraw them really shitly and screenprinted them on boards. It was that level of production. And he kept that secret until they were made, and it was like, 'Here's your boards'.

We really cared about making something good, but what's the point if someone's ideas are not good ideas. We wanted to try and do something else, me and Rob Selley. Alvin could still be sorting out people's packages and stuff like that, he could still be part of it that way. It was like, 'You do Panic, and I'll do Blueprint, but you're still involved with it'.

It's hard to talk about the history without talking smack on Alvin but in the beginning it was a fight of ideas, and they did some really stupid things and there was a stigma harking back to old distributor stuff, but Alvin was very much instrumental in setting it all up even though his ideas weren't very good. I wasn't creative; I was just a kid who'd gone to college, but the thing was that I'd moved to London where you would get the shit ripped out of you for riding those Panic boards.

You've got to remember that a lot of people had been kind of left by the wayside, where they'd lost their distributor deals when Panic started. Ed Loftus and all those dudes who went out to America to ride for Experience or whatever had got on direct. Simon Evans had gone, Matt Stewart had almost given up skating, Loftus was in San Francisco... Even though in your head you think that those were guys who skated for years and years, people would give up and they'd give up very quickly, and a lot of those guys – Jonny Wilson and people like that – were like, they skate, and now they don't skate. Winstan Whitter still skated a little bit, Jagger, who was on 101, wasn't really part of that crew but by then he was living in Chicago and down with all the Antihero guys.

Alvin Singfield

Blueprint didn't come out the gates successful; Panic for a long time was by far the bigger brand, and the segue of those two changing places happened over time, it didn't happen over one phone call or one discussion.

A bit like with Panic, it was a bit of a hard sell. People didn't really go for it initially. The thing that made Panic and Blueprint a success was the tours, the demos. Having something tangible. It wasn't like having an American brand with an American pro you were never gonna see.

I wanted Panic – and Blueprint – to be a national company, and that's why Matt was pro from Wales and Colin was pro from Glasgow and John was pro from Aberdeen and Paul was pro from London. It wasn't like the Six Pack from Southbank, it wasn't just, 'Here's a group of friends who skate together every day'. Those guys didn't even know each other, really. It was me bringing them together, going out doing demos and tours and filming for *A Mixed Media* that they all became – I would like to think – close friends.

They were definitely clearly defined in my mind; we wanted a different aesthetic for Blueprint. Blueprint moved through several different incarnations of what it was actually called. At one point it was The Blueprint 216 Project, then it was The Blueprint Project... Me and Dan Magee were both into this sort of Masonic/Illuminati graphic stuff, and obviously Flynn was seriously into that stuff, and that's why a lot of his graphics were very Masonic-y.

From the off we wanted a different aesthetic for it, and that's something that Dan 100% delivered, on everything. That was always going to be his thing; he would ride for Blueprint but he was always going to be the artistic mind there.

Over time Dan became more and more involved. He was at college and doing this outside of his college work, and then he finished college and I managed to talk Joe into paying him – not a lot – so he could do stuff for us, and he had to do →

Blueprint & Panic

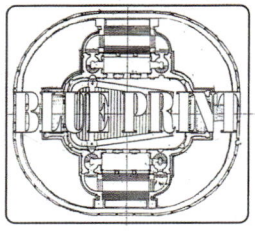

Elsewhere

other stuff for Joe as well, like lay out all the adverts and that kind of stuff. Me and Dan both got Macs, but Dan being the way he is, and mentally inclined that way, took to it a lot more than I did.

Pete Fowler

The first graphic I did for Matt Pritchard was the guy in the shell suit. That was the era of getting shit from scallies in tracksuits, so it was a pisstake of that. Everyone loved it and I was so proud because I'd seen Pritch come up from being this shy kid to just destroying spots.

I was really tight with Pritch, and he was aware that I was doing artwork, and at the time I was just doing a graphic for my mate. Matthew liked my work, I was part of the skate scene and we were good mates, so I was like, 'Yeah, of course I'll do your graphic!' I didn't get a board and I don't think I got paid but I was just happy to do one. Pritch didn't even get many, I think he got two in each package from Joe, and he'd go through boards quite quickly, as you'd imagine, doing massive stairs and stuff. He owned that double set at Milton Keynes.

Colin Kennedy

Alvin invited me down to one of their Faze 7 team-meet things where it's all the people that were on their roster of brands and you spend a weekend in Milton Keynes, which was their hub of skating. I shot an ad down there, but I'd already travelled around the skateboard circuit quite a lot by that point, whether it was Wakefield, Northampton, Sheffield, all those places.

I got on with all the crew, whether it was Selley, Cattle or Pritchard, and I was ambitious. I wanted to keep going and make something happen, and it went really well in Milton Keynes, and when they started Panic they made me a part of it.

Mark Baines

Paul Shier was quite instrumental in picking who was going to be on Panic, and he actually said he didn't like the way I skated – he said something about my style – so thankfully I didn't get put on Panic, and I was part of the better thing that came later.

Paul Shier

There was a Wakefield contest where there was the Faze 7 ad where it said, 'Class of 1995'. I skated the contest and joint-won the best trick contest with Neil Urwin, and he won a Stüssy t-shirt and I won the Mad Circle video, 'Let The Horns Blow', and we swapped because I wanted a Stüssy t-shirt. Then I asked Alvin if I could be on Panic, just asked him outright, and he said no, straight to my face. So then I drove home, back to Croydon, and didn't even think about it.

I don't know, but I assume Magee must have said something, but I didn't really know Magee at the time. I knew him from Southbank, but I got to know him when I skated for Panic, because we all skated for etnies through Faze.

So then I didn't ride for Big Spin anymore, and I rode for Panic. I don't think there was even a question asked. I got sent a box of boards from Alvin, and it was after the Little Chef board, when they made a board that just said 'Panic 95' on it. They even had a t-shirt to match the board, a Panic 95 t-shirt.

There was never a moment in my whole youth where I wanted to be sponsored for skating. That was something that just didn't come into your head, you just skated. So when the Big Spin thing came round it was sick, and I thought it maybe was a thing. And after the Panic thing started, it just completely changed. It was one of those Radlands contests that I went pro for Panic. Alvin phoned my house and he goes, 'You want to skate the Northampton contest?', and I said, 'Yeah, but it's a pro contest and you've got to be pro to skate it', and he said, 'Do you want to be pro then?', and I'd been on for a month and a half or something.

I wasn't into the board at all, the graphics were terrible. My first board graphic was obviously already done, and they added my name or something, but it was three kung-fu dudes and my name and I've never liked kung-fu in my life. They were all pretty bad, but it was that thing again, when it's free skateboards, so do I really care that much? Magee cared. I just got on with it. Colin was the only one who had a good graphic.

Alvin came to Croydon and he shot photographs, and he shot a sequence of me doing a back tail on a ledge and that was my first Panic ad. A sequence that had no roll out, it just had me landing on the board. And it was leaves on the page, just leaves and a tiny sequence at the bottom. When the ad came out I was stoked to have a Panic ad, but it kinda sucked. The ledge looked small, the sequence ended on me landing on the board and there was nothing past the land. →

Elsewhere

YOU BET!
Colin Kennedy

In those times you were chasing after any opportunity to do something, or any sort of vehicle to get you to London by train rather than having to take the National Express and pay for it yourself, and *You Bet!* was one of those opportunities that came through Joe. Me, Matt and John agreed to do it, and we did get paid, and at the time it was probably pretty good, like £300 or something.

Matt Pritchard

They had the skate course made, and they told us what they wanted us to do, and we're like, 'Yeah, fucking cool', and we did a few warm-ups and we fucked up a few times. I remember when it came to actually doing it they asked us who wanted to talk, and of course me being shy as fuck, I was like, 'No chance, I can't talk'. I was petrified, literally petrified. When it came to the actual shooting you can just see I'm there with my head down, and John Cattle agreed to talk.

When we got to do the actual challenge I never fell off once, which is unbelievable because I was so scared. How I didn't come off, I don't know. Cattle had a fucking nightmare, but we managed to do it. It was just fun, it was a great experience, and Cattle did a really good job of talking, considering none of us wanted to talk.

John Cattle

This is my weed-smoking time, but my happy weed-smoking time. So, we get there, and Jet the Gladiator will not shut up about how dangerous *Gladiators* is, and I'm just trying to get my head in the right place. I'm a bit stoned anyway, and she's talking too much about that, and I want to get a practice in. We do the routine perfectly, and no one falls over. And then Darren Day – I don't know if he's spotted that I'm the weak one, or the stoned one – comes up to me and he goes, 'Yeah, just keep doing what you're doing, this is great, you're going to be seen by ten million people'. And my brain just visualised ten million people because I was so stoned, and it just broke me and my legs turned to jelly. And then, 'Here we go, here's John and Colin and Matt', and off we go... I like to think I added drama to the situation. If we'd all done it too easy it would have been boring. ●

LEFT TO RIGHT
[1] Paul Shier, Croydon, by Wig Worland
[2] Colin Kennedy, Shepperton Studios, by Andy Horsley
[3] Matt Pritchard, Darren Day, John Cattle and Colin Kenndy on *You Bet!*

Sharon Tomlin

There was always drama between different skaters. It was like running a school, trying to manage all of that, and the fallings out, while taking crap myself. Certain skaters would think they were part of the gang and they'd be in the shop expecting to meet everybody, but I'd know that they'd already been in and were all, 'He's coming, let's all go before he gets here'. You know how it is; it's skating in the '90s so everybody talked shit about each other. I shouldn't take it personally because they were not only dicks to me but to everyone else and to each other as well.

I always felt like I had something to prove but it was kind of a waste of time because it never got to the point where anybody said I did a good job. I was always looking for some validation that never came. People, would be all, 'Yeah, you think you're all that, working there'. Are you kidding me? The only thing that kept me going was, 'I'm going to fucking show them'.

Matt Sherman

With Slam it always amazed me that it was as successful as it was as a business because just so much shit got pilfered from there. Just incredible amounts. My best friend Ben used to work there on the weekend and it was quite near Southbank and it was good to street skate round there, so I'd do a lot of hanging out on Saturdays in Slam, just being obnoxious, I think.

I remember being in there one time and Björk came in there with Tricky, and I really don't like the music of Björk, and I was being a knob. I was just making snide comments about Björk with Björk in the shop and I remember her just going, 'Let's go somewhere else where the people aren't knob-ends' or something, and I look back on it and I'm not particularly proud of my behaviour, I must say. How Paul Sunman

allowed it... I mean I'm an economics teacher now and I look back on it and if that was my business and I had kids in there doing that I'd kick 'em out, but he never did. He just let us get on with it, it was amazing. What a dude.

Paul Sunman

We launched and supported a number of standalone brand names across hard goods and clothing and they all had varying outcomes, but in nearly all the brands were the driven and visionary individuals who created or managed the brand. Some of those people are still at the forefront of their brands today.

Sofia Prantera

I was folding t-shirts in the warehouse, which was not what I came in to do, and that probably lasted a few months, and then that's when Russell said we should start something else, and we started thinking about Holmes.

Because we had the distribution of so many other brands at this point – there was Fuct, X-Large, Foundation, Poot, X-Girl – we had so many people coming in, and we were getting invited to all the parties. It was a real golden time. We knew that we had a captive audience and we knew we could start something.

There was a conscious decision at this point by both me and Russell not to be at the beck and call of a graphic artist. We didn't want it to be linked to one specific person because I think when you're a vehicle for someone else's creativity, there are a lot of problems, so we thought we would work with lots of different people because there were so many interesting artists coming in. It was the merging of two different passions: logo culture, which was more like merch that people were making, merged with my passion for making clothes that were interesting. There was no vetting process from Paul at all, because we were

a fairly successful business, so it was not questioned. Whatever we were doing must have been OK.

Paul was really computer-savvy from early on, so he got me a computer and I learned to use Illustrator, Photoshop and InDesign – which was called QuarkXPress – in the mid-'90s because I was sitting there drawing by hand and Paul said, 'You know Sofia, you can use this program to do it'.

Russell was very price-conscious, and realised that you needed to make margins. Paul was also using FileMaker Pro which was kind of an early version of Excel, and I designed a production program on it.

I would get into the Yellow Pages and find someone that would make army stuff, and I found someone in Salford who was working for the MOD, and they said they could make army pants, and then we'd find someone that makes the next thing. So we would buy the fabric and work with factories that were specifically good at one thing, and I think that was an approach that not that many people in fashion were taking. In America the quantities are greater so you can afford to be a little slack, but we had to run a really tight ship.

I was really good with relationships with the factories; I made sure they got paid and I made sure they were making stuff that we could sell. The growth of what we were doing with Holmes was very organic, so we would buy, say, 500 metres of fabric and then we would make 200 pairs of trousers.

I also worked out this way of making womenswear by putting it into the same production chain as the men's, but doing a shrunken version. The same with a skirt, you'd ask the factory if they could make that as well as the pants, and I still use that system now, with Aries. Russell and I were really conscious that the stuff had to be commercially viable. →

LEFT TO RIGHT
[1–11] Holmes garments
[12] Holmes ad, Sidewalk, September, by James Jarvis
[13+14] Holmes zine by Russell Waterman and James Jarvis
NEXT PAGE TOP TO BOTTOM
[1] Paul Sunman
[2] Lizzie Finn, Ben Sansbury, unknown, unknown and Russell Waterman
[3] Stuart Horner and Sofia Prantera

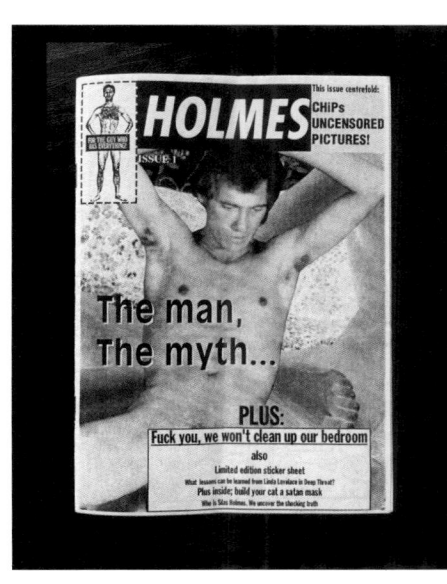

Russell Waterman

Paul gave first opportunities to a bunch of people. Will Bankhead, James Jarvis, Fergus Purcell, people that have gone on to be really important culturally, Paul gave these people opportunities to do ads for Slam and Holmes and stuff. Paul is so important and really undersung, and he's never going to big himself up about all that stuff, about what he did. He gave a lot of people opportunities and I'm always going to be thankful to him for that.

Holmes came out of bad stuff. It came out of a falling-out between Ged Wells and Slam, for various reasons. It was a shame that fell apart, but for me personally, there were positives in the collapse in the relationship as the new direction we went in changed my life.

What had happened was that we were left with an infrastructure to make clothes and produce stuff, but no graphic artist and no figurehead. With Holmes, Sofia Prantera and I spoke about it and then persuaded Paul that we didn't need to bring in a graphic artist for it because we knew enough people to do graphics. We had contacts everywhere from doing Insane, Sofia could design, we had our factories so we could create a concept ourselves and design our own clothes and it could work.

It took some persuading. Paul, at first, wanted to bring in a new graphic artist – a new figurehead – so hats off to Paul because he let us go and do it, and it worked. We knew enough talented people that at the time were at college, people like Ben Sansbury, James Jarvis, Martin Wedderburn, Fergus Purcell, Lizzie Finn – all these people that were around that were doing their thing, and Sofia was really talented, as an up-and-coming designer.

What was left was the concept, and Silas Holmes was the concept. This was at a time when X-Large, Fuct, all that East and West Coast US stuff was blowing up and no one was interested in anything from the UK. It predates stuff coming out of Japan, so it was all about the US. We came up with a concept where Silas Holmes was this character that we'd met in the US, he wanted to do a clothing company and we said we'd do it for him, and it was him that was giving us the inspiration and the designs to produce Holmes. We'd constantly refer to Silas Holmes, and we made up a backstory for Silas Holmes and we stuck to that concept.

James Jarvis

Russell said they weren't doing Insane anymore, and they were doing a new brand called Holmes, and he asked if I wanted to do something, so I did a t-shirt graphic. It was pretty much exactly the same with Fergus; we were lurkers in the shop. We were different because we weren't the same as all the skaters. The skater kids who'd hang out in the shop were a bit younger, and wanted stickers, and me and Fergus didn't really fit in, but that kind of made us cool. We were drawn to this thing and we wanted to be involved in any way that they would allow it, and it was just serendipity that they were starting this label, and it was carte blanche to do something.

Sofia was very approachable, and I kind of 'got' Sofia, and Russell was mildly terrifying: he was older, he'd had kids, which seemed like the most insanely grown-up thing, and he knew about shit. He knew about music, he knew about literary culture – not just Bukowski and JD Salinger – and he knew about politics and anarchists and philosophy, so I was kind of scared of Russell. Sometimes we'd have conversations about something like Iggy's mixing of *Raw Power*, and the fact that I knew about the different iterations of The Stooges meant Russell was a bit, 'Oh, he's not just one of Sofia's fashion friends'.

People make jokes now about bringing back gatekeeping, and at every stage of all these things, from going into Rough Trade to buy a record to going into Slam and asking for a sticker or buying a board, there were people quietly vetting you, somehow. Subtly. In some ways I feel like that was great and I kind of loved it because if you passed the test and got to the next level, it meant something. Especially with skateboarding.

Slam was my 'in' and what kind of made me legit. Paul saying, 'Yeah this guy can do our adverts', was a big deal. I realise that now, because I wasn't so aware at the time.

I became friends with Sofia and Russell, and working for them was just fun, and the fact you got paid was a bonus.

I got paid some money from Holmes, but it wasn't 'I'm making a living!' money. But it was a paid job because Holmes was a business. I was doing t-shirts, and then they said they needed to do a catalogue, and they wanted me to design the catalogue, and that was the first time I got to do a job where I was doing everything – the illustration, the art direction... I took photos of all of the people around Holmes and Slam – so Sofia, Rachel who worked for Slam, Luke Davidson, Chris Turner, Ben Sansbury – in the Holmes clothes and I redrew the photos with my weird minimalist characters, but more humanoid than the characters people know me for now. Then I put them in the catalogue.

I didn't quite know what I was doing, but it was at this point where I had to work out what I was doing because I'd been asked to do this job, and it did kind of force me to go, 'Well, how do I go about making artwork and graphics that are mine, and relevant to the wider world?'

They had this weird story of it being the wayward brother of John Holmes, the porn star, and in my prudish way I was always a bit uncomfortable with that, being brought up quite right-on. That was another of the things that was quite scary about Russell; he was quite open about things whereas I would be quite reserved. I think the backstory was because they wanted it to not be about them, which, in retrospect, is a really brilliant thing. It's become part of the template of DIY brand-building, and artists do it as well. I can see why you do it, because it gives you the opportunity to stop it, and move on to something else. As my career's progressed I've wished I had a nom de plume for different things, so that I could retire that persona and be whoever else next.

Holmes had been explained to me and it had this energy in making a company that people don't understand now. To be somebody from Russell's background, and start a clothing brand, was sort of revolutionary, it was subversive, and it doesn't seem subversive in any way now.

Russell and Sofia are sophisticated people, and I don't mean that in a wanky way. They know so much cultural shit. Sofia is so cultured, she knows a bit of Latin and she's really well read. Russell's incredibly well read but Sofia's knowledge of fashion is also amazing, so you met these people and although you could talk to them about William Burroughs, they could also talk about John Galliano and BodyMap and Katharine Hamnett. That's a cliché now, but it was refreshing for me and it wasn't as ubiquitous then to have people who could reference high and low culture at the same time and not apologise for it.

For me, I was boiling down all these things that I'm into, and obsessed with, and trying to refine them so that they can somehow function in my world, which Russell described as me trying to 'minimalist' it, and reduce it to an essence. In the Holmes era, *The Face* era, I wasn't conscious of the stylist decisions I was making, I was just doing stuff because that was how it felt I should be doing things.

In terms of being a participant in the energy of London in the early '90s, I think the period was really interesting in that you didn't know what you were doing, you were just reacting to opportunities.

People would have to contact me on my pager, and having that was obviously inspired by Kareem Campbell in '20 Shot Sequence'. The first graphic I ever did for Holmes was me learning to use vector graphic software on the computer, and I did a really technical drawing of a pager that said 'Live the fantasy'. It was 'Live the fantasy' because of lyrics like, 'Fucking with me 'cause I'm a teenager, with a little bit of gold and a pager', and I was that middle-class kid driving around in mum and dad's car playing NWA. It was excruciating but I loved that shit. It's that thing of loving the culture and wanting to celebrate those things, but I knew I couldn't participate because I wasn't part of that culture.

Sofia Prantera

We'd been featured in *The Face*, and we got approached by fashion TV to do a fashion film. We ended up renting this open-top bus and getting all our friends to come wearing Holmes clothes, but it was raining so everyone had waterproofs on – which were from outdoor brands and not Holmes – and it ended up being complete carnage and the TV guys never talked to us again. I always think the footage must be somewhere. ●

Elsewhere

1995

Elsewhere

Ali Cairns

I was living with the Flip guys, and there had been a tour that I went on, the first US Flip tour. Shortly after that there was a demo at this Lollapalooza rock festival thing in LA, and there was a guy called Chris Robinson there who used to skate with Allen Losi for LSD – a really nice person, and he died a few years ago, he fell down a glacier – and he was just filming that day. He took the footage back to his friend John Lucero and he was showing him, and Lucero told him to give me some boards and get some more footage. He'd told Skip Pronier, so Skip brought some Black Label boards from Lucero for me at the Flip house. That was my first eye-opener that people get given boards from a distributor in their own country and they actually think they're on the company, and then they go out to where the company is and they've got absolutely no idea who the person is. So it came full circle and in the end I actually did get Black Label stuff from Black Label.

Jeremy Fox had taken the same footage to Blitz, where Flip was, and Birdhouse, and Hook-Ups, and they all looked at it, and Per Welinder said he was going to ask me to ride for Birdhouse.

I didn't have any money, so Jeremy had hooked me up with a job in the warehouse, shrink-wrapping wheels, and Per came down from the offices and said, 'Do you want to ride for Birdhouse?', and I said yes. When I next came back I had all Birdhouse stuff, and I skated Radlands, but all I wanted to do was get back out again because I was on a skate company

then. Bucky Lasek had hooked me up with Airwalk as well, so I had a bit of money.

There was a lack of communication, there were no mobile phones or email then, and I went back to the Flip house and the Flip house was gone. There was nobody there. But by then I knew a few people, and I knew Ed Templeton, and I knew where Ed lived. Ed was always really nice to me, so I thought I'd go round Ed's house because it was only up the road. I asked him where everybody had gone, and he told me Jeremy had moved down the beach, Tom lived with Muska somewhere, Rune was somewhere, but Andrew Reynolds had just moved in up the road and he'd give me a lift round there because I was probably supposed to be staying there anyway.

Andy Scott

It only became a hassle when I actually did move to the States. I was doing gardening with my dad at the time, for my grandad's firm, so I was making good money, whereas through skateboarding I couldn't. I think I got one cheque, one month for $20, so I couldn't live off this. We had somewhere to stay, but it was tough back then. There wasn't that many boards selling, I don't think, and we were just doing our thing and we were all struggling at the beginning.

I was 19, so I couldn't legally drink. I'd been going out to pubs with my mates, and then you go to America and you're treated like a kid again, so it was a bit weird for me, all that.

I went out there with Ali Cairns when it first started, and we didn't really have anywhere to skate. The nearest ramp was in San Diego and we had to travel a few

hours to get there, so that was a bit rubbish. We'd just be skating street all the time.

I was probably the last one to go, and with everything happening so quick, I guess Ali was kind of just expecting me to be there.

I missed home a little bit. I had loads of friends over here, and we had a place to skate – we had Wakefield at the time.

I just didn't really vibe on the scene over there. When I was out there, there wasn't really anything happening. There was no X-Games or anything, we'd just be doing little demos at festivals and stuff like that. The scene was just dead.

I was there for three months then back for three, then I got the six-month visa but I'd come back for six just so it didn't look sketchy, but you never really knew where you stood, legally. I wasn't really getting along with that, and I just never went back one time. Jeremy said that if I did want to go back, he'd be there for us and look after us.

There was no pressure on me. He said I could always get stuff, but I kind of needed to be in America to make a living out of it. When I came back to England, that was it. It just kind of fizzled out.

I was still working for my dad, gardening, when I came back, but it wasn't long after that that I started working at the park in Bolton and I was doing little bits with Dave Arnold, building skateparks and stuff like that. Then I was making a living off of skateboarding, from competitions. I was getting paid to go there, then I'd win a little bit of money. Doing vert demos were quite a good payer too. ●

Radlands

Damien Ince

1995 was so special, the way Tom just blew everybody away. Probably a lot of the pros that were there in '94 were there in '95 as well, and it probably was a bit of an 'Up yours' to all of them. Or maybe not; Penny was just skating. It was just what he did all the time anyway. He was so nonchalant it was as if he wasn't even trying, or doing anything. It was just the way he was. He'd do a run like that anyway, so for me to see it, it was just like, 'That's just Penny', in a way, but everyone else wasn't seeing it all the time, were they? That was the typical thing he did; he'd just show up and do something absolutely out-of-this-world amazing.

It went wild in there. It was probably one of the best atmospheres ever, in there, I would say. That moment was... I don't know. It was like Jesus had just risen from the dead. It was that amazing. I don't think anything else has ever been that good in there. I was still blown away, even though I'd seen him do stuff like that every week.

Sean Goff

Tom won the contest, and when we came back he just left the trophy in the car. We put it in the shop, and asked him about it, but he just didn't care and it ended up being the pen holder in the shop. It ended up covered in ink, with bits of broken Biro in the bottom, just there because Tom left it. It just happened to be from the biggest European contest that year, won by a local kid. ●

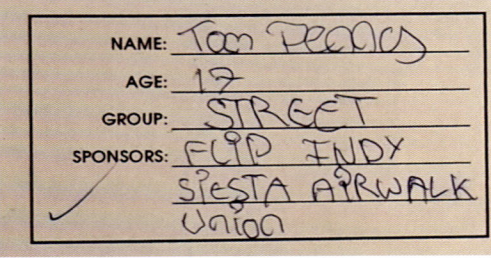

MiniDisc Radlands British Open Skateboarding Championships 1995			
SPONSORS :- SONY, FAZE 7, NEW DEAL, SHINER, VANS, SLAM CITY, NSK-RHP			
		STREET	STREET
COMPETITOR'S NAME	SPONSORS	SCORE	PLACE
TOM PENNY	FLIP	289	1
RAY BARBEE	THE FIRM	279	2
ED TEMPLETON	TOY MACHINE	276	3
JAMIE THOMAS	TOY MACHINE	272	4
PHIL SHAO	THINK	264	5
TIM BRAUCH	SCS	262	6
ERIC KOSTON	GIRL, ETNIES, ORION	261	7
GEOFF ROWLEY	FLIP	257	8
TONY HAWK	BIRDHOUSE PROJECTS	255	9
BOB BURNQUIST	ANTE HERO, SPITFIRE	251	10
TOM KNOX	SONIC	249	11
MARK JOHNSON	MAPLE	247	12
ETHAN FOWLER	STEREO	246	13
ANDREW REYNOLDS	BIRDHOUSE PROJECTS	242	=14
RICK HOWARD	GIRL	242	=14
WILLY M SANTOS	BIRDHOUSE PROJECTS	242	=14
GERSHON MOSLEY	POWELL	240	17
MOSES ITKONEN	MAD CIRCLE	239	18
SIMON WOODSTOCK	SONIC	236	19
EZEQUIEL FALCON	METR, RACE, STAR WEAR	230	=20
CLYDE	101	230	=20
RICARDO CARVALH	CORPORATION	228	22
STEVE OLSON	FOUNDATION	221	23
KEITH HUFNAGEL	REAL	219	24
CHRIS PASTRAS	STEREO, THUNDER, VANS	216	=25
LANCE MOUNTAIN	THE FIRM	216	=25
JAYA BONDEROV	ADRENALIN	214	27
JEFF TAYLOR	RHYTHM	213	28
MIKE SANTAROSA	POWELL	212	29
KAREEM CAMPBELL	WORLD	207	30
CARL SHIPMAN	STEREO	203	31
GARY CHEVALIER	INSANE, KRUX, DEAD END	168	32
SEAN MANDOLLI	REAL	XXX	33

NAME: Tom Penney
AGE: 17
GROUP: STREET
SPONSORS: FLIP INDY SIESTA AIRWALK Union

CLOCKWISE FROM LEFT
[1] Contest overview, by Skin Phillips
[2] Street contest placings
[3] Tom Penny's entry details
[4] Tom Penny, by Skin Phillips

199
6

Ben Rodriguez, Liverpool Street, by Wig Worland

Magee kind of said, 'This is skateboarding in Britain, and it's not like skateboarding in America', and it becomes its own culture. You don't want to be wearing Jimmy'Z, in Los Angeles, you can be standing at the bus station in Milton Keynes in the rain, and that was really inspiring. What Blueprint did was very open; it gave something to people but it never said, 'This is what it is, and these are the limits of it'; it was more, 'This is what it can be', and people went off and did great things. There's no way Palace would have existed without Blueprint. They were people that made you feel that you were allowed to do your thing.

JAMES JARVIS

Colin Kennedy, Sheffield, by Andy Horsley

Ian Deacon

Geoff had a lot of ankle problems early on in the States, he was hurt a bit, and Tom was just doing Tom stuff, so I don't know if that intimidated Geoff or if he didn't feel he could skate to Tom's level at that time, so I feel like once Tom had gone, that was his time. Geoff was just a bit delayed. If those two had been hitting at the same time, in America, that'd have been pretty crazy, but it didn't really happen like that. Tom helped Flip from nothing, and then Geoff kind of took over once Tom had left, and then obviously we got Arto Saari and Mark Appleyard, who made a kind of posse around Geoff.

Tom used to lose skateboards all the time, just leaving them. 'Oh, I'm going to go and do that', and then not keeping the board under his arm and going to do that. He's pretty loose, he's just floating through.

Tom's just ridiculously gifted, that's the thing. Sometimes when skateboarders are gifted, they kinda get a bit lazy because it's too easy for them.

You've got people like Geoff, who've obviously got ability, but they haven't got that supernatural ability. You never really get somebody that's got all the natural ability in the world and has that same drive, I don't think. It's pretty rare.

It's not that Tom was lazy, it was just, 'I can do this', he didn't have to think about it. Geoff would be like, 'OK, I'm going to go to the spot and I'm going to do this and I'm going to do that'. With Tom you'd just take him there and he'd do something. Geoff was in the middle ground between Tom and Jamie Thomas. He'd plan stuff but he wasn't super overt about it. Tom never thought about his career, Geoff did think about his career, and then Jamie fully planned every second of his career.

Alex Moul

Jeremy wanted me to come out to the States to help out, and Geoff said he'd pay for it, so they flew me out for a couple of weeks to see what I thought of it. Then I quit my job in the record store and started skating again and lived off the money from the DJ gigs and the records. I needed the sunshine so I moved out there and stayed on floors.

Tom Penny

I went to the States when I was younger, I came back when I was 18, and I ended up living in London. When some people wondered where I went or what happened to me or what I was doing, I lived in London for about a year and a half and just spent all my time at Southbank, all day every day from morning to night, then travelling across the bridge at night to the city for the nightlife. Just the same thing on repeat every night for about a year and a half or so. I was living around the Loughborough Junction area near Brixton with a friend of mine called Lewis Goodyear. All that generation I know really well, like Lewis and Ben Jobe and Winstan Whitter and Clive and Barrington.

Southbank is probably my favourite place to skate, worldwide.

Toby Shuall

Tom was just at Southbank all the time. This was the end of the era of the Southbank crew that I grew up with; lots of the people I grew up with would still be at Southbank but no one skated anymore, so Tom was hanging around with Lewis and loads of my friends but I was one of the only people skating in that period, and I was always trying to get Tom to skate.

Quite a few times I got called by Ian Deacon, because they couldn't get hold of him. They knew he'd kinda run off back to England to let off some steam, but they didn't really know where he was or what he was doing. And he wasn't doing very much, really.

There was a period of about a year where if I could make him skate, he would skate, and I would be giving him set-ups from Slam and they would get refunded because he'd never have a set-up, or he'd just lose it. One time we left Slam, went somewhere, got off the bus and we're walking down the road and I'm like, 'Where's your board?', and he'd left it on the bus.

He was really ripping and I think he was really enjoying skating and not having to document it. Not being part of that whole thing.

I used to sell his shit for him quite a lot, and one day I got to Southbank late and he was selling a pair of etnies Sal Barbier to a kid for £5. I was like, 'What are you doing, you can't sell those for five quid!', and he's like, 'Eh? That's alright, isn't it?' He just didn't give a shit. He didn't want any money and just wanted to be anonymous, really. I don't think people reflect on that, I don't think he really enjoyed being a famous skateboarder. At that point. It didn't gel with his world.

Andy Horsley

We all went to Radlands one evening, and Tom was skating the street course and the small mini – just fucking around as usual – and I was shooting a few photos. Just a regular Wednesday session. Tom disappeared for a while and turned back up skating the vert ramp by himself. I clambered up on to one of the platforms and started setting up flashes and all that.

Tom popped up on my side of the ramp and said to me, 'Don't shoot any photos man, I'm trying to keep vert underground'. Ha! The photo[1] that was used for a Speed Demons advert was shot from the hip as I pretended to pack up my flash gear. ●

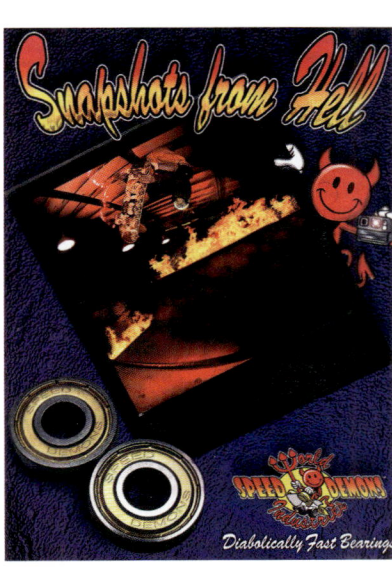

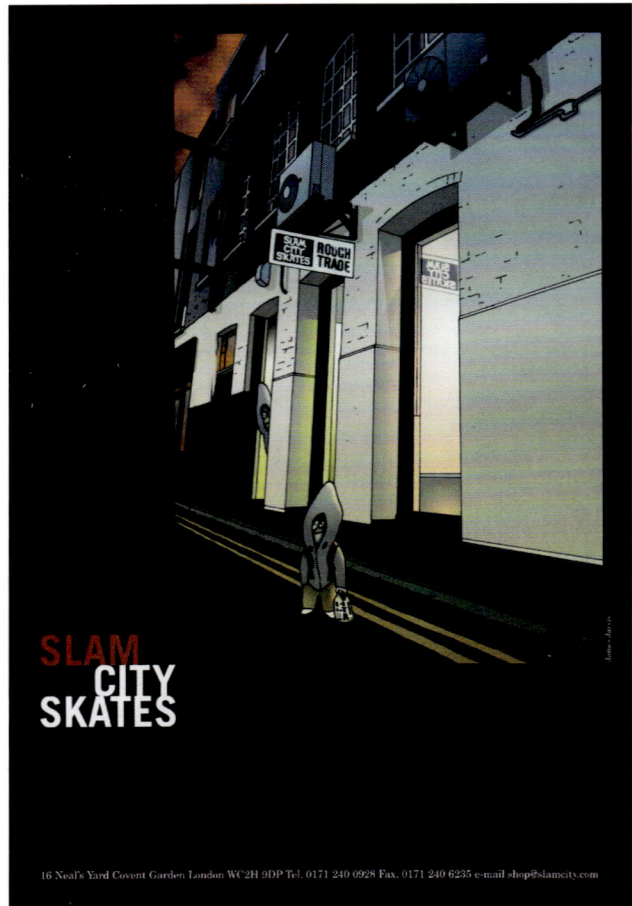

SLAM

Toby Shuall

I just begged Sharon to give me a job in Slam so much. I was sponsored by them before that, and then I just begged her and she gave me the job and it was the best thing that ever happened to me.

I worked with Sharon, and Andy Hartwell and Dave Cushway, so I didn't work with any skateboarders when I worked there, which was kind of cool, but it was also really difficult for me because loads of the skaters I grew up with hated Slam. I got a lot of shit for taking that job, but it was like, 'Fuck you, I've got a board and I've got some money in my pocket', but it caused me a lot of trouble.

When I started working there, the whole generation of skateboarders that I'd grown up with had quit, nearly all of Southbank had quit. When I started working there, the skate scene in London was really weird. It was very fragmented, and had sort of collapsed.

They were still selling a lot of skateboards, but nobody who skated Southbank would go to Slam to get a board, because they either couldn't afford to or they didn't want to, still. There was still animosity, and the Slam skate scene was really small by then, it had really shrunk, but we were still selling loads of hardware and DC was still in there when I started.

James Jarvis

Those ads were all done while I was still at college. I didn't get paid for the Slam ads, I got a pair of the first DCs for one, and a pair of purple Stereo jeans for one. You didn't get cold hard cash for those.

While I was in the Royal College I was thinking about how I wasn't a landscape artist, but how could I make a living out of these environments that I'm interested in, so I was thinking about what would live in them. I never wanted to draw people so I created these kind of hybrid things to populate these spaces. Doing the airbrush drawings was labour-intensive, because I'd go out with my little fishing stool and do observational drawings of the spot, then I'd go home and enlarge them and do them large format with an airbrush, freehand. As an illustrator, that didn't seem very efficient, but then you discover the computer, so instead of drawing the backgrounds I could photograph them and trace them, which I did for a bit. Then that seemed labour-intensive, so then I wondered if I could just use photos.

You can see that happening in the Slam ads. The first one is exactly how I was working when I was discovering the computer at the Royal College. I was taking a slide photo, scanning the slide, printing it out, tracing it on a light box, then scanning that drawing in with a little character in it, then scanning that and recolouring it.

That would take a couple of days to do, so you start working out ways to make it more efficient and streamlined, and the computer sucks you in. Instead of using Tipp-Ex you can retouch everything on the computer and you end up getting less analogue and more digital. You can see the process happening across the ads.

I was so excited to be in print, because for me that was the equivalent of getting a skate photo in a magazine. I was never going to get a photo of me skating, but I was in print, and I was doing something for these people who are the most legit people I've ever met, so that was reward in itself.

I was into environments. My degree show at Brighton didn't have any funny characters, it was just big-format airbrush drawings of car parks and skate spots, and that's how I got in the Royal College.

Sharon Tomlin

Even though Russell didn't want certain people hanging out, he had this thing where he wanted core skateboarders coming in to Slam, that I never really understood. As the person that gripped most of the boards, we had a ton of skateboarders coming in and buying stuff. The reason that we were selling Stüssy and DC is so that we could keep the price of the hardware low, and also because we were supporting Rough Trade. They made good money, but at the end of the day we'd both cash up together and it was pretty obvious. I get pissed off when people say that Slam just started selling sneakers to trendy people that weren't skating, because I didn't use to have fingerprints because of how many boards I was gripping.

I'd go to grip a board and the dude would be all, 'Err, can one of the guys do it?', and it was like, 'Well, no. I'm going to do it for you', then, 'Well don't put air bubbles in it!' It was that thing where you had to do everything fifty times better than the guys would, and I remember having battles with Ben Sansbury about it, where he'd say there was no way I could grip a board faster than him, and I'd be like, 'Yeah I can'. There were always challenges.

We sold so much hardware. Ray and Gary were my best friends because we would sell so much hardware, then I'd still hear the, 'It isn't a real skate shop!' Those two were the only people that validated me. They'd often give me a little pep talk and one time it was, 'Sharon, there are leaders and there are followers. You're a leader.' They always had my back. Christmas time, birthdays, they would take me out. They were friends but they would spoil me, and that would annoy Paul and Russell, who'd be like, 'Look, they're bribing you', and I'd say, 'No, I'm selling a lot of their stuff. It's kinda what people do in business.' You would get kickbacks for shifting van-loads of DCs, but we were friends. We'd hang out a few times a month.

They were really generous. If there was a group of people, skaters or whatever, they take everybody out for dinner and pay massive, massive bills for people. Skaters always had problems with them, like if they said anything wrong it'd be, 'Ray and Gary said this!', if they made some off-colour joke or something, but they were builders, not the cool guys. They might say weird stuff sometimes but they spent a lot of time fixing the skatepark and they weren't just about money.

I remember Kris from Ideal coming in and looking at our prices, and being like, 'Oh shit, you're cheaper than we are', and it was because I could put a massive mark-up on Stüssy, and the trendy stuff, to keep the price of the hardware down. And to pay the Covent Garden rent.

Slam was basically the living room where everyone could hang out, but then we got busy, and the skaters would have to move out the way so someone could sit down to try on shoes. I could see how that was a little bit upsetting for them, because it went from being the clubhouse to there being a bunch of people in there. I guess they kind of lost their safe space, from when they could hang out there and there was no one else to bother them. The trendy people – the Slamites – were the ones that paid the bills, because if you thought you were going to run the store off of the Southbank skaters, who mostly got their boards and stuff for free... We had a lot of trouble. There was always someone either robbing us, or junkies, or weird stuff happening.

There was this Portuguese kid who was always a little bit salty, but he kept buying boards and he kept snapping boards. For a while I'd be like, 'Oh, your board's snapped, it must be faulty – I'll get you another one', because we had a certain amount of leeway because of all the stupid shoes we were selling. It got to the point where it was, 'You keep breaking boards! It's not the board's fault!', and he came in one day with a broken board – he was never friendly, never nice, he was always a pain in the arse to deal with – and I just said, 'Look, you've got to learn to land above the trucks, you keep snapping boards', and I triggered him. He didn't like being told that by me. I told him just bail and he got really hostile, and he was going off at me and yelling at everyone else in the store.

I was trying to push him out the store because he was telling Andrew Hartwell he was going to kill him and basically having a meltdown. He got the drill that we used to put the boards up on the wall, and just swings for me, and stabs me in the neck. The pressure of it, the punch of it, pushed me out the door and he ran away.

They tried to land a helicopter in Cambridge Circus to take me to hospital, but they couldn't, so it was an ambulance, but he nearly killed me. I went to hospital for about a week, then went straight back to work. The one thing that fucked me up was that I could have sued Slam and Rough Trade, but I didn't really want to do that, so I went through the criminal injuries bureau or whatever, and they told me it was my fault because I'd told him to fuck off. It said on the letter that I'd acted unprofessionally. Reading that was kinda worse than getting stabbed. →

→ **ROLLERSNAKES**
Ben Powell

Rollersnakes' business model had relied on mail order, and big lists of products in magazines, and mail outs and whatnot, so once *STM* stopped being a zine, it turned into a glossy catalogue. It went out with *Sidewalk* eventually, but the one with Johnny Morrow cutting Scott Underdown's head off was mailed out to existing customers. That one ended up in the paper and it generated lots more business for Paul.

→ **MISCHIEF**
Robin Sunley

Cleveland Bod came up with the name, after Souls of Mischief. They were going to do it together, but Bod couldn't get it together. I was working for Bingo's dad at the time, at his electrical engineering company. I was in the shop when I came back from uni, and he said to me, 'You're tall, Robin. Are you afraid of heights?', and when I said no he asked if I wanted two weeks' work. Then I worked with him for five and a half years.

Stockton was a bit rough, and Bingo used to have to take all the stock out every night. He would pack it all up and put it in his car and take it home, then put it all back in the morning. Then

he started leaving it in, and he got robbed. He moved location, and it was in a tiny mall which would get locked at night, so it was a lot safer.

Danny Calow

In 1996 Mischief opened. Bod was obsessed with skateboarding; he was a skate geek, he was meticulous and he was really fucking good. You hear about people spending 20 hours trying to do a trick, but he would do that. Originally Mischief was going to be called B and B's, because it was going to be Bingo and Bod's, but Bingo managed to get the money off his parents and Bod didn't manage to get any collateral together.

→ **SHEEP**
Chris Hamer

By 1996 it had petered out a bit. We got raided by the police, a massive raid by the police because they thought we were laundering money and drug dealing, and they just trashed the shop and locked us up for hours and hours then let us go and didn't do anything about it. The police raid was a major deal, it was highly talked about within the hierarchy of Manchester city centre people with money, because it was to do with some quite famous people. My mate James, his wife worked at Granada, so he got all the ins on what was going on and they'd spent hundreds of thousands

of pounds surveilling us on Tib Street before they raided us. They sent a stooge in in the morning to come and try to buy drugs, and then when he went out they raided us, all in boiler suits with dogs and stuff like that. They thought we were some big-time drug dealers, it was fucking mental. They kept an eye on us for months and months afterwards because they couldn't understand that people would want to rob us of clothing, they thought it was drug dealing, not clothing. They couldn't get their head around that people wanted ACG trainers and Stüssy and Supreme more than they wanted bags of drugs. We were the only shop on that road then, and it's a really posh off-licence now. It was Hoi-Polloi's first shop too.

We closed in spring '96, and it was horrible. I didn't have a choice, my hand was forced by all the violence, which I was so fed up with that it was fucking me up, and then my bank manager retired. He was really cool, and he saw what we were doing from day one, but then they brought a young guy in and the young guy said that unless we got money to him in four days we were done. I'd have still been there if that hadn't happened; I'd have put up with all the violence because I knew that within three or four years everything would be easy. ●

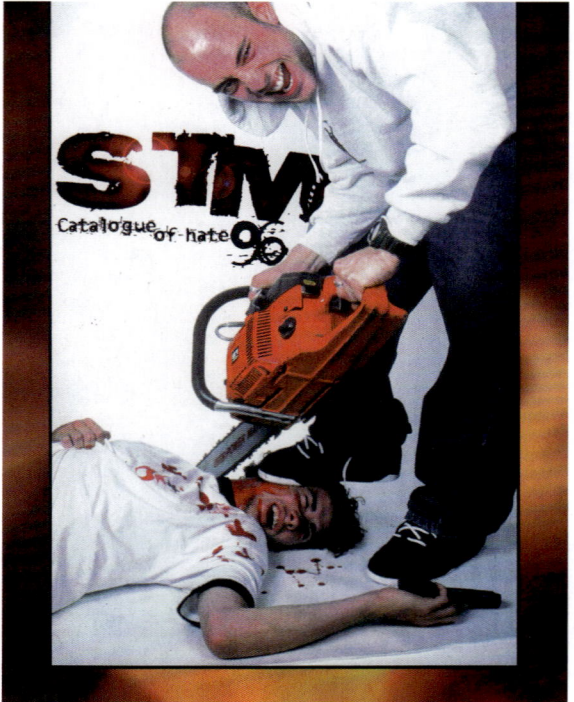

PREVIOUS PAGE
Slam City Skates ads, from Sidewalk, by James Jarvis
CLOCKWISE FROM LEFT
[1] STM catalogue, Johnny Morrow and Scott Underdown, by Leigh Haynes
[2] *Nottingham Evening Post*, 20/01/97
[3] Scott Underdown, Nottingham, by Wig Worland
[4] Paul Haynes, unknown, Johnny Morrow, Luke Wenban, Claire Ashmore and Ben Powell, Rollersnakes, Nottingham, by Leigh Haynes
[5] Steve 'Bingo' Binks and Dean 'Cleveland Bod' Broderick, Middlesborough Boulevard, by Colin Fitzgerald

1996

Paul Shier

A lot of people came to Croydon at that time, and my mum would go away on trips so they'd all stay at her house. That was frequent, and that's why there's so much Croydon footage in all these Blueprint and Panic videos. Colin Kennedy came, Matt Pritchard came... When I think of Panic I think of Pritchard and I think of Colin. Mainly, because those were the two guys I got the tightest with and who I was around.

Everyone got real close real quick, and we would go to the places where the people who rode for Panic lived. We went to see Colin in Scotland, we went to Wales to see Pritchard, and John Cattle lived on the Isle of Wight but we didn't go there.

Pritchard was more of a mosher. He fit the image of what Panic was. At the time I probably didn't think about it. Selfishly. Blueprint was obviously the better thing, with a future. It had an ideology, there was a sense of what it was, and Panic was just a little mumbo-jumbo. But I was still on Panic after Blueprint had been going for a while.

I guess back then graphics meant nothing. There was no communication between the guy who does the board and you. The Cat in the Hat board was the only one I never kept, because I hated it that much that I never wanted to see it. I had that Cat in the Hat board when I filmed that *411* profile thing, and I can remember scratching the graphics off on a wall, to get the graphics off the board. I hated it. It was so bad. It said 'The Cat from Croydon' on it. Who's going to buy that board? Who's going to go into a shop and a buy 'The Cat from Croydon, Paul Shier'?

Magee just started Blueprint. There was just another team suddenly. The first I knew was probably an ad in the magazine. I would have had no idea about it before that because it was almost like it was nothing to do with us. It was just another company that Faze 7 were doing, although it ended up becoming this sister company to Panic. But immediately it was way better, and I wanted to be a part of it. It was when Blueprint started that Magee got serious, and he started doing the graphics. Someone's definitely going to want to buy a KRS-ONE board over the Cat in the Hat.

Dan Magee

At the beginning when I started doing Blueprint I was still doing some bits for Alvin and Panic, but it would be him asking me to do stuff. Like he'd want a graphic and I'd do it but I'd mostly be doing Blueprint stuff. I got a Mac for my 21st birthday, so I was learning how to work that so I could actually start doing graphics in Photoshop and CorelDRAW, and they were getting vaguely better over time. I was still shit but stuff like the Mark Baines Starbucks one, stuff like that, it was like, 'Alright, that's not bad'. Then Paul Shier would get his Cat in the Hat one and he'd see the Baines one or the Flynn Trotman Illuminati one and he'd be, 'Fuck', he'd be bummed because he was on Panic and Blueprint was getting better. So even though he didn't say it, there was always this thing where he wanted to ride for Blueprint but he wasn't really into it because he wasn't a part of it, kind of thing.

Mark Baines

At the time, with Blueprint, I was just a bit, 'Alright, cool', and it didn't seem like such a big deal. It was going to be the sister thing to Panic, and I remember being stoked on the opportunity to do something legit in the UK, but I just took it in my stride. Kind of like the next step, like, 'Let's do it'. I was stoked, obviously, but I just felt like, 'Why would we not do this? We've got all these people that are really good skaters who know each other because we'd been doing these little trips that Alvin had been putting together.'

Blueprint was having the chance to be part of our own thing that we can create and we get to film videos and do video parts. I was hyped because that was what I wanted to do. Skating was my life so much back then that I just wanted to film. I was so keen. Me and Magee have always had a weird relationship – I've always loved filming with Magee, and it's weird because he's so harsh and he's so strict with a lot of things that it totally raises your level of what's acceptable, footage-wise. Almost too much sometimes, but I always loved going down to his place and staying and going out all day and filming around Liverpool Street or just skating the whole city, filming all the time.

There's times where we just completely didn't get on, and it's probably to do with me being older and perhaps thinking that I know better, and him just being the fucking nightmare that he can be sometimes. But we always got stuff done, and I always 100% trusted everything he did. Sometimes we'd clash quite a lot, but I think that's just young men being around each other so much.

He'd be harsh, he'd say some harsh stuff about your clothes or something, and when you're young and you think what you're wearing's sick and he's just being a dick, you want to punch him, but he just had his way and I've always respected Dan and what he's done, and what he does. He's always wanted the best for all the dudes that he's filmed, he just doesn't always show it. He wants to make everyone look the best they can, and he was always like that with me and I had times when I hated him but I always filmed with him. And if he was like, 'Yeah, that was sick', I would be stoked, because he doesn't give compliments, so when he does film something and he's hyped, it hypes you up. →

blueprint

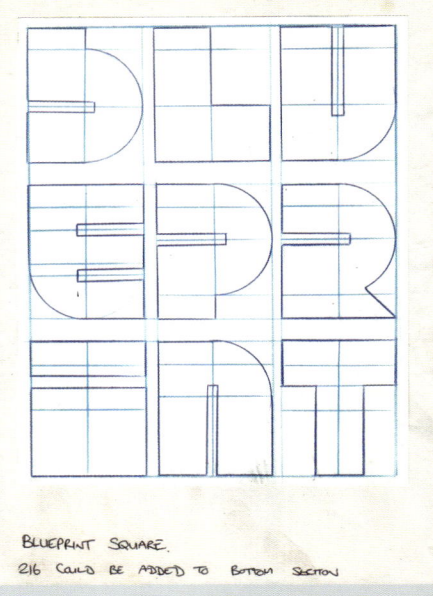

BLUEPRINT SQUARE.
216 COULD BE ADDED TO BOTTOM SECTION

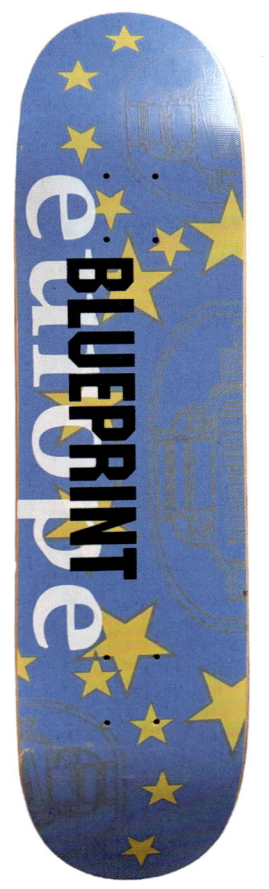

Elsewhere

CLOCKWISE FROM TOP LEFT
[1]   Blueprint KRS-One, by Dan Magee
[2]   Panic Paul Shier Shapes, by Dave Bagnall
[3]   Panic Colin Kennedy Irn-Bru, by Colin McInnes
[4]   Panic Colin Kennedy Speedy J, by Colin McInnes
[5]   Panic Colin Kennedy Ghostbusters, by Colin McInnes
[6]   Panic Field of Bulbs, by Ben Allnutt

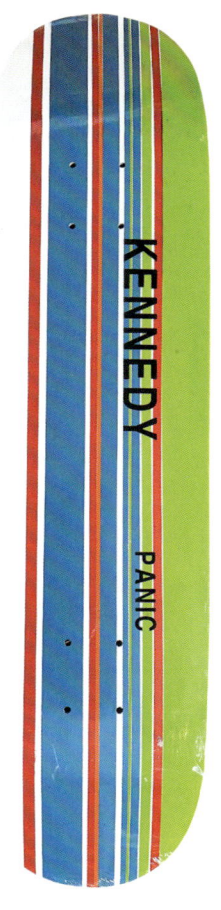
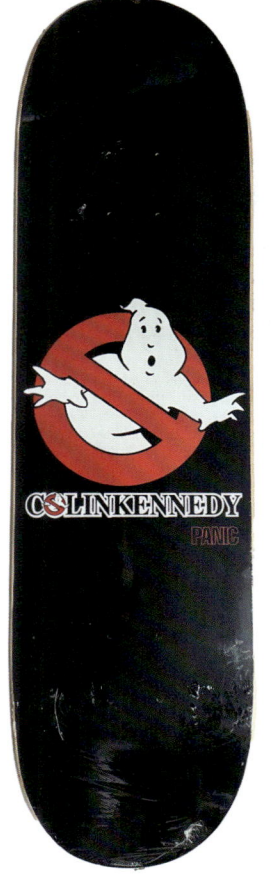

Colin Kennedy

Joe Burlo, even in the worst financial moments for the business, always made sure we got paid. It's not like we were making a million pounds, but considering the size of the business, he always took care of us. The first pay cheques that we got were royalty cheques, so you might get a pound a board. I don't specifically remember about the first board, but the Irn-Bru board sold really well and I ended up making some money, and at that time it was a shock to be making any money at all. Mick at MBC ordered 100 of that board, and I remember them arriving and how exciting it was.

As the brand grew we all got a steady wage. Some were maybe making more than others, perhaps – maybe Mark Baines because his board was selling a lot – but it was royalty cheques to begin with, then it moved to a standard base compensation every month, and it remained like that for as long as the brand remained. Joe stood by his agreements.

The name 'Panic' is just bad, I was never a fan of it, but it didn't matter because I was just happy to be part of something. Did I prefer it when I became a part of Blueprint? Yeah, 100%, because it was something that everyone respected. When we moved over to Blueprint we felt like it was a lesser commodity of Faze, because the aesthetic was so strong.

My first board, it's not that that isn't significant, but it was pretty nondescript. Was I still stoked to get a pro board? 100%, but I think it was that they needed to express something by giving me a pro board.

A pro board wasn't something I was expecting, or even working towards. I just wanted to be sponsored and make something happen around video or whatever, and be recognised for what I was doing, maybe. Thinking back on it, my turning pro was maybe a bit premature and I wonder why, and why the Irn-Bru board [p.272[3]] wasn't my first. Irn-Bru made sense because that's what we all drank.

Colin McInnes

When I did Colin Kennedy's Irn-Bru graphic there were two versions that I sent. I sent it to Dan and I was like, 'Obviously it'll need to be scanned and the lettering will need to be done properly, but here's that set-up and here's the mock-up of what it looks like', and he used the mock rather than the finished item. I eventually got somebody at work to finish the lettering on a computer so I had the right one, but he'd used the first one, which was just a rough. So when you look at the first board the colours are off for starters. That wasn't my doing. Who cares, right? But the colours were not as intense as they needed to be, it was a bit more watery, but I think that was because it was printed on white. They screenprinted the whole thing white in order to get the white lines, and the printer probably thought that would be the best way to do the board, and they were probably right but they probably didn't do the test that they should have done. Actually, it's probably fuck-all to do with that, the guys were probably just, 'Fuck it, print it, get it sold'.

That didn't bother me at all but what did bother me was the fact that they'd used the mock-up lettering and actually printed it red as well. I was like, 'That's black! It's supposed to be black!' I'm not annoyed at Dan for that though.

Dan Magee

I think I first met Colin Kennedy on a distributor trip to Wakefield, when we were all on Faze 7, and he was on Acme or whatever. Shortly after that, he came down to London and he stayed with me when I was staying in the halls of residence and he slept on the floor after getting the Megabus down. Ooft. Then Ewan Bowman did the same thing. He phoned like, 'I'm coming down, and I'll be there at four in the morning', because obviously that's the cheapest bus. He came down and fell asleep and then he started talking in his sleep, saying all this gnarly shit, all this violent stuff.

Colin went pro really quick and I remember that his board graphic was laid out by Ben Allnutt, who works at Palace now, because I didn't have a computer at the time. There were a couple of times when I got stuck with college or university so I'd ask Ben if he could lay it out in QuarkXPress at his college.

Then there was Irn-Bru, Ghostbusters [p.273[5]] and Speedy J [p.273[4]], all these rip-offs. Everybody's having all these ideas and there's not really any filter. Whereas with Blueprint it was like, 'You can't have that because it's Blueprint and it's going to look like this'. That's where I came in, the hard-nosed aspect of it, but I think by that time I'd done some bits and bobs that looked better than Panic so people were happy to roll with what I was saying because it seemed to be working. In a way all these random little ideas seemed to help me out because it gave those guys confidence in me.

Colin always had a lot of cool ideas but they were not always sellable. He wanted soft wheels at one stage, and that's a cool idea and a good idea for now, and he wanted a really big board, but that was dead in the water at that time too, in terms of actual sales.

Ben Allnutt

Magee asked me to do some Panic graphics. At this point I didn't even know how to use a computer. It was just QuarkXPress, I don't think Illustrator was even on the computers at college, they had black-and-white screens, so I could print type off.

He asked if I wanted to do some boards, and I said that I didn't really draw. I was doing graphic design but I didn't draw. I did this one Panic graphic [p.273[6]] and it actually came out really sick. It was a team board, and it was a landscape with leaves in a field and the flowers were lightbulbs. I hand-drew that but I did a couple of others that were awful, and I can't believe they even made them. →

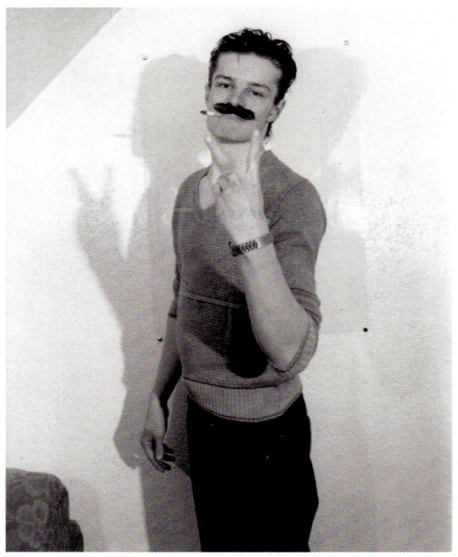

1996

FROM LEFT
[1]   John Rattray, Mitchell Library, by Andy Shaw
[2+3] Panic Matt Pritchard and Friends board and artwork, by Pete Fowler
[4+5] Panic Woods board and artwork, by Pete Fowler
NEXT PAGE
A Mixed Media van arrest screenshots

It's so sketchy when I think about it. Colin's first board [p.272[7]] was the face of the woman from the Illustrator packaging from the famous painting, in halftone. It's an inflated version of that in the background so it's this halftone speckled effect and then the face is in the middle. In my mind it's amazing but it's actually really embarrassing. I did it in Quark on a wing and a prayer and I had no idea what I was doing. I don't think Alvin or anyone else did either. I gave it to them as a printout, like, 'Here you go!' 'OK, what colours?' 'I don't know!'

I did Colin's second board, which was also a disaster. A hand-drawn mountain scene, and I remember Magee saying he wanted to have 'Highlander' written on it. I was just stoked to be doing board graphics, but I was like, 'Oh my god, these look terrible', even then. It was still full-on do-it-yourself times. I think they gave me 50 quid and a board for doing a board graphic.

I'd scanned all the background bamboo artwork for Shier's board [p.272[8]], and drawn these flowers in the middle, and it was very much the same language that I had with Colin's board – it was a background with a frame in the middle.

I was friends with this guy called Jim, and he was a really good illustrator. I said to him, 'I need a frame around these flowers, and I know you draw bamboo really well', and he said he'd do it. He literally drew a bamboo frame on a piece of A4 and I used it on the paper artwork and sent it off. I told him I'd give him £25 when it came through, because I was 16, at college, and I didn't have £25.

Months had passed and he's going, 'When's that board coming out? When's that board coming out?', and I'm telling him I have no idea. There was no time schedule to when things came out. Then he comes into college one day and he opens up Sidewalk and he's like, 'There you go, the board's out'. I'm like, 'Fuck! Amazing', I'm stoked that it's out, and he's like, 'Where's my fucking money?', and I'm like, 'What? I didn't know it was even out!', and I remember that day trying to speak to Joe or Alvin and asking if they could send me a board, or maybe send two, but by that point the kid didn't want to wait. I'm at the bus stop going home, he comes over and just knocks me straight out.

When I think about it I could have asked my mum or dad for £25 to pay this guy, but I didn't even think it was a thing because he was a friend, and he was a friend right up until that day when he knocked me out. I gave him the board maybe a month later, but he was kicked out of the college for doing that. It got quite gnarly, because I was out cold on the floor for about 40 minutes or something.

Magee had said they were taking some of the Panic team members and doing this new thing as an offshoot of Panic, and it'd be called Blueprint. I thought it sounded really sick, and I loved the name. There was no Seth-script at that point, it was 'Blueprint '96', and 'Aesthetics Project' and all this, and it was so up my street.

Magee wasn't very sure what to do, but he was thinking of a globe board, and he gave me this blueprint to a building in London and this Polaroid image. We mucked about with a few ideas and we came up together with those three boards. The globe, the tower, the camera with 'aesthetics' and then the European board, with the European flag [pp.272–273[9–12]]. We did those together but he led it, for sure. I just laid it out, but I remember being really adamant on the colours on the yellow and blue board.

I'm super happy with how they look, but I don't think people really remember those boards because they were in the time and space before Magee learning, and just accelerating into doing amazing things. I remember being fully envious, like, 'Fuck, I'm here at art college and he's gone and done these'. I was blown away by what he did, what he did with that brand, with the aesthetic and the storytelling and the visuals.

Blueprint was Dan's baby, his everything, and there's no Palace without Blueprint. Gareth and Lev will be the first people to say that.

John Rattray

I was getting boards flowed to me from New Deal UK, through Jamie at Clan. They were sending up some little boxes with boards and things, and I got DC shoes from them through Jamie Blair's contacts with New Deal UK.

I was skating with Matt Grey, who was doing Physics as well, and Toby Paterson, and through them I met Colin and started skating with Colin, and Gary Browne. That MBC crew was my squad that I started to skate with more, because they were much more into going street skating at night, every night, in town, and that's where my head was at. Colin helped facilitate getting me on Panic.

Seth Curtis

Dan Magee had got wind that I did art or whatever, and he asked me to do some graphics and said he didn't give a shit what they were, whether they were drawings or writing or whatever. I think I did some handwriting stuff and some crap logos. Supreme had just come out with this shirt that said 'Supreme' in joined-up writing – they still use it quite a lot now – and I had a sweatshirt with that on it, and I thought that was wicked. I was never very good at joined-up writing at school but I wrote 'blueprint' in joined-up writing [p.271[2]] like it is in the Supreme style, or what I thought looked like that, and I just ended up giving all these bits of paper to Dan and they ended up using that one as the main logo. It was just a bit of writing but I got one board and one t-shirt for it, which I don't think I even skated or wore. The boards at that point were fucking terrible. So bad.

Dan Magee

I was into stuff like Cream – Rick Ibaseta's company – and Zoo York and Silverstar. So it was just me trying to steal those ideas. The first bit of Blueprint was just me pilfering shit that I'm into, whereas Panic was literally, 'Alvin's got an idea!', 'Alvin's girlfriend's got an idea!', 'Joe's got an idea!', 'Pritchard wants to do this!', and that's how things happened. With Panic there was always too many voices.

The best ideas were when someone went to someone who's actually creative, like Pete Fowler, and they'd discuss an idea. Like the Pritchard and Friends graphic. That was a result of people talking, and then going to someone who was creative to get it done. But other stuff was so random, people would just do it in the office. Even the first Panic logo was done in Microsoft Paint or something. It was that level. Like, 'We're going to do this company!', and then Alvin just handed us a printout with the name on it.

So I've got my Macintosh, I'm working out how to do it, I scan a load of stuff from *Sidewalk* at 72dpi because I don't even know what resolution is yet, send it to Alvin, and then it's printed as an ad [p.271[4]]. And Alvin hasn't asked Wig if we can use the photograph of Ewan Bowman that's in it. I think I sent it to Alvin as a mock-up, just as an idea for an ad, but it got printed. It was like, 'I've got my Mac! I'm using it!'

It was a photo of Bowman doing a noseslide on a high ledge that I've messed with in Photoshop because I've just got my computer. It was some awful Photoshop job because I was just learning and I wanted to show Alvin, like a proof of concept kind of thing. It wasn't 300dpi so when they printed it, it was all pixelated, and Alvin hasn't asked Wig if he can use the photograph, and it's been in the magazine before, so now Wig is bummed. At the time it didn't even register that that was a big deal.

Alvin Singfield

Pritchard and Friends[2] were Morrissey, Naomi Campbell, John Lennon, Kate Moss, Jim Morrison and Homer. As for why, I can't honestly remember, but at least in the case of Naomi and Kate and Homer they were definitely icons of that time, so I guess that's why we picked them. Pritchard and Fiends were Vader, Jason, Grim Reaper, Hannibal, Alice Cooper and Charles Manson, but again I don't remember why those apart from just thinking about iconic fiends that people would know.

Pete Fowler

That[4] was actually supposed to be a Pritch pro model, then they changed it to a team board. It said 'Matt Pritchard' where it says 'Panic Skateboards'. When I saw that, I was pretty pissed off. I wasn't angry, I was just a bit confused.

Alvin Singfield

There was a lot more effort going into Blueprint, into the boards, the wheels, the product, because Dan was 100% on that. Everything that was done for Panic, after Blueprint, became a bit of a... not an afterthought, but Dan wasn't there to do Panic graphics, although that was his job because he was employed by Faze to do that. →

Every time I'd go to Dan and say that we needed another Panic graphic, he'd be like, 'Urgghhh'. All of his time and all of his effort would be focused on Blueprint boards, Blueprint wheels, the catalogues that we started to produce, the adverts... I think, in retrospect, maybe I should have fought harder for it, but I don't know.

Colin McInnes

Dan's got something to say about everything. He's got something to say about fucking shoelaces. He'd be like, 'I'm not filming you if you're wearing that'.

→ **A MIXED MEDIA**

Martin Kennelly

I remember Sumo showing Blueprint's A Mixed Media, and Alvin was there. Dan Magee was there, and pretty much the whole team had come to Sumo and put the video on, so it was kind of an unofficial premiere. Magee and those guys were constantly in Sheffield. This Blueprint and Panic link with Sheffield was always bananas.

Colin Kennedy

A Mixed Media was the first video when Panic and Blueprint became a thing, that I was part of, and the majority of the footage that I have in that, I filmed remotely in Edinburgh or in Glasgow. I think Pete Kelly filmed most of it, because he was pretty proficient with that same Video8 camera that goes back to the *Sons of the Hounds* video. Videos used to be like that, where you didn't have dedicated filmers, and it was just using any resources we could to get footage for the video. The rest of the footage in that part was filmed on those meet-ups that we had when Panic and Blueprint was becoming more of a collective, where we would all cross over at Wakefield contests, or at Milton Keynes.

Pieter Janssen

So Mike de Geus was on Blueprint, and I was on Panic for some reason. Pretty soon after, we were invited to that tour. This is our first meeting with the team. I'd met Shier years before, when he politely denied us staying at his house, but I didn't know all the other guys so I was kinda nervous.

I hadn't seen Mike for a bit, because I didn't live in the same city, and we met at the airport to go there, but he was kinda weird and he didn't really speak. He was mumbling to himself and just listening to Mobb Deep on his headphones the whole day, and I was thinking he was a bit off. I think this might have been the early onset of him having some issues, mentally.

So they pick us up, and Alvin was driving the bus. He was playing the Beatles, and I'll never forget that because he played it for two fucking weeks. The only thing he wanted to play was Beatles tapes. We get in and meet everybody, and obviously Mike is the star and I'm Mike's friend and I feel like an idiot because I'm only on Panic because they want Mike. I'm the extra weight.

I keep quiet at first to feel out the vibe, but I'm a pretty social guy so if you put me in a van with people, I'll mingle, I'll make it work. I'm cracking jokes and I think everything is going fine, and then I look at Mike and he

hadn't spoken, he hadn't said one word apart from 'Hi', and he sat down in the corner of this van with his headphones on. Then he taps me on the shoulder and he's like, 'Piet, Piet, I have to piss', so I ask Alvin if we can stop because Mike has to pee, and Alvin says he can't because we're in traffic, in the middle of London. Mike gets up – hunched over because he's pretty tall – opens the window and starts pissing out the window, ten minutes into the trip. The pee goes all over the window, because we're driving, and I just remember Colin Kennedy being like, 'Who the fuck are these dudes?'

Pritchard was super nice but also unhinged and wild. But I remember one night when I was in my room I heard all this commotion, and I thought I'd see what it was tomorrow, because they were going out every night and coming home late and I was sleeping already. In the morning Shier came to get me and he's like, 'Look at his room! Look at his fucking room!', because Pritchard had trashed the entire room. Everything was broken. The whole toilet bowl was gone. Then Alvin was like, 'Let's get out of here!', I don't think he told the front desk of the hotel anything about the incident when we checked out and we just rode away.

We drive for about six hours, across the country and up north somewhere, and we'd kind of forgotten about it. We were cracking jokes and amusing ourselves on the bus. Then we arrive at a branch of the same hotel, and Alvin tells us to wait while he checks us in. I remember people getting their bags, getting ready to get out, and Alvin comes running back from the hotel, he jumps in and just hauls ass, just drives away. We're asking what's wrong and he's like, 'We've gotta get out of here!', and the minute he'd said that, there's police cars in the background, because the last hotel had called this one, like, 'Hey. There's a group of thugs coming'. There's another police car and another, and there's a helicopter. I was paranoid that I couldn't find my passport, and I couldn't even imagine being arrested, but that happened. You can see it in the video, me freaking out looking for my bag.

Everybody gets taken out, and then pretty soon – within ten minutes – they know what we're about, and they're like, 'Wait a minute, these are not thugs, these are skateboarders'. They clearly were misinformed; they brought out all the big guns, then they just started laughing a bit, and it was pretty humorous by the time we got to the police station, but they still said that we had done some serious damage to the hotel.

We got thrown in cells, and I got thrown in a cell with my roomie, the filmer Marshall, who was even more stressed out than me but he didn't really talk much so he was internalising it. His eye started drooping because he'd filmed all week, and because of the stress.

The cops, those fuckers, they let us out in the middle of the night on purpose. It was four or five in the morning. Nobody was speaking, and there's this palpable tension.

Alvin didn't say anything other than, 'Get in the van', and he pops in another Beatles tape. He doesn't say anything, drives to a nearby train station, and just tells Pritchard to go home. The remaining part of the trip was a little more mellow but Pritchard was missed nonetheless.

After the tour Mike and me went back to Holland, and never heard from Panic or Blueprint again. I think we got kicked off immediately. There was never a follow-up trip, and I've never been back after that. I think Mike quit, but I think that Alvin also saw that Mike was not the old Mike from a couple of years prior. He hardly skated. The three tricks he did do are beautiful and I'm so glad they were captured on video, |but that was it. That was the last time I skated with Mike, even. It was the last for everything. It kind of marked the end of Mike's career too. He was getting more mentally anguished. Hopefully it's easier for people to talk about that stuff now, but I had no clue what to do at the time.

No shade on Panic or Blueprint at all, they just didn't know what to do with the situation, and I presume the tour was kind of a bust for them. I was more bummed out for Mike, that his last professional experience was just shit.

Alvin Singfield

That was probably the hardest thing I ever had to do. Everything about us getting arrested and missing the demo the next day was on Pritchard, and what he'd done. You can look back and laugh about it now but at the time, it was horrific. Everyone got put in the cells, and Pritchard's in the cell at the end singing 'Oggy oggy oggy, oi oi oi!'

All of us were young, so if you put eight or nine skateboarders into a van with some alcohol and drugs and drive round the UK, shit's going to happen. It was the hardest thing I ever did, but I was never going to throw him off, there was never any doubt about that.

Matt Pritchard

Now, I was a fucking nuisance. I was that shy skateboarder, and then I found alcohol and I could fucking speak to people with alcohol! I really had this fondness for alcohol. I used to go to competitions and get bollocksed, and fucking do my run naked – you couldn't do shit like that nowadays, fuck me, you'd be arrested – or do my run in fancy dress, and I just used to be bollocksed.

I remember most Mondays after a comp weekend, I'd get a call off Alvin giving me a right bollocking for not putting the company in the right light. I mean, I used to be puking on the skatepark floor and everything, in front of everybody; I thought it was hilarious.

It was Alvin and Joe telling me off, but at the same time I think they were genuinely worried about me because obviously I was losing the plot a little bit. They docked my wages, but I can't remember that. But fucking hey ho. I suppose that's what you get for acting a tit. ●

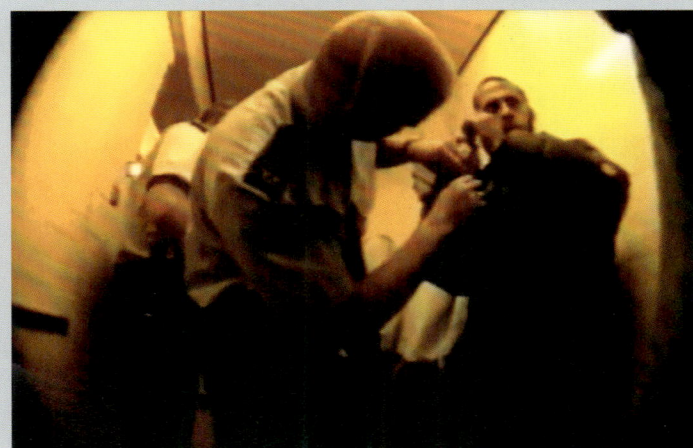

1996

Liverpool

CLOCKWISE FROM TOP LEFT
[1] Ali Boulala, John Moore's University, by Wig Worland
[2] Olly Todd, Cotton Exchange, by Wig Worland
[3] Brian Sumner, St James, by Wig Worland
[4] Brian Sumner's Transworld Check Out, December, photo by Wig Worland

Elsewhere

Brian Sumner

Wig is just funny. Wig shows up and it's like, 'Who is this tall, curly-haired dude who is handsome and together?' He kinda looks like he's going to go for a run or something. He'd be like 'Try this', 'Do this', and most stuff with Wig I did it in one or two tries. Some of the things were first try, and I was like, 'How did I just do that?!' Some of the rails were massive. The Law Courts was scary, it had cracks in it and only Geoff was jumping on it then. Shooting with Wig was amazing; it was solid, it was business, and I'm going to show up and get things done.

Ali Boulala's just a sweet kid. He came and lived in our house and we'd get McDonald's every day and he just ripped. He was fresh, into his hip-hop and he had Craig Mack on all the time. People in Liverpool just loved Ali, and he loved them, and he started sounding Scouse.

I got knocked out on a handrail. I hit my head and got knocked out and when I woke up I said I'd seen God, and everyone's laughing at me. My parents were out of town, my sisters were watching me at home, so we go home and I'm throwing up and I keep telling people I've seen God. I kept saying that God had a plan for my life and I was going to ride for Airwalk and live in America. I woke up the next day and I'm in my room and Ali Boulala's there, sleeping in the other bed, and I'm like, 'Who's that?', because I didn't know who he was. And all I did was talk about God for a week.

My 'Check Out' in *Transworld* was a photo of a Smith grind that I hated because it was a butt shot, and there was a nosegrind tailgrab photo that they used somewhere else. I'd had a switch 180 5-0 down a ten stair, so why go back to a Smith? It was just me being OCD with tricks on it. The nosegrind tailgrab would have stood out then.

Olly Todd

I moved to Liverpool in 1996, when I was 18, to start uni. I didn't know a single Liverpool skater. I obviously knew how good the scene was because I knew of Geoff Rowley and Brian Sumner and I'd seen all the Percy [Dean] photos in the mags. I knew how sick Liverpool was but I'd never met anybody from there, or even been there before.

On the first Saturday I skated into town with the clear intention of just walking around until I saw somebody with a skateboard. When I found somebody I was either going to ask them where the skate spots were or just follow them. Soon enough I saw two kids with skateboards in the distance. I followed them to the Quiggins Centre and they led me straight up the stairs into The Fleapit shop. Robbie Reid was working there that day, and I just said, 'Look man, where are people going to be skating today?' and he gave me directions to the Courts, which was the main meeting spot.

In that Wig Worland photo[2], that's Frosty's board, he just gave me his old set-up. It's a Think Matt Pailes, and the griptape job on it was insane; it was this huge spiderweb.

When I moved to Liverpool I had a 7.5-inch Eric Koston board. It had one Thunder truck and one Venture truck. The whole set-up was just trashed, but that was all I could afford. The guys – Joel and everyone – credit to them, they just picked it up and went, 'What the fuck is that?', taking the piss. *Eastern Exposure 3* had just came out, and everyone had suddenly started riding wider boards and bigger wheels, so the locals hooked me up with their cast-offs, which were more suited to what people were riding at that time.

This was one of the days in Liverpool when Wig had come up to shoot Brian Sumner, for his interview in Sidewalk. It seemed like he was there every Saturday for a couple of months. We'd follow Brian and Wig around the city, going to the spots that Brian wanted to skate, which usually meant the rest of us just sitting down at the bottom of a massive handrail while he handled business. It was incredible to watch him in that era when he was just fucking incredible at skating and so consistent and would jump on any handrail with no fear. It was amazing to witness that.

It just so happened we were at this spot called the Cotton Exchange. Brian wasn't shooting anything in particular, and I had a line where you roll along a wide step, and ollie over a wall and a bar, and then you land on this higher level which sets you up for a transfer from this flat bar to flat. I was doing it that day and Wig was kind enough to want to shoot it, and Ben Powell was there as well so he quickly interviewed me on the spot, so I knew it was going to be a 'New Blood'. ●

Smith grind

Dan Cates

Radlands and St Albans were really how I learned to skate in a contest and I used to really love it. I'd plan my run, I'd sketch it out in a notebook beforehand sometimes. The atmosphere inside that room was just incredible and getting almost the entire skate scene under one roof, as one, there was such a brotherhood and you knew just about everyone because there was so few people involved at that time. It just made everything so much more special.

Greg Finch

Gareth Skewis and myself arrived in the summer of '96, round about Radlands time. We went along to Radlands and figured that it was cheaper for me to enter the comp than go backwards and forwards, so I entered the comp and I can't remember where I placed but it was fun as fuck.

We blagged our way everywhere. We were on a bus to Northampton and we didn't think where we were going to stay for the night – or for the week for that matter, because we were a week early – and we went into the city centre to see if we could sort something out. Bearing in mind Gareth and I had maybe all of about £30 to rub together. We were broke. Gareth let this lady on the bus before us, proper South African manners, and she sat in front of us. We sat behind her and we were still talking about what we were going to do and she turned around and said to us, 'Do you boys need a place to stay?', and we were kinda like, 'Well, we don't know you and we're South African and everyone's sketchy'. We were a bit taken aback but then she said, 'No, look, I live with my two sons but let me just call them and make sure it's mellow'.

So we got off the bus with her and she called her kids from a payphone, and they're like, 'Yeah, of course', so we went around there and it was on a council estate and she put us up for the full week. She washed our clothes and she made sure we got to and from the thing OK – her son dropped us off a few times. It was outrageous.

When we first arrived in London the first thing you do is go down to Southbank, don't you? We met Boma Jaja, Terence Anthony, Ralph McKeown and Toby Shuall.

From going to Radlands I met Gary Chevalier and we became super good friends. He took pity on me – he saw my board was fucked – and he leaned over and said, 'Hey, you look like you need a board', but I needed money more than I needed a board. Someone had asked me if I was selling boards five minutes earlier, so Gary gave me this board and I literally turned to this dude and sold it to him for £15. Gary said it was such a ballsy move and we instantly became friends.

We worked offloading crates of Coke from trucks, and shit like that. Odd jobs around building sites. Gareth got a job in a bakery so he was working from three in the morning to about one or two in the afternoon, and I got a job in a pub, so we had these overlap times when we just used to skate. ●

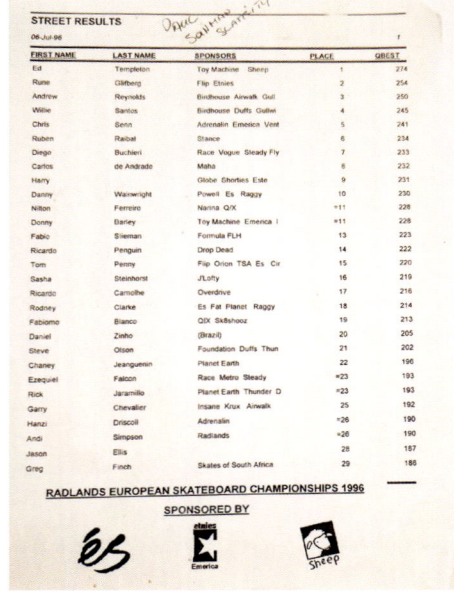

FIRST NAME	LAST NAME	SPONSORS	PLACE	QBEST
		STREET RESULTS		
		06-Jul-96		
Ed	Templeton	Toy Machine Sheep	1	274
Rune	Glifberg	Flip Etnies	2	254
Andrew	Reynolds	Birdhouse Airwalk Gull	3	250
Willie	Santos	Birdhouse Duffs Gullw	4	245
Chris	Senn	Adrenalin Emerica Vent	5	241
Ruben	Raibal	Stance	6	234
Diego	Buchieri	Race Vogue Steady Fly	7	233
Carlos	de Andrade	Maha	8	232
Harry		Globe Shorties Este	9	231
Danny	Wainwright	Powell Es Raggy	10	230
Nilton	Ferreiro	Narina QiX	=11	228
Donny	Barley	Toy Machine Emenca I	=11	228
Fabio	Sileman	Formula FLH	13	223
Ricardo	Penguin	Drop Dead	14	222
Tom	Penny	Flip Orion TSA Es Cir	15	220
Sasha	Steinhorst	J/Lofty	16	219
Ricardo	Carmolhe	Overdrive	17	216
Rodney	Clarke	Es Fat Planet Raggy	18	214
Fabiomo	Bianco	QiX Sk8shooz	19	213
Daniel	Zinho	(Brazil)	20	205
Steve	Olson	Foundation Duffs Thun	21	202
Chaney	Jeanguenin	Planet Earth	22	196
Ezequiel	Falcon	Race Metro Steady	=23	193
Rick	Jaramillo	Planet Earth Thunder D	=23	193
Garry	Chevalier	Insane Krux Airwalk	25	192
Hanzi	Driscoll	Adrenalin	=26	190
Andi	Simpson	Radlands	=26	190
Jason	Ellis		28	187
Greg	Finch	Skates of South Africa	29	186

RADLANDS EUROPEAN SKATEBOARD CHAMPIONSHIPS 1996
SPONSORED BY

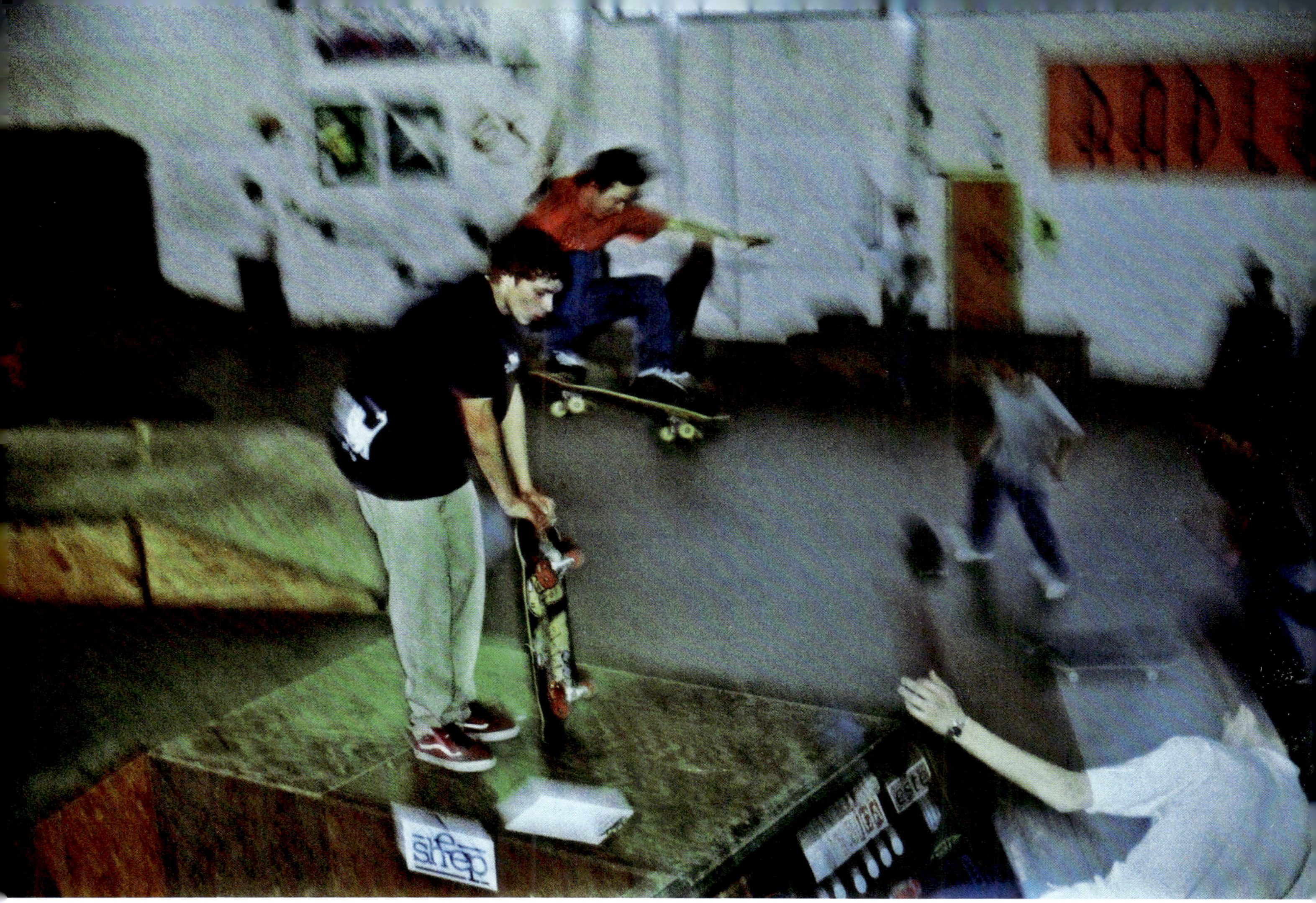

CLOCKWISE FROM LEFT
[1] Tom Penny, by Daniel Turner
[2] Street contest placings
[3] Dan Cates and Howard Cooke, by Jono Atkinson
[4] Greg Finch, St Albans, by Wig Worland

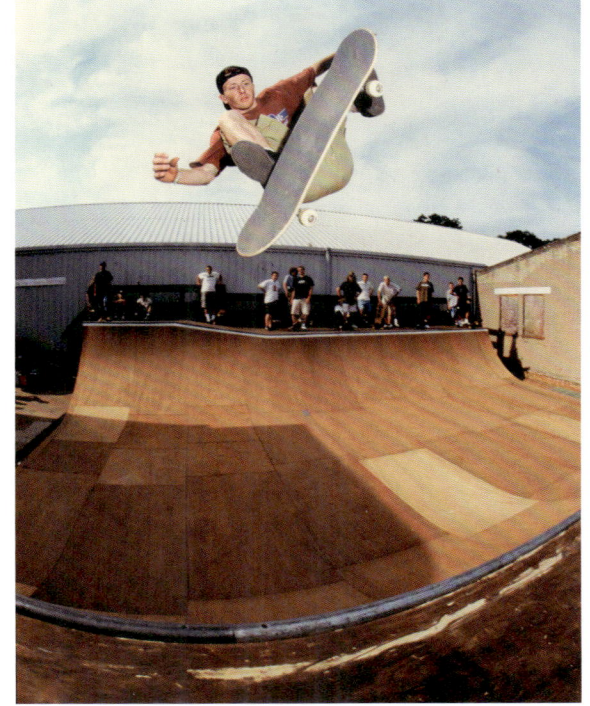

POWER DISTRIBUTION *power*

PROUD TO DISTRIBUTE:
**CONSOLIDATED
BLACK LABEL
DAREDEVIL
ONE FIFTY ONE
SUPERNAUT
MAPLE
CRAFTY CLOTHING
HALOS BEARINGS**
TEL: 0181 958 6990
OR: 0956 855 259
FAX: 0181 958 6990

Nick 'Zorlac' Orrechio

At the end of '95, New Deal Distribution asked me if I wanted to be sales rep for Droors and DC. They knew that I'd done part-time sales work as a student, and I was still a Harrow local, and I was on good terms with them guys. I said I could only work part-time because I wanted to skate all the time while I was young and I was living at my folks' house, meaning I didn't have many overheads. They said I had to do it full-time, but the selling point was that they'd give me a company car.

I'd been driving smashed-up old bangers, £400 cars, so I said yeah. If I had a company car it would mean I could take it on skate trips at the weekend, so in January 1996 I started my role as UK rep for DC shoes and Droors clothing. The job was great in one way because DCs were the new thing and they were hot and everyone wanted them. But difficult in another as I was rep for the whole country so clocking up mega miles and mega hours driving before I even got to speak to anyone. It was really tiring, and as the weeks went by I started to get back ache which quickly got worse. After about four or five months of doing it I busted my back, lifting the bags of shoes and clothing up into a store. Something went 'click' in my back as I stood up and it was never the same.

When I spoke to one of the bosses about being injured, he showed no concern whatsoever about my health or my future. I'm not gonna repeat exactly what he said. But I can tell you that the conversation with him made it crystal clear to me that after working so hard for them and breaking my back working for them, I was just disposable. The thing was though, his disregard for my welfare actually really pushed me to start my own company. Well not only start it, but keep pushing it no matter what.

So, mid-'96, I'm at home with a busted back wondering what I'm going to do. My favourite company at the time was Consolidated, and they had two of my favourites – Alan Peterson and Karma – on the team. They were this little independent company from Santa Cruz but they had this massive presence, and as well as that they had loads of really good riders.

I loved Consolidated, and I thought that I'd be really psyched to distribute it, because at the bottom of their ads in *Thrasher* it would say, 'Not available in the UK'. I knew I'd never make any real money out of it, but I really wanted to do it, so I hit them up by fax, told them I was just a kid with a skateboard and a bad back but I wanted to distribute their stuff, and they faxed back. I was so blown away that Consolidated, my favourite skateboard company, had faxed me back. I had no track

record of running a company or anything like that, but they were like, 'Yeah! Just go for it!', so that started around October '96.

I got some Consolidated stuff and it sold, and then I hit up Black Label because that was my other favourite company that wasn't available in the UK at the time. NDUK hadn't bought any Black Label stuff for about three years, so no one was distributing Black Label.

I was at my folks' house and there was a bit of space at the back of the living room that I could use, and they had a landline, so when I ran an advert for Power Distribution in *Sidewalk*, the phone number was actually just my parents' landline number! My dad ran a classic car parts business, and he had a fax machine, so I used that too. He made me some shelving for the skate stuff and off I went.

Soon after I started Power Distribution, I got told that one of the bosses at NDUK was talking BS to magazines and skate stores to try and sabotage what I was doing. Long story short, they did not succeed. It was pretty absurd looking back at it though. Someone that has never been a skateboarder, going round telling skate mags and stores not to support a skater-owned company. Delusional. I don't blame Steve Douglas for this as he was in the US away from what they were up to in the UK. ●

Carl Shipman
When I went to Münster and Stereo asked me to ride for them, Danny Way asked me to ride for Plan B. I'd just agreed to Stereo so I said to Danny that it wouldn't be right, because I'd just come with one company and jumped to another one, and I didn't want to jump again. They respected that, and I said, 'If you do anything else that's not a deck sponsor, I'll be part of it'. He respected that, and a bit down the line he got in touch with me and asked me to ride for DC, on the full team. I was really stoked to be on that team, being from England.

It started off laid-back, but with more pressure than what Stereo were giving me. They were like, 'Right, you need to come to San Diego, we need to get these ads, you need to do this', and at first it were great, but the shoes sucked. To me they were hard to skate in, and the only shoe that I ever liked of theirs was the Lynx.

Dan Cates
People I knew were getting sponsored, and Dave Allen got on Vans, and Wig Worland was doing all the ads, and I think he was maybe 'consulting' for them a little bit, in a way. At that time, globally, Vans was not what it had been. It was a low point for Vans, when I got on! The distribution was in Wandsworth in south London, and there was nobody who worked there who

was from a skateboarding background, so they didn't really know who was who and I think I kinda pestered Wig loads, and maybe Dave, and I thought, 'Fuck it, everyone else is getting free shoes, I'll have some of that!'

I wasn't really ready to be sponsored, although I'd won a couple of competitions and I was getting regular coverage in the mags and I was determined that that was going to continue. I was going to every event, and I didn't really have the talent yet – or ever – but I was doing everything else so I think Wig might have put in a word and I photocopied all of my coverage and sent that to the boss there, and they said they'd put me on.

I got two pairs a month, but they wouldn't send you two pairs together. You'd have to phone up every two weeks for a pair, and then they would try to drag it out so you didn't get your shoes.

Eventually we got them to send two pairs at once, and I lived in London so I could go down there sometimes and in theory pick some stuff, which never really ended up being that frequent, but I did technically have free shoes. You think being sponsored is this incredible thing but it was just me on the phone going out of my mind, saying, 'All I want you to do is just send me one pair of shoes!' ●

Global accessories ltd. 100 Garrat Lane, Wandsworth, London SW18 4DJ. Tel: 0181 877 9907

VANS
Since 1966

Dan Cates

frontside rock 'n roll

1996

1997

Mark Baines, Milton Keynes, by Wig Worland

You could see it creep in; everyone wanted their own shit, and not just a bunch of American boards on the wall of a skate shop anymore.
TOBY SHUALL

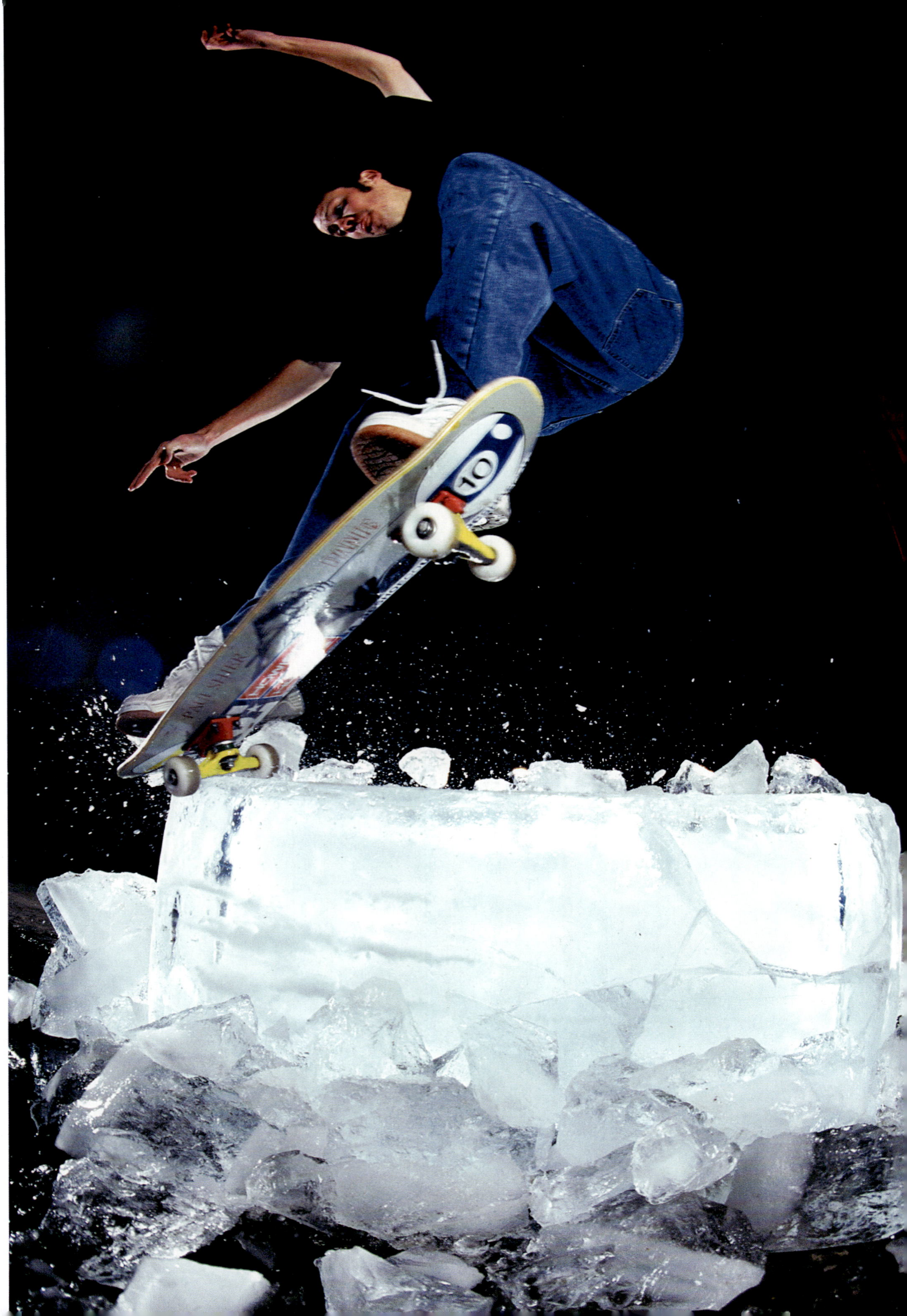

Ben Powell

I was the editor from issue 13 but I didn't want to be called the editor because I didn't feel like I deserved to be called that because I didn't know enough people and I wasn't like Jake Phelps or whatever. Then eventually Jim said that since I was the editor, we needed to say it. It's like once you've got the word 'editor' next to your name you're expected to be able to do McTwists and to know about everything.

Nobody wants to write. That's another reason I didn't want 'editor' next to my name; there's no kudos to being a writer. It was just a job nobody else wanted to do. If you were writing for a magazine you were 'establishment'.

I always felt a bit of imposter syndrome. The way to ward that off was to give that unwarranted opportunity that I felt that I'd got to other people who were telling me how shit I was. Kind of like, 'Go on then, it's not as easy as you think it is, you have a go and if you're good you can do it every month'.

That was kind of the ideology of skateboarding at the time; if you find a spot you tell people where it is. If you've got an opportunity you give it to other people, if you've got a video camera you film everyone and not just the cool guys. That was the skateboarding I grew up with. If someone came to our town I was always the person who went and spoke to them straight away so they didn't feel left out or whatever.

Paul Shier

Andy Horsley hit me up and said they wanted to shoot this picture on some ice, at this ice factory somewhere. There was no conversation that we were going to shoot the cover photo, it wasn't going to be for the cover. We just went there, and these people brought out a block of ice; it was just a block of ice on the concrete, and it was soaking wet everywhere.

Then we skated it, and it just didn't seem very exciting at the time because it was just a block, four-foot long max. I did a backtail on it and then just did crooked grinds on it. Then we smashed the shit out of one of these other blocks, and put it all around it, because we thought that might look better. It seemed pretty basic at the time, because I felt the level of skating was pretty high in the UK at that moment, and then I'm doing a crooked grind on a four-foot-long block of ice. We turned up, had a laugh, and there was nothing special made out about it.

It was very basic at the time, and then it was on the cover, and it was like, 'Wow, that's a good cover', and it was something that I was proud of having in my life. I'd never been on the cover of a magazine before.

Wig was interesting because he didn't skate. It was similar to Tim Leighton-Boyce, where he'd turn up with no skateboard. It'd feel a lot stranger now than it did then, because I was so much younger and so in it, but it was definitely weird that he didn't have a skateboard.

Before shooting with him, you knew who Wig was. You knew his photos, and how well he shot photos, so it was like an honour to shoot a picture with him, and he was a photographer that you knew that when you shot a photo with him you were going to get in a magazine. →

LEFT TO RIGHT
[1] Paul Shier, London, by Wig Worland
[2] Gordon Skrezka, South Shields, by Wig Worland

291   1997

Channon King

That photo[3] was from hanging around Southbank all the time. One night my friend John put his board on there and stood on it, just mucking around really, but we were like, 'Oh, that kind of moves!', and the board sat in there perfectly. We dropped in and went all the way to the end, but John was like, 'You can ollie that high', because I was going through a phase of trying to grind the highest things I could.

Back then there was no video cameras other than Magee, Manzoori, Frank and Channer, and other than that I don't think anyone else had cameras, but obviously I had to save it because I needed to film it. Channer was there one day and I just took him to the tunnel and told him I thought I could grind it, and he filmed it really well, riding down with me. It was an amazing feeling because I had loads of my friends with me, and there was all these fishermen at the bottom watching me, because it's a pier for launching fishing boats off. It's tidal, so as you were trying it, the longer you took, the steeper and steeper and faster and faster it's getting.

At the end, the rail doesn't just finish, it curves back into the wall, so when you get to the bottom you have to kind of pop over the hook, and what I should have done is go and buy a hacksaw and just hacksaw that off.

I'd go through phases of having a camera with me, and that time with the fountain and Buckingham Palace, we turned up to skate it and it was full of water and no one was crazy enough to actually skate it apart from Spence. If there hadn't been water there, that photo never would have got taken because I would have been skating.

I think I've got a good eye for composition, just from looking at thousands of images of skateboarding. My bedroom as a kid, every single surface was covered in skateboard magazine photos. My door, my ceiling, it was creepy. I just wanted to completely immerse myself in it.

Ben Leyden

To know Livingston you need to be there every day. If you spend a couple of months away from it, you come and go, 'What is going on here?!' It'd spin you out. It's a bizarre design anyway, and the kinks in it have been there since day one. You've got a certain patch of the bank next to the wall where it was concreted and it rained, and it was all divotted, and that's been like that since day one, so I think certain aspects of it just take people by surprise. I seen Howard Cooke come to the park and wipe himself out. I was skating, and I did a melly over the hip and landed on top of Howard Cooke. I was only young and he looked at me and he was totally pissed off with me. I told him I was really sorry and that I didn't mean it, and he never spoke to me for about eight years after that. He came in and just went to grind the pipe and was a goner.

I think if you skate Livi every day and you turn up to a five-foot miniramp, you're in your element. You know that it's playtime! If you put anybody that doesn't skate Stevenage into Stevenage, it's the exact same contrast. Or Romford or something.

You had tours in the nineties, so the Blueprint team would turn up, or the Panic team, and sure, they could do some stuff, but they'd never touch the bowl. Those guys were studying a totally different way of skateboarding.

At that time I was going skating, then going home and taking Valium and listening to Belle & Sebastian and painting everything magnolia. I wasn't really that gnarly, I don't think. ●

1997

Jonny Robson

I'd stopped doing things for *Sidewalk*, but I was still living in the *Sidewalk* house on Cowley Road, and I thought to myself that I knew so many amazing skaters... Frank Stephens had just bust out and I don't think he was getting any product at the time, Vaughan Baker had just started coming up at contests, and there was Alan Rushbrooke and Pete Hellicar who I was obsessed with because of what they did at contests.

I wanted to do a skate company and I thought, 'How hard can it be?' Turns out, not hard at all! And that was even before the internet so if you want to converse with someone how do you do that? How do you get their number? What do you do, do you write to them? How do you get their address? So I called Paul Haynes – who owns Rollersnakes – from a callbox and says, 'Listen Paul, I've got an opportunity for you, OK? I've got a bunch of skateboarders together, but I'm not going to tell you who they are...', and of course Paul, who's a successful businessman, goes, 'Jon, Jon. Let me just stop you there. I couldn't give a fuck who they are, just get to the point.' So I was like, 'You're putting out branded gear, Paul, and to be honest it's a load of shit and it's a miracle that anybody's buying it. So you've got the flow but I've got the designs and the personalities in the skateboarders.' All I wanted to do was make skate videos, so this was just an elaborate way of being able to do that. I told Paul I'd got everybody together and I'd bullshitted them that I had a skateboard company, and all I needed was for him to give me the resources to do that. And he's like, 'What do you mean resources?'

I said I needed one of those new mobile phone thingies, and access to a car, and he told me to get the train to Nottingham and we'd sort it out.

So I got the train to Nottingham with my last 30 quid or whatever it was – with nowhere to stay and no return ticket or anything – and I didn't even tell Andy Horsley or Chris. I think they just thought, 'Whatever Jon's planning is going to be shit and he's never going to do anything'. And in some sense they were right.

I arrived at Rollersnakes and Paul's not there. I asked them to call him and he arrives at five to five, just when the shop's closing, and he takes me into the back room. I've got a big bag of speed in my back pocket that some hitch-hikers gave me a few weeks before. I start chopping up this speed, telling him it's coke, and as soon as he hit it he goes, 'Why are you telling me this is coke? Is this what our relationship's going to be like? This is going to go a lot better if you realise that I'm smart! I'm building an empire here, what are you doing? Just tell me what you can bring to the table and don't bullshit me.' And I said, 'Well I'm afraid I can't tell you anything without bullshitting', and he goes, 'OK, well just bullshit me, and then tell me what's real'. So I tell him I just want to do a skateboard company, and he says he's sick of talking to me so he gives me a mobile phone and the keys to a Ford Fiesta parked outside, and says, 'Make me a skateboard company and I'll see you on the first of March, right here'. This was the first of February, 1997.

I just got in the car and tried to figure out what the plug he'd given me with the mobile phone was. I didn't know what a charger was, I didn't know you had to charge a mobile phone and I didn't know the calls were like 97p a minute or something like that.

Eventually I get Vaughan's number, Mark Channer's number, and Paul Silvester's. I think. Obviously I had Harry's. And we were going to call it Borstal. I'd done the design like the HMP prison gate logo, with 'Borstal' underneath and it was going to be a cross between early Alien Workshop with Polaroid-type images and an olive and orange palette and with things torn out and a little bit cut-and-paste, mixed with a gritty British *Scum*/*Kes*-type film aspect. If we could pull that off. We were going to do boards and t-shirts and make a wicked video. That was the idea.

I spoke to Pete Hellicar on the phone and I think that was him asking me if he can be on the company because he's heard that Harry's on it. He said he'd heard I was working with Paul Haynes, and that he loved Paul Haynes, but that he'd rip me off. I'm like, 'No, no! Because I'm planning on ripping him off! I'm kind of ripping him off right now!'

Pete tells me he's with a guy called Ben White and he had a warehouse in the Square Mile – and at the time I was obsessed with the Square Mile – on Charterhouse Street next to Smithfield Market. He tells me to come down to London and meet this guy because this guy wants to do a skateboard company.

When I arrived in London they were so cool to me. Pete was so cool to me and I really liked him. At the time Pete didn't really know me; he didn't know that I was untrustworthy, but he was a real skateboarder and just assumed that I would know something about skateboarding and that I'm valuable in it. He thought he was working with someone who was shit hot and he wanted to come up with a different name. At the time I was reading the *Unabomber Manifesto* – it wasn't that I was into anarcho-primitivism – and Ted Kaczynski was on the loose at the time, and there was an old anarchist in Oxford who sold his manifesto, this little green Xeroxed thing, and I just loved the name 'The Unabomber'. I think it was the *Washington Post* who actually coined that term because he'd bombed United Airlines and he'd bombed universities. At the time I was super pretentious and I liked the idea that'd we'd just blow everything out in the UK.

So this guy Ben White owned L'Esprit D'Equipe, and he'd made so much money from those Northwave shoes with the jazzy soles that everybody was wearing for a while, and Unabomber rode off the back of those sales. They had a really cool warehouse, the kind of thing that you'd dream about, with people skating around and it had a miniramp in there. Indoors in central London! They made me my own flat! I wasn't even grateful! They'd decorated it, they'd built a bed, I had this enormous gothic-arch leaded window about 15 foot high and 10 foot wide with the Hammersmith and City line going directly underneath. It was just incredible. I'd get to my office by going up this wrought iron spiral staircase. That's where the Unabomber office was. So I'd sleep on one side of the room and then go to my big-bastard ergonomic table that just had a phone and an A4 pad on it. I didn't even have a computer or anything and I was running a skateboard company, but Pete basically did it all. I did a few designs and I came up with the name, which was actually 'Virus Unabomber He/She/They' because the original *Washington Post* article said, 'Unabomber: He/she/they is still on the loose' or something like that. →

Unabomber

PREVIOUS PAGE
Franklin Stephens, Pentonville Road, by Wig Worland
THIS PAGE CLOCKWISE FROM TOP LEFT
[1] Jonny Robson, Oxford, by Wig Worland
[2] Vaughan Baker, Droitwich, by Wig Worland
[3] *Daily Torment* issue 1 (extract)
[4] Alan Rushbrooke and Vaughan Baker, Bristol, by Pete Hellicar

Pete said that we had to meet Pete Fowler, and I said, 'Isn't that Chris Fowler's kid brother?', and he's like, 'Yeah, yeah, he's done all the graphics for Super Furry Animals', but I didn't hold that against him, and Pete said he was good, and he was a real character too. He said there was another guy called Thomas Barwick who's currently doing cartoons for *Penthouse* magazine. Pete Fowler had done Panic stuff, and things for *RAD* and *Viewfinder*, and of course his aesthetic is amazing. He's a visionary and he's amazing at what he does. He was very 'London' at the time, he had black-rimmed glasses and a Manhattan Portage bag and selvedge jeans with six-inch turn-ups and stuff.

So they set up my office and my own phone line, we had a distribution line, Pete had sorted out who we were going to get printed by and he wasn't going to take the first quote he got, he was bargaining and he was trying different wood; he was doing it proper. Getting the right wood and the best deals on the printing, he was getting the artwork in and he was working on a Mac.

I just smoked weed. When Ben White would come in every couple of weeks he'd tell me it smelled like a doss-house and ask me if I was ever going to do anything for the company and I'd be like, 'Hey, I'm the ideas man!'

Paul Haynes

Jon could sell snow to the Eskimos. He can talk and he's very charismatic, so obviously I fell under his spell. It wouldn't happen today, but back in the day I wanted to give him a chance, so I gave him the keys to the car and a phone.

Those guys knew everybody in the skateboard scene, so I could sense that something was happening, and I believed in Jon's hype. I gave him free rein, and Pete was in Nottingham, so they got together and their creative juices started to flow.

I had too many other things to do, and you can take too much on, so I was concentrating on my business. I didn't have time to run a skateboard company so I was more than happy for them to carry on with it. There was no animosity when they went to better themselves and go on to bigger things. We helped him start, and we watched them fly because I was all for people having opportunities themselves.

Pete Hellicar

I'd started working at L'Esprit D'Equipe so I spoke to Ben White and said to him that there was this opportunity to start a skateboard company, that there was a load of people up for it but we just needed some fucking money and a distributor. At that time he was a big distributor, he had a good thing going on, and when I first met Ben one of the first things he ever said to me was, 'If you want something, just ask for it. Do not fucking steal from me.' He looked me straight in the eye and said that, and to this day I completely respect that. If I have people working with me today, I say the same thing to them, because I really appreciate that level of frankness. So I said

to Ben that there was the opportunity to do this company, and he said, 'Right, get me a business plan'.

So I spoke to Jonny Robbo and said that I could get an office, and distribution, and that it was right in the middle of London, and so I put a business plan together with him, and went and shared it with Ben. I mean, it can't have been more than two pages... 'Boards. T-shirts. Adverts'. And Ben was like, 'Yeah, alright', and he gave us enough money to do the first run of boards – I want to say about 13 grand – he sorted us out with an office, which Harry and I painted, which was next door to what is now Fabric – it's what is the entrance to Fabric, in this weird building next to Farringdon Station.

We needed someone to go out and sell the boards, and Jon was best for that. I needed to be in London because I wasn't getting paid in the initial first phases of Unabomber – we'd only budgeted for Robbo to get paid – so I was working in the warehouse but in the rest of my time helping to make Unabomber happen. Jonny Robbo got the van and the phone and the card so he can go out on the road and sell all the shit. As I saw it, he was full of beans, a smart guy and a really good operator so he'd sell it on the road and I'd do packages, ads, board graphics and try to make it work in terms of being in the office, and also make some money for myself working in the warehouse for L'Esprit D'Equipe. So Jonny Robbo got the job with the money and I was just stoked to be working on it.

At that time I didn't really want to be on the team, I was more interested in working on the company. I was skating with them, but I was 27, early 28, and I was at that point where I was in a bit of a lull where I wanted to skate but I didn't really want to be part of a team.

The name Borstal didn't really work for me but the *Unabomber Manifesto* has turned out to be quite important... That's the thing about Jon, he's a real thinker. Him and Ben and all those guys were really thinking alternatively, and it wasn't just hearsay, it was, 'Read this fucking book, look at this, listen to this'.

Part of our agenda was to bring an element of politicised perspective to skating because it's the perfect space for it. I look out of the window now and I look at the kerb down there and I can tell you how the kerb works and I've got a completely alternative perspective on architecture and on materials, and if you choose to be engaged in that way, that then leads to alternative perspectives in other areas. It was about poking holes in the geopolitical landscape but also in the skate landscape.

It was pre-internet, so lots of reading, lots of VHS tapes and lots of hot knives. I think it was a bit 'the style is no style', the cut-and-paste, DIY, *Sniffin' Glue* aesthetic, and I think that really just came from not having a lot of money or equipment. It was a question of making things work with what we had. Standard skate stuff, make do with what you have. →

The Gospel according to UNABOMBER

Wherein we outline the reason for our collective disdain of the ill-informed nostalgics who would make a mockery of our own vision, our loud and blusterous applause for the riotous and righteous, and why our hallowed and media contrived name is synonymous with the leaving of one's mark on the destruction of civilisation.

Spitoons and sabers at high and ready...........
...........To pounce with purpose upon those cities all abandoned to the ruinous wake of it's modest berth.
The vessel, built without any corners to cut, shadowed by the manifesto we use to sell it shall weave childishly on four wheels which demand a fifth, threatening all the while to split asunder the duel pressures of Joy and Anger – reactions pertaining to the knowledge of the metomorphisis, the explosion wrought by coming collision of virus 'Unabomber' against the fat and diseased Babylon.

And all the while, Unabomber, (he/she/they) speaks. Yes! Blessed with the 'Affliction' of autism, nimble fingers and dextrous oral cavity which grant that coveted capacity 'Be All You Can Be' soon inspiring others to cast off the contrived images of the new west and raise their voices above the instinctive perpetuation of deriguer banter and into the loftier pitch of UNA-doctrine; the dissemination of the program for tonight and tommorow where we suck in the validation of our title well won 'The Best Skate Company Since Records Began'.

As the cherubs of repose dollop your brow with the puckered promise of the world of dreams, and the lateness of the hour devours your extremities with the needlings of an empire far away from the everyday. Gather up your final ounce of resistance, scrub the slumber from your sockets and elect this company UNABOMBER to the place of prominence in the sensory landscape of your life. It will help you to grapple with the base instinct which keeps you in sync with the square world. and will be the vanguard of the violence vented when we vanquish 'Wake up To the impossible dream'. the coma, the death-like state, which people pull over themselves like a blanket, and is to us a rehensible condition which must be obliterated.

Mark Channer

Jon had assembled Harry, Alan Rushbrooke, Frank Stephens, and they'd just seen Vaughan Baker at a Custard Factory thing, and credit to Jon for having an eye for talent, so it was those four. I was floating around looking for some purpose, and I was really into that ethic of no possessions, and just skate, and live it, and I knew that that was a good, solid, small team. Pete had mentioned it to me, so there was the two of us to make it six people, then Paul Silvester got on.

It probably sounds clichéd nowadays but at the time it was new for me, the idea of having no possessions, no nothing. That still influences me, not being bound to having stuff. I didn't keep anything, because I think any insecurities I had about skateboarding have been filled with having so many people say nice things. It's overwhelmed any insecurities. I've had so many nice things said; I'm topped up.

Vaughan Baker

How it happened for me, because I didn't know that Jon was really thinking about it, was that I was at a contest in Liverpool – Brian Sumner and Toddy and all those guys were there – and I came fourth or something like that. After the contest Jon pulled me aside and asked if I'd be interested, and he reeled off the names and I kinda crapped myself because I just thought that those guys are the 'sponsored guys'. I agreed on the spot, as you would, and they invited me over to Nottingham to meet with them. So I collected my dole cheque, glued my delams in and went to Nottingham to meet all those guys.

The initial meeting was at Rollersnakes, and it was me, Harry, Frank and Alan, and we sat down with Paul and discussed it through. The next thing I knew, that wasn't happening and it was something else completely. It felt to me, with no experience of being sponsored, really big. But then I think to Harry and Alan and Frank, who were already hooked up, it was a bit different for them. But it did feel like 'ours'. I was on a board company with the guys I looked up to and it was essentially our company.

Jon always had that nervous, frantic energy. He was a new person to me, and I don't think I'd ever met anybody like him before. Him and Pete together, they had a lot of ideas, and it was all really cool. It was almost ahead of its time, I would say.

Alan Rushbrooke

When me and Harry were in America I had a message on my pager which was Hellicar asking us to give him an urgent call. This was when Harry was getting stuff from Toy Machine, and it was basically a trip out to see if Harry could get on an American company, and I was tagging along. I was the Bez.

I rang Hellicar back – reverse charges – and within the space of about five minutes Hellicar had blurted out the whole thing about Unabomber and asked us if we wanted to ride for it. I'd known Pete and those guys for years, and I was in the US and not really kicking with what the whole US vibe was, just not really feeling that, so it was a no-brainer to say yes to him and he said we'd sort it all out when we got back.

We all got invited down to London, to see Ben White, and Pete Turvey, who was working for Duffs at that point – Pete's an absolute legend who has hooked up so many people over the years – and they discussed what they wanted to do. Me and Harry would be the first pro riders, and we were all assembled as a group. I wouldn't say there was any business discussion, it was more just that they'd started a company called Unabomber and we were all stoked.

We had some blank boards, and we said we'd talk about shapes and ideas. My board was the same as the Julien Stranger Antihero board with the pirate ship on the bottom – that's exactly what my board was because that was my favourite board. I just gave them that board and told them to make it, and that's why it was blue as well, because I wanted it exactly the same.

For those early boards, they'd show us the series artwork, and then we would pick our shapes. It wasn't just, 'Here's your wood with your name on it, there you go'. I'm not creative artistically, so I might have offered some ideas but I think Pete and Jonny had very clear ideas for that stuff. With 'Bomber it was about using artists and giving them a platform as well, so each series was always the same artist. I absolutely loved it, 'Bomber was incredible at that time.

Paul Silvester

It was at G97 when Pete asked me, and I was drunk. I thought, 'Fuck it, why not?' I'd heard of it because Ben Powell had mentioned something about it, but I didn't really know much about it.

For the whole time with Unabomber I never really got paid, even for my pro board, and I had no idea who was funding it or anything like that. I just left that to those guys. I was just skating. I'd get a package of three boards a month, and t-shirts and hoodies and that kind of thing, and I'd just skate. For the first year or so I was just stoked to be riding with them, although I didn't really know them that well. I'd meet them to skate with and it was weird to start with because it wasn't what I was used to. It was good going to different cities and staying in people's houses but it took me a while to get in the flow with everyone.

It was weird to get to know them all and skate with them. I'd always felt uncomfortable when I'd see them skate, especially Rushbrooke on miniramp, Harry ollieing up massive things, Vaughan's consistency, Frank doing gnarly stuff, Channer's style and Pete skating the way he did, and I always felt like I was not as good as them. I always found it very hard to go out skating with them, but then seeing what they were doing when I wasn't skating with them also pushed me, and they all introduced me to a lot of stuff I wasn't used to, different cultural stuff, so that was a good thing.

I was the last one to turn pro, and I didn't want to do it anyway. I didn't

CLOCKWISE FROM LEFT
[1] Unabomber logo, by Pete Fowler
[2] Mark Channer, Hungerford Bridge, by Wig Worland
[3] Alan Rushbrooke, Nottingham, by Wig Worland
[4] Pete Hellicar, Leather Lane, by Wig Worland

1997

Elsewhere

think I was good enough, I didn't want the pressure and I was just happy to skate and get free stuff. I still wasn't making any money from Unabomber, but through Unabomber I would get more free stuff off people, and I would just sell it, apart from what I needed. I'd get the Megabus up and down the country, and was still living that lifestyle of not having much money to eat or do stuff, even though I was a sponsored skater. Going pro didn't make any difference because I didn't get paid. I got some travel paid for but I think they got other sponsors to put money in for that.

My photo for my first ad[4] is on a Zero board, because I hadn't even started riding for them when we shot that. That was from a month before, and they went ahead and used that photo for an ad straight away. They had them five on, and the ads started, and then when I got on, my ad went straight in and it had all their names on it.

I hated my first graphic, the Man one. I never really got much of a choice in that stuff. The second one was the Knife series so everyone took what they got, but then that double-fist thing was not what I asked for, so after that I didn't really care.

Rushbrooke and Channer and Vaughan were getting paid off Converse, but I just never pursued it. I'd get a call from someone asking if I wanted to do something, and I'd say yes, but I didn't ever go chasing anyone down. I never marketed myself because I didn't want to because I was just happy skating.

Harry Bastard

I'd seen the standard of some of the American skateboarders who were considered gods, and were living that high life, when really they weren't all that good at skateboarding. They were good, but they weren't as good as I thought they were. Maybe that's because I didn't realise I was a good skateboarder until a lot later on.

Pete Hellicar

Harry was a fucking mess, he really knew how to drink. He's proper. I've never met anyone like him, he's an absolute machine, he can smoke and drink everyone under the table. It was the beginning of all that stuff, that whole scene of English skaters being a little bit more rambunctious.

I remember being at a party once and being a prick and Harry just slapping me in the face really fucking hard. He just looked at me and he went, 'Stop being a prick'. It was straight up. He didn't beat the shit out of me but he called me out for being a prick, and rightly so. That was the attitude we had as a group. We were quite straightforward with each other and we wanted to highlight that same frank approach to the wider world.

Pete Fowler

I met Pete Hellicar from skating at the Southbank, through Ben Bodilly. Ben was the only person that I knew in London at first. Pete had this mad little office and he was working for a ski, surf and snowboard distributor called L'Esprit D'Equipe, and he asked if I wanted to do some graphics.

Harry lived in a little dungeon there, which was hilarious.

Pete definitely had a vision for what it was about: quite disruptive, with a real punky grit, he was an agitator. It's mad that he had the He/She/They thing back then.

Doing the artwork for Super Furry Animals was my big break in London, but I'd always still do stuff if I'm really into it if there's no budget. When Pete approached me I knew he was an interesting guy; he was really smart, he was very much interested in the beginnings of the 'Surveillance State', and he was very much aware of how things were going with society. He had a vision for what he was doing, and we had a long conversation about it, then I went off and did some drawings. Me and Pete got on like a house on fire and we were both interested in similar things. Doing the Super Furries stuff was pretty good income and it generated a lot more work for me because that was back when record labels had marketing budgets for fly posters and magazines ads.

I came up with the Unabomber gimp mask. When I stopped doing Unabomber, Pete said he'd like to carry on using the gimp, because it had been their logo, so he started doing variations on that. I totally trusted Pete, and he had a vision for it, and he wanted to have a brand identity. ●

ALAN RUSHBROOKE
FRANK STEPHENS
HARRY
VAUGHAN BAKER
MARK CHANNER
PAUL SILVESTER

0171 490 8650

LEFT TO RIGHT
[1] Paul Silvester, Leeds, by Wig Worland
[2] Unabomber He/She/They sticker
[3] Unabomber Bomb Builder, by Pete Fowler
[4] Unabomber ad, Sidewalk, October, Paul Silvester, by Wig Worland

Mark Channer

I was floating around, 20 or 21 years old, with no qualifications, and essentially, I was searching for what I learned later in life were the basics of happiness: feeling connected, feeling that what you are doing is making a difference, to be part of something bigger than myself. I wanted to be part of a team that was doing something good.

There were these *Video-Log* videos coming out, and there was the connection to those through Mat and Frank and Ben Powell; there had been a few of those videos and I was stoked to see them, but they just weren't that good. As someone who had made videos and watched videos relentlessly, it was a bit, 'That's not as good as it could be'.

I was the one who came up with the name. I was on a train back from Norwich with Mat and saw a newspaper headline about some local playing fields, and suggested it to Mat. Mat said it could have all sorts of different meanings, but I just thought it sounded cool. I'd blundered upon a title and Mat could see a concept within it.

I think we'd already started to film around the same time *A Mixed Media* came out. You can tell it's the same era because it was the first time you were digitising Hi8 footage on to a computer to edit, rather than it being tape-to-tape record/pause. There's a look to it.

We knew we could do it well and we knew we had the connections to do it. I had the savviness to edit, so I sold a bunch of product, bought a Hi8 camera and started videoing with Mat Fowler and Colin Kennedy. You can tell my stuff because it's got a slightly thicker submarine-window look to it.

I love that there was not an ounce of thinking about who anybody skated for. There was no premeditated company thinking, it was just about who had a bit of footage, who had the time and would be up for it.

Ben Powell's footage sewed it together – he contributed all the stuff that he'd been doing on his travels and gave it more of a UK-wide feel.

Frank, Ben and I got access to an editing facility just off Tottenham Court Road. We took most of the footage there and we only had a day so we got about half of it done. That didn't work out but Rushbrooke's now-wife Michelle had a student house in Nottingham with a spare room, so we all rocked up there and Simon Kotowicz took his editing gear there. People would come and go, and people would rock up for their parts, and we were there for five days. Simon really helped us out with the equipment, so we were basically directing it all and he was doing the buttons.

We did 1,000 copies, but then Simon did a bootleg version with a bonus section of him skating vert at the end. It was a really odd thing to do. It's the 'bonus' thing that really gets me, as if anybody's going to be like, 'I was thinking about buying *Playing Fields*, but Simon's vert footage at the end, that's really tipped me over the edge'.

Mat Fowler

When we knew my mum was going to die, my college tutor said I should go back home and spend time with my mum, so in the last term I moved back with my mum and dad, and I started signing on the dole. My mum had cancer so it was her last months, as it spread, and we kept her at home instead of going to a hospital. I would just look after her and take pockets of time to go off skateboarding, to have some clarity, I guess, to be able to cope with it all.

When she passed away I didn't have to go back to finish the last term for almost a year, so I stayed at home, just me and my dad. I have a brother but he'd left home and was living with his partner by that point, and I would help look after my dad or try and cook different meals and then I would go off skateboarding and signing on, so I would be signing on in High Wycombe and then going off skateboarding with Mark and Frank. That was when we were doing *Playing Fields*, that year in between having to go back to do my last term. I was essentially not working, not doing anything other than signing on and living with my dad, so I would go off on adventures to Scotland or to Nottingham or Ipswich and we would film. ●

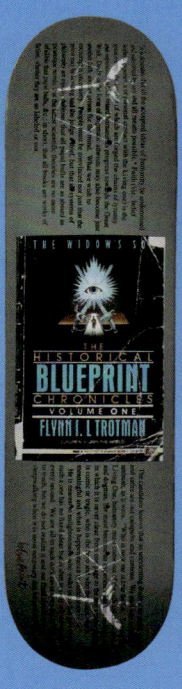

Alvin Singfield

With *A Mixed Media*, everything was shot in a year, and a lot of it was shot on the tour that we ended the video on. *Anthems* was more planned out; I had a guy named Adrian Frearson who was a snowboard videographer, and he'd got a 16mm or an 8mm camera, which is what we shot the opening sequence in *Anthems* with. That was all kind of choreographed, how each rider would appear. Like with Paul Shier and Mark Baines getting off the bus and kicking Matt Pritchard who was sleeping like a homeless person at Trafalgar Square. It was all meant to be fun, it wasn't meant to be taken too seriously, having a skit as a way of introducing quite a vast team. When you get to the bit at the Freemasonry headquarters in Great Queen Street, and it's the entire team in front of those giant doors, it's a big team, Panic and Blueprint all together. It probably went on for far too long but it was an interesting way of introducing them all.

Seb Palmer

It was my idea to do a skate premiere, because I'd been at *Ban This* in London, and nobody had done a skate premiere in the UK since that, I don't think, so that's how we ended up doing all the premieres for Panic and Blueprint in Sheffield before they were done in London.

They were filming a lot where we were, I think we were the biggest Blueprint stockist in the UK, and we were in the middle of the country. Colin Kennedy and John Rattray were coming down, and everybody was coming over to Sheffield.

Flynn Trotman

My first graphic[2], Dan Magee asked me what I would like and I just sent him the cover of a book I'd been reading. Looking back now, I think that fitted pretty well into the image, and maybe Magee got some ideas of where to possibly take it a little bit, because the graphics thereafter were around that kind of Masonic-y vibe. It was a little bit different.

Colin Kennedy

I think Mark Baines was a big catalyst of Blueprint being successful, because he just had such a huge profile, and he was doing stuff that no one else was doing. No one was doing things as proficient as he was. ●

SLAM

Sharon Tomlin

Seth was working at Sumo, and Seb didn't like Seth's girlfriend and he was worried she was going to trap him with some kind of anchor baby. He said he needed to get him out of there, and he asked if I could help out.

Seth Curtis

Slam was a fucking swearword down there at the time. The main guys at Southbank thought Slam had changed and it was a fashion shop and it wasn't a hardcore skate shop. I think I almost kind of made it my mission to put Slam on the map more, and be all, 'Nah, fuck that, Slam is skater-owned and operated'.

So much happened so it's hard to quantify my years at Slam. It was seminal in everything in my life. Having Rough Trade downstairs we took it for granted at the time, but looking back, oh my god. I had a fucking school in music at my fingertips. Free CDs, free music, going to see bands, going to clubs, music video shoots, fashion stuff, being in Japanese magazines, having a clothing brand and selling that in Japan, all that stuff was all from Slam. It was all amazing.

You'd go downstairs and ask Jamie – who was one of the saltier members of staff but he had insane music knowledge and he actually works in the British Museum now, as a music curator – what was playing and he'd be like, 'What's this? Really? Oh my god. This is Iggy and the Stooges, you philistine.' And he'd pull out all the CDs by the band and say, 'Take these, go and listen to them, come back when you're done. Philistine.' The education that I got there with all that stuff was so good.

Daniel Johnston was in a couple of times, he was good. Joanna Newsom was amazing. She did a couple of shows and we got really into her music. She went on to be quite successful. I remember Lev got really into her. He'd always fan out. The White Stripes played and we went to see one of the first White Stripes gigs in the UK, and I remember being blown away by that. We were all there for that.

In Slam, Blueprint was almost like the wave after the time of Toy Machine and that stuff. There was a real shift. I think there was always this perception within the UK that UK skate brands were a bit homespun and a bit shit and not as good as the American stuff, which was kinda true, really. There was a lot of that so nothing really 'stuck', and Panic had a faltering start, and then when Blueprint came around it was still a bit hokey, and the Faze connection was a bit hokey at the start.

As it gained momentum, as a shop we got really behind it. And as it caught fire, there was almost this wind of change that blasted through skating in the UK where it was like US brands just became completely irrelevant and everything was about UK skateboarding. Blueprint really was the first thing to surface like that. It was like Powell was in the late '80s. We were selling over a hundred Blueprint boards a week at Slam. We were ordering them in fifties. Fifty of each rider. It was mental. They were cheaper than the US brands, and we were all friends together. Everyone was coming to London, whether they were from Scotland, or up north, and Slam was the London clubhouse. That was where Rattray and Kennedy would come to for griptape, or where Shier and Baines would come to hang out.

Toby Shuall

When Seth started working at Slam, other people started coming, and about a year after Seth coming, the London skate scene really started to change, but nearly all of the old guard that I'd grown up with had just gone. Pete Hellicar came to London, Snowy came, Joey Pressey came, Blueprint started getting bigger and everyone started staying with Magee, and all of a sudden the skate scene got really good. Everyone started coming to London and everyone started coming into Slam all the time. That was the best bit for me, as a skateboarder, getting past this really tribal London scene, and the northern scene. We were really over that shit.

When Pete turned up with Unabomber it was a really good time, and London felt like Philly or something. It was cool. There was different people coming into town that ended up living in the city and skating and being together, and they were all from different places and it was really refreshing. There was still a lot of skaters from London, but it was very mixed and there was no more, 'You're from here, you're from there'. We were all quite excited to be in London at the time. I've left London now because I'm so over it and it was so expensive, but at that time it was a really good scene and it was fun to be there.

Slam finally got better, and no one was banned from Slam anymore, just as the UK industry began to start. Hellicar had Unabomber, Magee was getting a lot of momentum with Blueprint and it was just good. →

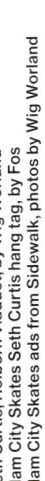

Fos

I drew the Slam Slayer logo, in '97 before I worked at Slam. I was thinking, 'Why don't they do this? This would be the coolest shit ever!', and I showed it to Russell Waterman and he loved it but he didn't have any say in it. Then I showed it to Sharon and Paul, and I think they paid me £50 for it but I was just stoked that they did it as a logo and I got stickers. It was like, 'Yes, I did that!', and I think that was the first graphic I ever did for anyone.

I happened to be in the shop one day when they put a notice up on the wall looking for a warehouse manager, so I sent them a CV. I was working in the shop, and Russell Waterman called to ask if anyone could help them unload two wagons of DVS shoes tomorrow, so I said I'd do it. When I went over there the next day, that was when I first met Russell, and they got me working there every day from then on. I worked there for five years from that day, after going in to take a bunch of shoes off a truck and I ended up becoming the warehouse manager, and then the sales manager.

When I started at the warehouse it was me, Chris Turner from Orange Goblin, Russell and Sofia. I think Luke Davidson had got fired, and I replaced him. I love Luke but I think that's how it went. Chris was the one making the sales, I was the one packing the orders, Russell was doing Holmes at the time, and Paul Sunman was sitting around and doing what he does.

One of the shops in Ireland never paid their bills – and bless 'em, they were

great, but it would take them about a year to pay a 30-day invoice – and the guy called me up because we had a Zoo York order for them. I'm telling him they owed us £200 from a year ago, and I ask if he can get that cheque to me so I can ship the Zoo York order, and he was like, 'Ship. The Zoo York. NOW!' It was the funniest shit, and I was dying laughing. I still say that to this day, 'Ship the Zoo York now!'

Paul was buying sports cars and not paying his bills, which delayed orders. He would literally buy a sports car 'for the company', and be like, 'This is my company car', and it's a Lotus Elise. I'd be like, 'Never mind that, where's the 20 grand that you owe to DVS, so we can get the shoes so that I can sell them and get my commission?' It was pulling teeth all the time, trying to get him to pay his bills. There was one order that was horribly delayed and when I came into work there was a Welsh guy on the phone going, 'Hello. I ordered DVS for summer, and it's now winter.' That was a classic line as well. It was so rad talking to all the shops.

I graduated in '97 and my final year project was genetically engineered sneakers, and it was in *Lodown* magazine. Somebody had been throwing away a freezer, so I had this freezer at my degree show with all these things that looked like they were growing in it. I almost failed the course because of that, but I think I got a Third for it.

Greg Finch

I really badly wanted to work in Covent Garden; I was working in shitty

pubs and whatnot, and that was just not conducive to my skate life. I used to go through Covent Garden and hand my CV out, just go round the shops, and I knew that Slam was an absolute no, but I knew all the people there so that was alright. We were all cool.

I went down to this place called High Jinks in the Thomas Neals Centre, and I was like, 'Fuck it'. There were loads of pretty girls there and it was right next to Slam, so I wanted to work there. I handed the dude my CV and just went back to him a week later and asked if there was any news. Then a week later after that, and a week later after that, and eventually just wore him down and he was like, 'Fuck, if you want to work here that bad then come on in'. His name was Theo and he ended up starting Superdry, then selling it off down the line. He started Skate of Mind, but it was all my idea.

As soon as I got in I saw this dead patch in the store at that back, and I started a skate shop there. We went to San Diego to look at the ASR trade show, bought a bunch of things – Dukes shoes and stuff, things Slam didn't have – and we started this store.

Paul Sunman is quite mad competitive, and really protective, and when he heard about it he offered me a job in Slam. I sort of played the two off each other for a minute, but I got a really good offer and I went to work in Slam. It happened quite quickly. He didn't want me in any senior position, and Slam was like a shit-show, so I just went in at a higher salary and that was kept between us. →

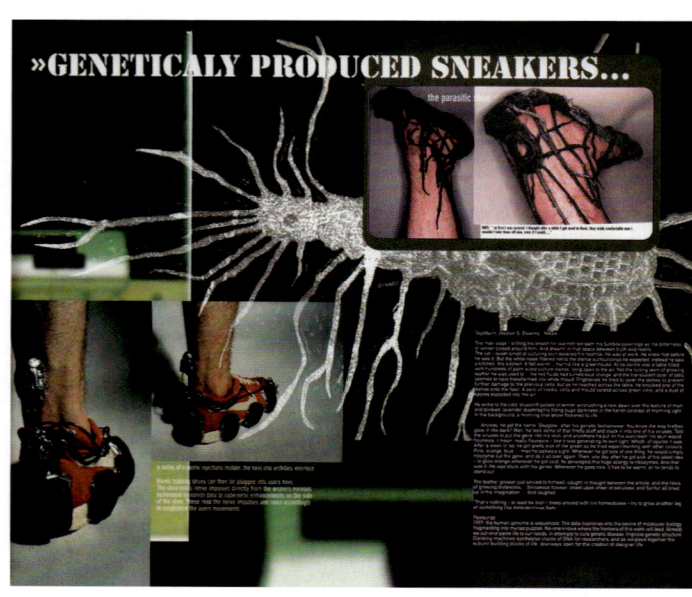

CLOCKWISE FROM LEFT
[1] Slam City Skates Slayer logo sticker, by Fos
[2] Genetically Modified Sneaker project from *Lodown* magazine issue 1, by Fos
[3] Nik Taylor, Greg Finch, Harry, Seth Curtis and Pete Hellicar, Stockwell, by Mark Channer
[4] Mark 'Zippy' Preston, Ideal, by Kris Ludford

Elsewhere

→ **ROLLERSNAKES**
Paul Haynes

When HSC were New Deal, we used to buy lots from them, but then they went into retail, so they were a distributor and a retailer, so we became competitors. We stopped buying from them, and we were importing – grey marketing – their products, which is a bit naughty, but it's business.

We fell out, and it got quite tense because they were a big deal. They were taking out lots and lots of full-page adverts in the magazines, so they started to become really powerful. They said to Jim Peskett at *Sidewalk*, 'If you let Rollersnakes advertise in your magazine, we're going to pull our adverts'. It was totally illegal, but what could Jim do? So I couldn't advertise my mail-order products in the magazine, and it was quite worrying because that was our main source of income because mail order was massive for us. They used their power and stopped us advertising in *Sidewalk*.

I got around it, I spoke to Chris at Shiner and asked if he could place an ad for me, just selling Birdhouse products, and then soon we had a double-page spread with all Shiner products because Jim couldn't refuse Shiner.

→ **FIFTY FIFTY**
Danny Wainwright

We came up with the idea one night smoking bongs. Me, Joe Habgood and Syd, and it was meant to be all three of us but it ended up being me and Syd. The summer of '97, I went on tour with Vans and there was Generation '97, there was Münster, there were all these contests, so I was like, 'Right, I'm gonna go because I need to make some money at these contests'. I made about six grand skating those contests, and I spent about a grand on tequila and weed, so I put five grand into the shop. Syd saved up money and he put five in, and while I was away he did a business plan, so when I got back it was like, 'Right, we're gonna fucking do it'. Habgood came up with the name.

We opened in October '97, and the first stuff we bought for the shop, we bought from Nick Zorlac out the boot of his car in a petrol station. We pulled up, he pulled up, boot's open, he had a bunch of shit in the back, paid him and off we went. Proper Del Boy stuff.

We had a relationship with Shiner so that wasn't a problem. There was certain things we couldn't have because Tony Coffey had them at Rollermania. Tony was in business and supporting that Bristol skate scene for years, so we were cool with that.

Bristol just needed refreshing really. Bristol was popping off. Skateboarding had changed and that's why we needed to make a shop. We were involved in making videos and skating and doing graphics and art, and painting, and we had all these people around us. There are artists everywhere in Bristol, the graffiti scene's super good, and there's a lot of painters. Banksy was meant to do a hundred hand-painted boards but we never got round to it. That would have been a nice little retirement... He used to come into the shop and hang out and drink tea, and I haven't seen him in years but he was a cool guy.

I've always painted, and I did all of the Fifty graphics, all the clothing and stuff. I go through phases of doing a bunch of canvases and then I get rid of them and won't paint for a year or two.

Nick Zorlac

When Fifty Fifty were opening and they asked if I could supply them, I said yes because I wasn't supplying anyone else in the area. They were at a trade show or event in London and they were going on the A40 to go towards Bristol to go home, so they said they wanted to buy a load of stuff but they didn't really know how to get to Edgware, so they asked if I could meet them. I put a lot of stuff in the boot[4] and back seats of my car and went to meet them in Acton or somewhere, on their way west out of London. Must have looked well dodgy to anyone passing by.

→ **AIR**
Dan Joyce

My video camera got stolen out of my flat in Harrow, and I was gutted, and there was no reason for me to stay there now. Then a friend of mine, Danny Gooding, who was the manager of Air in Leeds, well his dad was a vicar and he got the job as the local vicar in Liskeard, which was near where I lived, so he started coming down and hanging out with us.

He said they needed somebody to manage Air, and Wakefield skatepark had just started, and there was a really good scene up there, so he got me the job as manager of the shop and I moved to Leeds. When I first moved there I decided to hold a little jam there, and had a little street comp.

The owner of Air, Dickie Garland, he was best friends with Dave Beer who used run Back to Basics. They grew up together.

So I arrived there and I was just fully into skating. I had a girlfriend, and we split up and I was gutted. Dickie saw that and he goes, 'Here, do you want some coke?', and I'm like, 'Hmm... Go on then'. He had a little recording studio at the top of the shop, and he told me to go up there and he said there was some coke on a record on a turntable for me. I pressed play on it and did the whole lot, this massive line as my first one. And that was my introduction to raving and partying.

I used to sort Dave Beer out with DCs at the time, and he gave us free entry to all the clubs, and I ended up being a gimp in a fetish club in Leeds, I moved in with a coke dealer and I ended up losing my job and it all went to shit.

I phoned up my mum and I was like, 'I've fucked up here, I need picking up', and Alex from Siesta hired a van, drove up and picked me up. I was in Leeds until I was 21. ●

Ian Gunner

When we got DC it was new, and we knew it was a good brand, so we took DC to the 40 Degrees show, which was the big brand trade show. We were next to Vans and Airwalk, and all these surf, snow and fashion brands, and that's where the DC shoe growth escalated, from that show, because it wasn't just a skateboard shoe anymore. We were lucky enough to be able to offer pro shoes to skate stores and the big bulky shoes to the high street. The range was solid, the shoes were great and they were selling fast. It was a very rapid rise in popularity for skaters and non-skaters alike.

At the time I was very heavily into drum and bass, and I went to Goldie's club. Literally walked in, and Goldie walked past me with a pair of DCs on. I was like, 'Wow, this is serious. My hero's wearing the shoes that we've got in our warehouse.' So that Monday, I called up Gimme 5, because I knew he was a part of Stüssy, and asked for his size, and said I wanted to send a package. I sent all that out, went down to his club the following week, and he walked past me again, in the shoes that I'd sent him. I introduced myself, and he told me they were amazing, and couldn't thank me enough. He asked if there was anything he

could do, so the first thing I said was that we need an afterparty venue for an event that's coming up, which was the DC Super Tour, and he was just like, 'Done. How many people?' Not even a problem. That day set up a lifelong friendship and an amazing period for DC and music.

The DC Super Tour happened on unfinished ramps that we just put stickers on – the PlayStation park was half finished at the time and we were against the clock – but they seemed to love it. I also booked a DJ to play in the park and it got pretty rowdy and chaotic, the locals were trying to come in, so we had to cut the demo short. Some of the Americans were confused by the afterparty, by the music and crowd, but Damon Way was absolutely blown away by it and is still friends with Goldie now. DC even made him a signature shoe. Fortunately, me going to that club that day raised my profile at New Deal and I was tasked with helping with more marketing and promo duties. Through links with Goldie and music, I even gave shoes to Noel and Liam Gallagher. Everything just blew up.

I quickly started pulling together a UK skate team as well, which was super good – we had John Rattray, Paul Shier, Colin Kennedy, Rob Selley, Neil Urwin and a bunch of others – I purposely made sure

it wasn't a New Deal UK team. This had to be a DC Shoe team, not a New Deal UK team. It was still DC, in the DC style – you had to like wearing shell suits – but it was a good mixture of UK skateboarding and people from various board companies.

Paul Shier

DC was great. We never talked about ever getting paid, or asked to get paid, it was just such a cool thing to be a part of that it made no difference. NDUK were making a lot of money off DC in the UK, by the cars they were driving.

I was just hyped on the clothes and shoes. It was great product. I can't even think how many pairs of swishy pants Colin wore, which is weird because Colin doesn't seem like a swishy-pant person.

Colin Kennedy

I think I was just so influenced by Josh Kalis, and I just like that aesthetic, full head-to-toe. The brand had a strong impression on me, and it was a big part of my look, the DC logo. I don't look back on that negatively in any way.

I skated for etnies for a long time under Joe – well, 'skated for', I mean 'got some etnies' – under Faze, because he was trying to use his stable of riders to promote the brands that he was selling of course. He lost all of his soft goods, and

Sole Tech moved on, and DC moved over to New Deal. Paul was on DC and I was close with Paul, so I actively went after getting flowed DC from New Deal, and it was only flow because there was no money involved at that point.

It was such a strong brand and there wasn't that many distractions in the industry at that point, there was maybe only a few businesses taking up a huge market share. It wasn't like today where there's endemic shoe brands, corporate shoe brands, clothing companies, this, that and the other. You were either etnies or DC, and for me it was DC on the strength of their branding as well as more opportunities to do something, whether it was travel or UK tours.

DC were having huge commercial success at New Deal, and it felt good to be part of something like that, and they took care of us. To begin with it was a couple of pairs of shoes, then we'd get more product, and latterly I pushed to make sure we got a salary and whatnot.

I was round at Matt Anderson's house when Goldie came round, because those guys were taking care of him. That all definitely elevated your experience of London, and you felt like you were part of something special. The guys at New Deal valued what we brought to it even though we were skating for Blueprint, and by that point Blueprint was very successful. I think

they wanted to have members of Blueprint representing their shoe brand.

Neil Urwin

I used to get Dub stuff, but I was on Duffs, so when DC started they asked if I wanted to skate for DC, so I was like, 'Yeah, can do'. They'd just put my name to stuff. I remember not giving a fuck about the money they paid me, but I gave a fuck about the money I made from selling the shoes. That was by far the bigger prize. I'd get fucking massive packages, all the time. Even now, I'm constantly ordering stuff from Mr. Porter or whatever, and I'm creating anxiety for myself with all this shit that comes to my house. I realised about six months ago that the reason I do that is because it's re-enacting what used to happen.

Mon Barbour

Before you knew it, HSC were going great guns, doing these really slick brochures, doing two or three double-page spreads in the magazine, and they had everything. I remember Sean going down to see them and coming back telling me they had this room with a hundred telephones in it, for when people call in. It was a massive operation, they had DC, and hats off to Steve Douglas, because if it wasn't for him, none of that would have happened. Steve has given more to skateboarding than anybody else, but as the saying goes, 'Skateboarding owes you nothing'.

It changed skating in the UK. It made it more professional. It brought it to another level and it showed that it was becoming an industry, whereas before it was just a bunch of skaters and a bunch of distributors and skate shops here and there and there was nothing that was particularly joined together.

They bankrolled *Sidewalk*. If it wasn't for them putting in as much money as they did, *Sidewalk* wouldn't have been able to do what it did. That was when we stepped up our game, and realised we could start doing big adverts, and that's when I started developing the whole collaboration thing, doing adverts with a particular brand. We used to do really silly adverts, which were all paid for in hash – I used to give Chris Forder a quarter kilo of hash and that would pay for a couple of adverts – and that was how it went for many years, until we started doing these double-page and quadruple-page adverts, and at that point we had to really step up the game.

Carl Shipman

I shot a DC ad[3] on the White Wall in London, and I remember going down in my adidas, putting the DC shoes on for the shoot, and then getting rid of them and putting my adidas back on. I were used to skating in shelltoes and Gazelles and stuff like that, and I felt better on my board in them, or some Reeboks. ●

FROM LEFT
[1] Neil Urwin, Holborn Viaduct, by Wig Worland
[2] DC arrive at HSC, ad from *Sidewalk*, October
[3] Carl Shipman DC ad, *Thrasher*, December

running order

friday 11th july

4.00PM		Doors open
4.00PM-	11.00PM	The Pro's Open Practice
8.00PM-	8.45PM	Horny Toad on Stage
8.45PM-	9.45PM	DJ Peshay
9.45PM-	11.00PM	De La Soul on Stage

saturday 12th july

11.00AM-	12.00PM	The Pro's Open Practice
12.00PM-	12.15PM	Practice Vert Heat 1
12.15PM-	12.45PM	Vert Heat 1
12.45PM-	1.00PM	Practice Vert Heat 2
1.00PM-	1.30PM	Vert Heat 2
1.30PM-	2.00PM	BMX Demo (see below)
2.00PM-	2.15PM	Practice Street Heat 1
2.15PM-	3.00PM	Street Heat 1
3.00PM-	3.15PM	Practice Street Heat 2
3.15PM-	4.00PM	Street Heat 2
4.00PM-	4.15PM	Practice Vert Heat 3
4.15PM-	4.45PM	Vert Heat 3
4.45PM-	5.00PM	Practice Vert Heat 4
5.00PM-	5.30PM	Vert Heat 4
5.30PM-	6.00PM	BMX Demo (see below)
6.00PM-	6.15PM	Practice Street Heat 3
6.15PM-	7.00PM	Street Heat 3
7.00PM-	7.15PM	Practice Street Heat 4
7.15PM-	8.00PM	Street Heat 4
8.00PM-	8.45PM	Vitro on stage
8.45PM-	9.45PM	DJ Doc Scott
9.45PM-	11.00PM	New Kingdom on Stage

BMX DEMO

Matt Hoffman- 25 Years old owner of Hoffman Bikes & the worlds No 1 bicycle stunt rider.
Steve Swope- 27 Years old Vice President of Hoffman Bikes, 10 years as a top stunt rider.
Jamie Betswick- 25 Years old, Britains No 1, 4th on vert at the 1997 San Diego Espn X- Games.
Simon Tabron- 23 Years old, previous World Champion on vert currently riding for Hotwheels team.

sunday 13th july

11.00AM-	12.00PM	The Pro's Open Practice
12.00PM-	12.30PM	Vert Semi Final Practice
12.30PM-	1.30PM	Vert Semi Final
1.30PM-	1.45PM	Street Semi Final Heat 1 Practice
1.45PM-	2.15PM	Street Semi Final Heat 1
2.15PM-	2.30PM	Street Semi Final Heat 2 Practice
2.30PM-	3.00PM	Street Semi Final Heat 2
3.00PM-	3.30PM	Best Trick Street
3.30PM-	4.00PM	Vert Final Practice
4.00PM-	5.00PM	Vert Final
5.00PM-	5.30PM	Best Trick Vert
5.30PM-	6.00PM	Street Final Practice
6.00PM-	7.00PM	Street Final
7.00PM-	7.30PM	Highest Air Vert
7.30PM-		Announcements of Placings and Awards and Distribution of **$50,000.00**

Prize money split

	STREET	VERT	BEST TRICK		
				STREET	VERT
1	$10,000	$10,000	1	$1,000	$1,000
2	$4,500	$4,500	2	$500	$500
3	$2,500	$2,500	3	$200	$200
4	$1,500	$1,500			
5	$1,000	$1,000			
6	$700	$700			
7	$500	$500	HIGHEST AIR ON VERT		
8	$400	$400	1	$1,000	
9	$200	$200	2	$500	
10	$150	$150	3	$200	
11	$100	$100			
12	$100	$100			
13	$100	$100			
14	$100	$100			
15	$100	$100			
16	$100	$100			
17	$100	$100			
18	$100	$100			
19	$100	$100			
20	$100	$100			

CLOCKWISE FROM TOP LEFT
[1] John Cardiel, by Wig Worland
[2] Wig Worland shooting Moses Itkonen, by Kate Harahan
[3] G97 event guide (extract)

Phil Calvert

I think the real breakthrough for UK skating was students. When students changed the de rigueur student uniform from loose cable-knit sweaters with holes for thumbs and Dr Marten boots to cargo pants and DCs, that was it. G97 happened around the same time, the DC Supertour rolled into town just before that. Suddenly skaters went from being the geeky punks at the end of the street that were bullied in the UK.

America had a skateboard scene and within it was its own kind of ecosystem with all the other demographics that normal college kids had, within the skateboard scene, so they had the hip-hop kids, the Jocks, the footballers, but here we were all just one little group all the same. At that point in 1997 when G97 happened, we all became fucking rockstars overnight. And it was incredible.

Damian Ince

That came about because a guy from a promotions company used to skate back in the day. The promotion company used to put on gigs, and they'd seen that we put on a comp every year, and they came to my dad and asked if he'd want to make it bigger. When someone says to you, 'Do you want to put your comp on at Wembley Arena?', what are you gonna say?

There'd been all this trouble at Münster with security guards, and people boycotting it, because it's in a big arena and skateboarders are our own breed. We had our own little world and people from the outside looked in and didn't look kindly on us. We were the reprobates in society, and we didn't mix with the outside world, so you put skateboarders in a big arena and it doesn't mix, and we were a bit, 'Do we do it?', because of that. But when it's not your money that's being put up for it, it's like, 'Yeah, let's do it', because you're never gonna get a better chance than that, are you?

So we had a few meetings with this guy, and we said we'd go for it. They said they'd put the comp on and pay for everything, and we rolled with it.

We probably could have built the course, but Dave Duncan was building all the competition circuits in Europe, all the X-Games ramps, so at the time he was the world's best competitor course builder, and the promotions guy said they wanted the best in the world, so we got him over. We had the best time for two weeks building those ramps. Dave Duncan basically said, 'What do you want in the course?', and it was like, 'Fuck, what do we want?'

The car went in the middle because one time we'd put mine and my brothers' car in Radlands, so we wanted a car for

people to jump over in Gen 97, and one of our mates donated the Jag that went in there. Phil Jones, God rest his soul. He was a skater from Northampton who used to have a vert ramp in his garden back in the day, a few years before Radlands.

I wanted a bank-to-block, because I'd asked Rowley what he would want in a comp, and he said he'd want just a flat bank with a block on top. I loved skating the hip so we built a hip and a pyramid with a grind box. Dave Duncan was like, 'Yeah, all the Americans like these big fuckin' banks next to the vert ramp, so they can fly out the vert ramp', so we had to have these big, high, massive flat banks.

I thought it would be rad to skate a big kicker ramp, but then you had a step to go up as well – so you had a flat bit to clear, and you could do tricks over the gap – and that's how the G-gap, or the Euro-gap[2], was invented. That one was a beast, as well, that one was eight foot long. It weren't just like what you get at most skateparks now where it's a little three-foot thing, or a four-foot thing. This one was an absolute beast.

Penny got thrown out. He was skating, he hurt his ankle, and he had loads of weed stashed in his shoe. A medic came over, and security saw that he had loads of weed in his shoe, and kicked him out. ●

1997

1998

Tattoo Al, Police Bank, by Wig Worland

The happiest skating times I remember were skating with my mates for fun. It's something you do as a hobby, it's recreational, it's something you do because you enjoy it. When it becomes a business it changes. You've got such a short shelf life in skateboarding to make the money that you need to carry on in life. Making the money was good but the pressure was too much for me to be happy.
Carl Shipman

Elsewhere

Jonny Robson

Pete Hellicar and Ben White came into my office one day and woke me up, and they sat opposite me and go, 'How can you have done nothing?' I hadn't done nothing, I'd went round the country twice or three times in the little Astra van with an example of each product we did and an order book and I went to 88 shops from Thurso to Essjay's and everywhere in between.

So when those guys came and told me it was over, it was a surprise, because I just thought I'd be able to tread water doing nothing. I did those sales but they found out I'd been selling boards out the back of the van. Taking people to cash machines so they could buy a board off me for £25. I'd come back in the Astra van with half the boards and all the hoodies gone and I'd say I'd given some away to the shops as a goodwill gesture, just to get it moving.

There was so much stuff I didn't video. I didn't video Vaughan Baker killing Norwich town centre, I didn't video Frank at Bristo Square... Just couldn't be arsed even getting the video camera out of the bag. I'd come back and Pete would be like, 'So Frank tells me you weren't that keen on videoing?', and I'd be like, 'Oh yeah, he did ask me a few times...' He used to ask me to get the camera out and I used to say no! Because I couldn't be arsed.

The problem is that I knew how to do marketing, I knew how to form relationships with shops. I'd already been coached by the accountant on what to do. He'd said that when they go to place the order, that's your one chance to just get

a couple more. Sell it. Tell them there's a new advert coming out, and hammer them. And I didn't hammer a single person. I'd go in like, 'This is a new company. I don't know if it's gonna fuckin' last or what, but the boards are here. Who gives a shit?', so I wasn't much of a salesman.

So they came to me and said, 'Jonny, you're a nice lad but you're rubbish, so it's over for you. You're no longer getting paid, you're no longer part of Unabomber, but if you sign your name here we're going to give you £2,000 but you'll never be here in a business capacity again.'

I was finally revealed as a real charlatan. You know how people have imposter syndrome? I had the opposite. When people have imposter syndrome they're actually doing it and they feel like an imposter, and I wasn't doing it but I felt like I was on it. It's bad. It's like what you would get from a millennial at a start-up nowadays.

We started on July 4th 1997, and it was exactly a year to the day. They'd basically given me a year. They must have been talking about it for six months, these guys. What they were going to do about me and whether they could afford to carry me.

Pete Hellicar

It was Ben that said to me that Jonny Robbo was taking the piss and we had to either get shot of him or it'd be toast. He put it on to me and told me I had to deal with it because I'd brought this in. He was backing me, but at that point it was not working. We weren't getting any orders, he's selling all the samples and pissing money up the wall.

So me and Ben woke him up at about half eleven, twelve, and said, 'Jon, you're taking the piss'. And he knew he was taking the piss, and we had to knock him out the mix, which was awful. He was really part of the texture of the company and he was the start of the whole project. To have that removed... It's collaboration, isn't it? I got into it because I liked the idea of collaborating with all these amazing skaters that I have loads of respect for. I really rate Jonny Robbo's headspace, in terms of the way he thinks and the things he thinks about, he's a very astute and smart operator on some levels. On other levels he's a fucking idiot who just can't get it together.

You can't just go, 'We've got a skateboard company!' The idea is that we've got to sell some skateboards. I don't know what was going on in Robbo's head. I don't know if he was feeling insecure about stuff because there's always that thing that sits in the background of all of us... Our own doubts, more often rooted in insecurity and feeling like we can't do it. Fear.

Paul Silvester

I shot that photo[3], then I put another table in there, and I slid two of them, but that never got used. Maybe I wasn't locked in, or it was the lighting or something, but there was witnesses! I was stoked to be on the cover, but I was stoked that I'd done it on two, so I thought it was going to be a photo of the two. But I quickly moved on and carried on skating. →

CLOCKWISE FROM TOP LEFT
[1] Mark Channer, London Fields, by Wig Worland
[2] Unabomber ads and logos, *Unapromo* video cassette, Paul Silvester and Frank Stephens, by Wig Worland
[3] Paul Silvester, Leeds, by Wig Worland
[4] Alan Rushbrooke, by Skin Phillips
NEXT PAGE LEFT TO RIGHT
[1] Mark Channer, Bow, by Wig Worland
[2] Pete Hellicar, Upper Ground, by Wig Worland

Elsewhere

1998

Nick Zorlac

When I started Death I honestly thought it wasn't gonna sell and I was just doing it for me and some mates. It was honestly more like a skate club kind of thing, more than a skate company. It was more something that you were part of, rather than getting product from or being part of a proper team. It wasn't like you'd get loads of stuff riding for Death; you might get the odd t-shirt or whatever, and it was a bit like being on a shop team to begin with, where I'd give people stuff at cost price because I didn't have any money and I didn't think it was going anywhere.

I started Death just because I wanted to. What had been popular at that time had been Flame Boy and all that sort of stuff. The World stuff was so popular that kids would be asking you why you weren't riding those 'proper' boards. So against that backdrop, me starting a company called Death with a skull and crossbones, I thought no one was going to be interested, especially not younger people. It was literally that I wanted to start something that represented what my vision of skateboarding was, and because I didn't care if it made any money or not, I wanted to do something that had longevity and was always there for people that may have felt rejected in the early '90s when their kind of skateboarding was no longer popular. The early '90s was an exciting time, but in my mind it alienated a lot of people that I think were really important to skateboarding. Death was something that I wanted to be a home for people who may not subscribe to the current trend in skateboarding.

When I started doing Death stuff, it started selling pretty good, so starting something for the love of it – and as a bit of a 'fuck you' as well – that became a good selling thing, became the thing that enabled me to give up doing part-time work and actually make a very modest living out of being a skate distributor. The company that I did just for the hell of it became the thing that started selling good.

In a way it was selfish that I wanted to do something that I was into, and not try and please everyone. I had a bit of a problem with companies that were just starting and trying to jump on the bandwagon and please everyone and be really middle-of-the-road. To me, that's not what skateboarding is about and I wanted to do something that represented what I thought skateboarding was.

Dan Cates

To his credit, most of the stupid things that I wanted to shoot, Wig turned up for. I didn't really have a clue about photography for many, many years but I knew I was really lucky to know Wig, and be on good terms with him and be able to somehow get him out to shoot a lot of my stupid ideas[1]. He was very patient and he was very encouraging. He made you think that you could do something that you'd have probably given up on.

If you shot with Wig you knew that it was almost definitely going to go in. ●

LEFT TO RIGHT
[1] Dan Cates, Bromley-by-Bow, by Wig Worland
[2] Death Laughing Skull board
[3] Nick Zorlac, Portsmouth, by Wig Worland
[4] First Death ad, Document issue 6

DEATH
SKATEBOARDS
Every cloud has a jet black lining
Power Distribution 0181 9053777

Fos

Superhero had ended, it had its time. Me and Hiro Nakata were working and we couldn't do it, and it wasn't working anymore so we knocked it on the head. For a couple of years I wondered if I'd do a board brand, but the board brand just seemed like such a huge undertaking.

The name has roots to Superhero. There was something about this word 'hero'... I'm straight-edge and I always have been – I don't have the X or anything, it's just always been my choice not to do drugs or to drink. I'm not vegan and all of that, but that's always been my thing. I was just skateboarding all the fucking time, and I broke my wrist really badly. I went to hospital, and they said it was bad, and I needed pins in it.

They woke me up the next morning at 8am, and you can't eat all day because the surgeon might come in to do it. By nine at night they're like, 'OK, you can eat now', because the surgeons have all gone home. This happened four days in a row. I'd just seen *The Texas Chainsaw Massacre* for the first time, and the book I was reading in hospital was *Fear and Loathing in Las Vegas*. The lease had ran out for my house so me and my girlfriend were supposed to be looking for another place, and I was in hospital with a busted arm.

So I needed these pins, I was being starved, I was reading *Fear and Loathing*, then my girl broke up with me, I didn't have a place to live, and I was like, 'Fuck it, I'm going to start a skateboard company and I'm going to call it Heroin', because I just wanted to skate. All this terrible shit had happened, and skateboarding was my heroin. That was all I could think about and all I wanted to do.

They gave me morphine for the pain. The irony of being straight-edge your entire life and going into hospital and then being given morphine... There was so much irony going on that it just had to exist.

I drew the Good Shit logo in hospital, when my arm was in a sling, waiting for the pins to get put in. I drew it with my left hand, I drew it switch.

To start Heroin I was calling manufacturers in the US going, 'I need 50 of this board, and 50 of this board', and they were just going, 'Yeah, nah'. They don't want to deal with some little brand in the UK, especially one called Heroin, when they're making thousands of boards for Deluxe or whoever, so it was really hard to get stuff made. It was only through working at Slam that I met Greg Chapman, and he was like, 'Hey, I'll make 50 of each board for you'. I was at Chapman for ten years, until the financial crash. ●

"All this terrible shit had happened, and skateboarding was my heroin. That was all I could think about and all I wanted to do."
FOS

Elsewhere

Original Heroin artwork, by Fos

white deck

black graphic
red? →

red text
black border

Banned Horrorposter
is av

The Heroin
board massacre

fade?
red to white
beige to white
silver nose to white
flourescent green!

really
dark grey
red.

The Heroin
skateboard

HEROIN SKATEBOARDS
NEW CROSS LONDON

The Heroin
massacre

THE
HEROIN
SKATEBOARD
MASSACRE

FOS 98"

Heroin Skateboards.
— Good shit —

Colin Kennedy

We saw Blueprint as something way more aesthetically pleasing, from a graphic perspective, with whatever Dan was doing. Panic was naturally moving into the shadows of Blueprint, and I think there was this threshold moment where they said they were going to put this focus more on to Blueprint, maybe because it was more commercial. We could see that this was going to be the more successful thing, and we just wanted to be a part of that.

Dan Magee

I think people wanted to ride for Blueprint for a little while but Joe and Alvin didn't want to let them go. You can see that the John Rattray Northern Lights graphic[2] looks like a Blueprint graphic, and that was meant to be to convince Alvin to let Rattray ride for Blueprint, and that would be his Blueprint graphic. But then it was just a 'no', and they took the Blueprint logo off it and stuck a Panic logo on it.

I used to have huge conversations with Alvin to try and convince him to do stuff. Hours and hours. And that – getting them all on Blueprint – took a long time.

John Rattray

Colin Kennedy and I got the train a few times, from Queen Street, through Edinburgh and down to London, and stayed at Dan's when he lived in Brentford. We'd stay there and Alvin would come over, and not too long into that there was a decision made to spin Panic off as more of a price-point brand and maybe focus on Blueprint as a more premier offering that they were trying to take more global.

At the time I didn't care; I didn't pay attention and I didn't notice. They told me I was on Blueprint at some meeting at Dan's place, and it was like, 'Alright. Cool. If that's what you want to do.' Once it happened, and we worked on it, I was psyched, because Dan's creative point of view was pretty strong at that point. Dan might hate me – or agree – but a lot of what he was doing with Blueprint was super derivative of things like Silverstar, with the whole Masonic thing, but it had this whole twist on it because it was through this UK filter of grit and weather, and it had this strong thread of its own, which was good. Either way it had a clear art direction, and Panic was just a yard sale of I don't know what.

I liked that graphic[3]. Leo Sharp shot that sundial, and sundials are really interesting. I was studying Astronomy and Physics, and interested in that sort of stuff, so it was based on that, plus it played into Dan's Masonic vibe. That's why that one is a particularly good one.

Colin Kennedy

All my great graphics are just plagiarisms, but that's in the spirit of iconic skateboard graphics, as far as I knew them. It's easy to make a great graphic by just plagiarising something because you know it works. From my point of view, there weren't many Scottish skateboarders who'd had a pro graphic, aside from Chris Lonergan on Bash, so it was easy to have that identity. It comes back to how strongly we felt about our scene, and representing your community, because at the end of the day I never fully left Scotland.

It was easy to do Irn-Bru, and it's not like I was going to do whisky because I'm not a fan of whisky, but then we did the Margaret Macdonald Mackintosh[4] and that was just straight out of a book that my mum had. It's pre-internet time so you don't have access to all that imagery, so I took the book to London and gave it to Dan and he bitmapped it – or however the fuck you do it – and he built that whole graphic based off of that Scottish art history book. It's not like I'm a crazy Mackintosh fan, I was just thinking of something that represents that I'm Scottish, and relates to Glasgow.

This was perfect because it was a rectangular shape and it fits on a board. The silk-screen just came out looking so good.

Paul Shier

Magee just asked me to ride for Blueprint, it was just a smooth transition. It just seemed like an obvious thing to happen because Panic wasn't going anywhere. →

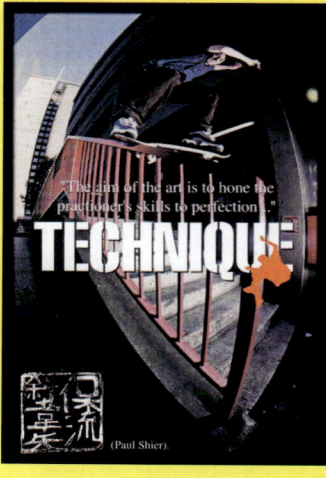

CLOCKWISE FROM BOTTOM LEFT
[1] Paul Shier, first Blueprint ad, photo by Oliver Barton
[2] John Rattray, Panic Aurora, layout by Dan Magee
[3] John Rattray, Blueprint Sundial, by Leo Sharp and Dan Magee
[4] Colin Kennedy, Blueprint Mackintosh, layout by Dan Magee
[5] Colin Kennedy, Glasgow University, by Wig Worland
[6] Colin Kennedy, Euston, by Leo Sharp
NEXT PAGE
Chris Massey, John Rattray and Dan Magee, Brentford, by Wig Worland

1 Eversholt Street

Elsewhere

Dan Magee

We had Blueprint wheels, and they were on Creative USA, which is good, but then Joe would always be trying to find cheaper manufacturers. In order to have the ones that Joe's not making much money on, but that were really good, my sacrifice was to let Joe have other lines that he could experiment with and lower the quality on and have proper margins. So he let me use Creative for the Blueprint wheels if he could use a cheaper manufacturer for Octagon, and that's what he did, and they flat-spotted and became octagons and that's what killed it off.

John Rattray

Alvin once told me it was called Octagon because, 'An Octagon is as close as you can get to a circle without being a circle', and I was thinking, 'No it's not. It's a flat-spotted wheel.'

Dan Magee

Mark Baines went to America on holiday and got piss drunk at the Warner House. He was really fucking good at the time, so you can imagine everyone out there asking him why he would want to be in the UK. And he's really young and he's never been anywhere. And he ends up staying out there and ends up riding for New Deal, but that might just have been Steve Douglas helping him out, I don't think there was an ulterior motive because Baines had already quit.

Baines basically got given a bit of an ultimatum. We were starting something new and he needed to be here to do stuff, so he can't live in America because it just goes against the ethos of what we're trying to do. So Baines quit. The people he was hanging out with at the Warner House said they'd get him on something, and he got on Recs and New Deal and some various other things, and he got caught up in the hi-jinx of Warner.

And he got really depressed out there.

He came back just too late for that *Build and Destroy* promo, and basically in the last two or three months of filming for *Waiting For The World*, and filmed everything for that part in that time. Joe paid for him to come back. This was the thing about Joe, he was fucking weird because he wouldn't pay for stuff we needed but then he'd pay for someone's fucking surgery. And Alvin Singfield convinced Joe Burlo to pay for Baines to come back from the States. This was the thing about Joe, he paid for game-changing shit like pro salaries, but then he wouldn't pay for the basic essentials. It was a double-edged sword.

Alvin Singfield

That was horrible. Joe was like, 'This guy isn't even in England anymore, he's living in America', and I think we'd seen photos of him riding other brands' boards. He could have got boards out there because that's where the boards were getting made, but Mark was young, and I'm sure he would admit that that situation of him leaving and going to New Deal was just down to the circumstances and the environment he was in at the time. To me it was heartbreaking because to me Baines was Blueprint. He was the kid from Worksop that I sponsored when he was twelve years old.

Mark Baines

I was really young at that point, and I remember Carl Shipman was on New Deal at the time and I think he'd spoken about me riding for New Deal, and Ches – Neil Chester – said I should ride for New Deal. So I went out with Ches and Carl, and it was just really difficult. When you're young and people tell you you can do this or you can do that, it's very difficult. It's like, 'Fuck, what do I do?', because I was just happy to

skate. Yes, there's a point if you turn pro you need to make a living or whatever, but I was genuinely just wanting to skate.

I looked up to Carl so much, and when it was presented that New Deal could happen, I ended up going to America, and it was just kind of weird; nothing was really on the table. I remember having conversations with Geoff Rowley, like, 'We'll go out filming and get you in *411*, it'll be good for you and good for Blueprint'; because I was skating with that lot, I was skating with Geoff, I was skating with Alex, Ali, all these people. So a lot of that early footage from America, I'm skating Blueprint boards. I don't think my Blueprint board had even been out for a year at that point. It wasn't long.

I don't think Carl gave a shit by that time. He had his comebacks every now and again and it was always good to see him skating but he wasn't even in America for that long. When I initially went out with him I think he only stayed there for two or three weeks and then that was it, and I was sort of left there with Ches.

Whilst I was there Alvin called me and said that if I stayed out there they weren't going to pay me, and that kind of upset me, and I said that I was out there trying to do good, and yes, perhaps there were conversations that other people had had that were put to me, but I just wanted to skate and film and all these good opportunities were coming up. I was out there skating with all these people, and I think Alvin and Dan were thinking I was getting tapped up by other people and wanted me back, and I know they did give a shit at the time. Again, at that point, it's people in your ear going, 'Nah, just stay out here, you'll be fine', and I ended up just quitting. It felt lame that they weren't going →

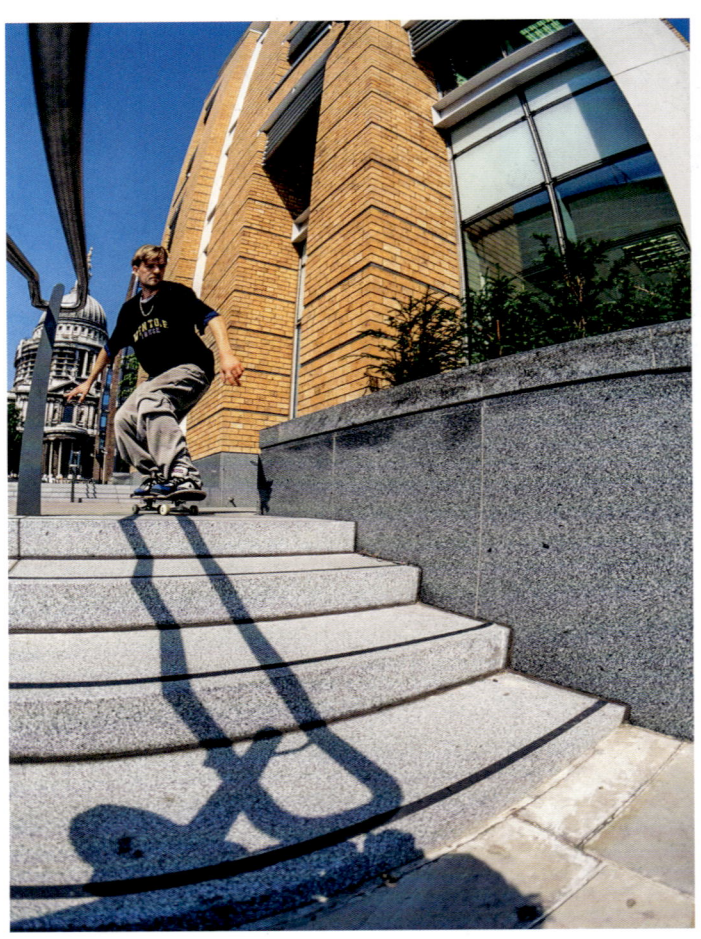

Elsewhere

to pay me, and when you're getting that reinforced by other people who are in a similar position, it's like an echo chamber.

I suffered really badly with anxiety, so at the time I didn't know what the hell was going on and there weren't really people that you could speak to, like there is now. I essentially put off coming home for so long because I was scared to get on the plane because I thought I was going to have a panic attack and not be able to deal with it. I literally didn't know what was going on. I didn't really have a stable set-up going on, but I just carried on anyway, thinking I'd be alright. There was a lot of people drinking and just living that lifestyle, and it wasn't the best all round, from quitting Blueprint then staying out there for a year-and-a-half... It was a rough period, to be honest.

That whole time was weird, because I did ride for New Deal and I was out filming things, but it never felt right. It always just felt like there was no longevity in it and I didn't want to stay there in the country. I just wanted to be at home and go back to how it was.

When Paul Shier and Colin Kennedy came out to a trade show it might have been the start of me feeling really homesick, and with being a bit older, I think they saw that. We chatted about it, I was pretty upset, and I just wanted to come back to Blueprint. Colin and Paul listened to what I was saying, and I think I said I shouldn't have ever quit, that it was a mistake and I wanted to be back on Blueprint. Thankfully they all spoke, and it was like, 'Yep, let's get you back in the UK', and it put the wheels in motion.

Dan Magee

Joe was starting to see that having this video stuff, this promotion, was working. Blueprint was selling over Panic, so he was seeing something now. He also let me hire my friend Chris Massey – who went on to do Landscape's *Portraits* video – to work as international salesman from this flat in Brentford Dock that we'd just got. So Chris was like the liaison between Joe and Alvin, and the Americans. I wasn't talking to anyone, I was just letting Chris handle it and believing what Alvin was saying.

So we're going to have our Industry section in *411*. I got all the footage, edited it, and sent it in. We're told it's going in, so Chris rings up and speaks to Chris Ortiz, and Ortiz is like, 'Here at *411* we pride ourselves on the quality of the footage and of the skateboarding, and this is not good enough quality for *411*' or something. I can remember Massey on the phone, like, 'What..? This is the best thing to come out of the UK!' and so on. Trying to give it the big one. I was hearing that but obviously not hearing what was being said on the other end, and Massey slams down the phone and goes, 'It's not going in! Fucking wanker'. And he says how Ortiz said it wasn't good enough quality.

You've got to remember that at this time UK skateboarding is so far away for Americans. It doesn't exist for them, Europe is just a place you go to for the competitions to make some money and party. It was only Northampton and Münster to them.

There wasn't even Cliché at that point. The only reason we did it, or wanted to do it, was because of Zoo York. The East

Coast at that stage might as well have been England, compared to California.

Chris Ortiz

If anybody ever thought that Giant Distribution dictated what went into *411*, that is completely 100% false. Never once did anybody from Giant come in and say what could go in and what could go out.

Steve Douglas would give input to try and make an edit better, but he never once said that something couldn't go in due to competition. If you think about it, why would he even start *411* if he was worried about promoting the competition, because that's all we did. Any input that Steve had was pushing the European scene. When we started the 'World Report', to give exposure to people from outside the United States, that stemmed from Steve Douglas.

The decision makers at the time of Blueprint was myself, Josh Friedberg and Kirk Dianda. I can't recall the exact reason, but it was not because of the quality of the skating whatsoever. There was a certain point where we were trying to supply NTSC cameras to our filmers in Europe, and if anything was ever submitted to us in PAL, Kirk was very vocal: 'This looks like shit, let's not use it'. It was to try and keep the standards of the video up, and at that point we wanted to be like a *Transworld*, as far as quality. After one or two issues the biggest thing we cared about was the quality.

I just want to clarify that it was nothing to do with the skating, because the skating was good, and it had nothing to do with Giant Distribution whatsoever. ●

LEFT TO RIGHT
[1]   Mark Baines, Huntington Beach, by Wig Worland
[2]   John Rattray, Southbank, by Wig Worland
[3]   Mark Baines and Alex Moul, Huntington Beach, by Gary Woodward

339   1998

Elsewhere

Gareth Skewis

Silas wasn't a skateboard brand, but all the top people in UK skateboarding wore Silas.

Sam Griffin

They'd constructed this whole universe and they'd open the door, just a bit, and you'd be like, 'What the fuck is going on in here?' All due credit to Sofia Prantera who now does Aries. The product was always fucking sick. It was taking all the best bits of skate culture and then taking it up to this whole other level where, yeah, they're getting the denim made in the same factory as Gucci in Italy, and they're not printing their graphic t-shirts on Hanes t-shirts, they're making their own t-shirts, which everybody thinks they're insane for doing but they're doing it because all the other t-shirts are shite, so they're just going to make their own.

Russell Waterman

Silas came out of mine and Sofia Prantera's parting from Slam City. Effectively Slam City owned Holmes, and we'd very quickly built up a decent reputation, made some clothes that people were interested in and had a really good worldwide network of people, and we felt restricted. I had three kids, I had no money and I needed Slam and Rough Trade to step up, which for their own business reasons they wouldn't at the time, so we decided to leave.

Sofia had this wonderful flat at Maida Vale, it had a little mezzanine level where our office and studio was and we had a clothing rail downstairs. We were making samples and things started to roll. We knew how the cycle worked and we were always late, but that was our thing. We did a deal with our brilliant Japanese guys – who were crucial to what we were doing – where they would pay us in instalments as things went into production, based on their order, and suddenly that money started to go down. I'd been taught how to do cashflows at Slam, so I knew we were down to our last 5K. We were meant to be getting sent 10K from our Japanese guys, and whoever did it accidentally put another nought on the money, so we suddenly got hit with 100K. Next thing I'm on the phone to Japan telling them that they accidentally sent us the money, and asking for their details so I could send the rest of it back. They're like, 'No, it's OK, we're going to have to pay you that eventually anyway, just keep it'. At that moment we knew we were going to get through the first 12 months. We kept having good breaks.

We quickly got out of Sofia's place and we got ourselves our own office. We were working out of self-storage units for a while, shipping stuff out of storage units.

We were really influenced by brands like Patagonia, well before Patagonia became anywhere close to fashion. Sofia and me were both very into that tech outdoor gear, that performance stuff, so we tried to make our versions of it and I really like that stuff.

We made some mad tech pants that were not actually very technical at all, and we did make a few jackets that were probably pretty good, that you could take on a hill and might survive. We made really good fleeces as well, using proper fleece companies like Polartec and Pontetorto. And we used brands like Pertex, which is used to make sleeping bags, which we used to make insulated jackets. It's that Silas stuff that I really liked.

The other thing that really set us apart, I think, was Sofia being really into Massimo Osti, and that military utility stuff with a mad twist, and I was still really into that football style, which meant everything was much cleaner looking and a bit casual.

Our guys in Japan, who were really important, asked us to develop a toy because suddenly these guys – these kids – could make toys. We were like, 'Fuck yeah!', because it would really suit the stuff that James Jarvis was doing, so we started to design a toy. Our guy knew the guys from Bounty Hunter, so he hooked us up and they helped us do a toy. At the time Bounty Hunter had only made a couple, and Bathing Ape had only made a couple, and it was the beginnings of what became the rotocast designer vinyl toy thing.

We'd started to develop this toy for Holmes, and the original sculpt had 'Holmes' on the t-shirt, so the first Martin toy would actually have said Holmes on it. It was a really good first product because James's stuff is so identifiable and familiar, so people would instantly know that Silas was the same thing because it was James's look on the first product. So the Holmes toy became the Silas toy and it was the first product that we made. That toy worked so well for us, and it ended up with a full page in *The Face*, it was in *i-D*, *Relax*, it was everywhere. →

LEFT TO RIGHT
[1]   Martin by James Jarvis
[2+3] Silas info/stickers by Russell Waterman
NEXT PAGE
Silas garments and ephemera by Sofia Prantera, Russell Waterman and James Jarvis

Sofia Prantera

The Japanese distributor was called Ken Omura, and he was really the person responsible for inventing drop culture. Him and James Jebbia were the two people that grew Supreme together; he was like the hidden business partner of Supreme and Silas at that time, but he had been involved in Holmes. It was him that had the connection to make the toys.

So we were making the catalogues, the posters and all the really amazing graphics that James did at the time, so Ken was like, 'Let's make this toy!', and he almost sort of suggested that he would help us if we would leave and do it independently. It was complicated with Rough Trade and Slam, two businesses that had complications of their own, so Russell saw it as an opportunity to do something new.

It was stressful working from my home, because Russell paces a lot, and both him and Rachel smoked, and even though they had to smoke outside, they would smoke with the door open, which was worse. When we did the catalogue with all the little stickers on it, we had about a million people round. The house was insane at that point, but I'm sociable so I didn't mind.

I think that method of working was kind of invented by us, and obviously financially helped by Ken – because you need to have some sort of financial benefactor when you're making it up as you go along – and then Palace and Aries went on to work in a similar way. We all have a similar structure to our business.

We never seeded anything. I remember one time we turned down Madonna for something. At the time we felt this real pressure to not engage with mass popular culture, which in hindsight is possibly not the best way to achieve commercial success. There was a real sense of shame around things that felt not politically aligned with what we did.

James Jarvis

Sofia and Russell were two brilliant people. Sofia is a brilliant designer, and she had this brilliant vision for clothes that was really original – it wasn't the generic streetwear that everyone was doing – and her vision for womenswear, making clothes for women that were feminine and not just women wearing men's clothes, that gave it an identity.

Russell had that background in music, and he had that understanding that you make a brand like a band, make it a thing that you want to follow and are into. That tribal, subcultural thing.

The big boost for me was that when they started this thing they wanted continuity, so that people understood that Holmes was the same as Silas, and the thing that was distinctive about Holmes was these funny catalogues.

Silas had this amazing following. There were certain people who could resonate with the drawings and the characters but wouldn't necessarily care about the clothes, because either they couldn't afford them or they just weren't interested in clothes, because not everybody is. We were proud of what we'd made, but you can't control the culture that springs up around something.

Russell Waterman

I was really into monster movies, shit like *King Kong* and *Godzilla*, and all the kaiju-type stuff – really crap big things smashing up cities – so I suggested to James Jarvis that we make a poster of this thing about to dominate London, King Kong-style. That was how that became the front of the catalogue that we sent out to our wholesale customers, with all the line drawings of the clothes.

James Jarvis

It was a spot I knew through the mags. If I was being some kind of cheesy BBC4 documentary with a slight youth-culture edge I'd be saying, 'It's like sampling'. I'm almost doing that thing where I know that Paternoster Square is cool because all this other stuff happened there, and then most of the people who saw that poster don't know about Paternoster Square or wouldn't necessarily recognise it.

He's got the Koston 1s, because I loved those shoes. The board he's got, I did that board a few years before for a marketing company that were doing a thing for Sony MiniDisc. They wanted to make some boards to give away, so that board exists. The graphic is a mirror of someone doing a kickflip.

Russell Waterman

A lot of effort and energy went into that stuff. Obviously we wanted to make money, and that was important – and we did make money, and it changed my life – but we didn't set out to do it like that. I needed to pay the bills but we set out to have control and do our own thing. Sofia's a brilliant designer, and she's still doing her thing with Aries because she lives and breathes clothes. For me, I love all the conceptual stuff, I love fucking around and I see humour in everything.

The people around us were brilliant. There's bits of James in there, there's bits of Ben Sansbury, there's bits of Fergus Purcell, bits of Will Sweeney, some of it's Lizzie Finn, and we'd sit there having conversations and just riff off each other.

They were an absolute ball-ache but I really enjoyed doing those catalogues. I didn't enjoy the later ones so much because they started to turn into fashion lookbooks, but the ones with the heavy concepts – concepts that you probably didn't get because I didn't get them because they got so convoluted because of all the ideas flying around – that's the stuff that I absolutely loved.

We were trying to portray our clothes in a way that no one else would do; it was counterintuitive, it was like, 'Don't make the clothes look good! Make them look goofy! We'll put them on mutants! If three people like this then fucking brilliant.'

Gareth Skewis

I was going to try to do fashion at St Martin's, or just a foundation art course, and I was ten Gs short. I was going to do a clinical drug trial, and me and Greg got in a massive fist-fight with some people and I got my nose broken so I couldn't do the trial. Greg was working at Slam, but he went off to LA with a guy called Gavin Morgan and Clint van der Schyf to skate, and I stayed in England waiting tables, and Greg got me a job at Slam. I was the Saturday dude, gripping boards, selling stuff, whatever.

Greg and I had skated with Arron Bleasdale and Ben Sansbury in Camden. Arron had always been super cool with us, as had Boma and Terence Anthony and all of those kids from Insane in Camden, and Ben was kind of the unofficial art director at Silas, at least in my opinion. I told him about my interest in clothing and he said I should meet Russell Waterman and Sofia Prantera, so I went to meet them and told them my plans, and they were like, 'Why don't you just forget university and come and work for us?', so I started work on the Monday. I was basically Sofia's second assistant, so I was in production because Sofia was the designer, and Sofia is one of the most proficient clothing designers I've met in my life. There are people with very big jobs at very high-end couture places now that very much understand what Silas was.

I'd go to the warehouse with Russell, or I'd do wholesale for their jewellery, or I would book wholesale appointments, or I'd liaise with their Japanese partners at One Gram. That's how it all started, but I didn't realise where it was all going to end up.

Silas was this amazing hybrid of Russell's 'Fuck the system, I don't want to be involved with anything', plus a fusion of hyper-independent music roots, and Sofia's love of high-end fashion and being an exceedingly good menswear designer. And you have Fergus Purcell, and James Jarvis, and this amazing thing going on in Japan. So as soon as I got there I saw it as my chance to really learn something, and I felt very privileged that I was in that room.

I kept working at Slam when I got the job at Silas, because I liked everyone there, and if it was raining I didn't want to just sit at Southbank; I'd rather grip boards, and we were selling Silas. It was a really interesting time for me, with Russell's provocative mindset with regards to running a clothing company, and Sofia's design aesthetic. ●

Silas: Megalopolis of dreams

Sidewalk & Document

Percy Dean

I got a phone call out the blue asking if I wanted to shoot for a snowboard magazine called *Snowboard UK*. That was Eddie and Stig. I'd never even been to a hill before, or seen proper snow, but I went and shot photos for them, and they gave me a bit more money, and then eventually they asked me to be staff photographer for that magazine, which I did for a year or two. During that time, I really hassled the publisher, like, 'You should do a skateboard magazine! You should do a skateboard magazine!'. They agreed and I managed to start doing the preamble to *Document*, which was making this little promotional portfolio. These little seven-inch fold-out documents with pictures in them, and saying what we were going to do, and rate cards and things like that.

I just knew that we could do it. I knew that my heart was not in snowboarding. I was always 100% a skateboarder and I wanted to do a skateboard magazine.

They said they'd give me £700 to make the promotional thing, and they'd take it from there, and I egged it on from there. I didn't even have a computer, there was one guy that had a computer so we'd write the stuff out and send it to someone to set the type and stuff like that. It wasn't a proper deal, it wasn't like running a skateboard magazine – it was just guessing.

I think we all embellished our reasons for why we were antagonising the other person. I definitely did. I'd get myself into a frenzy of, 'They said this about us?! They're trying to fuck us over!', and I'm sure Ben Powell was thinking the same about me and what I was saying. It's such a fragile line.

There was nothing to be jealous of but I think we were jealous of each other. I was jealous that their magazine was successful and I was jealous every time they did something first, or that was better than what we were doing. I think we were jealous of each other in idiotic ways, and that further added fuel to this fire of wanting to be the best magazine, because we all wanted to have the best stuff in our magazine, and when the smoke clears, that was the only reason we were arguing or kicking off at each other. Just because you wanted UK skateboarding to be shown in the best possible light, and in a selfish way, we wanted to be the people that were showing it because we felt like we were more connected to it. And we were both doing that, and that's why British skateboard magazine coverage is so good. Because of that thing between me and Ben, where we wouldn't back down and were fighting tooth and nail to make skateboarding as good as it possibly could be. Not in a big-headed way, but I don't think British skateboarding would be where it is now without me and Ben kicking off with each other and forcing each other to be as good as we were.

It was nothing about advertising or money, we didn't care where the money was coming from. I didn't know what advertising was, I was just writing about skateboarding and taking pictures of skateboarding, and sending people to take pictures of skateboarding. Then writing my shit about how British skateboarding made me feel, and what I thought should be happening with it and where I thought it should be going.

These battles between me and *Sidewalk* were all about skateboarding, it wasn't about money or success. In hindsight, if it was, it could have been good because we could have had money and success and we could have focused on that, but we just wanted skateboarding to be good. We just wanted to show the best of it, and I wanted to show it before them. That was it.

I think I could have made it a lot more harmonious between all of us. I'm sure Ben's feelings on us were probably down to me; I was the arsehole out of us all, making snarky comments in the magazine and putting straplines in that were obviously a dig at Ben. I was the one that was trying to get photos first, and I feel pretty bad that that was me. But it wasn't coming because of money, it was coming because I wanted British skateboarding – the thing I love – to be shown across the world and I wanted it to not be about Americans, and American money coming over here and dictating what British skateboarding was. British skateboarding is strong enough, and it's got enough people that love it and we don't need to be told how it looks and what you should buy by Americans. Especially when they're not putting the time in over here, and not supporting the scene.

I wanted British skateboarding to be about us, because we support it. We buy the stuff, we go to the comps, we look out for each other. It's not about Americans, no matter what the distributors wanted. And that was probably me cutting off my nose to spite my face more than anything, because every distributor that advertised in my magazine was selling American stuff, and I was antagonising skateboard culture by binning them off and making weird comments about them.

It wasn't gonzo journalism, but I'd write in a self-reflective style. It's quite a selfish way of writing, when you're writing from your perspective. Whether you're right or wrong, you're writing about how you feel about a subject. I think we implemented a lot of that in the end, and there was a lot of that kind of style in the magazine. We tried to keep to a documentary aesthetic as much as we could.

Ben Powell

It was an inevitable consequence of the fact that skateboarding was getting big again. We had adverts coming out of our arse, basically; it was so easy to get advertising. Pre-internet and we're selling 55,000, 60,000 mags every month, so there was room for another skate mag.

We'd got complacent by that point because it was fucking easy, because there was no competition. From the point of view of doing *Sidewalk*, *Document* happening – much as we didn't like it at the time because we saw it as encroaching on our territory – was probably the best thing that could have happened.

It was very adversarial, and it was *Sidewalk* versus *Document*, or *Document* versus *Sidewalk*, but ultimately the motivation for that was to get the best skating and to push skating as hard as we could. It wasn't to get more adverts, it was to get better tricks or be the first people to go to such-and-such a spot, or get the tour or whatever.

There was bants. I had words a few times with Sam Ashley about stuff that was in print, and he'd say it was Percy, and then I wouldn't say anything else because Percy would kick the fuck out of me, but we were all mates; me and Kingy used to go on the same tours together.

Document appearing was quite intimidating for us, but it kicked us up the arse when we needed it, and probably breathed life back into *Sidewalk* when we'd gone a bit flabby and lazy.

Olly Todd

I made that t-shirt[3] in my *Sidewalk* interview myself. It's a postcard of Jack Kerouac, and I typed out a little excerpt from one of his poems and stuck it round the outside and took it to a t-shirt printing place. ●

Elsewhere

1998

John Cattle

We had this resource where I was going away on trips, and filming these people, and Tom Moore was filming Flynn Trotman and all those people. I came up with the name *Viewfinder* because I love my double meanings, or a play on words. I was really into conspiracy theories and loved that kind of thought-play, that 'What if?' thing, so it was like, you look through a viewfinder to film, but if you watch this, you might find a view as well. A view you weren't aware of.

I knew Ben Powell a bit, and Ben had all this footage, and then Alan Glass was the guy that knew how to do it, so I was like, 'Right, I've got this rad idea, and this rad crew, let's all get together and see what we can do', which was what we did, and Alan taught us how to edit.

Alan Glass

Pete Evans told me that Cattle and Ben were trying to do this thing, which the only way to describe is a British *411*, although we were never going to live up to that expectation.

I had the equipment, because when I finished uni I went and got a job at a place called DVC in Brighton, that built edit suites, and then I got my own computer to start editing. I remember buying it and it just sat there for a few months because I didn't have anything to do, but after a couple of

little random projects for myself I hooked up with John and Ben, and Tom Moore from Wiltshire, and that became Viewfinder.

I lived in a cupboard in Colin Pope's house, in a cupboard that had enough room to sleep on the floor and have a desk, and Cattle and Ben would come down to Brighton on weekends and we just banged out the first one. We just edited all this shit and we all contributed footage and used all this footage of Carl Shipman, and Baines, stuff that people in the north had filmed, and *Viewfinder* One just happened like that, basically.

By the second one I had a new flat in Brighton and they would come down and edit. At the time it was fucking wonderful. We were sitting there smoking hash and editing all night long and it was a party. ●

LEFT TO RIGHT
[1] *Viewfinder* issue 1, artwork by Jethro Haynes
[2] John Cattle, Old Street, by Wig Worland
[3] Carl Shipman, Worksop, by Skin Phillips
[4] Carl Shipman's DC Euro Super Tour shirt

Carl Shipman

Carl Shipman

It got to the point where DC were like, 'You need to do this, you need to do that'. Everyone was saying I got kicked off DC, but I left. Me, Caine Gayle, Keith Hufnagel and Scott Johnston was all in line to get a signature shoe on DC, because it was a small tight team, and then Rick Howard and Mike Carroll come on, and Josh Kalis, and they started bringing their friends into the fold and the team expanded overnight, from seven or eight guys to twenty guys, and we all got put on the back burner.

The beauty with Stereo was that you never felt obliged. When you'd go and film, it was so laid back, and it was whatever you wanted to film. One time DC flew me out to do an ad, and they said they were going to replicate two lorry trailers, so they were going to build this so there was a gap and they wanted me to kickflip it. I went there and they'd contracted these big trailers outside the warehouse. Just square boxes basically, with a big gap.

I like skating shitty spots, like Broadmarsh, where getting anything on the shitty spot is a good feeling, but when you're manufacturing spots, it's so dodgy. I said I wasn't happy and I wasn't in it for this. It's not how it should be. It takes away from why you started. In this country the spots are shit; there's cracks and missing slabs and all that, so making a spot using Bondo takes away from the rawness.

The happiest skating times I remember were skating with my mates for fun. It's something you do as a hobby, it's recreational, it's something you do because you enjoy it. When it becomes a business it changes. You've got such a short shelf life in skateboarding to make the money that you need to carry on in life. Making the money was good but the pressure was too much for me to be happy. If you skated for these companies in the '90s, you were making them a shitload of money, and when I had visa issues and I needed them to back me, they weren't there for me.

I'd come home and made a life for myself here, and it enriched my life more – being here – than it ever did being a pro skateboarder in America. I were happier, I wasn't having to take pictures all the time even though they were on at me, and that was it for me. My fire to go out and shoot pictures or get footage had just gone. I was just going out skating with mates, and still pushing myself, but in my own time, and just enjoying it.

I remember people used to say I would sell my packages, and you're damn right I used to sell my packages. Of course I used to sell my boards, because your finances here in the UK aren't as good as what they are out there.

I love watching skateboarding now, but I'm not trying to grasp on to anything. I didn't want to be that guy still trying to do it. It were more rewarding to me to set up my scaffolding business, something that's got nothing to do with skateboarding, than trying really hard to stay in skateboarding. I've always got a set-up, but I only get the urge now and again. If someone asks if I've been skating, the answer will be no. I've been working, I've been running a business. That's what gets me out of bed in the morning, creating something for me and my sons. Something more I can leave them, than what skateboarding could ever give me.

I was brought up with a work ethic, and I always had the fact that I was going to have to work at some point. I can't just skate for the rest of my life, I need to work. Coming from a working family who grafted all their life, you have that instilled in you. I didn't want to just focus on skateboarding. ●

Ian Gunner

Mark Channer and a few others that we used to see around were basically scrambling around for support. I helped them out with a few boards, but while I was helping them out they were planning Unabomber. It left a bit of a weird taste, not massively, but we were helping them out and they were probably spraying the boards and putting Unabomber stickers on them. And that's fine, that's what they had to do.

So off the back of that, we sort of said, 'Well hold on a minute, why don't we do our own?' Everyone else was. Panic had been around a while, there was Blueprint, Unabomber was just starting, and there were a couple of other smaller ones. Ray and Gary said yes, Steve Douglas was undecided, but we started it anyway.

It was aimed at a younger demographic. Blueprint was already solid, and Unabomber was doing their thing and we almost looked at Unabomber like an Antihero. Blueprint was very well established, so it was going to be hard to compete against. But at the time we had all this data from HSC mail order, as we were sending out a stupid amount of catalogues, so we went down the route of a slightly younger demographic and it kind of worked. It was OK. It was doing good.

At that point Neil Urwin was on New Deal and was up and down to London on the regular, but he was a UK guy on a US brand, so felt a bit disconnected. Suddenly some of his mates were on a new thing that he wanted to be a part of, so Neil was the first pro, which was with the Coin Boy board, and the Fruit Machine board.

I think by the time Neil arrived, which was six or eight months into Reaction, Mat Fowler had got another job elsewhere, and that's when we got Ben Allnutt in. I knew Ben had done some early Panic boards, so he was good and he did the first Neil boards. There were many times me and Ben

just slept at New Deal, whether that was when we were doing the HSC catalogues, or board graphics, or coming up with ideas. It was a nice little partnership. Everything was all very collaborative.

Mat Fowler

Because I used to go to the skatepark and knew Ray and Gary, I think that they knew I'd gone away to the art school in Norwich and that I'd done Graphic Design, and so when I came back they were asking what I'd been up to, and they asked me to come in and chat about something. Initially it was a position that was a combination of things. They'd do those double-page spreads – I think HSC were the first people to do it – with loads of pictures of decks, trucks, wheels, shoes... They'd got TLB to come along and help and I think it was him that started that, and it was really radical at the time, those adverts. The funny thing is, before that it was a list, and it'd just be words, just lists of products, and it took quite a while for other shops like Rollersnakes to catch up. If you're going to order from a mail-order shop you're generally going with one where you can see a picture.

So first of all they offered a potential job doing that, which I did say straight away that I wouldn't really be that interested in doing because I'd studied art and design and I was more into creative work, whereas those adverts were more about being able to use a computer, just lots of layout. More mechanical. But they said straight out that they were also going to potentially start a UK skate company, so the theory would be that it would be a mixture of doing those adverts and laying out DC adverts that had come over from the US, so reformatting them into pages for *Sidewalk* and other magazines.

I moved into a house with Matt Anderson in Pinner for a year. It was really immersive and it became too much, between riding for Reaction and doing the graphics.

Those HSC ads did really well and they opened up an HSC in Nottingham, so there was a lot more demand for that kind of layout work, and I don't mind saying that I really hated doing it.

I only worked there for about a year. Initially when they brought me on it was under the premise that I'd be doing the graphics for a skate company and doing tiny bits of those HSC adverts, and they also said that they would get someone to do all that stuff, because there was a lot of that at the time, because that's what made New Deal Skates. They weren't just advertising in *Sidewalk*, they were advertising in music magazines – they were putting banners up at Metalheadz – so I wasn't just laying out the odd DC advert in *Sidewalk*, I was reformatting multiple things. A shop would call up and say they need a banner or poster and then I would get told to do that, and that became the focus and it meant that in the end the Reaction stuff was almost like I was lucky to squeeze that in.

Ben Allnutt

The Faze 7 thing is way behind me, me and Chris Massey aren't hanging out that much because I'm at work, and then one night I get a call from Marc Ball – who I knew really well, but certainly not for him to call me up – and he's like, 'Hey Ben, Gunner's told me you've just finished university and you've done graphic design, and we need a graphic designer.' He said that Mat Fowler was leaving them, to set up his own thing, and they wanted me to do Reaction.

Mat Fowler, to me, he's on the pedestal. Someone saying to me that they want me to come and sit where Mat Fowler sat, I can't do it but I'm not going to say no. So I go there, thinking I'm just going to be doing Reaction, stupidly, and I'm just straight in to doing everything. Resizing all of the ads for everything that New Deal was distributing for all the different magazines. I'm doing all the HSC catalogues. →

LEFT TO RIGHT
[1] Ian Gunner, Kensington, by Wig Worland
[2] Reaction team ad, *Sidewalk*, September, photos by David 'Styley' Steel
[3] Reaction flyer
[4] Reaction Mat Fowler ad, *Sidewalk*, May, photo by David 'Styley' Steel

I met Tim the first day I went through the door and I remember just being like, 'Fucking hell, it's TLB'. I vaguely knew Ray and Gary just from being at the skatepark. I mean, who didn't know them? They were just larger than life. My first day, Ray was like, 'So you're a graphic designer are ya? How much you fahkin' want?' At Yellow Pages I was on 12 grand a year, and it's bonkers that anyone could survive on that, but I was living at home. So I went, 'I want 16 grand a year', and he went, 'Fahk off'. So I went, 'Oh' – I had no negotiation skills, and when you speak to Ray there really isn't a negotiation – 'Well, that's kinda what I'm earning now', and he went, 'No you're not. I'll give you 14 grand a year and if you stay for two months I'll give you 16 grand a year.' Like a two-month trial. So that was it.

Mat's attention to detail, and cataloguing, was incredible. I could see everything he'd done, all the stuff he wanted to do, and I don't know if he left quite quickly but everything was like laid out, ready for me to go. I work with him at Palace now, and he's still creating the most beautiful artwork.

And then what happened was that it was all about price point. The thing with New Deal was that you couldn't really argue with them because they had the sales figures of every single board company in the world coming through New Deal at that point. 'What's selling? Wet Willy. We need Reaction to undercut and take some of those sales.' And that was ultimately the downfall of Reaction. Undercutting our own distribution. That's why Douglas killed it in the end, because we were making too much money out of Reaction, rather than the boards that we were distributing.

Reaction very quickly became this Professor thing, but we sold so many skateboards. Then we started a truck company called Transmit, which was basically a copy of an Indy; we had Jester bolts, we had Reaction wheels and you could buy a Reaction set-up. The idea of it was really good; we were selling cheap skateboards that were actually good.

Neil Urwin

To be honest I was not overly arsed about Reaction. They'd already started it when I was out in the US, and when I came back I didn't really know what to do with New Deal because I kinda wanted to hang out with my mates here. So I decided to quit New Deal, but I didn't know what to do because my loyalty to New Deal was massive because I was a kid when Ray first hooked us up. My loyalty to Ray was really deep, he'd given me the whole opportunity so I didn't want to stitch him up. I guess to some degree I probably saw him as a bit of a father figure at the same time.

So when I came back I spoke to Ray and Ian Gunner and I told them I was going to quit New Deal, and Gunner asked me to come and ride for Reaction. I'd thought that it was always going to be an option, to ride for Reaction if I wanted, so they said that if I quit New Deal I could ride for Reaction and

they'd give me a pro board and this, that and the other.

I said I'd probably talk to other people as well, so I got Alvin's number because they'd just started Blueprint at the time, and rang him up and I went, 'I'm quitting New Deal. What's the deal?', and he said he'd have a look into it and come back to me. I think it was the next day he got back to say they could offer me two pro boards and X amount a month, so I said I'd think about it.

I loved Blueprint. It was cool, I knew some of those guys – not massively well – and it was different. I think I went back to Gunner to ask him what we were going to do, and in the end it came down to loyalty, to Ray. The way my life was at the time, those guys were kinda like my family, and I felt like I'd be leaving my family to go into the unknown... Would I still even ride for Duffs? I couldn't get beyond the loyalty thing, and I rang Alvin and thanked him, and said I couldn't do it. So I worked it out with Gunner and that, and shot the ad with Horsley, so that would run before we'd told anybody I was on.

The Reaction team was Mat Fowler, Barry Dring, Matt Anderson, Gunner... The team was cool. Did it feel like a proper company at that point? No, because no one had a pro board or anything like that. There would be demos but they'd be at skateparks, and I wanted to skate the street.

Those guys were like family and I had that loyalty to Ray. Although they made that dogshit truck company, Transmit, and Ray's like, 'Ride for Transmit!', and I said OK and had to try and skate shit trucks and wondered what the fuck I was doing.

The funny thing is, before I turned pro for Reaction I'd kinda decided I wanted to bin skating off. I had this period where it was easy, then I stopped skating as much, and became a bit more into doing other shit. I was still skating for New Deal but I went and got a job in Aspecto because I was into trainers and shit. Just to do something different and see what happens. Then I remember Ray saying they wanted to do my pro board, and they sent Jake Barker up to film the Reaction video. Someone told us that Ray was sending up Jake to see if I could still skateboard, and I remember thinking, 'I'll fucking show yous...' Although to be fair I wasn't skating at all. I love skateboarding, it's the best thing in the world, but I'd go through phases where I didn't want to skate and I just wasn't arsed.

Jake Barker came for the weekend and I hadn't skated in three months, but I smashed it. It was like school, when somebody says you can't do something. Someone had to challenge us to do it, otherwise I wouldn't have cared.

Graphics-wise, I was into playing fruit machines and smoking tabs, so the fruit machine graphic[4] was mint. That professor graphic literally ripped my soul away, that. I think it was just, 'This is what we're doing', and there was a professor board with my name on it.

I don't think I was really overly arsed about it by that point.

For the Lion King one, we were in Soho skating around and you know when you go to Covent Garden you've got that corner which has all the shows? I was with Allnutt and Gunner when I saw that – it's still there – and I thought that would be a mint fucking graphic! So we made that into a graphic and that was it.

Ben Allnutt

Neil Urwin's Lion King board is one of my favourite boards I've done. I say 'done'... Thank you very much Lion King for doing that for us...

Greg Finch

Gareth Skewis and I would skate Harrow, Romford and St Albans in one day, and if we heard about a random demo going on somewhere we'd make a mission of it to go out to it, so we're bumping into everyone and skating with everyone. We made good mates and then at some point when I was working in Slam, Matt Anderson said to me that they were setting up a skate brand and that Mat Fowler was going to do the design, and the creative side of things. It seemed like a really rad bunch of people to be with, and so obviously I just said yes.

Colin Kennedy said he'd love to get me on Blueprint, and so there was this moment when I was getting boards from Blueprint as well as boards from Reaction, and I was trying to make my mind up. There was a good couple of months where I was umming and ahing but my whole standpoint about skateboarding was that I knew I wasn't that good. I knew I was a jack of all trades but I wasn't taking it mad seriously. I knew I was never going to not have to work in my life. I knew I was always going to need a job and I knew I really just wanted to have fun, so I made a decision to just stick with Reaction.

Chris Allen

When Faze 7 and New Deal did their own brands, immediately all those American manufacturers considered them to be competitors rather than just their distributor. So Shiner chose not to, and in a way it was a good thing because it helped us solidify our loyalty to distributing American brands, but that was at a time when localised brands became really popular because the product was better priced because there wasn't another manufacturer there selling the product to you as a distributor and you weren't having to pay their margin as well.

That was how in the late '90s and early 2000s we ended up gaining the distribution for a number of other brands, because they felt New Deal and Faze 7 were promoting their own brands above the American brands they distributed. That's how we ended up with brands like Alien Workshop, Destructo, Shorty's, Black Label, Acme and Habitat. ●

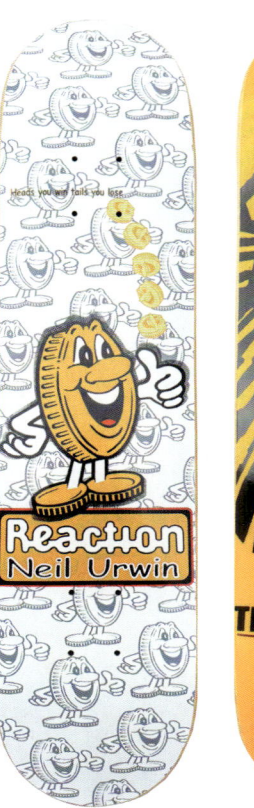

CLOCKWISE FROM TOP LEFT
[1] Reaction Neil Urwin Fruit Machine, by Mat Fowler
[2] Reaction Neil Urwin Coin Boy, by Ben Allnutt
[3] Reaction Neil Urwin Lion King, layout by Ben Allnutt
[4] Reaction Professor logo sticker, by Mat Fowler
[5] Reaction Neil Urwin Fruit Machine flyer, photo by Wig Worland
[6] Reaction Greg Finch ad, photo by David 'Styley' Steele

NEIL URWIN
PRO MODEL
OUT NOW

'THE FRUIT MACHINE' 8"
LOOK OUT FOR A LIMITED
AMOUNT OF GOLD MODELS

DEALER ENQUIRES CALL 0500 00 00 80

COLLECT

1999

Joel Curtis, Sheffield, by Sam Ashley

Our approach was just, 'You're in! Let's go!' Make your own shit, do your own thing.
PETE HELLICAR

Matt Pritchard

There was never any talk of me moving to Blueprint. Never. There was no way I was going on Blueprint because I didn't dress well enough, I wasn't cool enough, and I was Welsh. I knew it was all slowly coming to an end because Blueprint was becoming the main thing and Panic sort of started disappearing. I wasn't allowed on Blueprint because I wasn't cool enough, and slowly but surely everything just died a death. Panic went and Blueprint carried on, and that's when I went to Rookie.

Dan Magee

I can remember one time when Alvin Singfield bought Pritchard a Kentucky Fried Chicken meal and that was basically his pay. There was nothing. I think there was photo incentives, and Alvin would buy a meal for them. There was nothing.

John Cattle

Alvin phoned me up and he's like, 'How many times does someone get a second chance?' Because I'd quit. He asked me to come back to Panic and be team manager, and there was no talk of money, but I was stoked. Matt Davies, Stuart Graham, Ben Leyden, Greg Nowik, Gary Chevalier and Clint van der Schyf? I was like, 'Yeah, let's fucking do this!', not thinking about being paid my worth. I'd get boxes of boards, probably four boards at a time, but it was an opportunity, and I got to make a video that I'm really proud of.

What pissed me off about Joe, was when we first saw the new graphics and it was all skulls and stuff[2], and I was like, 'Yeah but this is what Death do, this is what Nick does', and he says, 'Yes, that's the point, we're going to put them out of business'. That really left a bad taste in my mouth because they didn't need to do that; they had a strong team and they didn't need

to start to try to fuck with people. They could have done it differently.

Nick Zorlac

At a trade show, I remember Alvin – who I get on with fine – saying to me, 'Those boards with the two-colour graphic, do people actually buy them?' He couldn't believe they sold. I told him they did, and then they came out with their ones.

Dan Magee

There was a time when Blueprint was on a knife-edge of, 'Is this going to work or is this not going to work?' It could only work if we could make something that people can't hate on, because people hated on it in the beginning. Rob Selley's amazing, but he wasn't putting in as much as all the people you know as staunch Blueprint riders now. Somebody like Shier, or Baines, they were going for it when they could have probably ridden for another company. And then we're sending Rob boxes and he's selling the stuff to buy weed. He didn't want to travel to London and he didn't want to shoot photographs with his mate Leo who lives 20 minutes away. That sort of thing.

Selley was fucking A-one in terms of pushing the boundaries of skating and he would never want to go anywhere, but one time we made him go to Scotland with us and that's why he's got all that footage in 'Build and Destroy'. For Selley, going on a trip outside of Milton Keynes and sleeping in a sleeping bag is out of the question, but there's times where we'd make him and he'd love it.

Alvin kicked Selley off just before he left. It didn't have anything to do with figures or anything, but there had been a few little things that had rubbed Alvin up the wrong way... When we first started I sorted out – with Joe Burlo – to get travel expenses paid for, so people could come down and film. Baines

and Flynn went round picking up travel card tickets and sending them in to get refunded, and they picked up tickets from the same day, so Joe was like, 'What the fuck is this? You're taking the piss now', and that was it. No one was ever, ever getting travel money ever again throughout the history of Blueprint.

So Rob was living in Milton Keynes and where he was semi-dealing. He'd skate one board and then sell the rest of the box. Rob would get his package and he'd be counting it out like money, counting the boards like, '£25, £50, £75'. There was one time we went to do a demo, and in those days you'd do the demo then go to the local shop and the kids would be hyped so they'd buy the boards. That's the idea of a demo, right? We'd got all these jackets – like the DC Super Tour – with 'Explore' written on them.

Rob had sold a board outside the skate shop, and the kid had gone in to get griptape. The guy asked where he'd got the board from and the kid goes, 'Rob Selley sold it to me outside'. And the guy in the shop that had organised the demo told us he was never going to order any Blueprint boards ever again. So that was when Alvin said that he had to go.

Alvin agreed a grace period for Rob, where he would do stuff over the next few months and then have an assessment kind of thing. Not how I would have done it, but fair enough. I said to Alvin that he didn't need to do the assessment, that he'll have got the message, but Alvin had typed it up in a letter to give to him. Rob had just been taking the piss, you'd ask him to film a trick or get a photograph and he'd be like, 'Mate, I did a switch whatever down the bus station the other day'. I'm like, 'OK, but you need to present that to the world somehow'. →

CLOCKWISE FROM TOP LEFT
[1] Rob Selley, Milton Keynes Bus Station, by Andy Horsley
[2] Panic skull board ad, *Sidewalk*, October
[3] Blueprint catalogue (extract)
[4] Scott Palmer, Knightrider, by Wig Worland

Flynn was cool, and he was really ripping, but I think because his name was Trotman his board never sold. It was kind of a weird name, and Alvin couldn't sell the boards, so he couldn't have Flynn as a pro, so he cut his pay. That was why Flynn left Blueprint, really, and went to Reaction. In some way that was a fuck-up on my part as well, because knowing what I know now about marketing skateboarding, I'd have been like, 'Well he's just "Flynn" then'. That would have been the way to do it. Alvin had turned him pro because he was fucking killing it but he just couldn't sell his board.

Flynn Trotman

I'd gone out and stayed with Alex Moul, chilling with all the Warner House crew, then Baines came out as well. That was when Baines was skating really, really good, and he stayed out while I came back. He quit and rode for New Deal for a little bit, then he came back and he got back on Blueprint. I got told things weren't doing so well, so they needed to cut my money.

So my money got cut, and I was a bit upset. Then I found out that my pay cut had gone straight to Baines, literally for the same amount. I might have spoken to Dan, but I was thinking, 'Well, if that's the vibe, I'm just gonna leave', so I rang up Ray at New Deal, because he was always nice. I told him the deal, and he asked what I was getting paid, and I told him, and he said, 'Nah, you can't live on that', and offered to pay me more. I thought that was really cool, and then I left for Reaction.

Everyone on Reaction, and all the New Deal people, were super nice, and

dare I say it, maybe a little less vibey than Blueprint. Blueprint was about image, and Magee could be a bit ruthless with his tongue, but image and aesthetic are definitely important, I would say.

It was a toy company, that's how I would describe Reaction. It was a budget toy company with an image to sell boards to young kids, and if you compare that to Blueprint, there is no comparison in coolness at all.

John Rattray

I think Andy Horsley was friends, somehow, with Jock, and Jock was just getting up and running with his illustration career, and was looking to do bits and pieces.

Dan Magee sourced the file from Andy and put it on the board. I don't remember the layout on the board[1] being very good, and I think that was maybe not Dan's finest moment as a graphic designer. Why's it in that little circle? He could have let the art breathe. It looks like a cupcake holder that your grandma would bake cupcakes in around the edge of it.

Also, I hate graphics that have me on the graphic. My pro model with me on the thing? To me that's awful and dumb and awkward.

Jock

It meant a lot to me to get to do this. It came about because a friend, Pete Evans, who lived in the same town as me, knew the *Sidewalk* crew. He was particularly friendly with Ben Powell, I think, and hooked us all up.

It was fully painted, collaged, and loaded with texture. As one of my earliest published pieces, I put everything I had

into it, and knowing it was for a skate mag, I knew I had the freedom to do that. And that's something I've tried to continue through all my work. This was an early touchstone, so thanks to John Rattray and everyone at *Sidewalk* for letting me do it. Andy Horsley asked me to do more in the following years, including another portrait of John[5], but it's amazing that this first piece is still on people's radars.

I was stoked it got used on the deck too. I still have one in my studio to this day.

Morgan Campbell

The ad[6] was cool, I was really hyped on that. The only thing that's sad about the ad is that they never paid Andrew Mapstone for the photos. I'd got on Blueprint that morning, went to a skate shop in the city, got a John Rattray board – the one with the sundial on it – then I went and got the sequence of the 5.0 bigspin, then I went and got the crooked grind photo, and it was all done by 3pm. I was so hyped. I love how in the crooked grind photo there's a kid who could easily have been plucked from Glasgow stood at the top of the stairs watching. I never noticed him on the day.

Carl Shipman

I always liked what Blueprint had done, and I can't knock what they'd done, but for me, I was totally over it by that time.

Blueprint were a good company with good branding, but I wasn't involved in it in any way, shape or form. I was on there for a little bit but I was completely over it, to be honest. They were over me as well, let's have it right, because I weren't doing anything. →

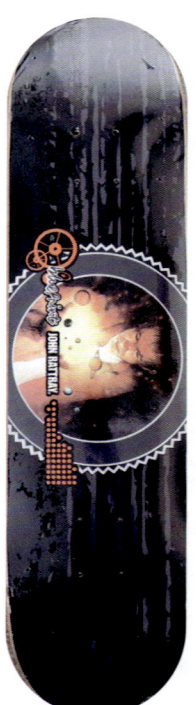
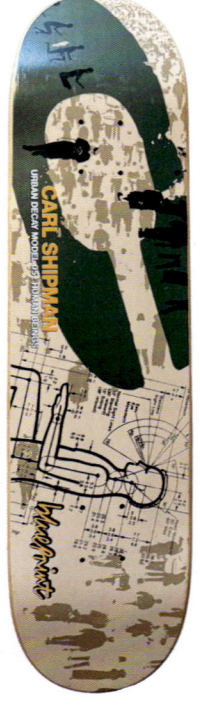

CLOCKWISE FROM LEFT
[1] Blueprint John Rattray Watchmaker, by Jock and Dan Magee
[2] Blueprint Carl Shipman Urban Decay, by Dan Magee
[3] Blueprint Carl Shipman US ad from Big Brother, October, photo by Oliver Barton
[4] John Rattray Sidewalk interview opener, by Jock
[5] John Rattray, by Jock
[6] Blueprint Morgan Campbell ad, Sidewalk, April, photos by Andrew Mapstone
NEXT PAGE
Channon King, Paternoster Square, by Wig Worland

interview **John Rattray**

Illustration by Jodie

ABUSE YOUR ARCHITECTURE.

Photos. Andrew Mapstoone.

FUJI RVP 37

MORGAN CAMPBELL

BLUEPRINT SKATEBOARDS

phn: 01787 269900 / fax: 01787 269888

Elsewhere

1999

Channon King

I was doing the Tum Yeto thing for quite a while, and then Slam just wanted to promote Unabomber. They took them on and started distributing them, so my flow changed to purely Unabomber boards for a while.

I went to America, I went to SF to stay with Jon Humphries the *Transworld* photographer because he had been over here, and he'd said to go over, and I only took Unabomber boards. Then I was staying with Judd Hertzler, one of the Foundation guys, and the phone rang and it was Alvin, asking if I wanted to ride for Blueprint when I came back, so I was quite excited about that.

Dan came down here, and we just went to the most random terrible places. He was visiting Faze 7 in Pebmarsh, so just down the road from Sudbury, and he had his video camera so he wanted to come down and do some filming. Obviously I was really excited and I wanted to get a lot done, but we went to a handful of the most dreadful spots.

One night, me and my mate John went to Paternoster, and I 50-50ed the last section, and it locked in nicely. I put a bit of wax on the wall to make sure my board would go down, and I probably dropped in to check I wouldn't just flat-out stop. When you're doing those against-the-wall things, I've had nasty experiences with that because your wheel nut, or your axle, bites into the wall.

John was saying that if I could ollie on to the bottom section, I could ollie on to the top section, because it's the same. I was pretty sure I could definitely do it, but I didn't want to tell anyone. I told Seth, but I wouldn't tell Wig because I didn't want to build it up in case I bottled it.

Seth said we could do it for a Slam ad, so I arranged to meet up with Wig, and he said he was going to shoot some stuff with some other people first because he had to travel down from Oxford at the time, and when he'd come down he'd try to fit a few people in to make his trip worthwhile. Unbeknownst to me he was meeting most of the Blueprint team, so it was Mark Baines, Paul Shier, Flynn Trotman and probably some others at the time. We all met at the Westminster Road gap, and I was completely unknown but I'd bumped into Bainesy before, so I knew him enough to say hello, but I hadn't met any of the others before.

I hadn't told Wig what I wanted to do, but I was thinking, 'God, I'm going to have all these people coming along watching me, this is the worst'. It felt like he'd come down, and he was with the whole Blueprint team, so he had an agenda and it was like I was derailing their agenda, so it was really bad.

I took them to Paternoster and I started trying it, and Flynn – because he's a beast – started bloody trying it with me, and that ramped up the pressure because he had a good chance of doing it. It was like it was mine, but he was looking convincingly like he might have a good chance of having it, and then on one try he nearly fell down the drop over the other side. Everyone had their hearts in their mouths and it was so close for him going headfirst down the drop, so then he just stopped.

So Wig did a sequence, and he gave it to the guy at Slam to lay it out, but Wig had an idea of how he'd lay it out. Nowadays you can do it on an app on your phone, you can layer the photos on top of each other and rub bits out and create a multiple exposure. Anyone can do that now, but back then you had a problem, especially in the daytime. So what Wig was going to do, was take a sequence, separate photos, and then he was going to rip the photos and join them together, which he did do. He sent it off to the guy at Slam who was laying it out, and no offence to him, but he just did not share Wig's vision. So Slam paid for a two-page thing and it got laid out not how Wig envisaged it, and you couldn't even really tell what I was doing so I don't think anyone even noticed it.

Wig was gutted, he said to me at the time, 'Are you sure you want to use this for a Slam ad? Maybe we could just use it for the mag?', but I wanted to do good for Slam, I had loyalty because they were giving me a lot of gear. Then it was a balls-up and nothing really came from it, and it didn't really have an impact.

Wig just wasn't happy, and he wanted to redo it, so we went back with Oliver Barton. The first time I did it, the first time I landed it, I looked at Wig and he was just shaking his head because his film run out, so I had to do it again. Getting on to that, the physical exertion of getting on to that, you would try ten times to get on and fail, so Wig would be using film every time. He'd shoot, and you wouldn't do it. Then I got on one and did it, and because I'd wasted film getting on to it, he didn't have enough film to shoot the sequence. So I had to go up there, knackered, and do it again.

It all came out perfectly, which is a miracle, because having somebody running down the stairs with multiple flashes, it's crazy to get that right [pp.362–363]. ●

CLOCKWISE FROM LEFT
[1] Colin Kennedy, John Rattray, Neil Chester, Carl Shipman, Brendon Body, Chris Massey, unknown, Scott Palmer by Mark Baines
[2] Fos, Ladbroke Grove, by Wig Worland
[3] Fos, Euston Square, by Wig Worland
[4+5] *Good Shit* slip case, by Fos

Alan Glass

I met Fos in London, when Seth Curtis introduced me. He told me he was doing a video for a brand he was doing soon, and he needed somebody to help with it, so I said I was down to edit it. Then he came to my flat in Brighton and we did *Good Shit* in one weekend. Then we realised at the end of that weekend that it could have been better, so he came back the following weekend and we polished it up. It doesn't look like that if you watch it. It was obvious – to me, anyway – that it had an Antihero vibe to it. I remember editing it and thinking, 'This is shit. Who are these randoms? What is that trick? Are you serious? I could do that!', and then it was like, 'Oh, I get it now, I get what the company's schtick is'. And that was not being part of the skateboard race. It wasn't, 'Our guy is better than your guy', or 'Our guy can jump down more stairs than your guy', it was a bunch of rough-looking dudes skating a dirty mattress or whatever it was. So *Good Shit* had to look like it was edited with scissors, and it had to look sketchy and shitty, and it did because the footage was sketchy and shitty because none of the people involved were 'filmers'. It was shitty quality but that was perfect for Heroin.

Heroin came out, no one could believe its name, people were like, 'Who the fuck is this Blindollie Softrock guy doing early grabs?' It was a breath of... not fresh air, it was bad-breath air, but it wasn't Blueprint. ●

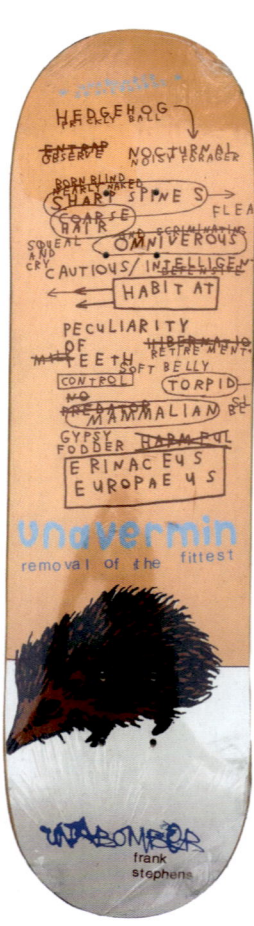
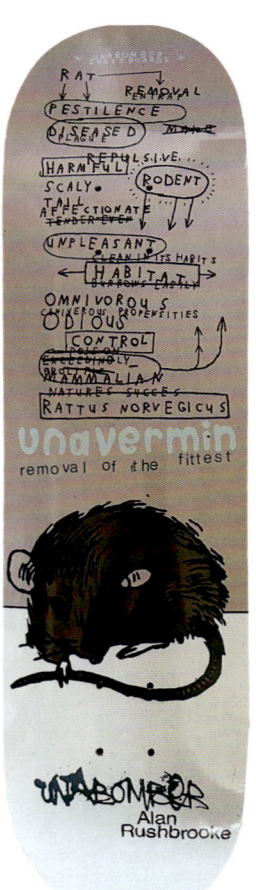
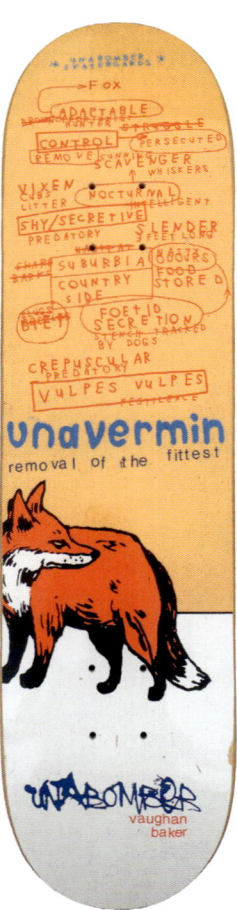

Pete Hellicar

We did a Unabomber ad [p.369[3]] that was a rostrum shot of bits of ephemera, and that's all based on the *Beano* fan club. It was something that gave you an idea of who these people were, rather than trying to present something fake and manufactured. People like Frank and Harry and Channer are all such solid humans, and it was about expressing that. It's giving people the opportunity to identify with that idea, and that's why we encouraged people to send us letters. It's about being heard, isn't it? The machine doesn't hear you, the system doesn't hear you anymore, you're shouting into a void. The idea of Unabomber was about being heard. *Sidewalk* was also about that. That whole, 'We're here, we've got a really solid scene, there's some of the world's best here' thing. So whether it was the cards, the stickers or the *Daily Torment*, they're like little broadcasts out, but they're broadcasts that are asking for a response. It's not asking people to take it as given.

Our approach was just, 'You're in! Let's go!' Make your own shit, do your own thing.

This all sounds really lofty but we were definitely thinking about it, thinking about the approach. It had to be like the *Beano* fan club. I wanted to get stuff back and start a conversation.

James Woodley

I remember when I was thirteen going down to London and staying with Pete Hellicar, and him shaving my head for me. I got a train down there on my own, Pete's flat was somewhere around Latimer Road, where the old PlayStation park was, and when I got off the tube I was literally about to get mugged by these two guys and Pete turned up in the nick of time and rescued me.

They were filming for *Headcleaner*, but I didn't really realise what was going on, I was just skating every day anyway. I think because it all happened so quick, I didn't have time for it to register in my mind. Pete was a big name back then and always will be a legend, he was on the cover of magazines and stuff, but I probably didn't even know that at the time.

Vaughan Baker

I was in the States when my board came out. I'm sure I knew about it but I can't really remember. I remember Nik Taylor did the graphics for us and we had to pick which graphics we wanted, but I wasn't in the country when my board was released. Frank Stephens came and met me in LA, and he brought mine and his first boards with him. I think they made about 100, 150. I think I only recollect skating maybe four of them.

Nick Hamilton

Peak Unabomber heyday. It was a privilege to be able to shoot with those guys, because they were as pro as you got, in London. It was always fun skating with Harry because he had just an insane pop. That's a frontside 180 [p.369[4]]. We went there specifically for those black bollards, because not many people could pop tricks over those. →

LEFT
[1–5] Unabomber Riot series: Harry, blue; Alan Rushbrooke brown; Pete Hellicar green;Pete Hellicar orange; Alan Rushbrooke purple; photos by Pete Fowler
[6–8] Unabomber Vermin series: Frank Stephens, Alan Rushbrooke, Vaughan Baker; photos by Nik Taylor
RIGHT
Pete Hellicar, De Beauvoir, by Wig Worland

NO PARKING
AT ANY TIME

Elsewhere

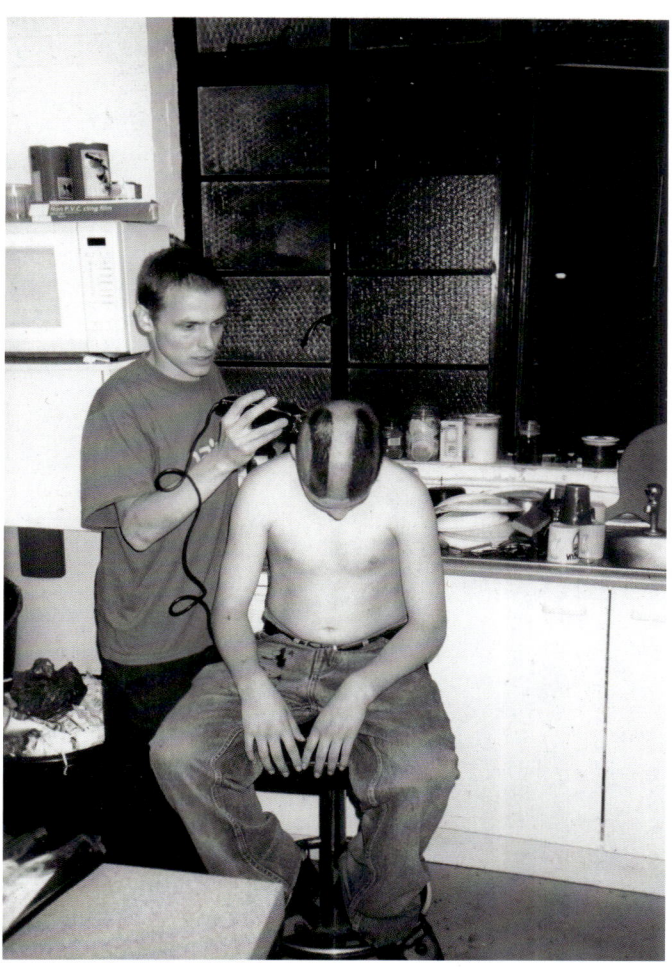

Greg Finch

It was so primordial and so amateur-hour, but so fucking hilarious.

Ray and Gary were just good at business, so they wanted to make something that would rival everything else in the UK and bring in money. That was their standpoint and it was never hidden. We were never led down a garden path or anything, it was always, 'This is going to be a brand, we want you guys to put in the effort, and then everybody gets the reward'. But they would do things, like one time we had a big dinner and they pulled out this massive video camera, like a massive on-the-shoulder BBC camera, and they're like, 'Here you go, we got you a camera, you can go out and film a video'. And I saw everyone just looking like, 'Oh my god', so I thought 'Fuck it, I'll take the bullet', and I just went, 'I don't think this is gonna work', and Ray just launched into a rage about how he'd managed to get this camera off some dude blah blah blah, and I said we'd try to work it out but there was no way we'd be able to tank around with this massive camera. There were so many moments like that where they'd come in with a hot idea and you'd be like, 'Errr...'

You could never complain, you'd get a package of more boards than you could imagine every month. I could never give them a hard time about that because they'd always be like, 'Do you need trucks? Here's trucks. Do you need wheels? Here's wheels. What do you need?' I'd speak to Gunner once a month and he'd be like,

'What are you after? Do you like Droors? I'll throw in some Droors bits.' They were always super, super sound to us and that was down to Matt Anderson and Ian Gunner managing it.

I remember the conversation around my board and I remember it being more like, 'You should have a pro board because it'll sell', so more from a sales point of view. I'd always joke, when people would say I was a pro skateboarder, that I was a promotional skateboarder, not a professional skateboarder, because it was sort of thrust upon me that that should be the way.

I skipped out on a lot of the ads. I thought they were really cheeseball, and a lot of the time it was a real cocked-up idea. Some of them were hilarious and I don't know if it was me being naive and a bit insular with skating but I think now I would have had a bit more of a fun time with it. I was really wrapped up in the skate world, and with what was cool and what wasn't.

Ben Allnutt

My favourite board graphic I've ever done – and I work with him now – is Greg Finch's first pro model for Reaction[3]. It's a white board and it's got 'Reaction' written like a dictionary definition, and it's got a little African finch. I did that and I felt like I was going to get in a niche. Mat Fowler had done series boards really well and I didn't have the talent to do that, so I wanted to do this thing where we had very different, personal, art boards.

Neil Urwin

I never owned a pager, so I don't know why I had a pager board[2]. I went straight to a mobile phone.

Tim Leighton-Boyce

So I was approached by New Deal, probably brokered by Steve Douglas, who at this point were beginning their astonishing explosive growth, on I don't know what basis: that I'd be a nice person to have around? That'd be a nice thought. Steve is always fiercely loyal, so maybe there was an element of 'We should sort Tim out'.

They got in touch with me – Ray and Gary – and I went and had breakfast with them, and they offered me a job and I went and worked there. Initially, I think I was aiming to make them a retail website, for HSC.

California Skate Supply had already done ads with pictures of all the boards, but doing it with more of them was probably me. The point I was making was that it wasn't so much about people looking at the graphics and choosing them by comparing them, the point we wanted to make was that we've got more than anybody else. Loads of different brands and loads of different boards. So the take-home from those adverts was meant to be, 'Oh my god, they've got lots of them!'

There was a constant squabble with Ray and Gary, about making them smaller and fitting more in. We also did the photographs, and this is pre-digital so we'd take a photograph of every single board and then scan it. It was shot on film and then taken down the chemist. →

FROM LEFT
[1] Greg Finch, Victoria, by Nick Hamilton
[2] Reaction Neil Urwin Pager, by Mat Fowler
[3] Reaction Greg Finch, by Ben Allnutt
[4] HSC ad, *Sidewalk*, August, by Tim Leighton-Boyce

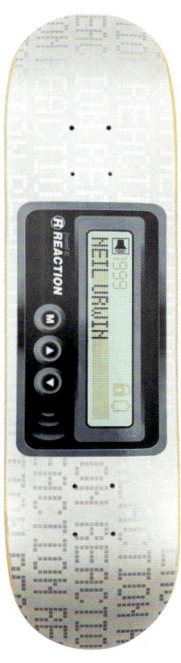

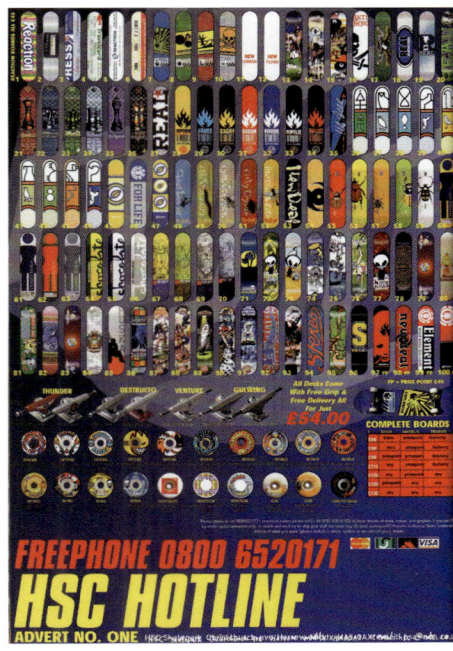

My job at New Deal at first was mainly to do the website, but what that meant was that in order to do that we had to have accurate stock control, which they needed to have anyway. So it turned into this monster, all-encompassing IT and computer software replacement process, which took forever. The people we bought the main software off hadn't done clothing before, so the concept of style/colour/size, having three options to deal with, was new to them, so they had to write that software into their system.

I was very much involved in many, many aspects of New Deal, and I really enjoyed it. I really liked working with them, but it physically killed me because I didn't want to move to Harrow so I was commuting from South London. I used to have this hugely bright uplighter with a 300w bulb in it, on a timer, and I also had one of those automatic tea-maker things, and all that stuff would kick on at 5.30am, waking my wife up as well. I'd get up, shower, and get in the car by 6.15am because if I wasn't, the traffic would be at a standstill. So if I got into the car at 6.15am I could be across London before the rush hour kicked off. If I did that it took forty minutes, if I got it wrong it took two hours. The other side of that is that because the same applied in the evening, there was no incentive to leave, so I'd stay and work late. I lived like this for years but it got to the point early on where I could fall asleep standing up. It was amazing I never fell asleep driving.

This was the cue for me to take care of myself and get out of there before it killed me. So I stopped, and morphed into a person who consulted on understanding how a person uses websites. People do not go where you want them to go, they go where they want to go, and that's this new world, so I went into consulting and helping people understand that process, and how to make it easier for users to do what they want to do.

I did that for a few years and it was very enjoyable, and I suddenly became aware of this new government initiative to do their online presence better, and what they were doing there sounded so good. They were so hardcore and purist about doing it the way the user wants and making it easier, making the language clearer, basing it on data and user research, and it seemed too good to be true. I applied for a job, and I got it, and I joined them, and it was the most wonderful, exciting period that I can remember since back to the early *RAD* days. It was mental the energy they had, and the devotion to doing it right. And 'doing it right' not as in 'what we think is right', but actually finding out what turns out to be right. ●

→ **ADDICT**
Andy Humphries

I started working for Addict, and I invested some money in Addict. It was doing really well – at that particular time, that was the look. Maharishi-type parachute pants, multi-zip jackets, pullover zips, asymmetrical zips. Basically what every teenager's wearing nowadays. The guy that does all the outerwear for Palace is Chris Carden-Jones, and he was the designer at Addict. Chris had never done that before, but he's a perfectionist. His dad was an architect so he'd grown up with that absolute precision.

There were a few other brands around but the Addict stuff was just made better. Chris Carden-Jones was heavily into his army surplus stuff, so that influenced the way that Addict was.

Flynn Trotman

Addict was Chris Carden-Jones and a guy called Dave Jeffries. It was good to be part of Addict because nobody was making clothes like that in England back then, with that kind of hip-hop/graffiti/skate-culture vibe, and they made good stuff.

James Hacker

Dave at Addict would just hook everyone up. He'd turn up at Bristol with a load of shit, and occasionally I would get a box. It wasn't like getting free shit every month. I think I did a couple of ads for them, but it was a real organic vibe.

We all went to Newquay – me, Paul Carter and Danny Wainwright, and I don't know who else – and they hadn't sorted shit out for anyone. There was nowhere to stay. All the Globe team were la-de-dahing it somewhere, Pritchard had that all sorted, and I'm like, 'So where are we staying, Dave?, and he's like, 'Yeah, I dunno'. We all stayed at this bed and breakfast, and Dave starts knocking on everybody's doors in the middle of the night saying, 'We're going! We're going!', so we legged it out of this poor lady's place. It was the era of no money. ●

1999

Alan Glass

I had some friends in London that had a music magazine called *Circuit*, this small, underground magazine about live music in London, and they had a conversation with a production company that were working for Channel 4 doing these ultra-low-budget programmes called *The Other Side*. They were basically giving people a camera and that was it. You get a camera, then you get to come in and edit it at some edit suite in Soho or something, and that's how they were making these super-low-budget documentaries.

My friends at the music magazine were in talks with the production company about doing one themselves, and they wanted a CV, I guess, so they asked me because I was the guy that'd done video stuff for the magazine before. Long story short, the production company looked at our CV and said that they had so many documentaries about music, and they didn't want one of those, and they contacted me separately and asked if I'd be up for doing one about skateboarding, because that was on my CV.

I had to deal with my disappointed friends at the magazine, and then I didn't really know what a documentary about skateboarding was, so I figured I'd try my luck with having some connections and knowing a few people to round up some of the best skateboarders. At the time it was quite funny to have guys from Blueprint and Death and Unabomber. The crew was really random; people who wouldn't normally have gone on a trip together.

We could only go in December, and if I could go back and change anything, it would be that because we could only go to indoor parks. At the time it wasn't really that bad, but now you don't put indoor parks in skate videos. I managed to con some money out of Vans, I don't know how I did that but I got them to chip in about £1,500 or something, which paid for the van and the Travelodges.

It was fucking fun. For me it was quite a trip because I didn't know everybody. I was almost kinda starstruck because there were guys there who I'd looked at in magazines and had been

editing into Viewfinder videos but never actually met. It was a nice opportunity for me to get to know people.

It ended up being broadcast at 4am or something, and they didn't give us any notice. I wanted it to be in the news section in *Sidewalk*, but they didn't give us enough notice for it to be publicised so if you caught it, lucky you.

Nick Zorlac

It rained the whole week, but luckily we had this network of indoor parks in the UK. I think myself and Dan Cates were invited as a bit of a novelty because everyone else were the top UK riders of the time. I'm not saying Cates isn't rad, but you had John Rattray on the trip! You could take them anywhere and they'd absolutely rip the place apart. It was a great week of drinking and having a great time. For the most part it was really good.

Flynn Trotman

John Rattray was a highlight of that trip. He was on that next-level tip, just a bit ahead of everybody.

Me and Paul Carter were being dicks, I think. I think we were smashing up glasses in the tour bus, just being arrogant. Dan Cates was there, and people that skate a little bit different, and in hindsight I wish I'd chilled with those dudes a little bit more now. I think I was a bit closed at that stage, and I should have been a bit more open. A bit nicer.

Harry Bastard

I hated skateparks, I hated indoor skateparks, but it was winter. It was a mix of random people, people you'd think would probably clash, but it was alright. It was a good laugh. I was constantly saying places were boring, but I think I was in a bit of a negative space.

Dan Cates

When you watch that video, Christ... What a nightmare I am. It rained every single day without fail and I don't remember it ever not being dark on that trip. I think we had a 17-seater van, and I think it might have had 17 people in it. It was rammed.

It wasn't negative and I don't remember it in a bad way, but it wasn't the dream that you were looking for.

Mark Channer

It's funny when you look back on it how obviously it's set in winter because everyone's just seasonally depressed, including me. I'd not been very self aware, and I was just talking about bad shit, complaining about miniramps and stuff. I know John Rattray had been going through some difficulties on that trip, Flynn's mental, Carter's half-cut... Weirdly, the sanest people are Cates and Harry, much as they don't seem it. Then you start cramming the Red Bull in.

Joel Curtis

I was down skating with Seth, and he was like, 'I think I'm supposed to be going on this trip tonight, I don't know', and then he said to just come along because it would probably be OK. That was the first

time I met Alan Glass, and he was like, 'Oh, yeah, just come, it's fine'. I had no money at all, I'd pay for a train ticket down to see Seth and then have about £5 a day to buy food, and that was it really.

Seth Curtis

Rattray was on the trip and he was on full on-fire mode, and he made everyone else on that trip look like an absolute beginner. Everywhere we'd go he would nonchalantly destroy the parks.

Alan Rushbrooke

I was still very young and I might have come across as confident but I was not confident in myself at all, at that period. I skateboarded, but I was very shy as a person, and I thought John was fairly similar. He'd obviously been skating for a while and was ridiculously good on a skateboard, but it's not like he was the crazy one on tour or anything. At the age we were, I don't think mental health was something we were aware of, or even us as friends were aware of.

People had dads who were – in hindsight – alcoholics, or abusive, and you'd maybe know that stuff was going on, but we'd just be skating with our friends and no one would talk about it. Skating was the relief away from it all, for some people. You didn't speak up at that time, but you probably wouldn't because you were still a child.

Yes, of course there's drugs and alcohol, and everybody has their fair share, but it's not like, 'Oh that person was pushing it more than anyone else', nobody was looking for that. It's not like you always do drugs and have mental health problems, because you could have mental health problems and not do any drugs.

John Cattle

That was absolutely the start of this energy-drink intrusion into anything youth-based, that I hate. I've talked to young people who have physical reactions when they don't have Monster. This shit should not be given to children. Or even adults, I reckon. That shit is fucked.

Rattray was there and he was having a really hard time with whatever had gone on previously, and he was in his hotel room, and we're having an argument about curry, 'Where the fuck's my naan?', and all that, and then everyone goes into Rattray's room. I'm the one like, 'I don't know about this, we should leave him alone, let's be maniacs in this other room', because John had something going on, poor guy.

John Rattray

Nobody can blame themselves for not knowing at the time. We're young, late teens, early 20s, so you don't know there's a question you can even ask. If you don't know there's a question you can ask, how are you supposed to do anything? Hindsight is 20-20, and we all live and learn. Hopefully.

No War for Heavy Metal really was a struggle for me. That was an interesting time, and looking back on it, I'm glad I got through it. ●

Screenshots from *No War for Heavy Metal* by Alan Glass

Danny Wainwright

I rode for Vans, and it was just impossible to get any shoes or anything, so I bailed and left Vans and rode for etnies through A4. It was etnies, then Emerica, then I was wearing éS but I wasn't on éS. I was doing a lot and I needed shoes but it was almost impossible to get shoes from A4. I was always grateful for what I got and I never needed loads of shit, but I needed enough to skate. I remember hitting up the guy at A4 one time, telling him I was shooting all this stuff and I really needed some product – some shoes – and he sent some shoes and when I took them out of the box, they'd been worn. They were returns, with sock fluff. I was just like, 'You must be fucking joking! Forget it', and I just quit right there. I had nothing else lined up but there's no point in representing a brand if they can't even send you fucking shoes. I'm not going to represent a brand if they're going to send me secondhand shoes and expect me to go shoot photos in them.

Christian Stevenson and Pete Dericks said to come back to Vans, and I was like, 'No, it's the same thing over there, same problems', and then Pete was all like, 'No, global', so then I started riding for global Vans, rather than UK Vans.

I had two Vans shoes, and the first one was a mish-mash of all these different designers working on it. They flew me to New York to go shopping and to hang out and look at shoes with them. A good friend of mine who does Clearweather, Brandon Brubaker, was one of the designers on that but then he left midway through and someone else picked it up, then someone else got involved, so it's like a Frankenstein that shoe, with three different designers.

It was bulky, it was big, it was heavy, it just wasn't what I wanted at all.

It didn't feel right, it didn't skate good, when you looked down on the toe it was rounded and I fucking hate that because I want to look down and see a more narrow, pointed shoe. Everything about it, I wasn't into it at all and I was kind of embarrassed about having my name on it.

When I did my second shoe, I called it the SUMS. I didn't put my name on it, which is weird and stupid, but SUMS is a graffiti name that I'd had for years. I used to write – and I still do now and again – SUMS. So I called the shoe the SUMS, and that turned out really good.

It was a weird time for shoes, and Vans probably were the worst. éS made bulky shoes but they looked good, and they all had their references to sneakers, and then you had DC making Lynx and stuff like that, which were still big and bulky but at least you could skate in them. I used to skate in DC, in iPath and in éS, all while I was pro and getting paid for Vans. I had a centre page in one of the magazines wearing a pair of éS, fully under contract with Vans. Pete Dericks phoned me up and he was like, 'What the fuck are you doing?' I was just, 'Dude, they feel good, they skate good, I need shoes to skate in and I can't wear these Willy Santos and all this stuff that you're making, it's terrible'.

My first Powell board[2]. was done by a friend of mine, Damian Neary, and his graffiti name was FEEK. At that time he worked at Aardman Animation as a set builder, but he was one of my friends from back them, one of the graffiti artists.

It was Park Row, the street where Fifty is and where Rollermania was at the time, and there's a monkey climbing up a pole breaking off the CCTV camera, and then there's a little robot down there with a wheelbarrow full of them. Fifty Fifty's there, but then as you go up the street there's number 52 closed down and boarded up, and that's Rollermania, because when we opened Fifty, Tony Coffey was talking a lot of shit about us. 'They don't know what they're doing, they won't last six months', all this shit. We were cool with them, I'd always say hi when I saw Tony or his wife, but they just got real, real bitter about it. So that was a little stab back from me, putting that in the graphic.

I wish they let me do my own graphics the rest of the time, because it was terrible. Boards would surface with my name on it and I wouldn't even know anything about it. I don't know if you're familiar with Cab's 'art', but he's got to be one of the worst artists in the world.

They knew I was into graffiti so they would do stuff with spray cans on, and I was just like, 'No, man, fucking chill'. Drips, stencil shit, just the tackiest shit ever. I don't even really like the first graphic, but I had one that had a white dove on it, it was just really simple, and that was probably the only board that I liked. I was more into design, and art, and things that look nice and clean. I was into Habitat-style shit, and I had a million friends who were graphic designers so I could have had sick graphics. One time they sent a board from a series and I was like, 'Have you made these?', and they said they had, so I said, 'Look, just don't put me in it, I won't have a board in that run'. Cab had painted a fucking teddy bear, some awful teddy bear stitched up and it had my name, and I'm like, 'Really? That's no reflection of me whatsoever. It's damaging for me.' It was really, really bad. They were saying it was sick and it was part of a series and I told them I didn't care and to give the board to somebody else. I didn't like it and I didn't want my name on it but it was too late, it was done. ●

Chris Allen

The Pro Skater game was 1999, and that was done because skateboarding had started to grow again. Of course, it's people like ourselves, being in the distribution business, who see that from the beginning. Shops don't realise it or take notice of it until a couple of years after we've started to see growth, and that's when kids are coming in looking for skateboards, and that's when things suddenly start to snowball.

When you're after a particular product you phone up a shop to see if they've got it, and if they haven't got it you phone another and another and you probably end up phoning six shops looking for one product. You're one consumer, but all six shops think there's a demand for that product, and that they need to get it in, and then before you know it there's six shops buying one deck each that's actually only really for one customer. There was an oversized demand for what the reality of the size of the market was. It just seemed that there were more people out there because if they couldn't get it from one shop, they tried another.

The numbers that we were bringing in of each board were much lower than it had been in the late '80s, early '90s, because now instead of being 50 pros, there were 500 pros out there and ten times as many brands as well. So even the top selling brands, in terms of numbers, weren't selling anywhere near as many as were being sold in the late '80s.

→ **LOST ART**
Dave Mackey

Fleapit closed in '98, and Robbie had moved to Philly. Adam was still trying to sell product from his house and we would go round and he would have some bits, but it was never gonna work, really.

I wasn't looking to open a shop; I had a job in a factory and I was just a skateboarder, but it was in the Christmas of '98 when we were expecting our bonuses that we got P45s. So I was signing on in the January, and me and my friend Ade, who was made redundant at the same time, decided to go to Spain, via an estate his uncle was working on in the south of France. So we were going to go and work a couple of weeks groundskeeping, and then carry on through to Barca, but we didn't really have a plan.

We were away for three months and I didn't have any clue what to do when we returned home. I'd had so much time in a car thinking about what I could do, and Ade was coming back to start teacher training and I still had no clue what to do, and I started to think about a skate shop.

When I came back I went to visit the Prince's Trust, and they seemed pretty down to assist me, so I started to formulate this business plan of opening a skate shop with zero clue about what to do, or even why I was doing it, other than that it would be sick to have a place for my mates to hang and buy boards. I'm assuming that's what most skate shop owners think when they start.

There must have been something in the water, or some energy in skateboarding around this time because a lot of retailers in the UK opened between '97 and '99; that was the period when Fifty Fifty, Casino, Lost Art and Note all started up. There was this sort of movement, independently, because none of us were speaking to each other. It just felt like we could open skate shops.

I looked at Quiggins, because Fleapit had gone, and I spoke to Adam Cooke and Robbie Reid and they gave me their blessing. Adam was over selling stuff in his house, and I think he was going to do teacher training anyway. I opened in the July of 1999, and the rest is history, as they say.

Nicky Ryan did the graffiti above the door. Nicky was the coolest skateboarder. The best style, he looked the best on the board, he was the first to pretty much do everything; he was super-fucking dope. Nicky had got into graffiti really young, so graffiti was always part of his life. I think he hadn't skated for a while when I approached him to do the shop sign, and Nicky doing the shop sign was like a real rubber stamp of approval on the scene for me. →

Shops

Elsewhere

1999

slam City skates

Chris Pulman
Retail Manager
chris@slamcity.com

RETAIL
16 Neal's Yard
Covent Garden
LONDON WC2H 9DP
ENGLAND
T: +44 (0)20 7240 0928
F: +44 (0)20 7240 6235
www.slamcity.com

DISTRIBUTION
Unit 9
343-453 Latimer Road
LONDON W10 6RQ
ENGLAND
T: +44 (0)20 8968 3333
F: +44 (0)20 8968 3388

SLAM CITY SKATES

get our mail-order catalog

ATTENTION PENNY PINCHERS

SLAM CITY
Chris Pulman

At the time Paul Sunman was running Slam, and Andy Humphries, Fos, Pete Hellicar, and Kirsty were working in the warehouse with Paul. This is when it was down Latimer Road way. I said I wanted to move to London and I wanted to pack boxes in the warehouse four days a week, because I was travelling back and forward to London so it just made sense that I would live there.

I had a meeting with Kirsty and Paul, and they said they'd figure something out. I went to America for a couple of months, and when I was there they emailed to say they wanted me to work at Slam, but they wanted me to manage the shop. I told them I just wanted to pack boxes four days a week so I could have a long weekend and enough money to live. I said I couldn't manage the shop because Slam was a cool-guy shop, but I ended up doing it, and I started in October '99.

Financially, it was a mess, and they just wanted someone with a college education to come in, someone who could work a fucking spreadsheet. Seth Curtis was running it and Seth is brilliant with people, brilliant at spotting things, he's much more sociable, he's much better at being a team manager, getting people to perform, really good at marketing, getting editorial placed against adverts in magazines, all that kinda stuff, but when it comes down to numbers I don't think he's that interested in it.

It was a leaky ship so I plugged all the holes. They were stupid things. They had a downstairs stock cupboard, and I said, 'We're tripping over boxes, we've got no space, why don't we use the stock cupboard?', and they were like, 'The light doesn't work?' Just before I turned the electrics off and put a new fuse in it, I asked if anybody had tried putting a new bulb in it… I was like, 'You guys have been tripping over boxes because one of you didn't think to change a lightbulb?!' So we had a stock cupboard. Slam was crazy for dumb shit. You could fix 20 things a day, and it just got better.

I didn't know what I was doing as far as fashion goes, but I knew that I knew skateboarding and I knew what it was like to work three paper rounds every day and then all your money goes on skateboarding. So when I started there, obviously there

was a fashion scene that we were coming out the end of, but my first and foremost thing was skateboarders. Skateboarding will always be kinda cool, but if you don't support the skateboarders you won't have that core.

I was all about skateboarders and making sure the business profitable again, and being sure that when skateboarders come in they get treated first and foremost. They get the best shit at the cheapest price we can possibly do it. We had everything but we had good advice too. If you're a kid and you come in, we had standard bearings, Reds or Swiss. Everything else is bollocks. 'These are the only ones worth spending your money on. £8, £16 or £40. You can get Pig bearings if you want, but they're fucking rubbish. If you really want them we've got them, but don't buy them.' There was a lot of that.

I'd never met a stylist before. Seth was well-versed in this, and someone would come in and they'd pick up 40 garments and go to buy them and I'd be like, 'Oh my god, this person's loaded', and Seth would be like, 'No, this person's a stylist. They're gonna buy all that and they're gonna bring it back in two days and want a refund.' So we used to charge those people extra, like, 'If you're going to bring this thing back in two days, there's a 10% rental fee. Buy it all, bring it all back, but we're gonna charge you 10%.'

People would always want free info. People would always call up and be like, 'Hey, can you tell us about skateboarding?' Seth had had a lot of that, and he was like, 'Dude, don't give those people your time. They're getting a free ride here.' I knew that, but the flip side of that is that if anybody's going to give them an opinion and it ends up on the news or something like that, I'd much rather it be me, because in that piece of information I could bury a little nugget about why we need more skateparks. I could always put a pill in the dog food when I'm feeding the news people. Like with the stylists, I'd be like, 'Hey, you've got to have this Landscape t-shirt in there!'

Alan Rushbrooke

There was a rad vibe in Slam. Seth and Pulman had got in and changed it. It was very cliquey, and there was a big backlash against it, and they completely changed it and wanted to make it more like a skate shop where anybody can turn up and walk through the door. Skaters are from different walks of life and different backgrounds so they should be able to go into a skate shop and feel like it's their home. The scene was amazing. Toby Shuall was so far ahead with what he was doing, and his style. Then Seth, apart from his moaning he was amazing. Pulman was like Oscar Wilde on a skateboard or something, then there's Greg Finch, and how amazing he was on street, ramps, the lot. It was a really cool period of time.

There was Rough Trade downstairs, and you'd hear something amazing and go down like, 'Oh, can I get that?', and they'd be like, 'You don't want that, you want this', but it was good vibes. Lots of late nights

and lots of fun. We'd always get invited to loads of stuff but we'd just go for a skate then go to the pub after.

Jacob Sawyer

When Pulman started at Slam in 1999 I was a regular, part of the lunch-break visitation unit, a crew which remained a part of the daily schedule when I began working there a year later. Chris was, and still is, completely obsessed by and interested in skateboarding on every level. He brought that energy to the shop, and was excited to talk to whoever came through the door.

Visible signs of him managing the shop were tidiness and better organisation but his motivation was catering to skaters, especially new ones. There were always completes, and pads, and he loved ordering and involving us in that process. He was also hilarious to work with.

His main skill was being able to talk to everyone who walked in with genuine interest and meet them on their level. I've watched him inspect the set-up of someone he didn't know, figure out if Smith grinds or feebles were part of their wheelhouse and have a half-an-hour conversation about those tricks with them. Foundation, Heroin, Indy, and Vans definitely benefited from his allegiance but primarily because of his enthusiasm.

Fos

I met Pin through Slam. When we were getting boards made at Chapman, the quality was a little bit… variable, let's say. Some of them would be really light, and feel lovely, and then you'd get another one and be like, 'What the fuck?! This is the same board but it's really heavy?'

Pin, bless him, has got this crippling OCD. He's gnarly, crazy about stuff, and I don't know if it makes me a terrible person but it's so entertaining to me. He would call Jake Sawyer at Slam and be like, 'Can you do me a favour? Can you weigh those boards?', so Jake would go through the Heroin boards and weigh them all, and one would end up being a little bit lighter than the others, so he would be like, 'Yeah, there you go. Told you!', and he would get all the light boards. Then he'd be like, 'Jake, wait! What brand of scales are you using?'

I didn't think that anything I drew looked good enough to be a skateboard graphic, and I was trying so hard. When I started working at Slam and they sold Toy Machine, I thought of the arm series[7]. I posted the drawings to Ed Templeton at Tum Yeto – each one was about the size of a bus ticket – and then he faxed Slam and asked me to call him because he wanted to talk about those graphics.

Me and my girlfriend only had a cellphone at the time, we didn't have a landline, but I called Ed Templeton and I was trembling, I was terrified. He's like, 'Oh, yeah, hey man, I want you to do those graphics'. I told him I'd learnt Illustrator so I kind of knew how to do it, and he talked me through a few things, like picking Pantone colours and stuff, and that was the first time that my graphics made it on to a skateboard. ●

Gordon Skrezka

That cover[2], that frontside crook, that was taken sometime in '99 but it wasn't on the cover until December 2000. It was sitting in the *Sidewalk* office for a year-and-a-half and I'd completely forgotten about it.

I was just on a trip to Oxford to see some friends, like Horsley, and I remember Newcastle was fucking shit around that time. It was literally just Urwin who – let's be honest – didn't skate that much. Nothing against the guy, but the desire to go out just wasn't there. You'd just go to the pub, then go for a skate with your mates; there was nobody coming up to take photos or anything, unless they were here to see Neil. But at the time it was all London-based, and even he had to go to London to get photographs.

When the magazine came out, and I was in the office about a week or so later, and Ed Leigh came in. He saw the cover and goes, 'Are they still not giving you any DCs? That's the best advert they could get in the country and you're not getting anything for it?' I would have liked some shoes, but I never got any. I've never been on anything.

Channon King

Seth found that[3], and took me there. I was just going through a phase of doing stalefishes, and I remember it coming really, really easily, and riding away being really stoked because I'd never done a pole jam stalefish.

Seth Curtis

We were out with Wig, and Channon wanted to go and shoot something on it, and I ended up skating it with him. Wig ended up getting photos of me skating it as well, and they ended up using my photo instead of his one. He wasn't miffed at the time, I don't think.

At this point I was kinda getting Toy Machine stuff from Fos, and some other Slam brands, and I had an FTC sticker on my board because I knew Joey Tershay and Kent Uyehara from when I used to go to San Francisco all the time. I went to SF a little after this period and I was psyched because they had my cover on the wall in FTC. Kent was psyched I'd got the shop on the cover of a UK magazine, and he said he'd give me whatever stuff I needed whenever I was in San Francisco. I was blown away by that. We used to always try to carry their product at Slam too.

This[4] was in south London, near Waterloo, and it was in a college – Southbank college, I think – but it's not there now. I don't know if it's the same architect that did Southbank, but basically it's the same as Southbank. The same material, and almost the same rail. I used to taildrop off the rail at Southbank for a laugh, just because I liked doing it and I was into doing taildrops and drop-ins.

I went down there with Wig and Mat Fowler to do it. I hadn't done it before but I'd looked at it and I thought it was possible. It was getting dark and Wig's all, 'It's getting dark, and you're wearing a navy jacket. We should come back', and I was like, 'Nah, fuck it, I want to do it'.

I climbed up there but I couldn't really balance but Mat had to kinda hold me up there. I was jumping down it and jumping down it and jumping down it but I just couldn't commit to landing in the bank. Then I just did it; I got up like, 'Fuck it, I'm going to do it', and I did it and rode out. There's not that much run-out, there's a generator thing and some windows, so when you come down you're fucking flying and there's not much room before you hit the generator so I ran out. Then Wig's like, 'Oh, my flash didn't go'. And he's going, 'Don't do it anymore! Stop!', and I'm just like, 'Fuck it, I'll do it again, make sure the flash is working'. He fired the flash off, it was working, and I climbed up and did it again. ●

200
0

Elsewhere

Danny Wainwright, Bristol, by Wig Worland

We had the whole of London as our playground. Looking back, I can see how everything was perfectly aligned.
OLIVER BARTON

2000

Elsewhere

Paul Silvester

One day after we'd been out skating round London all day, trying to film stuff for *Headcleaner*, Mark Channer and myself were heading back to his house and we passed that double set[5]. I'd been skating all day and probably had a couple of beers, and I started skating it. I had a couple of goes, and there were some other skaters nearby, and one of them was this guy Will from Oxford, who had a video camera and asked if he could film it. I never chased him for the footage, and I didn't see it until after *Headcleaner* came out. I just didn't care. It was all just spur of the moment.

Another time I was down there, and Wig Worland and Dan Magee were around. The first time I did it, it was low-key and it was at night so I never got busted or any hassle. When I went back with those guys, and Wig set everything up, we got busted by security after five or six goes so we packed everything up, went for a walk, and came back for another four or five goes and that's when we got it.

Ali Cairns

There had sort of been conversations about turning pro for Birdhouse, but it was a tricky one. I was technically pro for everyone else, and it was a weird situation. Tony said to me that Bucky Lasek didn't sell too many boards, but they were going to pay me anyway. I was getting paid to skateboard by my shoe company, my clothing company, by everyone, and even by my board company, but I didn't have a board with my name on it and I didn't think I was going to get one with Birdhouse. Vert was still not selling very much, and everything was still heavily geared towards the street.

I didn't want to be paid to be a pro skateboarder with no name, and I'd rather have my name on a board and not get paid. To have a vert ad for Birdhouse and not have my name on a board was really weird, considering I was pro for everybody else.

I'd gone to a demo with Bucky at Earl's Court, that 40 Degrees thing, and I'd met my future wife there, and we hit it off and we got married and we've got a lovely daughter called Ella so I decided to stay in Europe more. That was what sealed the deal.

Pete Hellicar had organised a trip to a competition at a place called Railslide skatepark in Frankfurt, and I was still on Birdhouse, but he asked if I wanted to go with them. I just saw the difference in how their team were a really nice, tight, united team and I thought I'd love to be part of that. To me, Unabomber was just cool. From knowing Jonny Robbo years ago, the seed was planted and I liked Unabomber already.

I might have been over-qualified for Unabomber in some ways, because when I spoke to Pete he was like, 'Are you sure?', and I said, 'Yes, I'd love to.'

Pete Hellicar

I never felt like Unabomber was working. And I don't mean that I didn't have faith in it, but it became abundantly clear that it was really fucking hard to run a skateboard company in the UK because you just do not have the market in terms of scale. The nuts and bolts of the company, the raw bits – how much shit you sell and how much money you make – were a real struggle to make work in any meaningful way.

Vaughan Baker

I'd started spraying out my Unabomber boards by this point. I was on this Emerica tour, and when we got to Edinburgh I knew that double set[6] was there. I saw that John Rattray had backside ollied them in *Waiting For The World* and at that time I believed that Rattray was the gnarliest, so I had to one-up something that he'd done, at any spot that he'd skated, just because that's where my head was at. He did the gnarliest shit, so I had to try to do gnarlier shit, to step ahead.

I battled the tre flip because I wanted to drop the better trick, so that people knew I 'meant business'. And I really had to battle that. That took an hour, maybe.

I just recollect being over it. So over it that I was just trying to toss it in and go to college and move on. It wasn't even like, 'I'm going to go and skate for Blueprint'. I'll say this, *Waiting For The World* definitely was a turning point for me. When I saw that, and I was trying to work on this Unabomber video – and it was a disaster and everybody was fighting internally and we didn't have a filmer and Frank Stephens still wanted to film on Hi8 even though I knew that filming on a VX was just better – when I saw *Waiting For The World* and saw how that presented UK skateboarding for the first time in that way, I knew that dealing with this company was not what I wanted. So I decided to leave Unabomber based on the fact there was no team anymore, there was no boards – I was getting boards from the skate shop. I was meant to be a pro skater and I just wasn't treated that way, so after a lot of phone calls to Pete Hellicar where he kept talking me back on, I just said there was no talking anymore, I was leaving and I was going to go back to college that September.

I was bailing regardless. I don't think I'd even spoken to Dan at that point, because I was dealing mostly with Alvin for Octagon wheels. There definitely was no stealing going on. I was overly frustrated; I wasn't getting what I wanted out of my time at Unabomber, and there was a lot of friction over there. →

And then funnily enough they call me a couple of weeks later. Paul Shier called me. I was tripping. I was with Olly Todd at the time, and we were watching *Waiting For The World*, before going out skating, and I think it was even Shier's part that was on when Shier called me.

They [Unabomber] were saying I was jumping ship to get a pay cheque, and to do this and do that, but no. It wasn't that.

Dan Magee

We did want Vaughan but we had a policy of not stealing anyone, even though that's kind of a funny thing to do.

We're at Birdshit Banks and Toddy – who I'd never met but we'd put him on Octagon – rolled up with Vaughan because Vaughan was going to ride for Octagon as well. We introduced ourselves and we kind of hit it off, and it transpired that he had left Unabomber about two weeks ago. I think we talked about it with Shier, and we liked that he had that kind of 'heroin chic' thing going on, so we thought it'd work.

Vaughan's bootcuts were so 'in' in skate culture at the time that you couldn't do anything about it, but he also skates to The Cult.

Vaughan Baker

Dan would definitely always take the piss out of my gear, all the time. I think I had the opinion that they wanted me to look like that anyway, but at times it was, 'Baker, that's too much, man'. I didn't get it too bad to be honest, I've seen it worse with other people. If he didn't like what someone was wearing he just wouldn't film them. I think Snowy got hit with that a few times, like if he was dressed head-to-toe like Chad Muska or some shit. I definitely remember Rattray getting stick, for sure.

Pete Hellicar

When *Headcleaner* was made we were all living together, and Mike Manzoori was staying with us, so it was a lot easier to get stuff together. It was just fortuitous that we ended up in this massive warehouse. It had a single room for a bathroom, and a kitchen, but no bedrooms. Rich Holland – Badger – built three or four bedrooms. There was a big German lady that liked Harry, called Ingrid, there too. We had it set up as a design studio, as well as a place to live, so a lot of the editing was happening in that space. There was a lot of video games too, Harry was looney on the video games. Always has been.

Mark Channer

Headcleaner I like overall, but it lost that feel and tightness. Nothing against all the extra skateboarders, but it had got too big. It's an hour-long video! If you compare that to *Unapromo*, and all credit to Frank for that, that video encompasses the feel, and so do the first ads. It was also an extension of *Playing Fields*, of me and Frank going round in his car. Some of his strategy for not having a driving licence was a clip-on tie. That was his substitute, for the police.

Toby Shuall

Frank was so obsessed with making that video, and he went and stayed with everyone to make their part, which is really sweet, so he came and stayed at my house for a few days and we travelled around. We went to Leeds with Mark Channer, to stay with Man, and he lived on a fucking mattress in a hallway. He didn't even have a room. Some skaters had a house, and in the hall in the house, between the kitchen and the bedrooms, he had a mattress that he'd fold down and that's where he lived.

That trip got crazy, and I remember thinking that I couldn't handle it anymore. We were eating unlabelled tins of food; we'd all stopped eating meat, and I asked Frank where he'd got them from, and he's like, 'I got it off someone!', and it turned out to be fucking chicken soup. I had a friend that went to university in Leeds so I just ejected myself to their place. I didn't even have 1p on me so he was the only reason I managed to get back to London. There was no money, there was nothing.

With Octagon I was just like, 'Cool, I'll get some wheels!' – these shit, giant wheels – but I was friends with Dan Magee so it was great. We went on a tour and someone actually paid for me to sleep in a hotel, which was unheard of. I quit Unabomber quite soon after Octagon started, and I'd wanted to quit Unabomber for ages, but because I was such good friends with Pete I was a bit worried about it and I didn't want to piss him off. It was just so shit, the deal for me. He didn't have enough money in the company to even give everybody on the team enough boards to skate.

Thinking about it now I'm older, I can't believe I rode for a company named after the Unabomber. It's a bit gnarly. I remember being a bit like, 'What's with this weird fucking gimp graphic?' A big influence on my life as a skateboarder would be Metropolitan or the original Stereo, so I didn't really want to skate for a company named after a terrorist with a gimp for a logo. But at the time I was just stoked on them and we were friends and it was fun. ●

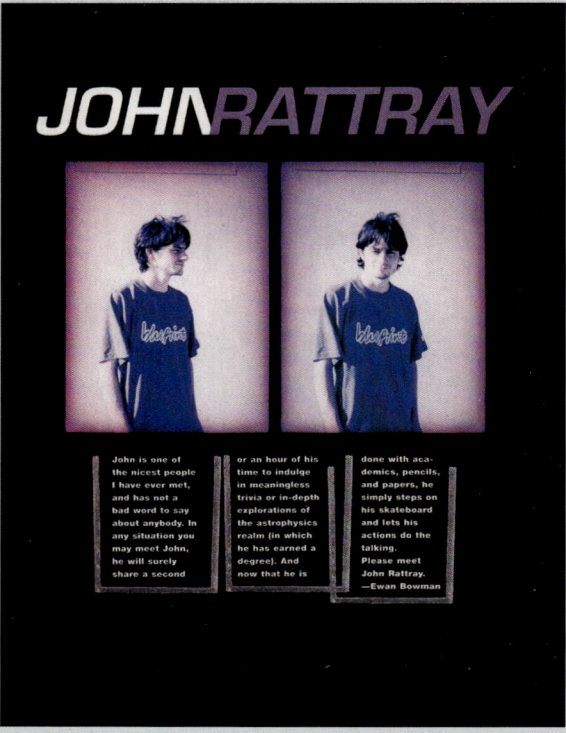

JOHN RATTRAY

John is one of the nicest people I have ever met, and has not a bad word to say about anybody. In any situation you may meet John, he will surely share a second or an hour of his time to indulge in meaningless trivia or in-depth explorations of the astrophysics realm (in which he has earned a degree). And now that he is done with academics, pencils, and papers, he simply steps on his skateboard and lets his actions do the talking. Please meet John Rattray. —Ewan Bowman

CLOCKWISE FROM TOP LEFT
[1]   Blueprint Mark Baines US ad, *Big Brother*, July, photo by Oliver Barton
[2]   John Rattray interview opener, *Slap*, March, photos by Joe Brook
[3–7] Blueprint Font boards, 'P' from Paul Shier's signature stylised to 'B', by Dan Magee
[8]   John Rattray, Clipper Street, SF, from *411VM* issue 37, filmed by Dustin Dollin
[9]   John Rattray, Paul Shier and Colin Kennedy, ASR San Diego, by Rich Hart

Dan Magee

When I moved to London for university and shacked up with my now-wife I was living in west London because she was out there. I got Chris Massey a job at Faze, as International Sales Manager, in order to get him to move to London because I wanted him to live in London because he was my mate, and then Marshall Taylor moved in with us because we were all friends at the time. We lived together in a couple of places. One was Brentford Dock and the other one was Cawdor Crescent.

When people would come down to London for the first time, they would basically live there. Massey would hook them up. People would just come and stay at our house and get jobs working at the warehouse and stuff, and eventually move to London that way. That was where people like Snowy and Olly Todd made their first port of call, through Massey.

I didn't really stay there much; I had a room there but my girlfriend lived with her parents round the corner so I just lived there, and people would live in my room or on the dirty sofas that we had. I was round there all the time editing, and it was like a hot-box of weed and footage and Blueprint or Octagon riders. We'd go and film, and come back and watch the footage and smoke weed and it was just a pure skate house.

We had a van as well, that we convinced Joe Burlo to buy, then weirdly enough it got stolen – which I'm still a bit suspect of – then Joe got us a piece-of-shit car called a Savanna, a Renault Savanna, that we called the Slamma, like Savanna Slamma, then that became the mode of transport. The van just got stolen randomly from a very safe crescent, overnight, after we'd been skating. In my conspiracy-addled mind I wonder if Joe took the car back in the night because he wanted a cheaper car or something like that. It was just weird how it went. Joe had this guy called Kev that he'd get to do stuff for him, so I wonder if that's how it went because when I told him

he didn't seem that bothered. Just, 'I'll get you another car', and then got us this super-cheap car.

So Massey was working for Blueprint for not very long; Joe got rid of Massey as an international sales person and got his son Simon to do it instead. Massey was the dude who could have taken it to the next level if he'd had a shot with it. He had a hard job too, like, 'Hey, we've got this company from England and you haven't heard of any of the riders', and that was his job.

Lucy Adams

I sent a sponsor-me tape to Faze 7, before I was getting boards from Reaction, but I never heard back. I used to ride Mark Baines Blueprint boards religiously. He wasn't my favourite, I think Scott Palmer was my favourite, but his boards were wide and I was trying to ride 7.25s back then. Fos did a 7.25 Organic board, but I was riding those Blueprint 'B' boards, the Mark Baines one of those. Loads of them.

John Rattray

Jamie Thomas came and found us at the ASR trade show in San Diego[9], when I was on that road trip. He talked about coming down to San Diego and hanging out and skating, and getting to know the team. It wasn't an offer at that point; he was coming at it from the Circa angle at first. I was still getting flowed DC, and Damon Way came to that trade show and dropped off some DC for me, to see me through the rest of that trip. I got those DCs and went up to skate Clipper before going home.

I went back to the UK, and we're filming for *Waiting For The World*. Mirko Mangum and his sales colleague were on a sales trip in Europe, so they came to meet me in Edinburgh, and he offered me a spot on Circa. He left it open-ended to me in terms of what compensation should look like, and I remember calling up Danny Wainwright and asking him what he was getting from Vans, and trying to get a sense of what the going rates were, but I couldn't get it too clear. I emailed Mirko and said $2,500, and he was like, 'Is that per month

or per year?' That's why you should get an agent to deal with this shit. I didn't know if he was joking or not. I think he was saying that I was overshooting on the monthly, and we could build it up based on milestones or something. At the time I'm just a kid out of college, going, 'Err, I dunno'.

When I was at home the *411* part and my *Slap* interview came out, then six months later there's another trade show, at Long Beach, so we go out for that as Blueprint – that's the one where Wainwright wins the High Ollie Contest – and I felt really out of sorts because I realised I didn't know anyone and everyone kinda knew me because of this stuff.

Wainwright had weed that was really strong, and I was in a room with him, and took a puff of a joint. I'd grown up smoking whatever Moroccan hash we'd get in Scotland, and drinking cider, so it spun me out so bad. High-THC weed was really gnarly, and was a catalyst for underlying issues that were already there. It really just accelerated anxieties that I had anyway, and that turned into this real bad almost-psychosis and I ended up in this panic, this chronic anxiety loop, all the way into this trip that Colin and I had planned up to San Francisco to stay at Joe Brook's. The weather wasn't that great and I wasn't really prepped and I couldn't get my head together, and I was really getting down into a depressive cycle and that ended up with proper suicidal ideation in San Francisco.

When I finally got home to Aberdeen from that, my sister took me to the doctor, and the doctor identified that I just needed to make a choice around what future I was going to pursue – oil and gas or pro skating – and gave me Fluoxetine. Shier had been calling me, Dan called me, Hellicar called me, a few people called me to try to get me up and about and I was just kind of recovering from that whole psychological cycle that had happened post-*411* in Long Beach. I made a choice, that I was going to pursue pro skating, then we finished filming *Waiting For The World* after all that. ●

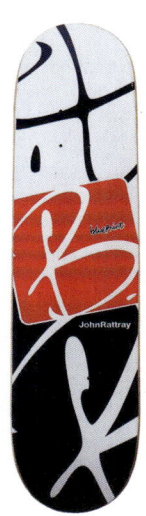

Dan Magee

With the first two videos, there was no process. We were literally just making it up as we went along; I'm learning stuff as we went along. I didn't know how to edit and I'm having to learn to edit on an A/B linear editing system, but by the time you get to *Waiting For The World* it's non-linear, because digital editing has come in, but you're still learning stuff.

I feel like we just got lucky... Back then you couldn't really tell people what clothes to wear because they haven't really got any trust in you yet, at that stage in time. At that time it was like a, 'Oh, you've got a good camera, but you're not going to tell me what to do' kind of thing.

A lot of it was two-trick lines because I can't be arsed to film a long line because I don't think they look good and it's really drawn out and it's really hard to insert in edits. I was working that out, and you can kind of see it in a lot of my stuff.

There's loads of two-trick lines because it keeps everything dynamic, whereas if you have anything more than a three-trick line – unless it's really good – you can only really have that stuff at the beginning of a video. Early on – and I don't know how – I kinda figured out that you need to keep it within those parameters. You need to have maybe eight lines which are all two tricks or three tricks, then I think it was 20 to 30 single tricks, to make a video part. I worked that out eventually, that's like what the sweet spot is in terms

of how I would do it. Everyone was up for travelling, it was only ever Selley and Chewy it was really hard to get to come. Even when John was going through his depression, we did that last-minute trip to Scotland which was Paul Shier's idea, to get John out. Even though we didn't understand the level of his depression at the time; we were so naive to it. Shier had the foresight to want to organise a trip to make everyone skate and make everyone stoked. That was really important. But to make Selley go somewhere was impossible. It was always that he didn't want to sleep in this, or do that, or he didn't have the right shoelaces or whatever. Chewy was equally hard because he didn't have any money and we couldn't really support him. Also he was intimidated by London, things like sitting on the Tube freaked him out. Obviously that's changed now. Chewy and Selley were the only really tough ones to get going anywhere. Everyone else was pumped for travelling.

It's not like, 'Hey, you've got to look stylish', all it is is future-proofing. If you've got a sleeveless top on with a Hoax graphic that's a Toy Machine rip-off, then you yourself are gonna be bummed in two years on that clip going in there, and you'll tell me not to use the clip with the Hoax t-shirt with the sleeves cut off. Or if you're wearing shorts in a clip, you're gonna be bummed in four years. If I'm like, 'Hey mate, just put this white t-shirt on, and blue jeans, and a white pair of trainers' or whatever, in four years

you're still going to think it looks dope. All it is is future-proofing.

If you're filming for a video that comes out in three, four or five years, your neon-laced Jedi Dunk footage is now not going to be useable.

A lot's been made of the tough love thing, but you've got to look at it like this: I'm a short-arsed little dude, and at any point in time all these geezers could just batter the shit out of me.

The one thing that I always did, was show you other people's shit. You'd have a timeline but you wouldn't show them their footage, you'd show them someone else's. There's a negative way and a positive way of doing that.

The negative way, is you can show them another skater's shit where they're fucking killing it, and they might be like, 'Fuck, I better do this'. For instance I'd probably show Ben Grove Smithy's shit, because I know in Grove's mind he's quite a demo champ, and Smithy's a kid who's not really like that but he's just an animal. So Grove seeing Smithy's shit, he'd be like, 'Fucking hell, I've got to do this'.

The positive way is, 'Right, let's put your footage in alongside someone that you respect', and they'll want to do this and do that because they want to be in the same line-up, or be alongside them. When we'd go to Mallorca, I'd basically make an edit of the whole trip and every night we'd just watch it together, and that's positive reinforcement. Barton was more on the positive reinforcement, but I might do a bit of snide nudging. Good cop, bad cop, kind of routine.

I don't think you could make an epic video with just positive reinforcement or negative reinforcement, I think you have to have both.

As time progresses and people's memories dim, or society changes, they tend to go back to the negative stuff. 'This dude did this, he made me jump down that', or whatever. But them riding away from that is probably one of the best memories in their lifetime.

It's sometimes hard if the person's having a bad day, or you don't know about shit they've got going on in their life, it can go wrong. But there are not many times like that.

Unless someone picked a song and it happened to be a good pick, no one had any input on music. People didn't know what they were having until the premiere, and the only person who did not stand for that was Colin. So what I had to do was get Colin to give me 20 songs, so he'd give me 20 CDs, and I'd be like, 'No, no, no, no, no... This one is kind of OK'. He's done that for every video except for *Make Friends*.

The thing that always made me just choose – because obviously the brand is aligned with the context of the company – was when Smithy asked if he could skate to Jamiroquai. It was basically, 'No, you can't

skate to Jamiroquai, and to nip this in the bud no one else is going to have a choice in it'. But then again, Travis.

I think I owned that Seahorses CD single, and I know I heard that 'Sugar Man' song on the radio, but it was All Saints singing it. It was a B-side to an All Saints single, and I found it on a forum or something.

I think making a skate video is a lot like making an album, and it's not necessarily that they're great songs, it's more that it goes from one song to the next and it makes sense. A full-length video has either got to be like a concept album in terms of soundtrack, where there's a reason why you're using these songs, and there's a reason why it fits this person, and there's a reason why it comes after this other song and before this next song. Or it has to be like a mixtape where it's like, it would just run.

The one I nearly fucked up, but I think is perfect for the video, was Skinnyman for Smithy. That track was given to me by Mark Harmon because I couldn't find a track, but I think it goes perfectly. There is no more a British skater than Smithy, because he's a random kid from a little town in Essex. It was originally gonna be Razorlight, and I'm so glad it wasn't. I think it got thrown in the mix and Sam Ashley – who's a muso as well – went,

'You cannot use Razorlight'. And that was it. There's nothing that I wish I hadn't used but there were a couple of close calls.

Paul Shier
Magee was good at what he did. I don't think I trusted anyone who has been a videographer more than him. With every video part I ever had, I never saw it before the premiere. I don't think he wanted to show it anyway, but there was just full trust that he was gonna make you look your best, and I feel that with every video we did, he made everybody who was on the team look as good as they could look. But he was definitely an arsehole to some people, as a filmer.

At that time we were drinking a lot, and smoking weed, and we'd go on trips, like we'd go to Mallorca for ten days, and he would be the sober dude – the only sober dude. That came at a price at the time, when you're hanging out with a load of shitheads who drink. But he just did a great job, and without him, Blueprint would not be what it was. Without him I wouldn't be doing what I do now, and I think that's the same for everyone. Vaughan works for Vans, Baines works for New Balance, Colin and John work for Nike. There's a lot of other people who've succeeded with their lives too, but for those who succeeded within skating, it was helped by Dan's work, what he did for them. →

LEFT TO RIGHT
[10] John Rattray, Mitchell Library, by Skin Phillips
[11] Paul Shier, Dan Magee (with camera), John Rattray, St Paul's, by Oliver Barton

2000

Waiting For The World was a massive turning point for British skateboarding. Still today, I'll be in the middle of America, and somebody will be like, 'Oh man, *Waiting For The World* was in our shop, we had one copy!' It hit in the places that could relate to being from the UK. People fucked with it there, people didn't fuck with it in California because it wasn't relatable.

I wanted most of my stuff at Fairfield. Most of my parts for Blueprint, 70% of my footage is in Croydon, and 60% is at that spot. I just knew it very well, I knew it inside out, and I had things I wanted to do that I don't believe were being done at that time in the UK. The spot was so special to me, and everybody hated it, outside of who skated it.

Alvin Singfield

Waiting For The World took it to another level and made it hard to compete against Dan. He pulled out everything on that one. In that first year, Panic was only in the UK. It was only overseas after *A Mixed Media* came out. I think we did something like 3,000 copies of *A Mixed Media* in the UK, and then a year later with *Anthems* we did something stupid like 30,000 copies and that went everywhere, and it was utter shit compared to *Waiting For The World*, but that was three-and-a-half years in the making.

That was the biggest selling skateboard video – outside of America – in the world, and then Blueprint went on to be the biggest selling skateboard brand – outside of America – in the world. Polar and those brands would whoop it now, but this was even before Cliché and stuff. At the time there was no other brand that got to the level Blueprint got to. And after I left, Dan and his guys were going out to China and Russia and all that. I knew that when *Waiting For The World* came out, it wasn't just a new Blueprint video, it was a fucking game-changer. There hadn't been a British skateboard video like that before, and there wasn't one for quite a while after.

I can watch *Waiting For The World* and *First Broadcast* now and I think they still hold up as good videos. Dan was so far ahead of his time.

Channon King

With Dan, if you did a good trick, you were in his good books, but sometimes he would kind of crush people; he wouldn't really bring the best out in them through being like that. I think sometimes that although Dan got results, he didn't always know the right way of getting them.

Back then I was dysfunctional, I didn't really know how to behave and I was a dick, so I don't really blame people for the

way they were towards me. I didn't have the right parents, I didn't have anyone guiding me, and I was just using all the dysfunctional mechanisms to get my way and to manage my feelings of powerlessness. Not wearing Blueprint stuff was just a dysfunctional way of sorting that problem out, rather than trying to do it properly. The only tools I had to sort it out at the time were to scream and shout and snap boards. It was just my way of dealing with things.

A lot of the reason people gravitated to skateboarding, and a lot of the reason I did, was because I'd been in school, which was like a 12-year jail sentence for a crime I didn't commit, and then when you're out of that, skateboarding offers you this unstructured freedom where you decide your own destiny. If you win or lose it's all down to you, and although you're with other people, you're an individual and it's not a team thing. So for then to be on a company who give you something, and as soon as they give you something you kind of owe them – not contractually, but morally – obviously I'm going to kick against that. So I stopped wearing Blueprint clothes and all the rest of it, and I didn't want to feel like somebody owned me. It's like not wearing a school uniform or something, just rebelling against it.

LEFT TO RIGHT
[12]   Paul Shier, Fairfield Halls, by Wig Worland
[13]   Channon King, Southbank, by Oliver Barton
[14]   *Waiting For The World* master
[15+16] *Waiting For The World* VHS slip case by Dan Magee, photography
        by Oliver Barton
NEXT PAGE
Al Collins, Sheriff Street, Dublin, by Leo Sharp

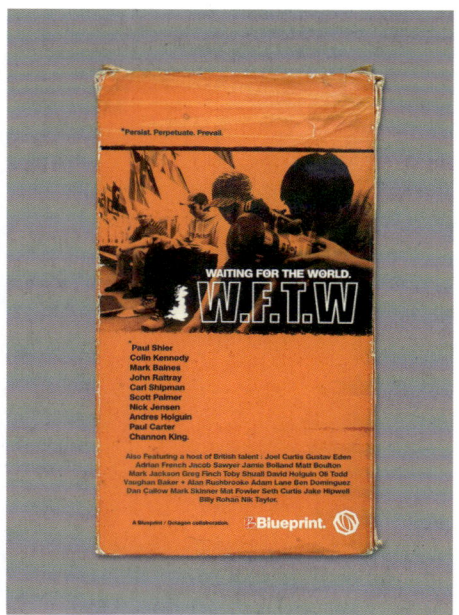

Oliver Barton

I don't think there's anybody in the world like Dan; they broke the mould after they made him. There's no one who can film, edit, do board graphics, create catalogues, team manage, book travel, work on collaborations... Yeah, he's a really special person.

It was so exciting, everything that he was doing. When I saw *Build and Destroy*, the promo, it looked so much more dynamic than anything that was coming out from anybody else at that point. Not just the skating but the production, and he was so talented with everything and he knew which computers did what, and what their memory was – this technical side – and he would geek out on all the cameras.

He would be really direct with his constructive criticism on what I was doing wrong, filming-wise. My stuff was quite over-exposed, and because the TRV didn't have a handle the footage would quite often be a little bit tilted. He'd be like, 'Jensen, make sure he doesn't film it crooked'.

He had a really strong set of rules, and no one had ever told me there was this set of rules before. Even clothes that people were allowed to wear. There's footage in *Waiting For The World* of John skating Dynamic Earth, and him and Paul Shier had found a Gap shop that had all these vests on special offer, and John got a bright orange one, and Dan had to black and white the footage. He was just looking out for people. He taught me a lot

of rules and pointed out a lot of things that weren't cool. I was really open-minded to everything, and he narrowed down what was and what wasn't acceptable. We probably argued about it quite a lot, but it definitely helped.

You hear a lot about coaches doing this thing where they create an 'us versus the world' attitude, and I think that with retrospect the *Build and Destroy* promo not being in 411 could arguably have been the best thing that ever happened to Blueprint because it did push everyone to be much more proactive and go out filming and wanting to make a full-length video.

The excitement around *Waiting For The World* was so much bigger than anything that would have happened if it had just been a *411* thing. I remember we went to do the soundcheck at the theatre in Sheffield and Dan soundchecked with Rattray's part, and I've never felt like that before or since. Just the feeling of excitement, knowing there was something really amazing that you could be really proud of. Not in any kind of competitive way, just being really proud for Dan and the team that they were about to prove how good they really were, even if they were going to have to battle the odds if they were going to get people to look at them.

The way Dan had it, everyone would just meet up and go on sessions and skate stuff. No one really thought about photos and it became quite natural to just shoot photos and film. It was never really

something that people ever thought about, like, 'I've got to get an ad!', or anything; it would just be, 'Oh, we've got this picture, we should use it for an ad'. We did shoot a series of portrait ads that was a bit more organised like that, for the 'Judge By The Monuments We've Destroyed Not Created' ads, but it was all really organic.

Gareth Skewis

Dan Magee played *Waiting For The World* to me, Greg Finch, Nik Taylor and Chris Pulman, just before the Sheffield premiere. I remember thinking that the calibre of skateboarding, and the execution of this, was so fucking good.

Me and Greg drove with Styley to the premiere, and I remember thinking that it was of such a calibre that it was going to change UK skateboarding. All of us agreed that one wall in Slam would become British boards, and we were just going to push UK skateboarding, and that fully changed things. It was huge and it was an amazing time.

What Russell and Sofia were doing with Silas, and what Dan was doing with Blueprint, they were never trying to be anything else but what they were, whereas a lot of time in skateboarding previously, and in streetwear, businesses that were non-American were trying to mimic certain things that were happening in New York or LA. To me, Blueprint and Silas were quintessentially British and didn't give a fuck what was going on outside in the world, which I felt was deeply attractive. ●

Elsewhere

SUBURBAN BLISS

Toby Shuall

Because I worked in Slam and sold Bathing Ape t-shirts, and other weird Japanese brands that I've forgotten the names of, and I knew Michael Kopelman, and from being in that scene in London and seeing that people were doing clothing companies, I just wanted to do it, because I needed something to do other than skateboarding.

I'd started drawing these funny little things, then I got the t-shirts printed, and I went to see Michael at his shop Hit and Run, and he was like, 'You can't just print something on a Fruit of the Loom t-shirt and bring it in here and expect me to buy it'. He basically said that if I wanted to make a label I'd have to try a lot harder than that, and coming from the skate world, that was quite good. It was harsh to hear at that age, because I thought I was going to walk in and he would buy some of my t-shirts, but he taught me a lot.

I started doing it and I thought it was a way I could make a living, which turned out to be completely wrong. I was always broke and I liked drawing so the idea was that I would put my art on t-shirts. Loads of things were inspiring me, and I was around people making clothing, so I just started doing it. Andy Hartwell had started a company called Ouef, which I believe means 'egg' in French, and I'd been exposed to quite a lot of fashion stuff, but I wasn't trying to start a fashion label. It was very small. I made 20 t-shirts, and then I made 30.

I started hitting up all the other shops, and Sibs at Focus took some, and Ed and Brian at Hanon in Aberdeen took some. I was stoked when I got in Hanon, because that was hard. It was like, 'Why am I trying to deal with these really hard-to-deal-with Scottish brothers?', but it was such a good a shop. I'd sell them maybe 30 or 40 t-shirts every time I did a run, but it was so shit when I did it that a t-shirt would cost me five or six pounds, and I'd sell them for £12, so it was mad. I'd worked really hard on it all year and worked out that I'd made ten grand... It was not viable.

I went to a trade show with Gareth Skewis and Greg Finch, and I was like, 'This is so shit, what the fuck am I doing here? Fucking twats buying stupid Nikes...', just being really jaded and pissed off, and I didn't really want to be there. They introduced me to some guy and he was such a cheesy 'streetwear' guy, and I couldn't even be fucked. I think I said to him, 'Don't worry, you won't even like it anyway', then I went out drinking with Greg and he's like, 'What are you doing? You literally sabotaged a sale', and I was like, 'What's the point? I'll sell him 20 t-shirts and make £302 out of it and it'll just be a nightmare'.

I just quit there and then. I didn't want to make 'streetwear' anymore, I didn't want to keep making all these cultural references to people who collect New Era hats and Nikes, I just couldn't stand it anymore. It just wasn't working. It was a dark time, in a way. When I started it I wanted to put drawings on a t-shirt, and I still really wanted to make art, and I felt like I had to get rid of the company to continue to make art. I'd always been scared to make art because I was worried about how I would make a living, but I wasn't making any fucking money anyway.

After quitting being a skateboarder, I can quit anything. I did not want to quit being a skateboarder but I had to, so I've been able to change my path in life a few times. ●

LEFT TO RIGHT
[1] Toby Shuall, St Paul's, by Daniel Turner
[2] Suburban Bliss logo and Lady of the Woods t-shirt, by Toby Shuall
[3] Suburban Bliss press shot, behind Lower Marsh, by James Moriarty

2000

Heroin

Chris Pulman

Fos dropped a board and a long-sleeve off at Slam for me, and I called up Wig and told him I was going to ride for Heroin. I put the long-sleeve on, set up the board, we went to Gas Banks and shot that ollie over the hip. The one he shot through the fence[1]. Apart from the fact that I'm wearing fucking Globes, that's still one of my favourite photos. The shoes are so bulky that my feet are barely on the board.

Dan would show up with all the guys he'd been out filming with, because Slam was a youth club on a Friday afternoon. It was like, 'Man, these guys are actually making a real skateboard video here. They're working properly hard and it's going to be good.' And then *Waiting For The World* came out, and it was a thing. We had every board in the world on the wall – Girl, Chocolate, Zero, Element, every brand – but under the counter it was just Blueprint boards. So every kid would come in like, 'I want this Girl board', and we'd be like, 'Have you tried a Blueprint board? They're £40 and it's the same wood shop.' So nearly every kid would go out with a Blueprint board, even though we had everything else.

This was when I was riding for Heroin. Heroin and Death are more of an acquired taste. In London you could put Death boards on the wall in Covent Garden and you couldn't sell them. Every time,

we'd always have a regular Death board and a Cates board, and no disrespect to those guys, but nobody would pick them up. If you went up to Harlow, every kid was riding a Death board, but in Central London, the kids wanted Blueprint.

I pushed the fuck out of Heroin boards, but at the end of the day, when a kid is coming in to spend money, this kid doesn't want a Heroin board, this kid wants something that's cool and fresh. He wants to be Nick Jensen, he doesn't want to be Ollie Payne.

I fucking suck at skateboarding. I just love it. Most of the time I'm just hanging on and the only reason I stay on my board is because of fear. It's passion more than skill, and everything I do is because I love it, and not because I have any innate talent. I never had any real gymnastic ability, and I knew I was never going to be *good* good. I knew I was never going to be good at skateboarding, but because I knew I wasn't going to be good at skateboarding I knew that I had to find another angle. That's the beauty of skateboarding, you don't have to be good to contribute, or to enjoy it. That's the big reason why people like me who aren't good at skateboarding hate skateboarding being a sport because as soon as you turn it into a sport it becomes a meritocracy, with rules and ideas about who's the best, like any other sport, and

it's so sad to take something and make it into a sport. If the only way somebody can understand something is based on who does something the highest and fastest, then that just becomes athletics. I'm more interested in ballet than in high jump because you have to really think and understand and appreciate it.

You have to make mistakes to have style. If everybody skates perfect, then nobody's got a style. You have to be doing it wrong in some way in order to have style. Whether it's a correction when you land, or a certain way you flick your board because you broke your ankle once. Style comes from imperfection. ●

LEFT TO RIGHT
[1] Chris Pulman, Gas Banks, by Wig Worland
[2] Heroin artwork, by Fos
[3] Fos, Slam warehouse, by Wig Worland

2000

GUNNER

NEIL URWIN, GREG FINCH, BARRY DRING, RODNEY CLARKE, ROB SELLEY, MAT FOWLER, FLYNN TROTMAN, GUNNER, PETER KING, LEO & JODY SMITH

REACTION

Ian Gunner

We were New Deal UK, we were commonly known as the Death Star, we had all the brands, and Ray and Gary were driving round in BMWs, but apart from Julie and Carol in accounts, every single person in that place skated. It wasn't this corporate entity that everyone portrayed it to be, until they wanted a board or until they wanted a bit of discount or until they wanted their jam sponsored. Even the likes of early Radlands, all the logos around it were painted by Mick Forster and New Deal paid him for it. Ray and Gary were always so chilled about the whole thing. They were 'geezers' but they weren't show-offs. Gary especially, Gary was the most relaxed guy you'd ever meet. They were just doing the right things in the right way, they were giving jobs to skateboarders, and they were doing good things for skateboarding.

Warrior was started up to distribute brands that competed with NDUK brands. Girl and Chocolate were up for grabs, and alongside that was Lakai, so Warrior was started and Matt Anderson was put in as the Head of Warrior. We were still going to absolutely go to town on DC, we weren't going to change our strategy there, and I think Warrior was there to tick a box. Some brands didn't want to be distributed by New Deal UK because they thought there was too much going on and we wouldn't be able to focus on their brand, so suddenly Zero, for example, were on Warrior. ●

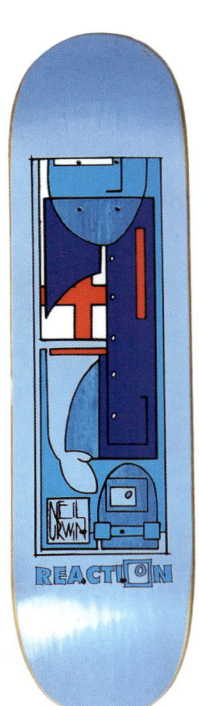

LEFT TO RIGHT
[1]   Greg Finch, Southbank, by Wig Worland
        Reaction Ian Gunner ad, photo by David 'Styley' Steel
[2]
[3–4] Reaction Country Series, by Ian Gunner

Dan Cates

We were fucking around in the house one Friday night, just drinking, and we were probably gonna go out to a club or something, and Zorlac had just set up a new board and it had a vert-gap in the griptape. There were sticky labels lying about, paper sticky-back labels on a roll, and I got one of them and I wrote 'Nick is fat' and just stuck it on his board.

He either scratched 'Cates is a cunt' into his griptape or he made a sticker with that and put it on my board, something like that. Then he goes, 'Yeah, I might bring that out as a board graphic. Yeah. You deserve that.' And he was just joking around so I was like, 'Yeah, go on. Do it. Go on then.' And I dismissed it as a joke, and then he went and made it.

It was a really limited run, about 50 of them, as a joke, but obviously it's a board with my name on it, so some people took it to be a pro model. I knew it was something that shouldn't really be happening, but I was just, 'Yeah, alright then', and that was that. It happened by default.

My griptape, I always use the traditional method so it wasn't pens, it was always coloured grip, cut out. All of those griptape jobs were done from as many different colours of griptape that I sourced from here, there and everywhere. Old skate shops or wherever.

I used to dread setting up a board because it would take me about ten hours so it was like a major event, but I was young then and I didn't have any responsibilities so I did have the time and the inclination. But they needed to become a bit easier as I progressed and went through more boards and things like that. Eventually I had loads and loads of diagonal-stripes ones, in all different colours.

As far as the wacky boards, I do enjoy making things and I'm reasonably handy, I suppose. I've got one that's a bed of nails, that was drilled out in a grid and then six-inch nails were banged through it, then one that's got Astroturf for griptape, an eight-wheeler, a twelve-wheeler which was three complete set-ups that are all the same, connected by two 2x2s. There's the crutch board, various longboards and various skimboards. I made a circular board that was pretty good, by cutting a 30-inch diameter disc out of 9mm ply. ●

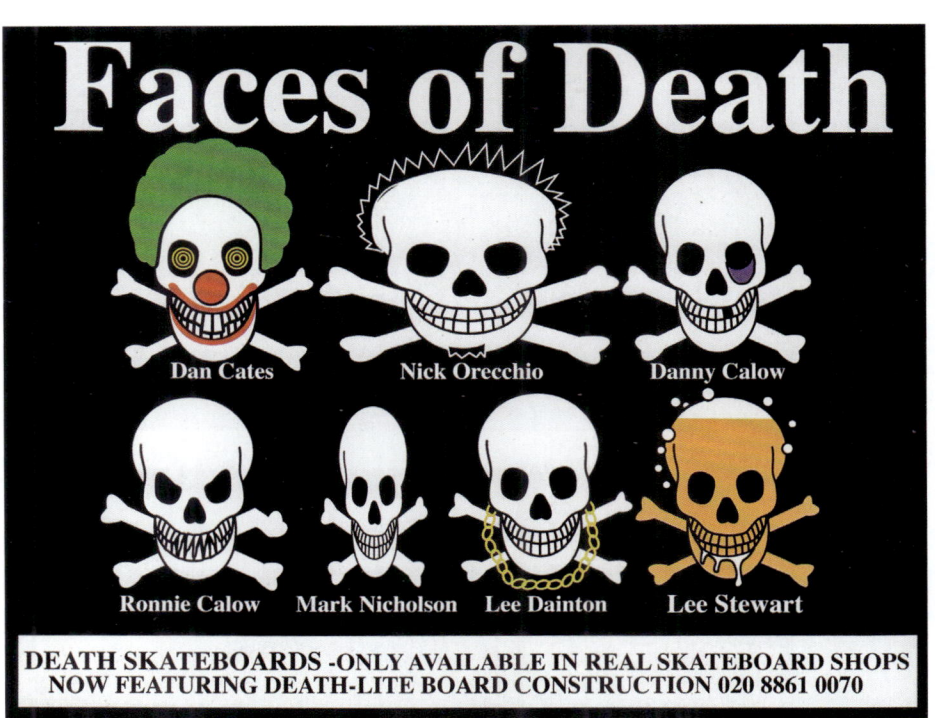

Elsewhere

CLOCKWISE FROM TOP LEFT
[1] *Document* issue 11, Alan Rushbrooke by Stephen 'Kingy' King, design by Rich Holland, published by Fall Line
[2] *Document* issue 15, Daniel 'Snowy' Kinloch by Percy Dean, design by Joel O'Connor, published by 4130
[3] Bruce Kelliher, Kerry, by Rich Gilligan

Rich Holland

The last issue I designed, issue 11, I was not getting on with the publishers by that point and there was tension between the publishers and what was going on. In the last issue I did I put '666 see the number of the beast' underneath the barcode in single-colour black on full colour black. You couldn't see it, but you could see it in the light, and it got printed. I Photoshopped the word 'War' on to the name of the shop behind Alan Rushbrooke too. You can tell I was angry with the publishers.

The publisher didn't spot it but WHSmith spotted it, and phoned up the publisher and went fucking nuts at them, and at that point I was like , 'Fuck it, I don't want to do it anymore'.

Percy Dean

Joel O'Connor's design was something that changed *Document*. The way that Joel really pushed skateboard magazine design forwards, with montage covers and using design elements and graphics within imagery on covers. That had never been done before, and Joel's layouts inside the magazine were through the roof sometimes. We just wanted it to be a bit more of a grown-up magazine than a kids' magazine. I think we thought that *Sidewalk*'s success was that it appealed to everyone; it appealed to kids and it appealed to the older guys, but we didn't appeal to them because I didn't understand the kids and I didn't understand the older crew, the Middle-Aged Shred kind of guys. We were about current street skateboarding, and the things that were happening right there, right now. I'm not saying that *Sidewalk* was a kiddies' magazine, because I know what Ben and Horsley did was so far beyond that, but I think that *Sidewalk* maybe had a younger demographic and because I wasn't a young kid I didn't give a fuck about that, which is wrong and selfish, like a lot of the things to do with *Document*. But I was young and I was into skateboarding and I wanted to do it my way, and that was it.

It didn't feel like what *Sidewalk* were doing was wrong, it just wasn't my approach. It wasn't what me and my mates were into, and it wasn't what we'd read about. We just wanted to show something that was a different side of the coin, something that was about music and about art and the things that supplemented skateboarding or were part of the lifestyle and were really important to us. We wanted to shine a light on that and incorporate a bit of a more serious approach, and be a bit more moody and a bit more antagonistic.

I don't want to say that we were for the educated grown-ups and they were for the kids, because it wasn't as simple as that. I think who I was permeated into how *Document* was. It was very serious and we wanted it to be right, so it was less fun than maybe it should have been. It was more about how British skateboarding has to have this pedestal, it has to have this showcase, and we have to do it right. Then you'd look over and see what they were doing and it looked like they were having more of a laugh than us, and that made me jealous.

We wouldn't put a knobhead on the cover. There were so many people who had good photos and we'd swerve them for covers. We'd swerve them out the magazine completely, even if they had good photos, because we just didn't care about the money. We didn't care about who was advertising, or the reasons why. We decided what goes, and I think it was lucky that we were at that stage in our lives where we didn't give a fuck about that stuff, because we could have been at a different stage in our lives where we cared about money and making things look nice for advertisers. Or putting things in the magazines for reasons that they shouldn't have been in the magazine for, rather than because it was what British skateboarders wanted or what British skateboarders liked, not because an American advertiser wants a new board on the cover. Some guy's coming over from America, and his company advertise, but he's an absolute cunt, so are we going to put him on the cover? No way.

We got told by Factory that we should always have blue skies on the cover. Jim Peskett told us we should have more blue skies on the cover, and it should only be a fisheye picture on the cover, and things like this, but we obviously never did it. I think my reputation preceded them trying to tell me anything to do with the magazine.

It scares me how much film I've thrown away. I used to think that once it was in a magazine, that was as good as it could be. I can remember throwing so much away, and now it's my biggest regret.

Mark Noble

4130 Publishing was doing well, and *Document* landed on us as an opportunity. Percy rang us up with the idea that we could do the magazine because his publishing company was having other ideas, and I thought it could be really great. It seemed like a good opportunity to do it, and keep the magazine going.

It looked a bit shitty, I thought, before we got our hands on it and before Joel O'Connor was given freedom. We knew we had to support those guys and give them what they needed to make a really good magazine. We wanted to grow it, and we did. We got advertisers that we already dealt with on board to advertise with us, and we were up and running. We switched distributor – we put it in with Comag – and effectively relaunched *Document* and pushed it to all the newsagents we dealt with. Sales were up to 15,000, 16,000.

Percy Dean

They saved us when no one else would have us. It wasn't my house on the line with the magazine, it was Mark's, and they stepped in and supported the magazine when Air Publications went and there was no other publishers for us. I didn't even have a camera; all the cameras got taken off us because they were the publisher's cameras. I had Kingy, Sam Ashley and Joel O'Connor underneath me, all twiddling their thumbs not knowing what they were going to do, or what was going on.

Rich Gilligan

Bruce Kelliher was the first person I really photographed. He'd just got sponsored at the time, and I would fuck up so many pictures with him, but he was so encouraging. Almost like this older brother thing. Bruce had this idea for this photo. He wanted to do this gnarly drop-in in Kerry, in this rural town, at this gnarly old railway bridge. We went and shot it at 7am, and I somehow managed not to fuck it up.

It was published in *Slap*, and then as soon as that came out, *Sidewalk* and *Document* were both like, 'Hey! Can you send us stuff?', and it was good because it gave me this confidence where I wasn't just trying to emulate their stuff. I wanted to shoot things with a more documentary eye, not just fisheye. ●

200
1

Stuart Duncan, Bristo Square, by Leo Sharp

You open a skate mag and everything looks perfect, but that really is not how it was.
JAMES WOODLEY

Elsewhere

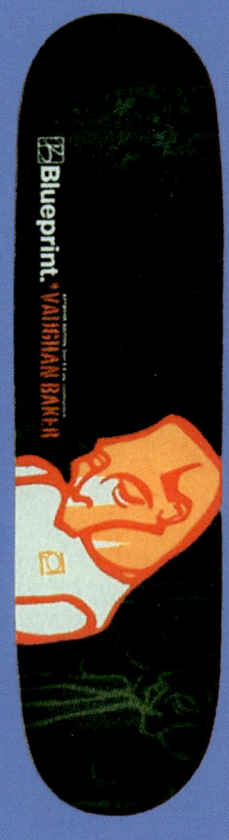

Elsewhere

Alvin Singfield

I left about six months after *Waiting For The World*, in 2001. It was the hardest decision I've ever made in my life, but I went to Faze 7 at 17 years old, fresh out of college, and I'd been there for nearly 11 years. I just felt like I'd done all I could do. Big Spin was dead, Panic wasn't far off it, Dan pretty much had control over Blueprint… There was a lot of problems because Dan is very opinionated and Joe was very opinionated. Joe controlled the money and Dan controlled the image and art direction, and I was stuck in the middle and that caused a lot of grief and it just became rubbish. I knew that if I left, then Joe would have no option but to deal with Dan directly, and would have to bow to Dan's requirements.

I'm so glad there was no social media back then, because the amount of shit I've taken over the years since then, for stuff that people don't even know that I did or assume that I did or hearsay says I did. It's just how people remember it. There's always a bad guy, you've always got to paint somebody as the bad guy, and it was always going to be either me or Joe.

Dan Magee

It wasn't my company, I never got any ownership of it at all. When Blueprint started I was literally doing it for free during my university years, just to have decent boards to skate. I wasn't getting paid, but when I left university and knew I had to get a job, Joe and Alvin said I could do mail-order stuff, and some of the rollerblade bullshit they did because I had a computer, and they'd pay me minimum wage and I could do Blueprint and Panic stuff. That was actually a lifesaver but it went on for far too long. Up until Alvin left, that was how it was, and when Alvin left I got a grand, or two grand, pay rise and that was how it was for the next fucking three years, and so on.

Mark Baines

I'd known Alvin since I was really young, obviously he'd put me on and I always had a really good relationship with Alvin. He did a lot for us all, and I think I feel like he took it as far as he perhaps could and it did need the creativity and the direction that Magee could give it, basically. Magee could do everything; he was doing the videos, the graphics, he was organising stuff, he was coming up with ideas for trips, he was very much on everything we were doing, basically. It kind of made sense.

Alvin did do a lot for everyone in the early years, he put everyone together, no one can deny that. We had some really good times, all of us together, and I think people should remember that Alvin is a big part of that.

Vaughan Baker

I did not skate the 6.5 ply board, I would not entertain the idea of that thing. It would just die, for sure. When I was on 'Bomber I would skate 8.25 boards, and then I got on Blueprint and I had to skate 7.5s. It was a fucking mission. I managed to blag a 7.75, and that's as far as Dan would let me go.

I was skating that top end of Southbank quite a bit at that time. I'd kickflipped the 12 before, which I'd shot with Wig when I was still on 'Bomber, and I was skating the three-set and the eight-set quite a lot, and I guess I'd only just started doing fakie flips down stairs at that point. I can't remember who it was, but somebody was doing fakie flips down stairs at that time I thought it looked sick. I remember it not being too hard[2]. I'd already filmed something there and I'd fakie ollied them in a line, so I had to one-up that, and it was the perfect set of stairs for a fakie flip. That was one of those days of showing up at Southbank, skating the seven for a bit, and then Sam Ashley shot that. That was my fourth cover. →

CLOCKWISE FROM TOP LEFT
[1] Blueprint Paul Shier ad (extract), *Sidewalk*, September, photo by Oliver Barton
[2] *Document*, September, Vaughan Baker, by Sam Ashley
[3] Blueprint Vaughan Baker ad, *Sidewalk*, November, photography by Oliver Barton
[4] Blueprint Denim ad, *Sidewalk*, November
[5] Blueprint Scott Palmer ad, *Sidewalk*, August, photo by Oliver Barton
[6] Blueprint Nick Jensen ad, *Sidewalk*, April, photo by Oliver Barton
[7] Blueprint Vaughan Baker 6.5 ply, artwork by Vaughan Baker
[8] Mark Baines, Eastcastle Street, by Oliver Barton

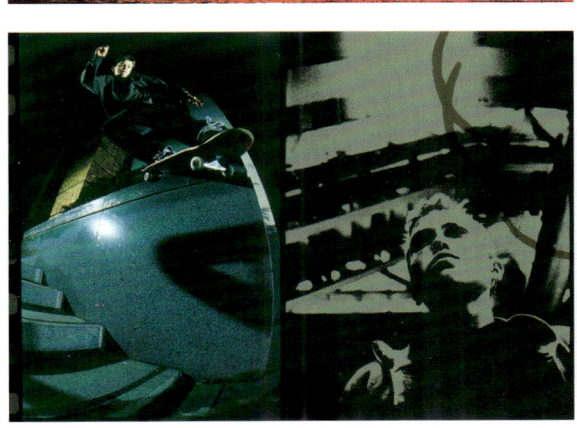

Jamie Thomas

Waiting For The World came out, and I loved it. Rattray was one of my favourite skaters. Then we went on that Circa *Videoradio* tour together, and spent a lot of time together. On tour you're on the road for weeks, and you hear about someone's hopes and dreams, and what they want to do, and I just felt like I would regret not trying to work with him more, and find a way to spend more time skating with him.

At this time I wasn't sure what his future was going to look like with Circa; he'd only travelled a bit with the team and I wasn't sure if they were really going to get behind him and give him a shoe and do the whole thing, so I didn't know if I was even helping him that much.

I thought that if there was an opportunity for him to ride for Zero, it would have been huge, and I thought his style of skating was different and unique to what everyone else was doing on Zero so he would be an incredible addition to the team. So after the *Videoradio* tour I talked to him about that concept, because I'd known him a lot better. It wasn't just that I was a fan of his skating, I'd actually got to know him as a person, and he'd gotten to know me a bit, and know the way we operate.

I spoke to John and he told me he wanted to talk to Dan, and I ended up speaking to Dan as well, because I really didn't want to take the wind out of a brand. I knew he was a major part of Blueprint, so I felt some level of accountability to not hurt a brand that was so vital to the UK scene, so it was a delicate task. I wanted him to be a part of Zero but I also didn't want him to be detrimental to the vitality of Blueprint.

I really tried to be respectful, because I knew the story of how I approached him was going to get out, and that's part of my reputation, and there's a code in the industry to be respectful. I thought it felt more above-board, and I wasn't just on a mission to poach him. I didn't think he felt that way back then, but maybe he did and I wasn't as respectful as I could be. It's such a tough thing because I respected the UK skate scene and I didn't want to disrupt that, but that's such a fine line. How can you respect that, but then not be willing to talk about the opportunity that could be way greater? I feel like it's such a 'damned if you do, damned if you don't' scenario. I felt that John's skateboarding was so special and I wanted to do whatever I could to get it seen by the world. Of course that's my narrative, and a bit selfish, but we had a platform at the time where I was able to do that.

John Rattray

When Jamie asked if I wanted to be on Zero on that Circa tour, I'd kinda already made the decision that I wanted to pursue this. Oliver Barton also gave me advice, and said that if I wanted to do this thing on a global platform, Zero was really an option that I should consider seriously. Then I just decided I needed to go and do that, for me.

When I came back from the *Videoradio* tour I went and stayed at Oliver Barton's place in Hackney, and I did that because I'd made a decision to move off Blueprint to Zero and I needed to talk to Dan. I didn't feel like I could go and stay at Dan's and also quit. I stayed at Oliver's because it was neutral ground, and I called Dan to tell him I was going to quit Blueprint and move to Zero. ●

"DYING TO LIVE"

ZERO WELCOMES JOHN RATTRAY

CLOCKWISE FROM LEFT
[1] John Rattray, College Street warehouse, Aberdeen, by Oliver Barton
[2] Zero John Rattray welcome ad, *Thrasher*, January 2002, photo by Adrian Lopez
[3] Zero John Rattray t-shirt
[4] John Rattray, Hilton Drive, Aberdeen, by Oliver Barton

Ali Cairns

I met Ollie Barton when we were doing stuff for the Dope video, and we just got on really well. Whenever we were doing stuff, if I had an idea he was always really accepting of the idea, and he was a pleasure to work with. He'd always be keen to do it, even if it was driving snow. He was as up for it as I was and he was so much fun to do stuff with.

If somebody ever wanted to take a picture with me, I was always very observant to how they did it, especially in the early days, and seeing how it turned out from where they were sitting. I'd see the result and remember how they did that and where they took it from, and I carried that on and I wasn't shy in coming forward – not in an arrogant way – when I knew how somebody else had done it and how amazing it could be.

Oliver Barton

Ali would always have an idea for a photo. He wasn't so much, 'We'll just skate and see what happens', he would be, 'I've had this idea...' He called me one time and it was snowing so much, and said he wanted to go and skate St Albans miniramp, so he brought a little blowtorch and we shot a photo of him doing a pivot to fakie in the snow. We got in a really bad car crash on the way home because it was a white-out.

James Woodley

You open a skate mag and everything looks perfect, but that really is not how it was.

My downfall was from around 2001, when the drink really started. My house was a loving family but there was always drink involved, there was always a party going on, or mum and dad's friends round having a drink. I was smoking when I was eight, I was walking to primary school smoking cigarettes. I had my first line of cocaine when I was 13, I was on a slippery slope.

There became a point where I couldn't skate without having a few beers, and it didn't matter what time of day it was, whether it was the morning or the middle of the night; I was having a beer. I thought it was part of who I was. Then waking up in the morning shaking, needing alcohol in my system. I didn't know I was going to be an alcoholic, and I didn't know I was going to be an addict.

Eventually I got booted off all my sponsors. I even got a letter of dismissal from Emerica. Then I was in jail. The first time it was an accumulation of stuff, all drink-related all the time, just being an idiot. Being aggressive, being violent, being my own worst enemy and hating the person that I was, as well as being a full-on alcoholic. I just fucked everything up basically.

Harry Bastard

I did all the photos for the *Spots* book, and I went to all the places. It was before skate spots became precious, and people wouldn't tell each other where places were because they wanted to get the footage themselves. It's from before

that thing happened, so everyone was totally open about it and skateboarding was still an open, social, community-type thing.

I always had the urge to just go places and find new things to skate; even when I was a kid I'd go skating on my own to random places because the rest of our lot weren't really up for that. I hitch-hiked to Barrow when I was 12 with Jimmy Boyes, and I got left there with no money or anything, but you learn a lot when travelling, and I managed to scrounge enough money from people for the train back.

I wanted people to fucking travel and see more than where they were from. Justin, Will and Kev at Dope Clothing were amazing, and they taught me how to use a computer and said they were up for doing the book.

Doing that book was the first time I'd properly used a computer, or used a camera. Dope paid me a little bit of money to create that book, and I managed to buy myself a £1,200 laptop and pay myself £100 a month for one year. That's what I got out of that book, and then we ended up getting them all pulped, because it wasn't selling. It was £15, which was quite expensive for the time, but there wasn't much mark-up on it because the shipping of books is expensive – especially back then – so a lot of them didn't move. ●

FROM LEFT
[1] Ali Cairns, St Albans, by Oliver Barton
[2] *Spots* book by Harry, front and back covers, Milton Keynes spread

2001

Heroin & Organic

422

Chris Pulman

When my own board came out I pushed that, like, 'Hey, if you want an 8-inch board that's got a long wheelbase, here's one, but it's got a picture of me on it'. Very often I'd have my board with me, so if they asked about an 8-inch board, I'd go, 'Well have a stand on that', and they'd go, 'That's cool, do you have that one?', and I'd say, 'Yeah. We've got loads'.

It was sick that people bought my board but mostly we sold Blueprint boards. We pushed the hell out of Blueprint boards because it was a proper skateboard company with double-page ads, riders that got paid, they filmed videos, they went on tours and everything was done properly; Dan was doing it properly, if there is a 'proper' in skateboarding, and I don't know if anybody would agree with me but basically all the other British brands piggybacked off that.

You would never have been able to build Heroin, or Death, or Landscape, or any of these other brands if there wasn't one brand doing it properly in the way they did. Paying the guys, filming videos,

having ads, going on tours. That's how you do it, that's the model for a skateboard company. The reason other brands were able to thrive is because Blueprint was the core of the British skateboard industry.

Fos

After doing the Toy Machine stuff, I think that proved to people that I was kind of competent and knew what I was doing, and I got asked to do more and more stuff for Slam, and that was when we started doing Organic with Slam.

I was the sales manager for Unabomber, and all the other brands at Slam, and in 1998 Unabomber left L'Esprit D'Equipe and they came to Slam. We were selling all these boards, and it was doing really well, and they decided to leave and do it on their own. I'd already started Heroin, and I knew that that wouldn't go through Slam because they already had Unabomber, so that went with Nick at Power, who's amazing. It was when Unabomber left Slam in 2001 that Paul Sunman said they needed another brand. I told him I did this brand called Heroin and I wasn't going to give it to them, but

I had four riders in mind that could do something on another brand. Organic was started through Slam, and bankrolled through Slam, and Heroin was a completely different thing, through Nick.

It was all Sunman. He knew that I knew how to submit graphics and things like that, so I was in the right place at the right time. We'd lost Unabomber, and Unabomber was a big thing for us, and we wanted something else.

We didn't try to emulate what Blueprint was doing and we didn't try to emulate what Death or Unabomber were doing. Or anybody. We just wanted to do something that was different from all that, but a little cleaner than Heroin. With the riders, it was Joel Curtis, Olly Todd, Toby Shuall and Snowy, and we took Snowy from Heroin because he was probably going to leave and ride for Blueprint or someone else. Heroin was going in a different direction and he wasn't going to stay with it forever, so we did this other thing and he was part of it. There were four riders, and the logo was four-sided to symbolise the four riders. →

LEFT TO RIGHT
[1] Chris Pulman, St Paul's, by Wig Worland
[2] Heroin catalogue and Chris Pulman's royalty cheque
[3] Early Organic sketches, by Fos

Toby Shuall

Magee and Shier were saying to us that they wanted to start something, and I was like, 'Yes!', I was going to do whatever was good for me because I was so over trying to keep it real, because I was broke. They wanted to start a company because Joe Burlo owned Blueprint, and they realised that they'd kind of given it to him on a plate. I never knew Joe myself but it became apparent he was never gonna give them what they wanted, so I think they were thinking of a way they could start it independently, but they were procrastinating.

I knew that they'd said the same thing to Olly Todd as they had to me, so I got Olly's number from someone and phoned him up and asked him if they'd been talking to him, and he said yeah, so me and him had never really met but we were the same age and at the same point in skateboarding, so we hashed it out on the phone and decided to just do it with Fos because it was more likely to actually happen there and then. Olly was on Third Foot and he was really loyal to them, but he wasn't really getting anything either, just a few boards here and there.

So him and I agreed to do it. I was really good friends with Snowy, and Fos brought Joel in, so that was how it started.

I didn't get any money from Organic, ever, but I got a lot of stuff. It was the same old deal, where it's like, 'Oh, you're not really giving us anything? OK, well I'm going to take quite a lot of these boards, and sell them.' Fair enough, Paul Sunman is a businessman, but we'd given him a company and it'd made money in the first year – not loads, but Slam had made a profit out of Organic – and he didn't offer us anything.

I had problems with it from the beginning because I didn't like the name and I don't like dipped boards, so it was difficult.

Joel Curtis

I was on Zero through New Deal and it was fine but they would send boards and that was kind of it, really. Fos was a friend of mine through Seth, and I was on Circa through Slam and that was how I got that hook up, really. Fos said he wanted to start an in-house company at Slam, which turned into Organic. Slam had connections with the Chapman wood shop, and they started making the boards and they were fucking awful. They were really heavy. They were all East Coast made but a lot of

them were dipped, those Organic boards. Once Organic got going they got better, but they weren't great. It was just good to be involved in something like that, rather than being one of those people floating around being sponsored by a distributor when the brand didn't have any knowledge of it or didn't care. It was something we could be a bit more involved with.

Olly Todd

I was in my flat in Liverpool when Toby rang up out of the blue. We'd never even met at this point but obviously I knew exactly who he was.

He explained the situation with Organic, and as he was talking to me all I could think of was, 'Shit, I'm going to have to ring Ken at A Third Foot and tell him I quit'. That was my first concern, and I started to get really worried about that before I could even think what I was doing with Organic. I probably built it up and made more of it than it was, but Ken was super cool about it, and supportive. ●

Elsewhere

Dan Magee

First Broadcast happened because there were a few guys on other companies that we were stoked on, and I wanted to film. But in order to get Joe to distribute it, I had to explain that the main section would be Blueprint riders. After *Waiting For The World* we had to give everybody time to decompress, and get the new team together, but some people were already ready to go, so we did it.

I always liked Unabomber, I thought it was sick. I just think it came too early. It was ahead of its time, it just got out of control with a few hundred people on there. Dudes skating the Copenhagen skatepark for five whole minutes. The first video was fine but you had glimpses of Unabomber's greatness in *Headcleaner*. Frank's parts are always good. They just didn't focus on exactly what it was.

After *Waiting For The World* I could kind of get people to do different stuff, or I had their trust. So by *First Broadcast* we could kinda have a theme, or go out with a generator, or only skate a certain kind of spot because they look UK-wide and that's what our USP was. Skating cobbled streets and all that vibe.

Adam Mondon

Working on *First Broadcast* was the beginnings of trying to be a middleman in managing situations of people's choices in what they're wearing, or their trick selection. Hearing Magee's side of it and trying to ease it in with the skaters so we can get the best out of the situation without completely destroying their self-esteem. I wouldn't totally disagree with what Magee was saying; sometimes you'd see an outfit that was maybe not going to fit with the overall aesthetic. It's amazing how diverse skating is now, it's incredible, but it just wasn't at that stage. It was about hearing the skater's side, and hearing Magee's side, and trying to meet somewhere in the middle to make it manageable.

I think it's been mislabelled over time as one, a Blueprint film and two, a Dan Magee project. I understand where that's come from, but it's always felt a bit undersold from my point of view. I felt right from the start that it was a 50-50 project for me and Dan. It was very collaborative; it was born out of filming Blueprint riders, and Cawdor, and it was something that we both put everything into.

Ali Cairns

Dan Magee was in touch to do *First Broadcast*, and because he filmed street skating a lot, I guess he filmed it in a different way, but because I had always been around street skaters, more than vert skaters, I noticed there was a right way of filming stuff. I would always look at all the old vert footage and it was always filmed standing a long way back, or just filming somebody crossing the ramp. For *Hating Life* they were filming me close up, with the Death Lens right under me, making me look ten times better than I was, it was brilliant, and then I got to film with Dan and he was making me look 30 times better than I was!

He'd find it quite cool, because I would tell him where on the ramp I was going to do the trick, so he would know where it was going to be, and I'd probably make it within a few goes, at least. He would say how different it was because he'd usually have to stand next to a block for an hour and they might not make it at all, but we could film five tricks within three hours. We'd nail bits of wood on the ramp, and get lights up and everything, and I think he enjoyed filming vert.

He said one time that that was the first time and the last time he's ever filmed vert. I love the Mogwai music that he put to that, and that's probably still my favourite video part that I've had. He put it together so well, it's really well done. It was nothing but joy, filming with Dan. ●

CLOCKWISE FROM BOTTOM LEFT
[1] Adam Mondon, Dan Magee, Joel Curtis, Seth Curtis, Vaughan Baker and Colin Kennedy on a First Broadcast filming trip to Barcelona, photo by Oliver Barton
[2] Toby Shuall, Euston, by Oliver Barton
[3] First Broadcast slipcase and artwork, 7" by Mark Jackson and Hattie Castelberg, photos by Oliver Barton
[4] Vaughan Baker's First Broadcast rider board

Simon Chayter

Pritchard vs Dainton and Stimulus are inextricably linked. The idea of the video was birthed before the company, and it wasn't really a company, it was four of us naively trying to do something.

It was Evo from City Surf's 30th birthday, in this place called The Warm As Toast cafe – which spells TWAT – in the heart of studentville. During that night we're having a big conversation, saying that we should make the next video the best thing we can. 'We'll make it look cool, get as many people involved as possible, it'll primarily be a skate video but it'll have some dicking around'. The dicking around wasn't meant to be the main thing, but we just wanted to make the best skate video we could, and include everyone so it wasn't just a Cardiff video. That night, *Pritchard vs Dainton* became a solid idea.

The thing that essentially killed Stimulus was outside parties getting involved, telling Matthew and Dainton X, Y and Z. I'm really pleased for everyone and how things have gone, and I'm in a super happy place, but without the advent of *Dirty Sanchez* I think Stimulus would have had a couple years further development and I don't doubt we could have achieved something with some real longevity and we could have put something back into the scene that we felt so dearly for. But the TV show ruined that.

Matt Pritchard

Just as the *Pritchard vs Dainton* thing was happening, Death came knocking, so I left Rookie, and me and Daint had a joint board on Death. That's how I joined Death, and then I had four or five boards on Death. I was on Death for quite a while, even though I wasn't skating much, and I was still having boards come out. In a way I was thinking, 'This is a bit naughty, having a pro board when I'm not really skating'. I was pretty much just a pisshead.

When I was working at Globe, I got a phone call and the receptionist said it was a woman called Martha Delap from MTV. She was a talent scout for MTV, and obviously *Jackass* had just hit the TV in America and they were looking for something similar, like they do with *Jersey Shore* and *Geordie Shore*. And I went to MTV with Daint for a meeting with them, and that's when we handed them the *Pritchard vs Dainton* video. They watched the video and literally two days later they phoned us up and asked us to go back in, but this time to bring Dan Joyce and Pancho. So the four of us went back, and that's when *Dirty Sanchez* was born.

Dan Joyce

I ended up getting a company car from work, and I got free petrol, so I used to drive to Cardiff every weekend to film *Pritchard vs Dainton*. One week they were like, 'What can we do?', and I said we should try to jump the car. We went to Celtic Manor, where there's two split levels of car park, and we tanked the car round there, went up this ramp and the car flew into the air and it smashed down and the gearbox just fell out of it. I was like, 'Don't worry, I've got this card, I just call them up and I get sent another car!' So I did and a brand new car turned up.

We were down in Newquay at Boardmasters, all off our heads early on Sunday morning, wondering what we could film, and Pritchard goes, 'You can fucking run me over if you want!', So I was like, 'Alright. How fast', and he goes, 'About thirty?'

So we did that and he just hit into the windscreen and totally smashed it, and he goes, 'Ah, sorry bud, I just fucked your car!', and I'm like, 'Don't worry about it, I've got the card, they'll just bring me a new windscreen!', so I rung them up and they come out and fixed the windscreen.

I was skating Plymouth loads, and getting right back into it, and a mate of mine had a wedding. I was skating around this fort at six o'clock in the morning, on the last day. We had to wake everyone up so I was skating round this fort banging this massive gong I'd found, and someone had spilled some beer so I slipped on this beer, slipped down some stairs and my knee got caught in-between two of the bannisters and it bent sideways. I had knee surgery and that was the end of skating for me. That was just as the *Dirty Sanchez* stuff was happening, so I could never really skate in it. So I put it on the back burner and just got into drugs again. For quite a long time. ●

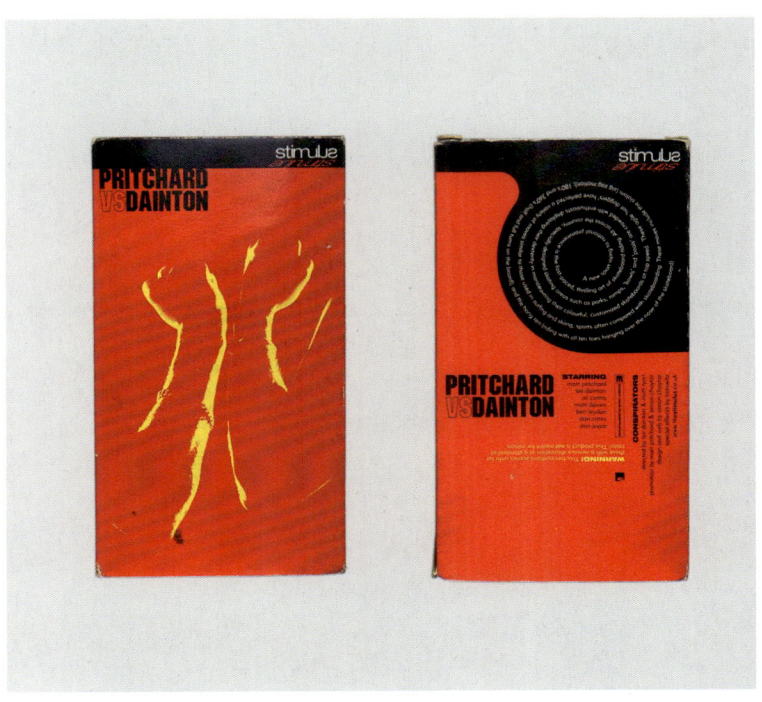

Ian Gunner

We were a distributor, and a distributor's role is to be the middleman, and being the middleman, you are vulnerable. So what we – which was Ray, Gary, myself, Marc Ball, Dan Evans, Alex Cock and Phil Penwarden – did was get together and do our own thing, it was a bit less skateboarding – so not like Reaction – but was something that New Deal UK could own that can't be taken away, because we were in a vulnerable position and we weren't the most liked. So we decided to start a clothing company.

It was kind of left to Phil, myself and Dan to come up with the concept. Phil is a seamster, so can make clothes, so we set him up with a tiny little office underneath Warrior with a sewing machine and a cutting table. Dan was the DC and Droors Sales Manager and there were a few stores he was selling to that weren't skate specific so we saw opportunities there, and I was the marketing guy and I had interest in fashion and design, so between the three of us we came up with this small concept.

We made a bunch of samples, I had an idea to vacuum-pack a bunch of clothing in black bags with a tiny little logo on them and send them to a bunch of influential stores, and it went through the roof. Instantly people thought it was cool, and what was needed. It was skate-inspired, but it was fashion, and it took off pretty big quite quickly.

Phil Penwarden

It had all the logistical support, and the marketing support, and the funding, from New Deal. Everyone was involved, everyone from New Deal was shipped in and we just had time and bandwidth to do it. There was no pressure to drive around and sell it or to make money, because there were sales and marketing people in place through New Deal and we just had loads of money so we could afford adverts.

The first range we designed, we just sent out free to people, so we didn't even retail it. A hundred pairs of jeans, packed up and sent out to magazines and to Goldie and whoever.

We had money to trademark the logo, and we spent money on the website and everything else. We did it properly. It was really good.

Ben Allnutt

We started Fenchurch and I was doing catalogue layouts, labelling, trims, all of that stuff, and I remember seeing the garment designs and I was like, 'I think I can do that'. They used the same software that I did, so I just started drawing stuff and giving it to Gunner, and asking him to give it to Ray, or to Phil who ran Fenchurch, because I wasn't that confident in doing that myself. In the end I gave them so much, and they weren't interested, and quite rightly so.

Then one day Ray went, 'What's that? What the fahkin' hell's that?', in a very classic Ray way. 'That's a bit alright, that'. And I said it was me, and that was it, and I started doing a few cut-and-sew t-shirt things.

New Deal was massively changing, everyone cool was leaving, and I was like, 'You know what? I think I'm going to go and become a design junior in garment design', and the first job that would take me was this awful, clubby, menswear shit called Peter Werth, which was like a poor man's Paul Smith. I went there as a junior, learnt how to do garment design and it was amazing. Then one day at a trade show I see Ray, and he asks me to come back to Fenchurch and do garment design.

Dave Mackey

I was getting Lakai and Zoo York through Warrior, and Warrior was across the yard from New Deal. It wasn't like it was a separate business in a different place, it was in the same zone. Phil was the guy that did Fenchurch, and Seb Palmer was the rep for Fenchurch because he was the DC rep at the time and I think he was showing Fenchurch to certain accounts.

Warrior invited me down to come and see some of the stuff. I met the design team, and they showed me how things were done, and it was pretty ahead of its time, to be fair. They were very knowledgeable on the subject, and they had the right people in place to do it, and it was the first time I'd been involved in something like this and I was excited to be a part of it. I was really stoked on it. I had my own sticker with my name on it, it was a big deal!

Neil Urwin

There was the white t-shirt, no-graphics on the board, point in time, and I was not arsed about that because I had all these different sponsors. When I got on Reaction, the main person I would take pictures with would be Leo Sharp. Maybe Andy Horsley a bit. I remember shooting that switch front crook on the table at Shields with Leo[3], and seeing where he was going to sit, and working out where my board would be so I could put the stickers on in the right place, and wear my hat at an angle, all for photo incentive. Fucking right! Why wouldn't I do that? I was paid every month – it wasn't that much, for boards – but I think I got paid per board, and I'd get photo incentives which could be pretty decent. If you got a cover you could make £600 or £700. And then selling shit. So I was fucking raking it in.

Greg Finch

I really enjoyed filming for the Reaction video. It was quite a free-for-all, and the footage is all shot on different formats. It was right on the cusp of people only using Hi8, or only using Digi or whatever it was. There was no real pressure, and I kind of regret that there wasn't more pressure, and a lot of the time when we did do stuff we'd lose the footage. There was lots of stuff that didn't go into that, that should have gone in, just because we were total idiots and we didn't film it properly or someone pressed record when it wasn't recording and stopped it when they should have been filming. Stupid shit. Full amateur hour. There were dedicated filmers, it was these two twins Sam and Jake, but they weren't always available, so you'd just give the camera to your mate and tell him to point it at you. ●

Toby Shuall

It was my idea, and I went to Badger – Rich Holland – and Marcus Oakley with it. Badger fully did it, and became a lot more proactive in it than me, but it was certainly my idea initially.

The building we did it in, in Borough, was about to be turned into lots of flats, and my ex-girlfriend said that she reckoned I could do something in the space, because they wanted to do something in the space before they developed it, so they could basically milk the cultural association. It was really her that gave me the opportunity, because she found this venue to do it. She worked in PR, and Badger had Bullet, so he knew how to deal with budgets and funding and stuff, so we went to PlayStation and got the money. They just gave us 20 grand and we spent every single penny of it on wood and just built this fucked-up skatepark.

It was only there for two days, and the guy who owned the building was like, 'You have to take it down!', so we started ripping it down and he came back when we'd half-ripped it down and he said, 'Actually, I quite liked it, it's kinda cool, you guys could have stayed for a couple more weeks'. Wanker. It was so lame.

It was all quite mad because when we got the money we spent it all on wood, instead of being like, 'Cool, let's keep a bit of money so we can buy some food'. We were just so stoked on it that everybody involved just galvanised like a psychotic youth club and started building it. There were no drawings or anything, we just started knocking it up and spent all the money and it was just wild. I think we paid Pin a little bit of money.

I don't know how I met Jimmy Boyes but he just turned up there, and he was great. He just fucking loved it. He drove back to Durham in the middle of the night and came back about 35 hours later with all his boards and built this weird teepee downstairs.

Rich Holland

The Jam Factory was an old warehouse that had been bought by a developer and was just about to be turned into jazzy apartments. It was a classic example of getting the cool kids in, make something buzzy, then get the corporates in and sell it for more money and push the artists out.

'A skatepark' didn't even cross our minds, it was essentially an exhibition about skateboarding, and the landscape was a sculpture. Because we were skaters, we had a focus of making it rideable but it was never about making a perfect ledge or whatever, it was more about making a sculpture that allowed skateboarding to be expressed on it. It was loads of fun. It was exhausting, but we were all just young, living it. We didn't have anything else to worry about other than making enough money to survive, getting high, hanging out and skating.

Sam Griffin

Jimmy Boyes had come down to London to help out. Heart of gold, but at one point he was using Pin's £400 Makita drill as a hammer, and if Pin's in a stressful situation he does this thing where he just goes, 'Chriiiist, I'm spinning out!', and that was getting said a lot, at four o'clock in the morning in this derelict Victorian gymnasium, as we were trying to get this thing finished.

Jimmy Boyes

Me, Pin, Badger and Toby especially, we were the ones that would always stay up extra late getting the job done. Me and Pin were two weeks deep and I left the building and skated to go and get some drinks and stuff, and just as I'm skating back, I notice on the side of an entrance to a garden, there was this suitcase.

It was locked, but the corner of it was wedged open, so my first impression of it was that it had been stolen, and someone had lifted that corner up and took whatever

was in there out. I thought I had to check it out, so I stick my hand in there and I'm searching inside, and I feel this pocket, and a plastic bag. I pull it out and it's white.

I go back into the space where we were, and I'm like, 'Look what I've just found', and Pin just wet his finger, stuck it in the bag, stuck it in his mouth, looked at me and went, 'It's coke'. Pin was stood on this poly-prop at the time, taking a break from work, but after his finger had come out of his mouth, within a minute this tic-tacking motion becomes really quick.

Fos

It was really the first skate art thing that had happened in London. It was just a bunch of kids who didn't really know what they were doing who were excited about skateboarding and art. Toby was a real motivating force for it, he took the reins and ran with it.

Nik Taylor

Simon True came up with the name for it, and he had the photograph of this wasted guy passed out wearing DCs we wanted to use for the promotion. It was the perfect image.

I did all the poster artwork and then this guy at X-Box, who were giving us the lion's share of the funding, was just like, 'Yeah, we're not having our logo associated with that picture'. We argued it but he said it wasn't happening and we ended up using this picture of a crocheted teddy bear. It was pretty stupid. I was really fucked off with the whole thing so we were like, 'Fuck it, let's just use this, and we'll tell him that a skateboarder's made it'. Looking back now it was totally cutting our nose off to spite our face. 'Here's a shit picture! This is what we're using'. The guy from X-Box said we couldn't use that image either, but we were like, 'Yeah, one of the skateboarders makes these things so we're using it'. I'd just plucked it out of some knitting book from the '70s. ●

2002

JIMMY BOYES, CHURCHILL SQUARE, BRIGHTON, BY WIG WORLAND
In the rain was sick. I couldn't see the security guard at the bottom of the rail, as I approached it. As I get on the rail I see the security guard holding the rail as I slide down it, and I'm thinking, 'He's gonna move, he's gonna move', and he takes his hand off at the last second but I pretty much take him out. As soon as he lands from the tumble he just goes for his walkie-talkie, 'I need back up! Man down! Man down!', and I just got the hell out of there. I had to make my way back to London.

1987–2002 was the important golden time for this stuff. Not because I was having a great time, but because at that time the big money was out of it. The freedom for people to do stuff was amazing. To do what we did then, I don't know whether anybody's ever going to be able to do that again. The freedom's just not going to be there. That time was crazy, with what was going on in skateboarding, in graffiti, in music, with what was going on generally in 'counter culture', and it wasn't until the early-to-mid 2000s where the money really caught up.
RUSSELL WATERMAN

Greg Finch

I was naive, and I think that's what drove that whole experience. Alan Rushbrooke, myself and Badger [Rich Holland] had become good friends – Alan was working in Slam with me, and Badger was doing the filming for Unabomber and stuff like that – so at some point we all linked up and we were all good friends. We were all smashed at the Dragon Bar one New Year's Eve and they were like, 'Let's start a skateboard brand!', and I was like, 'Nooo... Let's start a skate shop!' We were completely out of our heads so we left it.

Then a couple of weeks later I went to a Vince Ray show in Waterloo, when I was living in Lambeth. I went to this place called The Last Chance Saloon, and I got talking to the proprietor and she said she had this magazine that was going really well so she wanted to leave the space and move on, so I said, 'Funnily enough, I'm looking for a shop. Can I buy your lease off you?' She said I could take the lease but only if I promised her I'd keep the art gallery downstairs because it had a history – it was an art gallery for ex-convicts during the war and all sorts of things. It had mad history. So I promised her I'd do that and went back to Alan and Badger and I was like, 'I've got the fucking store and it's going to cost us 11 grand a year, but we have to have an art gallery', but we knew enough skate artists amongst us that we could do it.

None of us had money but we basically just begged, borrowed and stole as much money as we could get together and I think we raised around £38K, and we just went in. We started.

Rich came up with the name. It's the suffix from pesticide or suicide or whatever and it means 'to kill', basically. We were thinking of calling it South-something, because it's south of the river, but 'South-cide' just sounds so corny. That's cheeseball as fuck so we couldn't do that. He looked at 'Cide' and because of his graphic design brain he figured it out. The treatment was so far away from what Slam was doing, it was quite alternative and goth-y looking.

There was a show once a month – the first Wednesday of every month – and we had all sorts. Adam Neate was probably the most sought-after. Toby Paterson did something in there, and French did something in there. French was a big part of that and he helped run that store, basically. Sam Griffin, his show was really good. Seth Curtis had a show in there when he had has 176 brand.

It was a weird journey. Shortly after I opened it I split up with my missus and had to move out, and I didn't really have any money and I had nowhere to go, and I bumped into a girl in the Ruby Lounge, which was a little bit further down, where we'd all drink. She said her uncle had something to do with Greggs bakery – and there's a Greggs bakery along Lower Marsh – and he has a room going above that if I want, and it was £175 a month. And I was like, 'Fuck, if I can't scrape that together then I may as well give up now'.

So I dived in there, and we used to call everywhere we lived Palaces, so that's where Palace comes from. Toby Shuall lived in the Ice Palace, we lived in the Waterloo Palace. Slowly but surely as people moved out I got more skateboarders to move in. Edson and Snowy, then there was Lev.

Rich Holland

Because I had the design stuff, I could get things printed and help set everything up, and I was a dab hand at making stuff, and I'd built all the interiors of where we lived, pretty much, and I'd been building ramps since I was 15.

The opening was really brilliant; loads of people came together and there was no friction between us and the Slam lot because we all skated together at Southbank, we all hung out together and we all went to the same gallery shows.

Alan Rushbrooke

The gallery space was important because we wanted a 'home' for people. We were the first people to show Shepard Fairey; he'd never shown before, before that gallery space. Adam Neate, a friend of ours, showed there and he then got signed by Banksy's agent and he's gone on to be a really successful artist who went from living on beans and toast to buying two houses and living between Brazil and the UK. At that time that was the scene, and everything's evolved now and it's a whole new group of people, and so it should be. →

Sam Griffin

The art show side of it was really good. Just like there is now, there was this really creative community in and around skateboarding, and there were people that were already involved in quite serious projects like Silas, like Ben Sansbury who does the board graphics for Palace, and Fergus Purcell who did the logo, and Toby Shuall who went on to do Landscape.

It was around that time when quite a lot of London wasn't gentrified – and Lower Marsh Street was still pretty dicey back then too – so you could just do stuff like that. You could get the money together and just do a shop. It was feasible. Edson worked there on a Saturday, and Lev worked there for a bit as well, and that's when I first met Lev, because Greg and everyone else were living in the 'Palace', a few doors down. That was the Waterloo Palace. The shower in that flat had a current running through it, so you'd have a shower and get the occasional 240 volts through the water. That's how rugged it was. They've gone from that to where they are now, and that's not some simulated rags-to-riches thing, they really have done it.

Toby Shuall

Cide was a really good era, and it was just cool that some skateboarders started their own shop. Greg did so much for everyone, Greg was the one who was

there every day and trying to do stuff at Southbank and he was still skating all the time as well. It was a really good thing, it was the first time London had its own independent skate shop.

It was doomed to fail as well. Slam was still Slam and it had all the trade, and Lower Marsh Street is just about coming into the world now, but at the time it was dead, which was kinda cool but not good for them trying to make a living. Cide was the skate shop for Southbank and you're not going to make any money out of Southbank.

I coined the 'Palace' thing, because I loved the Palace Brothers, and we lived in this house that was literally like a palace in the summer but it was hell in winter, so that became the 'Ice Palace', and they called the one above Cide 'the Palace'. The Ice Palace was opposite the mosque at Whitechapel. It was amazing because I could skate from Whitechapel to Southbank, skate Southbank and then go street skating, and never have to get on a bus or a train.

Greg Finch

Round about 2002 we would skate Shell Centre, Southbank, Stockwell and Viccy Benches pretty much solely. That was my life. We met Lucien Clarke and straight off the bat we were like, 'We need to sponsor him'. He was this tiny, tiny kid with massive hands and massive feet and he could do the most extraordinary shit.

Gareth Skewis

Even though I was working at Slam and at Silas, when Greg opened Cide, to me that was hyper-important because that is the stepping stone to how Palace starts. Palace started five years after, but that's the precursor – everyone being together at the gallery, and in the space upstairs, and Greg living two doors down in what was the original Palace. That's where that group of friends all spent a lot of time. It was chaos but it was the best.

Sam Griffin

Lev and Gareth had that implicit understanding that they didn't have to ask anyone's permission to do that, and that they had more than enough talent around them in one shape or another. Whether it be riding a skateboard or designing graphics or running a warehouse. They knew people who were all exceptional at these things, and it was just putting it all in the right place.

Gareth is an incredibly talented businessman and Lev is an exceptionally talented creative, but as well as that, and it's a corny analogy, but they're also extremely talented conductors of orchestras. You can see that Gareth learnt a lot of that stuff from Russell at Silas, and I believe that Russell was very forthcoming with his mentorship of Gareth. ●

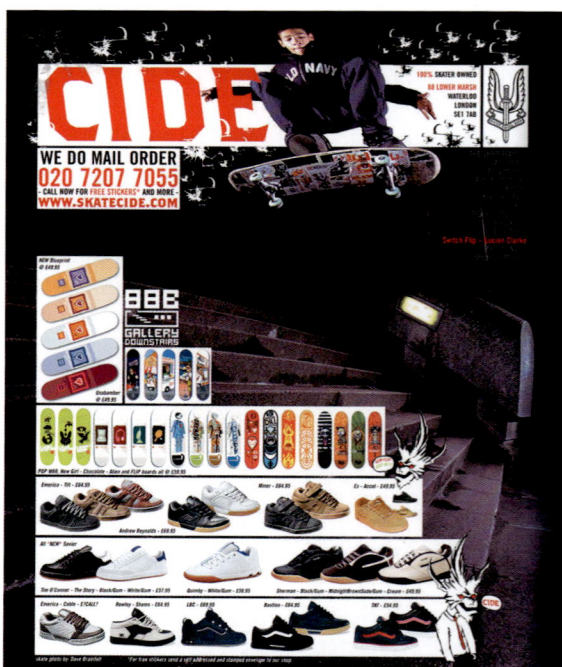

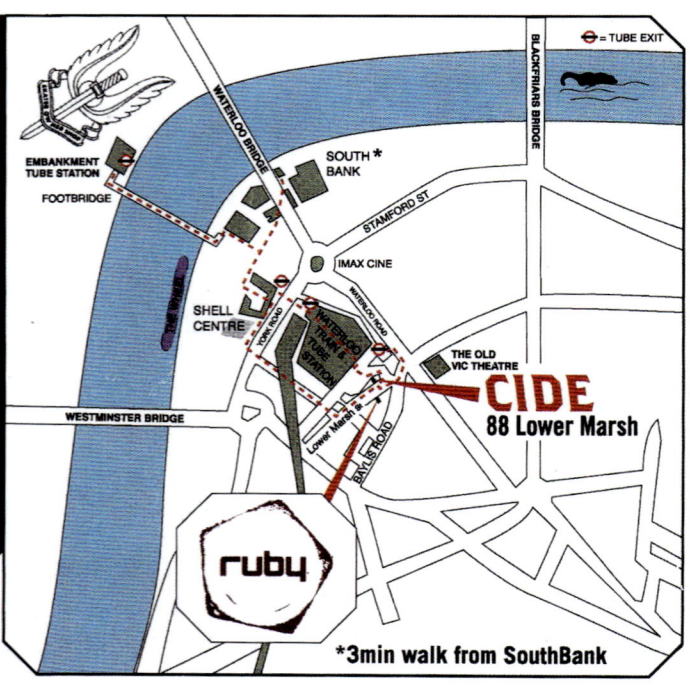

FROM LEFT
[4] Lucien Clarke, Southbank, by Brendan Ryall
[5] Directions to Cide
[6] Sam Griffin, Bristo Square, by Graham Tait

Fos

There was a while when I was getting so much grief for the Heroin name that I was going to change it to Ruin. It was a concept that I was maybe going to talk to Jamie Thomas about, and take it to Black Box.

In my sketch books from back then, some pages are Organic – or Landscape – and some are Heroin. Organic only really existed for about two years. When I wake up and draw in my sketchbook everything looks like Heroin, but with Organic I would clean it up a bit. It was me pushing myself as a graphic artist, a little bit. In a direction that's unfamiliar to me.

Alan Glass wanted to make Blueprint videos, he wanted to make professional-quality videos, and I always call *Everything's Going To Be Alright* our emotional video, because of the Aphex Twin piano, the Aereogramme song and all the stuff like that. He definitely brought a better quality of filming.

Alan Glass

Immediately after *Good Shit*, Fos said I was going to be their video guy, basically, and we became very good friends and I would be in London every week. Brighton to London was less than an hour on the train, so I would always be in London anyway, and now I was filming the new Heroin video. Crashing on Fos's sofa and filming all those guys.

I don't think there was a deadline, I'm sure it was as loose as everything else was back in those days, and it was like, 'When it's done, it's done'. We were so prolific and life moved on really fast. We were always skating, always filming, and it was more like it just happened, rather than, 'You need three more lines, mate'. Dan and the Blueprint guys were on that from an early start, and the Blueprint vids to me were high-end shit, but I wasn't working with a brand that that suited.

Heroin Skateboards was not Blueprint, it was not a *Transworld* video, it was a bunch of rag-tag sketchy dudes. It was a new thing for someone like Chris Pulman to have a board, and it felt like we joined the skateboard race then. It was like, 'Here's our pro, watch him do his thing', and even though that was Pulman and he wasn't trying to one-up the tech manoeuvres or do the biggest handrail, it did seem more like a serious project and I wanted it to be as posh as it could be. I was undoubtedly influenced by Transworld videos or Blueprint videos because that high quality was something I wanted, but I had to create it in post-production for the most part.

Fos

Slam bankrolled the whole thing and let me do whatever I needed, which was fine right up until the point where it came to me getting paid for my work that I'd done on the brand. On paper we had made 20 grand profit – it had done really well – so I was like, 'Look, you've got to pay me something for this'. I wanted to be an equal partner, and Paul offered me £500. He was like, 'Well, you work at Slam. This is your job and you get a wage', and I wasn't having that, and that's when I quit.

I left the name – they owned the Organic trademark – and we started Landscape. Karl Watson had started Organika, which was a little annoying, but it was nothing to do with that. When we left it was going to be called Forest, and it was all me and Toby Shuall, really. Toby was a huge part of it and we would sit down and have meetings and figure out what we were going to do all the time. Toby had been at Unabomber and he was so disillusioned by it, and he wanted to ask if he could ride for Heroin, but I wanted to do a brand with him.

The Landscape logo is the Japanese symbol for 'tree', because me and Toby Shuall had talked about calling it 'Forest', but 'Landscape' just seemed to work better for a skateboard brand.

Olly Todd

Fos always had my back, and I owe him such a lot. I'm really grateful to him for seeing something in me, because what he saw in me wasn't what was in *Portraits*; it was a much earlier version of my skating that he recognised and saw the potential in. If I'm being honest I didn't think I was good enough to be on a full, established UK team.

By the time *Portraits* came out, I think that my skating – and the way that I presented my skating – had reached its maturity. From then it plateaued and kinda

went down, so even my *Static* and Stereo years weren't my best. My *Portraits* years were my best years, for sure.

I didn't have a mobile at the time but you didn't need one because the whole thing was so organic. You'd go to Slam, you'd get some lunch, everyone starts to filter in – Jensen, Snowy, Danny Brady, Lev, Joey, whoever – and then you figure out where to skate and then you skate all day and then you go to the pub, then you wake up and you do it all again. For a young skater it's the perfect existence.

I was in Slam once when a casting director came in asking for people to audition for an Oasis video, so obviously my eyes popped out of my head. Christian Stevenson sorted it all out so I got this role as a skater in the video for 'Little by Little'. Being in Slam was the perfect opportunity to have something like that fall into your lap.

I'd never seen that fox graphic[7], that's so banging. I would have definitely gone for that. He probably had that as an idea for a board, but I presented him with an idea which he ended up using, without telling me about this fox graphic.

This[12] is directly below the first proper Palace office. The first actual office was in the basement of the second Slam shop in Covent Garden, but this was their first proper office.

This[11] was what we called 'New Spot', because we couldn't think of a more imaginative name for this new spot that appeared near Russell Square in London one summer.

We were looking for something else to skate other than Southbank and Shell Centre, so we used to go there every night after Slam, with whoever had been working that day, or whoever was out skating. We localised that spot for a good few weeks.

One evening Sam Ashley was out with us, and I just started trying it, through the curve. It wasn't in the days when you'd instantly see the photo on the back of the guy's camera, so I didn't see the image at all.

One day I walked into Slam – on my birthday, funnily enough – and it was there on the cover, total surprise.

Joel Curtis

Chris Massey was the right person to do the Portraits video. It's really unique and it stands up to other videos of the time. Blueprint was always ahead and there was always a broader picture with Dan and all the videos he made, but I think Massey really did bring something.

Massey was drastically underpaid and having to work full-time as manager of a Starbucks, so that's why there's so much night footage in that video, because we could only film after Massey's work so we'd be out until two in the morning filming on Oxford Street or Baker Street, or Elephant and Castle or somewhere weird. He really took the time on that and put his heart in it.

I was stoked on that video but I wish I could have done more, and I wish my part could have been better. ●

Magazines

Elsewhere

Oliver Barton

Paul Shier had met Cairo Foster, so we would go out to San Francisco a lot in the winter. That's another example of a door that Paul opened for me, because I became really good friends with Cairo, and he was talking about wanting to shoot an interview. I said offhandedly we should get in my car and drive up through the north of England, into Scotland, and come back down and drive all the way to Barcelona. I didn't really think much of it, and then all of a sudden he and Elias Bingham turned up in London, so we did this trip where we went to Sheffield, we went to Edinburgh, we went to Paris and we stopped in Lyon.

It was right about the time when Tom Penny sightings were Bigfoot-style, and then we saw him as soon as we got to Lyon.

That mushroom spot is in a really deserted part of Lyon, it's in a commercial centre, so if you go there at the weekend it's dead. There's a French photographer called Olivier Chassignole who used to shoot all of the Cliché stuff, but he had been shooting Tom a little bit because Ali Boulala was living there already, and Tom was staying with him. We came up to the spot and Tom was trying this trick, and myself, Elias and Cairo just sat down and watched.

We were amazed, actually seeing the man, the myth, in real life, and he was getting really close to it. French Fred was filming too, and it was amazing to see Fred.

Out of nowhere these street guys come up behind Olivier, and I don't know why, but one of them just whacked him really hard on the back of his head, just to fuck with him, and he hit his face on his camera, and he got really upset, packed his stuff up, and left. Tom didn't see any of this going on, so he just kept skating, and Fred was still filming. It was getting a bit darker, and I could feel Cairo looking at me, and I wanted to be really respectful to everything that was going on, and eventually he's like, 'Are you just going to watch this go down, or are you going to get the camera out?'

I managed to get it but it was quite dark. That film is 3200 speed pushed to the absolute limit, and Andy Horsley definitely did some magic on it to make it look cooler.

It was right at the time when I was leaving *Sidewalk* and moving to *Skateboarder*; I think I'd just started on a retainer there but I was really fiercely loyal to Ben Powell, so I felt that although that was shot on the *Skateboarder* budget, on *Skateboarder* film, I felt like that was my send-off. I didn't really think about it

too much, I just thought that Ben would be really hyped to have the sequence and that would be my thank-you to *Sidewalk*.

Everyone in America was really bummed when they saw it pop up in *Sidewalk*. People at Sole Tech were especially bummed because I think they'd been digging around for something of Tom for a really long time, and for them to see it come out in a regional magazine, they were disappointed. It ran in *Skateboarder* the next month, and that just goes to show the power of Tom Penny, really. He could have the same sequence run in two magazines.

I didn't realise how serious it was until I came to America and people were not very happy about it.

FROM LEFT
[1] Tom Penny, Lyon, by Oliver Barton
[2] *Document*, October, Mark Baines by Sam Ashley, design by Joel O'Connor
[3] *Sidewalk*, October, Joleon Pressey by Oliver Barton, design by Nik Taylor

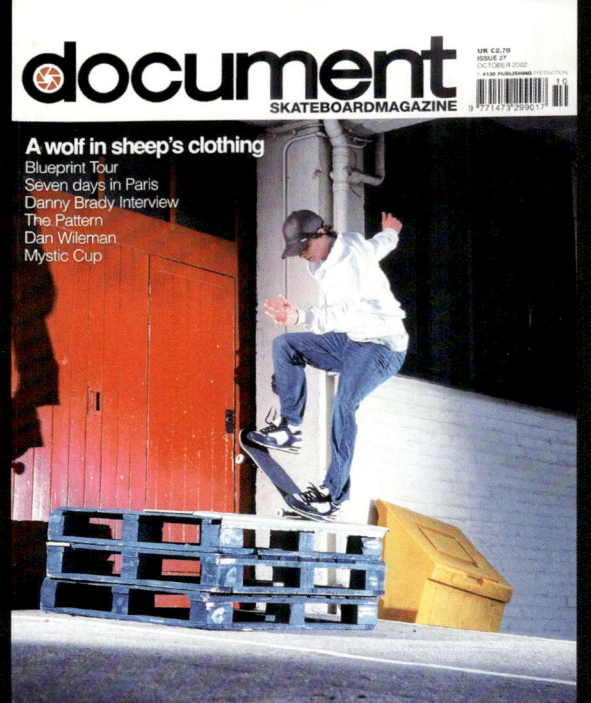

Nik Taylor

I was writing bits and bobs for *Sidewalk*, I was a freelance graphic designer and I was doing a lot of stuff that was pretty soulless, corporate crap. I guess I'd done those Slam ads so they knew I was capable, and I started doing one or two articles every month, using QuarkXPress and Photoshop.

Wig Worland told me that Leo Sharp was going to Australia for a period, and Andy Horsley was going to have to take on more photography, and asked me how I'd feel about designing the whole magazine. That was like the dream. I had two months of getting everything together for the changeover, and then I did a couple of issues before I sorted out a new logo and redesigned the layout.

I got pretty stressed working on *Sidewalk* because it was so much to do in such a short time. It was 80 pages of editorial usually in around two weeks because everything would be quite backed up. It was difficult coming in at a point where I was aspiring to be a 'professional graphic designer', and trying to impose some sort of order on something which had previously worked perfectly well in its own particular way. Andy was really good at putting everything together really quickly, and I was trying to make it a bit more organised, to keep me sane. Consequently I was just fucking running myself into the ground. It sounds really presumptuous, but I just wanted to change it to make my job

easier. The way Andy was doing it, doing it really spontaneously, is amazing. It's such a lot of work for one person. I couldn't work like he did. I had to have it regimented, and I'd got really into this idea of grid systems and all that sort of stuff. I don't think I made myself very popular. I thought it'd be easier to work to a stricter structure and I thought I'd just redesign everything. I was definitely the problem in that equation, trying to impose order on something that was already working. I see it like I came in and upset the perfectly functional apple cart.

For Andy to have done it for so long is a testament to his character because it is so fucking stressful and I never ever detected an ounce of that from him. I wouldn't be able to sleep because I would be thinking about everything I had to do, and then the last week before it went to print I'd have to go up to Abingdon, where the Permanent office was, to hand over all these files. I'd go up to Abingdon and I'd have to sleep under the desk on bubblewrap. There were people that did all the work getting it ready for print, and the scanning, so I'd hand it over to them and they'd work normal office hours but I'd still have stuff coming in so I'd be working in that office until three in the morning. I'd curl up under the desk because I couldn't be fucked driving back to London in Wig's car, which I was borrowing, only to have to drive back the following day. I remember I had a nervous twitch in my eye and a twitch in my knee for three or four months just from

the stress. That stress wasn't to do with Ben or Andy or anybody there, because I made it as complicated as I made it. It's that weird thing when you're gunning for something for so long, this dream, and then you get it and you're like, 'Shit, I can't do this'.

A couple of things were really unfortunate coincidences, like when I introduced the new *Sidewalk* logo, and about a week before that, coincidentally, *Document* had also brought out a new logo and they were almost the same. It was just like, 'Fuck!!' I'd been working on that logo on and off for about two months. Also, it had a concept to it that no one got, and I was constantly trying to explain to people what the little dot at the bottom of the 'S' was: a wheel of a skateboard. There was an idea behind it that was totally lost, I suppose it simply failed as a concept, and it just looked weird.

I don't know if Joel started doing *Document* before or after I started the bits of design work for *Sidewalk*, but we'd obviously studied at the same time and were coming from the same reference points. To anyone looking at it, it looked like *Sidewalk* was suddenly trying to rip-off *Document*. It was a really hard thing to constantly feel like we were the establishment and somehow the bad guys, constantly trying to claw back credibility. I don't know if any of the others felt like that, but I felt like everyone was rooting for *Document*. →

Wig Worland

Every now and again New Deal UK would go, 'That's it, we've had enough, we're pulling our ads from *Sidewalk*'. They'd ring up Jim Peskett and go, 'We're pulling our ads, we've had it with you guys', and then what I'd have to do – and I don't know why it was me, but maybe I was a bit more diplomatic than Ben Powell and Andy Horsley – would be that I'd get three or four back issues, tear them up and put all the pages that involved their riders in an A4 folder and drive from Oxford to Harrow and placate them.

Ben Jobe

I'm more into function than fashion. I had a tie-dye shirt that looked like the sky, and when I was jumping I really felt the effect, and people would look at me and I looked like a cloud because of the tie-dye. That was quite a powerful effect, but nine times out of ten a pair of trainers is just a pair of trainers and it doesn't make you feel like a cloud.

Skateboarding's kind of a dance, isn't it? I'd put my headphones on and I'd play around with things. There's a block by the riverside and I figured out that you can do a backside nosegrind, and if you relax and do a 180 out of it, the fact that you're relaxing when you're turning round means that the fact there are bars behind you doesn't make any difference. Your board goes around. You discover things like that when you play around.

The world is pretty crazy and you don't know what to believe or who to believe or how to believe, but when you're skateboarding you're doing something in the moment, you're exploring, you're feeling and you don't have to have any confusion. You feel around and play around and explore your surroundings and express yourself.

You're hyping up each other and bouncing off each other, and you spend loads and loads of time enjoying and appreciating everything and everyone around you. That's what skateboarding can be and that's what life can be.

Leo Sharp

One of my favourite people to shoot with was Woody. When I lived in Manchester he was always absit and he was always up for doing something photo-worthy. He was the first person to ollie that gasworks gap[3]. That was something we'd always look at, for years, because obviously you'd hang out at the gasworks and just skate whatever debris was there, and people would always look at this gap over the four stair, over the rail and down this massive drop and wonder if it was even possible.

Eastbourne Ben actually tried it before Woody, and there's photos of that, but he never landed it. Then Woody did it for that video *Leisure*, that Stu Bentley made, then I got him to do it again for that photo for his *Sidewalk* interview.

Dan Magee

Sidewalk, and eventually *Document*, gave us everything. There was no internet so they gave us everything; they gave us covers, back-to-back covers... No wonder New Deal was so stressed. They'd lost a bit of market share – I don't know how badly we affected them there – and they were losing a lot of coverage, and that was a really big thing to Steve Douglas, I think.

Nick Zorlac

I appreciate everything the mags did for us, but I think it's accurate to say that it was way more of a struggle for us to get coverage in magazines than it was for other UK brands. I don't feel hard done by by the magazines though. It was just part of the fight and the reality of owning a skate brand in the UK. Well it was for me anyway. Especially a brand that does not attempt to fit in with what is on trend in skateboarding at any given time. ●

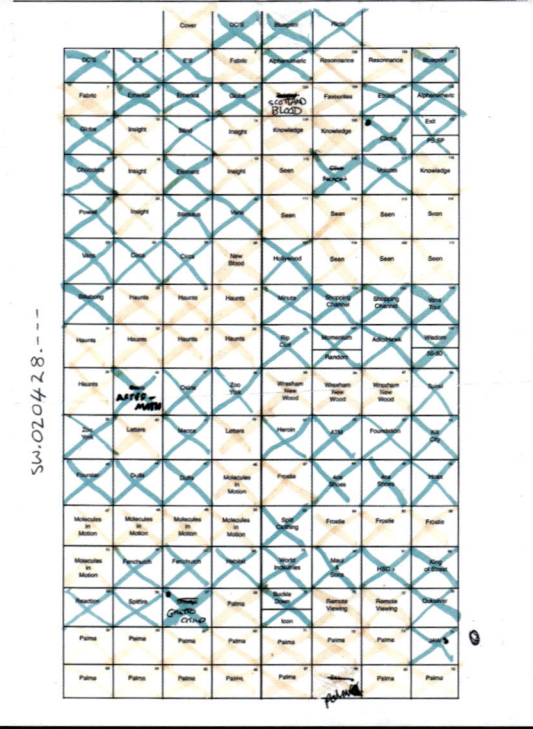

CLOCKWISE FROM TOP LEFT
[1] *Sidewalk* page plan, April
[2] Ben Jobe, Waterloo, by Wig Worland
[3] Gary Woodward, Gasworks, Manchester, by Leo Sharp

Reaction

CLOCKWISE FROM TOP LEFT
[1] Mark Brewster, Harlow, by Wig Worland
[2] Flynn Trotman, Bath Rugby Club, by Percy Dean
[3] Reaction Lucy Adams ad, photo by Lex Kemberly
[4] Reaction Greg Finch ad, photo by David 'Styley' Steel

Flynn Trotman

The way things ended with Reaction and DC was me being a bit of a dick, on reflection, and it goes back to being with the Warner crew. At that stage I left Huntington Beach and had a bit of the vibe from being around all those dudes, so I was drinking and partying a little bit, without a care in the world.

Louis Slater had also gone out there, after I'd left, and Louis was a bit more deep in the Piss Drunx crew.

We were on a Reaction tour, and we were all in a pub, with Ian Gunner and everybody, and Louis came to meet us. Me and Louis had the connection from Blueprint as well as the PD crew, so we chilled, and started drinking, and then we were like, 'Fuck this pub, let's go somewhere else', and as we left, Louis threw a pint glass – and I didn't even know he was going to do it – through the pub window, and the glass landed all over Gunner. I didn't think nothing of it, and I drank through the night, then the next morning I met up with everybody, and there were really bad vibes. Everybody's like, 'Flynn, you're a dick'. Which is fair enough. So that was a pretty bad strike. Gunner was pretty pissed at that.

I was living in Bristol at the time and we were all into spray painting our shoes, and spray painting over our graphics, and Gunner didn't say it, but he was probably getting a bit annoyed that we were spraying over our boards.

Then I broke my toe, and I turned up at Urban Games in a pair of etnies flip-flops, because I had a broken toe and I couldn't wear shoes, and I think Gunner was pissed off with that too.

Sometime later I got a letter from Gunner saying that I was off, for riding other brands and things like that. It's funny because he would even send me other boards, I would get Black Label boards because I couldn't ride the Reaction boards because they were too thin, and I'd spray paint over the graphics. That was quite a shock because that was all my boards, all my shoes and all my money.

I was off the team and they released the latest range of boards, and they released my board with the Spiderman graphic. I rang up and spoke to Ray, and Ray was just like, 'Yep, alright, cool', and he sent me 50 or 60 of them, to sell or whatever. And that's how I parted with New Deal.

I didn't know what to do after that. I remember joking with my friend Murray that I'd gone from eating salmon in restaurants to packets of crisps on a kerb. I just didn't know what to do. I spoke to Percy Dean, who was doing *Document* magazine, and he came back to me to say he'd been speaking to these guys in Europe about doing a company called Crème, so I got on Crème.

Lucy Adams

Reaction started happening for me in 2002. I'd been skating St Albans quite a lot, with Rodney Clarke, and I'm pretty sure Flynn got kicked off, and I took Flynn's place. Quite an awful state of affairs.

I got introduced to Gunner, and it was just like, 'Yep, here we go', although it was quite formal. Gunner sent out an email with a lot on it. Mark Brewster was getting the January ad, this is happening, that is happening, Lucy gets an ad in July... I was going to Australia, so I had to figure out who I knew that would be there that could shoot photos.

Mark Brewster

Reaction could've been so much better. All I remember was seeing Gunner in the advert in the magazine, in the limousine, wearing snakeskin shoes, and thinking how it was the most un-skate, most corporate, most out-of-touch thing that could possibly happen. Taste-wise it was just so off the mark on the cool-scale. There wasn't even a number low enough, it was dungeon-tier.

But then again it was full of cool people. I didn't really know Rob Selley but he was cool, Rodney was the person who first got me on Vans, the Smith twins were really quiet but also absolutely mind-blowing, there was Neil Urwin, who was a bit moody, but he was sick and had done the whole America thing. Pete King who I knew from Leigh-on-Sea, and Greg Finch who was sound as fuck, so I knew everyone on the team.

I got on Reaction just after they'd done their video, which I've still never watched in its entirety. I remember thinking that if Selley was on, well, he's dope as fuck, so there must be something going on.

I was talking to Ben Allnutt and he said they were going to rebrand it, and I said I'd really love to create some graphics. I designed two full sets of boards, for all the pros – a set based on airline baggage labels and a set based on old 45 record labels, but they were never used as it was just before the rug got pulled.

I remember the rebrand meeting for Reaction, where that new eye logo was introduced, which I still wasn't 100% into, but I think the font was one that I sent to Ben Allnutt. I got sent a few bits and pieces, and the new ads came out, and then apparently Steve Douglas stopped it all. Which was totally understandable.

I can't remember how they told us it was over, but it was really shortly after the rebranding. There was all this excitement about them rebranding it, and that it was actually going to be cool, and then suddenly it was finished and they told everyone to pick a company to go on distro flow. I picked Habitat, but they probably figured out that I wasn't really that into it when there was a Habitat video premiere at the Prince Charles theatre that I didn't bother going to.

Ben Allnutt

Reaction was coming to an end, and I had one last-ditch attempt, I thought we could rebrand it and I wanted to pitch something to them. I remember saying to Gunner that I wanted to have a go at it, at Reaction, on my own. I felt like I could do it. We had a team meeting, and I presented this logo to the guys, and this vision for what it could be, and everyone was fully onboard. There was the new logo, and it was going to be series boards, but series boards that I felt comfortable doing.

I was going to get rid of the Professor logo and finally get my chance to do my own thing with it after a long period of just doing stuff which we had to sell, which I totally get. And then that was it.

Ian Gunner

We had a good team, and we introduced a few more people – like Rodney Clarke, Flynn Trotman, Pete King, Leo and Jody Smith, Barry Dring – and we were doing some good stuff, but we almost were too successful, because Steve Douglas jumped in and told us that because we were a distributor for US brands, this had to stop. Steve made some big calls around that time, and fair play because he was protecting the home of skateboarding, which was the US. Steve said Reaction had to stop, because it was taking time and effort and money from the business, as such.

Also at this time, myself, Steve and Ben Powell had a meeting, and I think at the time I was putting an average of 36 pages of advertising into *Sidewalk* every month. At that point Steve said we needed to have US skateboarders on the cover. This wasn't a dig at the magazines or photographers, Wig was great, Ben and Horsley were great, Percy was great; they were all very welcoming and super easy to work with, we were friends. Steve wasn't trying to do anything maliciously, or trying to take over skateboarding, he was simply just looking after our return on investment and the US brands and skaters.

At one point I think I was spending about 11% of our turnover on marketing, which was heavy. ●

belong

Blueprint

BELONG
BLUEPRINT.

Dan Magee

The Investigation series [pp.454–455] came out of the fact that this was a time when everything was going very logo-based. Basically everything we did was a big bold logo because that was within the realms of what I could muster, in terms of my graphic skills. That worked, it sold, but in my heart I felt like we were always cheating it, just putting a logo on a board. On top of that it had got back to me that Hellicar had said something like, 'Blueprint is just different colourways', so I was like, 'Fuck!', and I knew we needed something more, but that would still feel like it was part of the line-up.

The guy that did it was called Jamie Bridson, and it was one of the only things that I ever got a budget to pay anyone for, but given how much work went into them, it was probably fuck-all. I think he said he'd do them for free, but I told him he needed to get paid for them. I went and had the longest meeting with Joe – about seven hours, and I always tried to avoid meetings with Joe – and in the end he gave me a grand to pay the dude for the boards.

They're all loosely tied to what people were doing at the time. On Rattray's one he's looking out with binoculars, which is a very loose hint back to an old graphic where he had a telescope. Shier's eating some ramen because he had a Japanese girlfriend and he had a couple of boards that were running that theme, Colin's got headphones because it was running off that 'Kinetic', music-making theme, Scott Palmer was a tradesman at the time so he's interrogating someone and he's got a hammer, and Baines has got a cup of coffee because he had that Starbucks board.

Those graphics were being done when Rattray quit, so when Rattray went to Zero, his board became Vaughan's board. That was one of Vaughan's first boards.

The other thing was that we had this problem with Scott Palmer at the time, where he was mental-obsessed with the two-fingers-of-flat Dwindle concave. He was always mad about things, he would drill holes in his DVS to aerate them; there was never anything that was right for what he wanted to skate. This obsession with the Dwindle concave went on for so long, and he ended up spraying Dwindle boards. Taking his Blueprint boards into the shop, swapping them for Dwindle boards and spraying the graphics out.

I was like, 'If we're going to do something completely different, let's just have a different section of Blueprint', which is maybe why that meeting took about seven hours, because I had to not only convince Burlo to pay for the graphics but also to do these boards at a different wood shop. This is the sort of thing that I was up against all the time.

When they came out they were so sick, but because of the market at the time, they were the worst selling Blueprint boards. Whether that was because the graphics weren't a logo, or because the wood was different, but Burlo obviously got scared and said I couldn't get any more money for graphics and he couldn't change the wood again. Because of things like that it was very difficult to move the company on because he was scared of anything that would lose him money.

I was stoked on Vaughan's *Headcleaner* part, and they used his artwork in that video and that was one of the best things about it. It just worked. One of those characters with the big heads that became the Artwork Series, I think he did one of those with a heart that was bleeding. That was the origin of the heart that was bleeding, but then I had a weird dream at Joel's – when I was sleeping in Seth's old bed – where that logo was sprayed and it had two drips. That was what made me do that logo.

Vaughan Baker

I definitely had a drawing in one of my sketchbooks that Dan had full access to. The first graphic I had, I'd drawn that character and that image was in my sketchbook, so the Spray Heart is definitely a digitalised version of a drawing that he might have seen in my sketchbook. The thing is, they were really good to me. Joe Burlo was good to me. I ain't complaining. ●

FROM LEFT
[1] Vaughan Baker artwork, and Vaughan by Dan Magee and Justin Atallian, from Belong series
[2] Danny Brady, Millbank, by Oliver Barton
[3] Vaughan Baker, Devonshire Green, by Percy Dean

  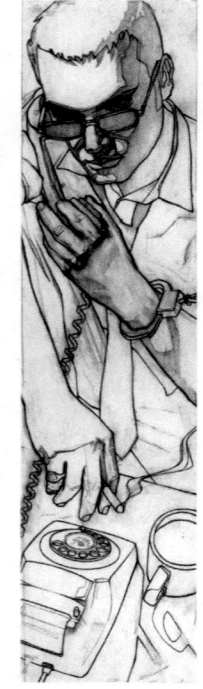 

KENNEDY   SHIER   PALMER   BAINES   RATTRAY

✓   ✓ close   ✓   ✗   ✓
to chop
sticks

Dear Dan,

Here's the ideas I've been working on. They are very rough, just to give you an idea of the compositions and look.

They're shaded with tone, but that's just the way I draw; they will be simplified to flat colour obviously for boards.

Still not happy with the Gainer, but that is where it's up to. Need to keep working on them all.

Hopefully I can get some photos of all the skaters in these kinds of poses, but for these drawings I used a combination of the mirror, & photos of friends.

I can get them looking like the guys if you like these original ideas.

Kennedy:

tapping a phone call, the headphones relating to his love of music.

Stier:

loves noodles (hope he still does!)

Palmer:

joiner/woodwork becomes good torture apparatus!

Bones:

being interrogated (still like his coffee?) possibly the coffee could be spiked?

Rattray:

binoculars there with his fascination w/ the stars

and astronomy. He is on a 'stake out' kind of situation.

I developed the use of phones so it was incorporated into all the compositions, so that it remains unclear who is communicating with who.

Hope you like the shit, sorry it is late in arriving.

Let us know what the general opinion is,

speak to ya soon!

Jamie

(thrive on cold winters)

James Jarvis

Eventually we started Amos because we all – Russell and I particularly – felt that the toy thing had its own momentum, and we never felt that toys should be part of streetwear and fashion, because toys had a wider remit, a wider connection to the world, whereas fashion needed to stay exclusive for it to retain its value. With toys there was no value in exclusivity.

When we did Amos we were thinking that we could do something like Beanie Babies. That was our original idea, just to see what we could do with it. It ended up being exclusive, but that was through the consumers. You make this stuff, but then the culture that it becomes wasn't ours to create. We'd made what we felt we could safely sell, because we didn't want stuff lying around. We didn't do the Supreme model where we'd make 150 of something knowing we could sell a thousand. If we knew we could sell a thousand, we'd make a thousand.

We never called it 'designer toys', although other people did. It was small-run, collectable figurines and in my mind it had nothing to do with toys and was more connected to ceramic shepherdesses that your granny would collect. It was that kind of thing, but for graphic designers.

Russell Waterman

We started Amos quite early in the evolution of Silas. It was separated to give James's designs room to breath away from the restrictions of fashion. It was sort of an accident because of the unforeseen success of the Silas promotional toys, but ironically Amos was with us for longer than Silas.

I've always liked the 'stop it when you're winning' thing. It's very hard to know when to do that. The 'streetwear' business was changing and we were under constant pressure to grow Silas. We were probably going to have to do trade shows, use sales reps and all the shit we hadn't done before, stuff I never wanted to do. Selling to people that I didn't particularly want to sell to. Being on time with our deliveries? Fuck that, I don't want to be on time with our deliveries. We could no longer be this maverick clothing company that had come up from the anarchic world of skateboarding, We were going to have to be more serious and play the game. Silas would have to become a very different beast and I honestly didn't have the stomach for it.

At the time we had money to pay off our staff, most of who went on to get great jobs because they were all talented and highly thought of. I think they seemed to understand why we chose to wind it down. In the end, selling the intellectual property

to Japan was just a bonus. We even tried to protect the artists involved by restricting the use of individual designs without a direct renegotiation with the creator.

As far as I know, no one hates us for what we did. There might have been a few shops that were pissed at us for suddenly bailing, but no one really hated us, and that was hard to achieve. Today I still have many good relationships from that time and I'm proud and grateful for this.

It's funny that with Amos, James and me were able to carry on with the playful subversive ideas that we'd used with Holmes and in the earlier days of Silas. For us Amos became a design company. It wasn't just about toys. By the time we stopped we had produced a bunch of toys, but we'd also written and published books, set up art shows, created public installations, and even curated a music festival. Really Amos is a whole other story which maybe one day we'll be ready to tell.

I'd come up on punk rock and Anarchist Situationist ideas, I'd spent my whole life trying not to work for, or with, large companies, But I could see the industry was going away from the smaller independents towards big business. For me it was done and time to get out. I've never really felt like we left any real legacy and I don't think that any of it was particularly special. Skateboarding's much more meaningful. ●

Gavin Hills

GAVIN HILLS
Neil Macdonald

This book probably wouldn't exist if Gavin Hills hadn't existed. When Gavin wrote for *RAD*, it felt like – and it turns out that this is true – you didn't need to be a proper journalist to get your ideas published. Gavin spoke about skateboarding and life in a real way, with none of the 'skate and destroy' posturing prevalent in the other magazines; he spoke about failure, depression and insecurity so openly, back when nobody else was, and he talked about the joy of life, of meeting people, of the ecstatic highs that life can provide, in the most human way, because it was real. He was living his life and writing down what was happening.

From *Bomber* zine to *RAD*, to editing *Phat* and the official England and Manchester United magazines, writing for *The Idler*, *The Big Issue*, *The Face*, *The Guardian* and *The Observer,* it was only in 1994 when he won an Amnesty International award for his reporting of the war in Angola that Gavin acknowledged he had in fact become a proper journalist. Three years later, on 20 May 1997, Gavin was swept off a rock while fishing in Cornwall, and drowned.

Gavin wrote about skateboarding, travel, war, football, style, drugs and *people* better than anybody. Live in the fast lane, but always make sure you have the bus fare home.

Rest in Peace, Gavin.

Tim Leighton-Boyce
Founder and editor, RAD

Vernon and Gavin materialised, and I was in awe of them because I thought they were proper journalists. This was quite early on in the days of *RAD*, and we didn't feel we were proper people at all, and I thought Gavin and Vernon were because they'd written stuff for *City Limits*, so I was slightly wary of them, slightly self-conscious... How wrong that turned out to be. There was no need to be self-conscious about that element of Gavin, although of course he was a proper journalist, but he was a mad maverick version of such a person. One of my favourite things he wrote was the rip-off of The KLF, 'How To Be The World's Greatest Street Skater (In 30 Days)'. Some of the stuff he wrote was really, really brilliant.

Vernon Adams
Journalist and photographer

When we were at art college Gavin was really into football. I understood it a bit but Gavin was fully into the whole casual culture. The casual look, with Italian Ball jeans, Diadoras, Sergio Tacchini and all that kind of thing. A lot of his friends were into that, and him and his brother went to a lot of that sort of stuff, but it wasn't my kind of world.

Munster 1989 was a classic. We flew to Germany, and Gavin didn't have any money. I don't know if he'd cobbled together a few quid from the office to get to the airport, but he didn't have any money. I bought the train tickets to get us from Düsseldorf or wherever it was to Munster, and they gave us one big ticket. Just this piece of paper. So obviously I had that in my pocket and when we got to the platform a train arrived, and Gav jumped on the train. Without any of his stuff. And the doors shut. And the train wasn't going to Munster, it was going somewhere else.

So he's on the train with no money, no ticket, no nothing. It was just a disaster. His argument was that he was sure the train was going to the right place, but my argument was, 'If you were so convinced it was going to the right place, why didn't you get on with your own bag?!' He had this classic Gavin story about trying to dodge ticket people and getting kicked off the train, and obviously he didn't speak any German, while I went to Munster with all our stuff. He had a nightmare. I don't even know if he showed up the same day or the next day, but I felt bad for him so I got us a hotel. Even though there was hardly any money.

There was a year where Gavin, myself, and another guy who came with us went by train all the way from London. That was pretty crazy, and then after the comp Gavin and this other friend of ours went to Greece for a holiday. Again, they didn't have any money, and they just winged it by hiding in the toilets with no tickets and all sorts.

Russell Waterman
Slam City Skates/Holmes/Silas/Amos

Gavin, coming from North London, knew a bunch of people that I knew, and he knew them in a social way because he'd be going to clubs. He knew them as not-hooligans, and I thought that was fucking nuts. He was into football culture and he was also into Situationism, and I was into Anarchism and Situationism so we could talk about that stuff, and I liked the zines he was doing. He was into skateboarding, Situationism and football, and I didn't think there was anybody else into all that stuff, so we hit it off really quickly. He was down with all the skaters and he was down with these football hooligans, and I'm talking proper football hooligans, not just kids wearing Fila and Ellesse. He knew some of the proper nutters, and it seems like he knew them well. He could just mix with people and move in different social circles seamlessly and effortlessly, which is why he could write like he could.

Simon Evans
Skateboarder

Gavin was special. It was really sad, it breaks my heart. I was just so lucky and I don't know how it happened, but suddenly the next thing I know I'm at the *RAD* offices meeting people, and I met Gavin. I felt like Gavin was a man, and he was probably just a few years older than me. I always think of him as a writer, but he was a fucking character as well. He was really kind and really smart, and he was like a proper writer. A journalist in training. He was the first person that I ever read that would write these lists, he was a list writer and he would do these funny lists and it was the first time I'd seen anyone use that format. He was just a really, really good writer. He was mad too; one time he fell off a viaduct or something walking home from a rave.

Then he started working for *The Face* and he got bigger and bigger but it was just the beginning. He was a proper writing talent, but also very kind to us even though we were just skateboarders. Very loving. We'd be like, 'What's socialism Gavin?', and he'd say, 'Oh, it's just different socks'. He would explain things to me that I didn't understand.

Marc Bultitude
Skateboarder

Gavin was really great. Gavin was an inspiration to Simon. He was this cheeky working-class lad who was living in a big house in Camden with Tom Hodgkinson – the guy who worked in Slam and started *The Idler* – and Ged Wells. I think it was Tom Hodgkinson's family home, because he was posh. Everyone knew that he was posh but he was a really cool guy.

Gavin was a chancer, and Simon really liked that because I think he saw it like, 'If Gavin Hills can do it, then maybe I can'. They used to encourage each other, Gavin used to really encourage Simon to write. He was always really funny in the *RAD* office. If you went there and Gavin was there, everybody would be laughing.

When Gavin started working for *The Face* I think that was like an 'in' for *The Face*, because Gavin could introduce them to outside things. He did great, powerful, journalism for them but he was the guy on the scene, the guy that was at all the parties. The style magazines were looking at skaters by this point, like, 'These people are urban, they're everywhere, and they look really good'.

Tom Hodgkinson
Founder and editor, The Idler

I think about Gavin every day. It's just so sad. He was such an amazing person. He was outstanding, and he was such an inspiration. He was such a big, lovely person, but he had some real sadness. He got married, and he had this lovely Shakespearean *Midsummer Night's Dream* wedding but it just didn't work out at all.

Without any money at all, he managed to have this quite free life, and that's what inspired me about him, and Ged, and others. They didn't really have any money but they were just doing amazing things and they had this incredible freedom, somehow, to a live a very, very full life without having a real job, and just get into incredible adventures.

In *The Idler* he was writing about men's mental health issues, when it wasn't really being done elsewhere, I don't think. That was quite ahead of its time. He'd had breakdowns and came out of them, he'd talk openly about sex, drugs and his own life. Just an amazing person and it's so sad.

He became a real star and he would have done incredible things. And he invented *Vice*, as far as I'm concerned. He was going to war zones, and people didn't do that before him, Young MTV-type trendy journalists going to war zones and hanging out with soldiers and putting on punk gigs? It was a completely new kind

of reporting. Whether or not *Vice* copied that I don't know, but he certainly did it before *Vice*. *The Idler* isn't big like *Vice*, but we've got our own studio and we're doing what we like every day, so thank you skateboarding.

Skin Phillips
Photographer

He became a football writer, and he went on tour to watch games, but he didn't actually go to them. So he sent the review in from watching it on TV. He was just winging it. He was little bit naughty, but in a good way.

Tim Barnes
loaded

Gavin certainly didn't know anything about football, and he didn't know anything about skateboarding to start with, but he was really good at picking stuff up and he was really good at making friends and find the people who were interesting and who mattered. Not knowing something was no barrier to him, ever.

We ended up doing an official magazine for England during Euro '96, and Gazza was supposed to be our cover star and our main interview, and it didn't happen. So Gavin said, 'Don't worry, I'll be Gazza, and you can interview me'. So he pretended, and I asked him the questions, and he answered as if he was Gazza and that was fine. That was our interview and nobody ever knew. He was good at that sort of thing and that sort of thing happened all the time. He was a great blagger and he was good at knowing what people wanted.

He was good at knowing what was going on. He wasn't particularly cool, but he knew what was cool, always. He could just spot things happening, and he was so much fun that he could draw people out and get in anywhere, and find out what was relevant and what people wanted. He really enjoyed himself and he really enjoyed doing everything that he did, and I guess that just came across and made things feel genuine.

Adam Porter
loaded

One of the first times I met him was at the Coach and Horses, and we just really got on. I'd call us, in the broader sense, naughty, but we weren't bad boys really. We weren't nasty, we just liked the adrenalin of running around and causing a bit of mayhem. I wasn't really into the skateboarding part of it at all, but it was around that time when he started doing *Phat* magazine. They were making that out of a tiny little office in Soho, about four or five of them, and it did incredibly well; it had a circulation of 35,000. To get a circulation like that out of such a small office in town was unbelievable and I think it showed to James Brown and Tim Southwell that here was an appetite from young guys for a magazine like that, but Gavin pointed that magazine at the skateboarding fraternity which was much smaller, and *loaded* was pointed at the football fraternity which is enormous.

James Brown
Founder and editor, loaded

I first met him backstage at Glastonbury, maybe four or five o'clock in the morning, when it was light, and he had a Richard the First Lionheart George Cross top on, and a belt, and his face was covered in chocolate. I was with Miranda and she introduced me to Gavin. I said, 'Who the fuck is this?', and she said, 'James, this is Gavin. You're going to love each other'. He was the same as me, really, he was just looking around for something to do, being nosey. It was very easy in those days to wander around backstage.

That must have been the first summer of *loaded*. We were all writers and clubbers and things, so we'd all run into each other, so I just got to know him like that. I used to see him out a lot, and because of what was going on culturally, and in music, there were just so many reasons to go out. There were no reasons to stay in. There was so much going on, and between the people that were doing things there was a common bond, and that didn't matter whether it was some guys running a club in Liverpool or some people running a clothes shop in Nottingham or some guys with a pub in Leeds or some guys running an after-hours club in Brixton. You just knew that you were all into the same stuff. I think what *loaded* was doing was sharing the knowledge of the things that we all loved.

I was in my late twenties, and it was an exciting time because you'd see the same people in the Coach and Horses in Soho, or in Vic Naylor in Clerkenwell, or up in Camden in the Good Mixer. Or maybe you'd go to a party and there would be people from *Select* or *The Face* around and Gavin would know them. This was before 'Cool Britannia' and all that stuff, and it just felt like we were young, we were going out all the time, and you'd bump into a lot of the same people. So Gavin and I became friends.

He had a recklessness that I liked, and he was the only person who wasn't actually in the *loaded* office who felt like they were the same as us. He was more aligned with *The Face*, he was a *Face* writer, and he wrote about things in *The Face* that we wrote about in *loaded* – football and trainers and stuff like that – that they hadn't done that much of. They'd not really covered things like that, the less elite, less fashion-oriented male culture.

In a way, now, with digital media and phones, you can find your tribe easily. You find it through your passions or your social media mates or whatever your hobbies and interests are, but back then you found your tribes through going out, or retail – you'd meet people in record shops or skateboard shops or comic shops or clothes shops, whatever people are into – or you met them in bars and clubs. In a way, it meant that with that random nature I would go to bars and there would be people I knew, but there was never much of a sense of organisation. Just the same big groups of people hanging about in different places, so Gavin was somebody I would tend to meet at random, like that.

When I think about Gavin now, it always seemed light. It always seemed like this stuff was going on in the daylight and the days were long and sunny. I can remember looking at him opposite this bar called Marathon in Chalk Farm, and he was with all those guys from *Select*, and Miranda, and all those guys who really looked up to him, and adored him, and I can remember he put his hand up and started walking, and they all just followed him. He was like a tour guide to craziness. They were probably going to go off and do something wholesome, whereas me and my mates were probably going to go and do something unhealthy.

I didn't think his writing was brilliant; what I thought was good was his opinions and his subjects. He went and did interesting things, and things that other people weren't doing, and his observations into this, and his coverage, is what was interesting and what he was good at. He liked things that were exciting, and going on, and he liked finding things that were exciting and going on, and telling people about them. In the culture and in the area of media that we worked in, that's all you had to be good at to get going. Find good things that people don't know about, and tell them about them. Interesting things. Whether it's music or skateboarding or whatever the fuck it is.

I did specifically hang out with him two or three times. We went to Ibiza together, and he had a bit of a breakdown when he'd taken too much coke. We met a couple of dudes who'd taken a lot in, maybe a crown-green-bowl-sized bit of coke in, so we had an awful lot of coke to do with what we wanted. I can remember being up at dawn and Gavin started crying really badly. With Gavin you never knew whether he was fucking around or not, but he started crying really badly. There was too much drink, too much drugs, and he got emotional and he just broke down and he was sobbing and sobbing, and at first I thought, 'Is he fucking putting this on?', but the others,

who didn't know him as well as me, were really concerned.

He was talking about when he was in a refugee camp in Africa somewhere – he did male culture, and youth culture things, but he also wanted to go down the serious reportage route – and he started talking about a woman who was dying of starvation giving him her baby. That was a very moving moment, and that moment was at odds with the lifestyle we were all leading. We spent the rest of that day on pedalos, driving round the harbour laughing and fucking around, and getting on people's boats who we didn't know, but there was that moment where there was this other side to him.

When Gavin died a lot of us got a phone call, and we just went to his flat, so there were about twenty people at his flat, maybe less. Miranda was really shook up, and she knew that my mum had died maybe five years before, but I don't think many of us had known anyone who'd died. That was what was unusual about it. The fact that he wasn't alive anymore made me realise how young we all were, and how young he'd gone. In his cupboard we were looking for stuff to drink, and he had a jar of hard pasta in the shape of tits.

Sheryl Garrett
Editor, The Face

Cynthia Rose – who'd been at *City Limits* around the same time as me – sent me either a note or an email that just said, 'Oh, I've met this kid, he works for a skateboard magazine and you should meet him', and every bit of that made me think, 'No I shouldn't'. But I like Cynthia, so we did arrange to meet up and he came into the office. I took him out for a quick drink and told him I had about 15 or 20 minutes, and about three hours later I went back to the office.

We just clicked. We were very, very compatible and I really liked his ideas. I still had no idea whether he could write, but I thought I'd try him out on some small ideas, and – as I often did with young writers – if they've executed the idea and the can't write, I can rewrite it. But everything Gavin did, he just did so beautifully, in terms of writing.

I can't even remember the first thing we commissioned; it'd have been something really crappy about computer games or trainers or dance styles or something like that, because we were running a lot of little funny articles like that. But I remember – as well as laughing out loud several times – thinking that he'd made some really good points. He wasn't just going after cheap laughs.

You never met Gavin and didn't feel like you'd just had your whole tank filled up with joy. Even when he was depressed he was hilarious. That's an awful thing because I'm not minimising his mental health but even when he was feeling low he always turned it into something incredibly entertaining. He was just a life-enhancing person to know.

What I loved about his reporting for *The Face*, when he started doing the really serious reportage work, was that he was great at finding someone that as a reader of that magazine you'd think, 'Well that could be me'. Whether it was a child soldier, or guerrillas in South America, whether it was football, drugs or music, he'd find someone he had something in common with. He would write people so that you just felt that by one quirk of birth that they could be you.

When he wrote for England magazine and the Man United magazine he used those to talk about what it's like to be a man in the nineties, and what it's like to be white. He never used the words 'white privilege' because that wasn't very common then but he was very aware of it. It was always there, in what he wrote, and I think that's what was so strong about it. If someone said they were going to write a thing about male mental health, how many of us would have read it? But because it's about skateboarding or football or trainers, everyone read it.

He was messy in that he was just chaotic, but you always got copy on time from him. Because of his dyslexia the spelling was terrible but everything else was pretty much as you read it. There was always some gratuitous quotation from William Blake or

Shakespeare that would get cut out because he only knew about three Blake or Shakespeare quotes. He used the same ones again and again and again, so it was always, 'Well, that's the paragraph to cut'. But most of what you read is exactly as he wrote it.

He was just a genuinely good person. He wanted to change the world. Not in a pompous way, but in an 'empowering people to realise that they could make a change' way. He wasn't, 'I've got all the answers, follow me', it was 'Here are some great questions. What do you think?' 'If I've managed to do this, you can do it too'.

He was thirty-one when he died. Thirty-one and a couple of days. I think that most of us don't really know what we're doing until we turn thirty, really. He'd just started doing a TV series with Miranda Sawyer, and I think– as a team – they would have been massive on TV. I think that would have started him on a TV career, so where he'd be now, I really don't know.

Miranda Sawyer
Journalist

I met him at a party. I don't know what the party was for, but I remember that it had some form of food; it had some form of burger thing and it had tomato sauce and mustard in squidgy bottles. I met him – I was pissed, obviously – and I went, 'Oh, you're Gavin Hills! I think your writing's really good', or something like that, and because I was pissed and lairy I squirted his trousers with tomato sauce. It wasn't aggressive, we were just having a laugh and I did it.

I woke up the next day and thought, 'Fucking hell, he's Gavin Hills, he works for *The Face*. Those trousers are probably Japanese workwear', and I felt really awful because I liked his writing and that's just really embarrassing. It was pre-email so I must have got his number somehow, and phoned him, and I said I was really sorry and asked him to meet, and so we met in the Coach and Horses in Soho, and it turned out that his trousers weren't actually Japanese workwear. I remember him laughing at the idea that he had very posh Japanese trousers, but that was my idea of what people at *The Face* wore at the time. I kind of thought it'd be alright because he hadn't been a twat to me when I'd done it. If you're in that situation and somebody squirts tomato ketchup on you for a laugh, if you're a certain type of person, you'll have a fight. You'd just think, 'You're a dick and I'm going to hit you'. Of course he actually didn't do that, and when I met him we got on immediately and we were friends after that.

The thing that was really good about Gav was that when he arrived, as a young woman you felt simultaneously protected – because he was quite tall and he was really good at getting on with people of all classes – and that you knew you were about to have a laugh. He would do things like organise a sports day for no reason, just so we would all go and have a sports day.

We got asked if we wanted to do *The Rough Guide*. It was pretty soon before he died. There were physical guides called *The Rough Guides*, that everyone took when they went away, and then they made it into a telly show. The two people before us who did it were Magenta Devine and Rajan Datar but they wanted to re-jig it and they somehow came upon me, and I think I suggested Gavin.

We tested for it, they said they'd make a pilot episode, and we went to Lebanon. He was thinning on top and he was always trying to hide his bald patch. I remember him trying to buy Regain in the airport.

It was the first time that Gavin had done telly, and I'd done a bit. There's a thing about television that's quite difficult if you've not done it before, especially if you're doing that kind of thing where essentially you have to be yourself but a telly version of yourself. Basically, telly pumps up your ego and smashes it into bits at the same time because there's a fucking camera on you – amazing – but then you don't know what you're doing because nobody's trained you. So when they ask you to do it again, you don't know if you've done it wrong. You don't understand. It messes with your ego, but what was really good was that we had each other on this trip.

At the time there was an area of Lebanon that was occupied by Syrian gunmen, and you would just get stopped by people, by Syrians. We had a translator, a fixer, so we never really knew what was going on. We got stopped and these two armed Syrian guys just got in the car – one got in the front and one got in the back – and we couldn't argue against them because they had guns, and I could tell that our fixer was absolutely shitting himself, so it wasn't an easy situation.

This guy said something to me, and Gavin was sort of laughing with him, going, 'No, no, she's my wife!', and then he was joking with the guy about the gun, and he says, 'I know how to break this gun down, I'll show you how to break this down, shall we break it down?' He diffused the situation completely. I was the only woman in the car, I was quite young, I had dyed blonde hair, and I probably looked really 'available'. The first thing they talked about was me, and that was quite scary, so Gavin was saying that I was his wife, and then just switching it over to talking about the gun and having a laugh about that diffused the atmosphere. The gunmen loved him! He was really amazing.

He's one of those people who could absolutely move through all situations and make friends in all of them. He knew about football so he could chat that football Esperanto of a working-class bloke, he could go to a rave and be really happy there, and he had loads of quite posh friends so he could talk to posh people too. He was just really able to deal with anybody, and then you take him out of the country, put him in a foreign country and he could do it there as well. It's a really amazing talent, and I feel I'm much more able to do that now, because I learned that off him. I learned a lot off him in order to be able to do that.

There's another aspect to him which is incredibly valuable in all people, in that he was always in real contact with his own emotions. He wasn't always jolly, he could get very depressed, and he wrote about that very well in magazines like The Idler. He definitely could get quite down and I think that also endeared him to people. You could sense that he was somebody who could, and did, get depressed. Life isn't always easy, and I don't think it's easy in your twenties no matter how much of a laugh you have.

He was never horrible to anyone. I'm sure he bitched about people a little bit, but he was never horrible to anyone. I never saw him be a twat to anyone. I really didn't. You know sometimes when people get drunk or they get wasted or whatever, a bad side will come out? That just never happened.

He was sad about his marriage not working and I remember him saying to me that it's like you've got to unroll your life out all again. He was further along in terms of settling down than I was. He was further along in terms of having a relationship and wanting it to work, and I was nowhere near that, really.

He was really romantic, though, Gav. I think anyone who believes in the power of rave, the power of football, the power of writing or the power of travel is a romantic. A complete romantic, and I think that's very admirable because what you're looking for is something that brings everyone together. He believed in youth culture and he believed in romance. Not like a Lothario, but as someone who believed in life and humans. He thought life could be good and he thought that it should be fair.

He was really great. He was a great friend, and obviously a massively talented journalist. He was inspiring, he was kind, and I just really love him. He was great. It was terrible when he died and it really shook up my world because I couldn't believe that somebody so positive could die, and that somebody who I felt so safe with could die.

I still miss him. He wasn't perfect, because nobody's perfect, but he was really great. He was a great writer, he was really good to be around, and I really loved him. He was brilliant. I wish he was still here. He'd have been a great dad and everything, it's just really annoying.

Matt McMullan

MATT McMULLAN
Will McMullan
Matt's brother

Matt McMullan was a brother, a son and a friend to many. But his identity was as a Skateboarder. It was in his blood, in his mind, it was the way he looked, the way he talked, it was everything. Matt died way too soon, after grappling with life and the struggles it can bring. But until the day he passed away on the 4th of February 2006, Matt was a skater, and a really good one.

Matt cut his teeth skating in the late '80s and '90s in London, gaining sponsorship from Death Box, and others. You would find him most days down at Southbank or Stockwell skating with his friends. I was ten years younger than Matt, so I looked up to him quite literally, but in so many other ways as well. Growing up he was my hero, though I probably did my best not to show it. I spent a lot of my time skating in his wake, hacking it down hills around South London, trying to keep up while watching him in awe. I remember falling really badly trying to keep up with him once, and I looked down the hill to see him trudging back up to console me and my grazed up face and knees. Painfully lovely memories.

Alex Moul stayed at our house around that time too, he was a legend on the UK skate scene, and Matt's best friend. It's hard not to be in awe when you're nine or ten years old and your older brother is a sponsored skater, surrounded by other skaters of a similar ilk. I remember he would get these huge packages delivered to the family home full of new boards, clothes, stickers, wheels, every bit of skate gear you can imagine came in these packs. I remember the smell of those boxes distinctly, the fresh decks combined with the stickers is a heady mix of newness never far from my mind or my senses when I think of my brother even today.

He would open these packs up really methodically with a Stanley blade, before setting up the board – another very methodical process, he was so precise at. Griptape was applied perfectly with the trusty Stanley blade and a filing tool, bolts screwed in on the tucks and wheels, then he would intricately apply stickers, placing them so the sticker would purposely overlap the side of the board before slicing the overhanging bit with the blade

to give it a neat aesthetic. I always thought there was a real craft and beauty to this process he had, and the delicate nature he took in it all before taking the board to the streets to run it ragged and basically destroy it slowly. Precision and carnage, quite an accurate description of his skating process.

Matt used to give me his old boards, then he would put a couple of the others he had spare on the front wall outside of the house for the local kids. I remember he would put them out on the wall and around ten minutes later they were gone. Skating was quite underground back then, but in our part of South London a lot of kids were into it.

Southbank back in the '90s had an aura about it, it had a sound, it had a smell, there was an edge to it with the backdrop of cardboard city and the homelessness. It could be warm and energetic but it could sometimes turn dark and feel dangerous, with fights breaking out and some crazy antics going on. Pretty scary for a ten-year-old me. Skating was frowned upon back then by society, and it certainly wasn't a means to a career like it is today, which is when Matt came to a crossroads.

When the Flip team moved out to the US in the mid '90s, Matt stayed behind in the UK and started working as a designer in various advertising agencies around London. Although his skating wasn't as prolific at this point, he still skated to work, he never wore a suit or conformed, he wore skate clothes to work, and every weekend he would be on his board, mainly at Stockwell with Reuben and that crew. Just because his team and some of his mates left, it never left him, he was always skating, up until the day he sadly died.

That's why I have such a love for skating to this day. I feel closer to him when I'm on my board, or when I see or hear a skater in the street, or even when I watch any video part. It's a connection to him, and it all stems from these memories of growing up skateboarding with him.

Credits

Thank you to everybody in this book who gave me their time and spoke to me on the phone, on Zoom, across a pub table or in their home. Extra thanks to all who let me sleep on their sofa while I was there, rifling through their slides, negatives, artwork or boards.

Thanks to Tim Leighton-Boyce for inspiring a generation, and to Ben Powell for letting me write about skateboarding in the first place.

Special thanks to Wig Worland, Ray Calthorpe, Nick Sharratt, Dan Magee, Skin Phillips, Dave Mackey, Seb Palmer, Mark Baines, Sofia Prantera, James Jarvis, Russell Waterman, Gareth Skewis, Vinny Evans, Robert Dukes, Peter Lee, Polly Powell and all at Batsford, Tijl Schneider, James Hudson, Tory Turk, Jagger, Vernon Adams, Kevin Banks, Oliver Barton, Jamie Scott, Kevin Parrott, Steve Douglas, Colin McInnes, Tom Hodgkinson, Toby Shuall, Neil Urwin, Ian Gunner, Pete Hellicar, Ben Allnutt, Gary Skinner, Dan Adams, Ian Deacon, Jacob Sawyer, Mark Noble and Grant Smith for all going above and beyond.

Everybody that helped with this book is essential to the story of UK skateboarding, and how it got to where it is today, but by no means is this the story of everything that happened or everyone that mattered – the village kerb is just as important a part of the scene as any legendary spot, and it was the people buying the magazines, videos and boards who allowed the scene to exist and thrive at all.

Thank you also to Adam Mondon, Adam Porter, Al Morrison, Alan Glass, Alan Rushbrooke, Alex Brindell, Alex Cock, Alex Craig, Alex Dyer, Alex Irvine, Alex Moul, Alex Osborne, Alex Turnbull, Ali Cairns, Ali Lowe, Alistair Kerr, Alvin Singfield, Amber Rawlings, Andrew Groves, Andrew Linaker, Andrew McDonald, Andrew Simmons, Andrew Stark, Andrew Warrington, Andy Coombes, Andy Horsley, Andy Howell, Andy Humphries, Andy Lincoln, Andy Rae, Andy Scott, Andy Shaw, Andy Simmons, Andy Smoke, Annie Macdonald, Anthony Claravall, Arron Bleasdale, Barrington Jeffrey, Barry Wong, Ben Gregson, Ben Jobe, Ben Leyden, Ben Powell, Ben Smart, Ben Wheeler, Bobby Puleo, Bod Boyle, Brian Sumner, Carl Shipman, Channon King, Charles Burrows, Charlie Stern, Chris Allen, Chris Atherton, Chris Aylen, Chris Hamer, Chris Mowatt, Chris Ortiz, Chris Pulman, Chris Stone, Colin Fitzgerald, Colin Kennedy, Corin Casey, Curtis McCann, Damian Ince, Dan Cates, Dan Gooding, Dan Joyce, Daniel Higginson, Daniel Turner, Danny Calow, Danny Wainwright, Darren Howman, Dave Duff, Dave Hopkins, Dave Olinski, Dave Turner, David Skrezka, Davross, Davy Van Laere, Dobie Campbell, Don Brown, Duncan Houlton, Ed Gill, Ed Loftus, Ed Toft, Elton Whybrow, Emily Regoczy, Eoghan O'Brien, Flynn Trotman, Fos, Fred McMillan, Gabriel Pluckrose, Gary Brown, Ged Wells, Geoff Rowley, George Horn, Gerhard Stochl, Gordon Skrezka, Gordon Wagstaff, Gordy Orr, Graham Tait, Greg Fabb, Greg Finch, Greg King, Guy Jones, Harry Bastard, Henry Kingsford, Iain Borden, Ian Deacon, Ian Lawton, Ian Passmore, Ian Read, Ian Roxburgh, Jackie Native, James Brown, James Burnett, James Davies, James Hacker, James Woodley, Jamie Blair, Jamie Bolland, Jamie Thomas, Jason Williams, Jay Doherty, Jeff Pang, Jeremy Elkin, Jeremy Henderson, Jesse Deville Fleet, Jim Thompson, Jimmy Boyes, Jock, Joel Curtis, John Cattle, John Dalton, John Rattray, Jon Exley, Jonny Robson, Jonny Wilson, Jono Atkinson, Joseph Millson, Justin Maule, Kate Harahan, Katie Hewett, Katie Macdonald, Kingy, Kris Ludford, Laszlo Beckett, Lee Yau, Leighton Dyer, Leo Sharp, Leon Parr, Lewis Threadgold, Lindsay Knight, Lucy Adams, Luke Davidson, Marc Bultitude, Mark Brewster, Mark Channer, Martin Kennelly, Mat Fowler, Matt Barr, Matt Dawson, Matt Gold, Matt Pritchard, Matt Sherman, Matt Stuart, Merlin Nation, Mick O'Neill, Mike Halls, Mike John, Mike Manzoori, Mike O'Brien, Mike Wright, Mini Mansell, Miranda Sawyer, Mon Barbour, Morgan Campbell, Neil Danns, Neil Davidson, Nick Hamilton, Nick Philip, Nick Zorlac, Nicola Newman, Nik Taylor, Oliver Kenney, Oliver Knight, Oliver Payne, Olly Todd, Patrick White, Paul Alexander, Paul Haynes, Paul Mittleman, Paul Robson, Paul Shier, Paul Silvester, Paul Stylianou, Paul Sunman, Paul Webster, Percy Dean, Pete Dossett, Pete Evans, Pete Fowler, Peter Tarry, Phil Calvert, Phil Penwarden, Phil Wilson, Pieter Janssen, Raydale Dower, Rebecca Armstrong, Rennie Spaczynski, Reuben Goodyear, Rich File, Rich Gilligan, Rich Hart, Rich Holland, Richard Hughes, Richard Stainthorpe, Rick Curran, Rik Cooper, Robin Sunley, Robyn Withawhy, Ross Crighton, Ross Milne, Ryan Grey, Ryan Mills, Sam Ashley, Sam Griffin, Sam Paterson, Sam Scott-Hunter, Sarah Epton, Sarah Feeney, Scott Wilson, Sean Goff, Sean Keef, Seth Curtis, Shane O'Brien, Shane Rouse, Sharon Tomlin, Sheryl Garratt, Sibs Roberts, Sim Higginson, Simon Batten, Simon Casey, Simon Chayter, Simon Evans, Steve Hicks, Steve Kane, Steve McQueen, Steve Pannell, Steve Rocco, Steve Wilshire, Tim Barnes, Tim Bladon, Paterson, Tom Penny, Tony Rivers, Tony Seddon, Vaughan Baker, Walker Murdoch, Wes Morgan, Wig Worland, Will Bankhead, Will Harmon, Will McMullan, Wingy, Winstan Whitter, and you.

Imprint

First published in the United Kingdom
in 2026 by
Batsford
43 Great Ormond Street
London
WC1N 3HZ

An imprint of B. T. Batsford Holdings
Limited

ISBN 9781849949422

A CIP catalogue record for this book is
available from the British Library.

10 9 8 7 6 5 4 3 2 1

Reproduction by Rival Colour Ltd, UK
  with special thanks to Dan Adams
Printed and bound by Dream Colour, China

Typeset in Neue Haas Grotesk
Design by Tijl Schneider

This book can be ordered direct from the
publisher at www.batsfordbooks.com, or
try your local bookshop.

Distributed throughout the UK and Europe
by Abrams & Chronicle Books, 1st Floor,
22–24 Ely Place, London EC1N 6TE and 57
rue Gaston Tessier, 75166 Paris, France

www.abramsandchronicle.co.uk
info@abramsandchronicle.co.uk

sound & vision

by michael a. manzoori

£500 fines set to knock skateboarders off course

Skateboarders who practise in Birmingham city centre squares face fines of up to £500.

The penalty has been increased from ... since the city passed its first ...

Council gets tough on skateboarders in squares

by Lucy Palmer

Face a fine or get your skates OFF

PNCBLUEPRINTFILMS

PNCBLUEPRINTFILMS

presents

Anthems

a 40 minute Skateboarding Film

PLEASE FIND ENCLOSED YOUR 5 VIP PREMIER TICKETS FOR SATURDAY 25/10/97

PLEASE NOTE THAT NO UNDER 18's WILL BE ALLOWED ENTRY FOR THIS EVENT

radlands